IN THEIR OWN WORDS

C. CHRISTINE FAIR

In Their Own Words

Understanding Lashkar-e-Tayyaba

OXFORD

UNIVERSITY PRESS

Oxford University Press is a department of the
University of Oxford. It furthers the University's objective
of excellence in research, scholarship, and education
by publishing worldwide.

Oxford   New York

Auckland   Cape Town   Dar es Salaam   Hong Kong   Karachi
Kuala Lumpur   Madrid   Melbourne   Mexico City   Nairobi
New Delhi   Shanghai   Taipei   Toronto

With offices in

Argentina   Austria   Brazil   Chile   Czech Republic   France   Greece
Guatemala   Hungary   Italy   Japan   Poland   Portugal   Singapore
South Korea   Switzerland   Thailand   Turkey   Ukraine   Vietnam

Oxford is a registered trade mark of Oxford University Press
in the UK and certain other countries.

Published in the United States of America by
Oxford University Press
198 Madison Avenue, New York, NY 10016

Library of Congress Cataloging-in-Publication Data is available
C. Christine Fair.
In Their Own Words: Understanding Lashkar-e-Tayyaba.
ISBN: 9780190909482

Printed in the United Kingdom by Bell and Bain Ltd, Glasgow

CONTENTS

CONTENTS

DEDICATION

Dedicated to the victims of terrorism and their families everywhere.
May they find peace and justice.

ACKNOWLEDGEMENTS

This project is the culmination of research I unwittingly began in Lahore in 1995 when I was a doctoral student studying Urdu as well as Punjabi through the renowned BULPIP (Berkeley Urdu Language Program in Pakistan, currently known as the Berkeley-AIPS Urdu Language Program in Pakistan). As a student of South Asian Languages and Civilizations, I frequented Anarkali Bazaar in Lahore, where I first encountered booksellers purveying the propaganda of Lashkar-e-Tayyaba (LeT), which now operates mostly under the name of Jamaat ud Dawah (JuD). I began collecting their materials that year and continued to do so during subsequent visits over the next couple of decades, until I was ultimately deemed *persona non-grata* by the country's intelligence agency, the Inter-Services Intelligence Directorate (ISI).

Due to the ISI's assessment that I am a "nasty woman," I have been unable to return to Pakistan since August 2013, but astonishingly, I was able to continue gathering materials for this effort through inter-library loan. Since 1962, American libraries have procured books from South Asia through the so-called PL-480 program, named after the eponymous public law which allowed the US Library of Congress to use rupees from Indian purchases of American agricultural products to buy Indian books. In 1965, a field office was opened in Karachi to oversee the acquisition of Pakistani publications. While the PL-480 program was long since discontinued, The Library of Congress continues to use the same institutional infrastructure to purchase these publications under the guise of a new program called the South Asia Cooperative Acquisitions Project.

I am deeply indebted to the Library of Congress and the other libraries across the United States which purchased these publications through this program and made them available to scholars through their institutions' inter-library loan programs. I am particularly beholden to Georgetown University's Lauinger Library, which never failed to produce a book I requested. The University of Chicago and the Library of Congress were the primary sources of these books and I am grateful that they continue to obtain and lend terrorist publications. As one US government official wryly noted when I explained my new sources of materials, "there is no better way to keep terrorist literature out of the hands of would-be terrorists than putting it in a library."

I am also extremely indebted to Georgetown University, which has supported my work unstintingly since I joined the Security Studies Program in the fall of 2009. The University and the Edmund A. Walsh School of Foreign Service at Georgetown University subsidized the writing of this book through a year-long leave through sabbatical and a senior research leave. Moreover, the School of Foreign Service provided invaluable financial support that enabled me to collaborate with Safina Ustaad, who did most of the translations used in this volume. (Ustaad and I are publishing a subsequent volume that contains these translations via Oxford University Press, entitled *A Call to War: The Literature of Lashkar-e-Tayyaba*.) The School of Foreign Service also subsidized a related and ongoing project in which I am studying the battle-field motivations of Lashkar-e-Tayyaba fighters. Through that funding, Ali Hamza translated a 10 per cent random sample of the over 900 fighter biographies I collected, the analyses of which I present in this book. I am also grateful to the Security Studies Program, my home program within the School of Foreign Service, for generously subsidizing other aspects of this project, such as my work with Abbas Haider and other ongoing collaborations with Ali Hamza. Both Haider and Hamza translated some materials (under my guidance and quality assurance) which I have analyzed herein. Ali Hamza has been a superb colleague and collaborator over numerous years on several quantitative and qualitative projects alike. I am extremely fortunate to have had the opportunity to work with such a gracious and talented colleague.

I also benefited tremendously from fellowships with the Institute for Defense Studies and Analysis (IDSA) in New Delhi, which hosted me as a senior fellow in the summer of 2016, the Gateway House in Mumbai during the summer of 2015, and the National Endowment for Democracy (NED) in Washington DC, which hosted me as a fellow in the summer of 2017. I remain obliged to Jayant Prasad, Rumel Dahiya, and Ashok Behuria at IDSA, and Sally Blair at the NED. Don Rassler and the Combating Terrorism Center (CTC) at West Point also provided important resources for the quantitative aspects of this project while I was a fellow at the CTC. It was a privilege to work with Don and the other members of that team including Anirban Ghosh, Nadia Shoeb, and Arif Jamal to whom I am deeply beholden. I would also like to express my gratitude to Oxford University Press which graciously allowed me to compress, update and draw upon significant portions of *Fighting to the End: The Pakistani Army's Way of War* (2014) as well as Taylor and Francis which granted me permission to draw heavily from a 2014 article in the *The Journal of Strategic Studies* ("Insights from a Database of Lashkar-e-Taiba and Hizb-ul-Mujahideen Militants," *Journal of Strategic Studies*, 37, 2 (2014), pp. 259–290.)

As this volume is the culmination of years of research and consultation, it would be remiss were I not to mention the superb community of scholars with whom I have discussed this project and data. Those who have been generous with their time and insights include: Daniel Byman, Bruce Hoffman, Jacob Shapiro, Praveen Swami, Ashley Tellis, Arif Jamal, Maryum Alam, the late Mariam Abou Zahab, Jaideep and his colleagues, and numerous others who met with me over the years in India, Pakistan, Afghanistan, and Bangladesh. Seth Oldmixon deserves a special mention. Oldmixon is one of the most under-valued assets in the community of South Asia analysts. He has a hawk's eye for details as he has scoured social media feeds and publications of militant organizations, reads the South Asian press more diligently than most intelligence analysts I know and has an extraordinary ability to recall events, identify persons and their associations.

I am also profoundly indebted to my husband, Jeffrey Dresser Kelley and our ever-evolving pack of canine associates, who have patiently, and at times, less patiently, abided my months away from home with grace and aplomb. They also endured long periods of my inattention as I sought first to comprehend the huge number of sources I processed for this volume and then drafted this book, which took much longer than I ever anticipated. They have foregone vacations and grown tufts of gray hair wondering when—or if—it would ever conclude.

Michael Dwyer at Hurst has been equally patient and supportive of this project. Without his belief in this project, there would be no project at all. Saira Wasim, one of the most intrepid and dauntless artists I have had the privilege of knowing, deserves extraordinary mention. Wasim has generously lent her courageous art to this cover and to that of my last two books. Wasim, masterfully subverting the tradition of the Mughal miniature painting, valorously confronts and interrogates the perversions and defeasances in Pakistani and international politics alike as well as the culpable dastards. When I have

ACKNOWLEDGEMENTS

writer's block, I peruse her body of work for inspiration. Her work is literally worth a million words.

Finally, I am aware that most readers who will buy this book will do so because of the hideous crimes this organization has perpetrated, mostly against Indian citizens. Thousands of Indians have been murdered by LeT, and if not for the group's lethal effectiveness, no one would care about it. The biographies of the martyrs weighed heavily upon my conscience as I studied their declared intentions to slaughter an enemy about which they knew nothing but lies propagated by the organization and the Pakistani state, leavened with rare fragments of truth. Because my ethical commitments preclude me from profiting from the deaths of thousands, I will donate any personal proceeds from this book to charitable organizations that assist victims of terrorism. Because Lashkar-e-Tayyaba mostly murders Indians, I will donate my personal profits to the Government of India's Central Scheme for Assistance to Civilian Victims of Terrorist/Communal/Left Wing Extremist Violence, Cross Border Firing and Mine/IED blasts on Indian Territory, as well as Save the Children India. Over time, I may adjust the charities to which I donate, although I will remain committed to donating to non-religious/non-proselytizing organizations in India that do relief work. Thank you in advance for supporting these institutions through your purchase of this book.

1

INTRODUCTION

On 23 November 2008, ten highly trained Pakistani gunmen from the
Lashkar-e-Tayyaba (LeT, Army of the Pure) set off from Karachi in a
Pakistani cargo vessel loaded with food, navigation equipment, sophisticated and diverse weapons systems, and copious munitions for what was to
be a one-way mission. As they approached international waters, they
hijacked a forty-five-foot Indian fishing boat crewed by four Indians. They
killed three and forced Narayan Singh, the lone survivor, to navigate them
to Mumbai, India's sprawling port city of over nineteen million people. As
they neared their destination, they murdered Singh and completed the final
leg of their voyage in two inflatable dinghies. Upon alighting on shore, the
men split into five teams and set off to attack high-profile targets, including
the Taj Mahal Hotel (at the Gateway of India), the Oberoi Trident Hotel,
Café Leopold in Colaba, which was popular among tourists and locals alike,
Chhatrapati Shivaji Terminus (formerly known as Victoria Terminus), and
the Nariman (Chabad) Jewish Community Center. Ultimately, they seized
the Taj where for three days they killed guests with small arms and set fire to
various wings of the sprawling hotel. During the siege, LeT operatives were
under the command and control of handlers who barked orders at them via
the command center in Karachi, Pakistan. When the hotel was at last
liberated by Indian security personnel, 166 people were dead and 293
wounded. The victims hailed from ten countries including the United States
and Israel.[1]

1

Indians were all too familiar with the group and its well-honed abilities to conduct sophisticated attacks against hard and soft targets alike. According to data from the University of Maryland's Global Terrorism Database, Lashkar conducted 205 attacks between 1 April 1999 and 19 December 2016, leaving at least 1,191 people dead and 2,411 injured.[2] In contrast, before this well-coordinated rampage across southern Mumbai, very few people beyond India or Pakistan had ever heard of the LeT. It lacked the brand-name recognition that Al Qaeda enjoyed at the time or that which the Islamic State enjoys now. This was true even though LeT had long become the most favored proxy of the Pakistani state to conduct terror operations in Indian-administered Kashmir and elsewhere in India, in an effort to compel India to relinquish control of that portion of Jammu and Kashmir it controls. Until the Mumbai attacks, American officials in terrorism and intelligence-related fora viewed the organization as largely India's problem, and consequently assessed that it posed minimal harm to US interests in South Asia or beyond. This insouciance was always misplaced. In the meantime, LeT developed a vast infrastructure for fundraising, recruiting and cultivating political support across North America, Europe, the Gulf, and South-East Asia.[3]

The 2008 Mumbai attacks were a rude awakening that roused American officials from their somnolence for several reasons. First and foremost, this attack played out over days, rather than hours, as had previously been the case with their attacks in India. Admittedly, this had as much to do with Indian ineptitude in responding to the attack as it did LeT's own competency.[4] Second, the multi-day siege was covered, minute-by-minute, in the international media due to the explosion of private media houses in India and their connections with international outlets such CNN. For American audiences, the attack took place during the long Thanksgiving weekend when television viewership is high. Third, unlike previous LeT attacks in India, this one targeted foreigners, including Americans and Israelis.[5]

Since the November 2008 attacks, the body of scholarship on LeT has grown, albeit not as expansively as the literature on Al Qaeda or the Islamic State. Tankel and Jamal focus on the history, development, and operations of the groups.[6] Others, such as Thorat and Waze, Unnithan, Sanghvi, Scott-Clark and Levy, and Rotella among others, have concentrated their efforts upon the November 2008 attack itself and its varied perpetrators.[7] Still, others have mobilized "big data" on LeT attacks to make predictive assessments about what the group may do in the future and what kinds of counter-terrorism policies may prove most effective in countering it.[8] With few exceptions, this emergent literature has generally overlooked LeT's institutional sources.[9] This is unfortunate because the organization sets a high store on outreach and publications, many of which are widely available.

In Their Own Words informs contemporary discussions and analysis of this organization by mobilizing the vast corpus of LeT's own writing. In this work, I analyze a sample of LeT's own publications and present new information about the organization, its recruits, the families that produce them and the external and domestic political imperatives that motivates the LeT's operations within and beyond Pakistan.

I draw from these materials to advance two key claims about the organization. First, as is generally accepted, I argue that LeT's ability to conduct complex terror attacks in India and Afghanistan—coupled with its loyalty to the Pakistani security establishment—render it incredibly useful as a reliable and obedient proxy. In fact, it is the state's most duteous and governable agent. While it has long been appreciated that LeT is useful to the Pakistani state for its loyalty and lethality in conducting its militant operations in India and, more recently, in Afghanistan, analysts have overlooked its *domestic* utility to the state. This forms the second principal focus of my study. LeT/JuD stands in stark opposition to Al Qaeda, the Islamic State and the various Deobandi militant groups savaging the Pakistani state and its citizenry because it vigorously opposes violence within Pakistan. This stance puts LeT/JuD at odds with other *Salafi* and Deobandi organizations in Pakistan that propound the doctrine of *takfiri* (excommunication and often murder) for Muslims who "misbehave" by failing to live their lives as these organizations demand and expect and for those Muslim leaders who fail to impose *shariat* when they have the opportunity to do so. Not only does it argue against violence against other Muslims, it also adopts the same stance against Pakistan's religious minorities. This yields a surprising paradox: while LeT decries Hindus and Christians outside of Pakistan as the worst polytheists and worthy objects of militarized *jihad*, *within* Pakistan it argues for their conversion through compassion, preaching and proselytization.[10] LeT is one of the state's most important partners in helping it manage the aftershocks of its long-term policy of using Islamist militants as state proxies. This explains, in large measure, I argue, Pakistan's aggressive and unyielding support of LeT at home and abroad, including the organization's August 2017 launch of a political party to contest Pakistan's 2018 general elections.

LeT is the deep state's handmaiden in prosecuting its external agenda while JuD and its Pakistan-based affiliates assert the state's internal security agendas.[11]

In this light, the announcement that the organization had established a political party with the almost certain assistance of Pakistan's army is a natural development in the partnership between the organization and the deep state, even though LeT has argued against such an explicit political role for itself since its inception. Moreover, its willingness to contravene its longstanding position against participating in elections to accommodate the deep state is a further testament to its unstinting fealty and symbiosis to and with the army and the intelligence agencies that support the LeT.[12]

What's in a Name?

While international attention to LeT is relatively new, the organization itself is not. As I detail in Chapter 4, the group came into being in 1986 or 1987 when Zaki ur Rehman Lahkhvi merged his Ahl-e-Hadees militant group with another Ahl-e-Hadees organization, Jamaat ud Dawah (JuD, Organization for Proselytization), which Hafiz Muhammad Saeed and Zafar Iqbal established. The organization that ensued from this merger was known as the Markaz al-Dawah Irshad (MDI, Center for Preaching and Guidance). Hafiz Saeed set up LeT as its armed wing within a few years of MDI's founding. The exact date of LeT's formation is not known but scholars generally assess that it was established in 1989 or early 1990.[13]

The US government did not recognize the group as a Foreign Terrorist Organization (FTO) until December 2001, reflecting American indifference to it. Washington only did so after another militant group, Jaish-e-Muhammad (JeM), attacked India's Parliament in December of that year, precipitating the largest Indian military mobilization along the Pakistani border since the 1971 war. (Many news outlets erroneously reported that the attack was carried out by JeM and LeT working in concert and this error perdures in the scholarly and policy analytical literature.) India's military mobilization was deeply problematic for the United States, as it had recently begun military operations in Afghanistan. As the US forces and their Afghan partners drove the fleeing Taliban and their Al Qaeda associates south and towards the Pakistan border, the United States needed Pakistan's assistance to kill or capture those crossing into Pakistan. With the Indian deployment of its forces towards the border, Pakistan swung some of its troops from the western Afghan front to the east. As a result, the Taliban, Al Qaeda and allied fighters ensconced themselves in various parts of Pakistan—including the Federally Administered Tribal Areas (FATA), as well as prominent cities in Balochistan, Sindh, Punjab, and Khyber Pakhtunkhwa—from which they would continue operating.

To prevent an Indo-Pakistani war and redirect Pakistani attention back to its western border with Afghanistan, the United States undertook vigorous diplomacy, mostly in effort to persuade India to stand down. Principally for this reason, the United States proscribed LeT and JeM among other Pakistan-based and Pakistan-backed terrorist organizations. The administration of President George W. Bush exerted tremendous pressure upon Pakistan's military dictator and president, General Pervez Musharraf, to ban LeT and other organizations designated by the United States. The United States also persuaded Musharraf to make a series of public statements that would ameliorate Indian concerns and even pressured him severely to curtail dispatching terrorists into India for a limited time after the events of September 2011.[14]

Ultimately, the bans that Musharraf enacted against these groups were merely a feint. Pakistani intelligence gave advance notice of the impending ban to LeT's Hafiz Saeed and the leaders of other militant groups. This allowed them to transfer their financial assets to new bank accounts and expeditiously re-emerge under new names. Saeed subsequently announced a reorganization of MDI, which was dissolved and replaced by JuD. In the words of one US official, "LeT's old offices merely changed the name on the door."[15] Saeed resigned as LeT's *amir* and assumed the leadership of JuD. Yahya Mujahid, spokesperson for LeT cum JuD and one of the founding members of MDI announced: "We handed Lashkar-e-Tayyaba over to the Kashmiris in December 2001. Now we have no contact with any jihadi organization."[16] In practice, the vast majority of LeT's assets and personnel were subsumed into JuD while the organizational nodes and operatives outside of Pakistan continued to serve under the banner of LeT. Despite his ostensible resignation from LeT, Hafiz Saeed remained the leader of both organizations; the placard above LeT offices was merely replaced with that of JuD. In the organization's various publications, Saeed is still referred to as the "Commander of the Mujahideen."

In subsequent years, JuD spawned numerous related organizations, such as the *Idara Khidmat-e-Khalq* (IKK, Organization for Humanitarian Assistance), set up in 2004 to provide relief to the victims of the Asian Tsunami.[17] At that time, the organization collected and dispatched considerable supplies to Sri Lanka.[18] In April 2006, the US Department of Treasury declared IKK a Foreign Terrorist Organization (FTO).[19] Later, in 2009, JuD set up another humanitarian front, *Falah Insaniat Foundation* (FIF, Foundation for Welfare of Humanity), which raised its profile by providing relief during and after Pakistan's massive monsoon-related floods in 2010. The United States also designated FIF as an FTO in 2010, and the United Nations followed suit in

2012 by designating FIF pursuant to UN Security Council Resolutions 1267 (1999) and 1989 (2011).[20]

Under the banner of JuD, the organization has been a part of several umbrella organizations with other militant and right-of-center political groups. For example, in January 2009, JuD was involved in a group called the *Tehreek-e-Tahafuz Qibla Awal* (Movement for the Safeguarding of the First Center of Prayer), which held anti-Israel protests in Lahore. (LeT/JuD attendees are easily identified by the organization's distinctive black and white flag.) Similarly, in 2010, JuD had a noticeable presence in the *Tehreek-e-Tahafuz-e-Hurmat-e-Rasool* (Movement to Defend the Honor of the Prophet), which organized protests against the Danish cartoons of the prophet Muhammad. Later in 2012, JuD was prominent in the *Difa-e-Pakistan Council* (Defense of Pakistan Council), which organized large rallies in Lahore, Rawalpindi, Karachi and elsewhere to protest American policies in Pakistan as well as the US/International Security Assistance Force (ISAF) activities in Afghanistan. In the spring of 2015, JuD also generated popular support for Pakistani military assistance to the Saudi-led alliance in Yemen. To do so, JuD formed the "*Pasban-e-Harmain-Sharifian*" (Defenders of the Sacred Sites in Mecca and Medina) and argued that the Yemeni Houthi rebels aimed to invade Saudi Arabia and assault the *harmain*—the Grand Mosque in Mecca, which surrounds the Ka'ba, and the prophet's Mosque in Medina.[21]

Subrahmanian et al. characterize these temporary, cause-specific organizational formations as ruptures in JuD's organizational coherence.[22] However, I do not. I contend that these efforts reflect JuD's initiative-based efforts to reach out to other similarly-inclined organizations who do not share JuD's sectarian orientation or to ensure that JuD is represented in umbrella organizations led by other militant or right-of-center groups and personalities whose causes JuD espouses and/or whose causes are embraced by Pakistanis generally. In other words, these are symptoms of JuD's efforts to forge temporary political alliances rather than revealing fractures in the organization itself. In fact, as of August 2018, JuD has only experienced one such split, which occurred in July 2004 when elements of the group's leadership became dismayed that Hafiz Saeed was appointing his relatives to top positions. Lakhvi, in particular, was perturbed by Saeed's blatant nepotism in making these appointments because he believed that he was being sidelined in the organization. Given that Lakhvi was a foundational member of MDI as well as the founder of the militant group that combined with JuD to form MDI, these developments were intolerable. Lakhvi briefly parted ways with Saeed and formed the *Khairun*

Nas ("Good People," a reference to the so-called Companions of the prophet). This fissure was temporary, and the organization soon merged back with JuD, likely due to the intervention of Pakistan's Inter-Services Intelligence Agency (ISI).[23] For these reasons, I use JuD, LeT and MDI more or less interchangeably, unless stated otherwise, because doing so is accurate, and because I hope to remind the reader of the fact irrespective of what the Pakistani government or the organizations say to the contrary.

In early August 2017, JuD opened a new front when it formed a political party named the Milli Muslim League (the "National Muslim League," MML) with the aim of rendering Pakistan a "real Islamic and welfare state."[24] The MML, which is headed by Saifullah Khalid, a close aide of Saeed and a foundational member of JuD, intends to field candidates in the 2018 general election. The organization wasted no time entering the political fray: after Prime Minister Nawaz Sharif was forced to resign on 16 August 2017 and thus vacate his seat in the national assembly for the NA 120 constituency,[25] JuD quickly fielded a candidate under the MML banner for the 17 September 2017 by-election to fill that vacancy. Because the MML had not yet been registered as a political party, the candidate (Muhammad Yaqoob Sheikh) filed his nomination papers with the Election Commission of Pakistan (ECP) as an independent candidate.[26] Despite being in existence for a mere four weeks, it received four times as many votes as did the Pakistan Peoples Party (PPP) in that by-election. This is most certainly due to the fact that it enjoyed the explicit backing and support of the security establishment.[27] It then fielded a candidate, Alhaj Liaquat Ali Khan, in an October 2017 by-election for the NA-4 constituency in Peshawar although he did not fare as well.[28]

While Saeed initially said that this party was separate from JuD, like many of his pronouncements, this too ultimately proved to be fiction. Campaign posters for the NA-120 and NA-4 by-elections clearly featured the pictures of the candidates as well as that of Saeed and, upon Saeed's release from "house arrest" in late November 2017, the MML leadership opined that "Mr Hafiz Saeed will soon start planning out our membership strategy and getting others on board through networking."[29] Saeed dropped the façade in early December when he announced that JuD is "planning to contest the 2018 general elections under the banner of Milli Muslim League."[30] In the end, Saeed did not contest the 25 July 2018 elections himself. Moreover, former dictator, president and army chief, General Pervez Musharraf declared his unstinting support for Saeed, LeT/JuD and the MML upon hearing that Saeed had been released from house arrest. He even suggested that he would like to contest the 2018 elections in alliance with the MML.[31] The path for this cleared in March 2018 when, after a protracted legal battle with the Election Commission of Pakistan (ECP), the Islamabad High Court granted the MML's petition to be enlisted as political party by the ECP, setting aside the ECP's refusal to do so.[32]

Based upon the available information about the MML, its ties to the JuD and its mentorship by Pakistan's security organizations, I reject the Panglossian viewpoint advanced by some analysts that the MML's formation signals a new effort by Pakistan to redirect the terrorist organization's external militarism towards a new domestic political role and thus serves as a state-directed "de-radicalization" or "demobilization" effort to bring Islamist militants into mainstream politics.[33] In fact, for at least two years, sources close to the Indian intelligence agencies and journalists who have the ear of Pakistan's military and intelligence agencies were claiming that LeT was forming a political party at the army's behest. While a comprehensive forensic analysis of the organization's origins is beyond the scope of this book, given its recent emergence, a few things are known about the MML and its ties to Pakistan's army and the ISI. First and foremost, one of its founding members and current information secretary, Tabish Qayyum has long been cultivated by the deep state. He first emerged as a writer for a website known as "*Pakistan ka Khuda Hafiz*" (PKKH, God Protect Pakistan), specifically in association with its now-defunct English-language magazine entitled *Fortress*. (PKKH has been a long-time collaborator with JuD and many PKKH, JuD and LeT activists have received training from the ISI to more effectively "engage in a social media war on behalf of these banned terror groups on Facebook and Twitter.")[34] In 2016, Qayyum completed his MA at Pakistan's National Defense University in the Department of International Relations, Faculty of Contemporary Studies. He wrote his thesis on the presence of the Islamic State (IS) in Pakistan and available means to defeat it. In this thesis, he highlighted the current effort of JuD in combatting the Islamic State (IS) and argues for a larger role for the organization in these efforts. He correctly notes in this thesis that the Islamic States has even declared JuD to be an apostate organization for its staunch opposition to IS and its deep ties to Pakistan's security establishment.[35] Qayyum's writings and digital footprint provide the clearest evidence of the support that the MML has enjoyed from Pakistan's security establishment as well as its inherent ties to JuD.

The MML has aggressively marketed its manifesto and Pakistan's English and Urdu media has obliged. The clearest exposition of its aims and goals are articulated in the October 2017 issue of *Invite*, JuD's newest English-language publication. In this issue, the party clearly states that it aims include, *inter alia*: ensuring that both Pakistan's society and state conform to the injunctions of the Quran and Sunnat; promoting domestic security; protect Pakistan's ideological, moral and cultural ethos; inculcating the ideology of Pakistan among the country's citizens; rendering Pakistan a modern Islamic welfare state; promoting a "political environment in which all members of the society, especially the lower and the middle class, get complete rights and prepare them for leadership roles;" restoring Pakistan's honor and place in the international system; to protect and safeguard the rights of women and minorities; to morally and diplomatically support the struggle in Kashmir; promote a foreign policy that promotes the interests of the global Muslim community (*ummat*); and "counter the Takfeeri extremist ideology of the *Kharijites*, educate the people in battling it, and to work towards curbing sectarianism."[36] (I describe these issues at length in Chapter Six.)

I contend that the MML will complement JuD's efforts to stabilize Pakistan internally and enhance LeT's external activities in the service of the deep state. Moreover, while the organization had long abjured politics, it has played a crucial role in discouraging violence within Pakistan. The aims and goals of the MML are very much in keeping with JuD's long-standing positions on not conducting attacks within Pakistan and resolving disputes with its problematic leadership and members of wayward interpretative traditions through preaching. The only surprising aspect about the formation of the MML is that this development had not been anticipated hitherto. Pakistan's deep state, which is the expression that Pakistani writers have adopted to describe the over-developed security institutions which dominate domestic and international affairs,[37] has an abiding interest in encouraging JuD to more firmly and formally ensconce itself in the nation's politics, and the emergence of the MML will likely help legitimize the deep state's use of militant assets in Kashmir and elsewhere. The timing of the MML's foundation is also notable because it coincides with the army's exhaustion with both mainstream political parties (the Pakistan Peoples Party (PPP) and the Pakistan Muslim League of Nawaz Sharif (PML-N)) and the ongoing failure of Imran Khan's Pakistan Tehreek-e-Insaf (PTI) to develop a national presence. In effect, the army has few options to engineer Pakistan's political leadership in the forthcoming general elections. While the MML fared poorly in Pakistan's July 2018 elections (no religious party ever polls more than 10 per cent in a free and fair election),[38] the MML could play a useful future role as a member of a coalition groomed by the army and its intelligence service, whether in the ruling parties or in opposition.[39]

Overview of Pakistan's Contemporary Militant Landscape

Pakistan has long used Islamist—as well as non-Islamist—militant proxies as a part of its foreign policy and national security strategy. First, these proxies are generally effective in securing Pakistan's immediate objectives. In Afghanistan, they have been employed disruptively to ensure that the country does not become a secure base for India. Within India, they have been employed to pin down hundreds of thousands of security forces in Kashmir, the Punjab and elsewhere. In Kashmir and throughout India, Pakistan uses these proxies to raise the stakes for the sake of international attention and intervention. With the explicit nuclearization of the subcontinent in 1998, international observers routinely opine that such terrorist attacks are what may precipitate an Indo-Pakistan war, with attendant risk of nuclear escalation. Thus, these groups advance Pakistan's perennial agenda of keeping the "Kashmir dispute" alive.

Second, it is relatively easy to stoke unrest in Indian-administered Kashmir and provoke Indian over-reaction, which inevitably results in Kashmiri fatalities, human rights abuses and even shocking violations of international humanitarian law.[40] In turn, Pakistan capitalizes upon these wearily predictable Indian over-reactions with its well-honed theatricality to highlight these real and exaggerated atrocities alike in Kashmir in international fora such as the United Nations. Indian excesses further alienate Kashmiris under its governance, which Pakistan exploits cynically and cyclically. Third, it is almost impossible for India or anyone else to compel Pakistan to cease using these groups permanently, and it is impossible to detect and disrupt every terrorist entering India. Fourth, using militant proxies to secure these objectives is relatively inexpensive when measured in direct economic costs. While it is impossible to know with any certainty how much financial support the Pakistani state provides to groups like LeT, Kambere et al. estimate that LeT's annual operation budget is about $50 million, of which about $5.2 million is dedicated to military operations.[41] It is unlikely that the state has to provide the full $50 million because the organization has a massive fundraising capability through its domestic and foreign charity solicitations, the sales of its numerous publications, and its annual collection of sacrificial animal pelts, among other lucrative endeavors.[42] However, even if one assumes that the state provides this $50 million in full measure, it is a tiny amount compared to Pakistan's annual defense budget of $8.7 billion.[43] This facile calculation excludes, of course, the opportunity costs that this strategy, rooted in perpetual conflict, imposes upon the state's economic growth and its ability to invest in the country's human and other development resources.[44] Fifth, Pakistan is able to use these proxies instead of its own forces, which is politically, diplomatically, militarily, as well as economically a more fraught option. Finally, the use of proxies under its nuclear umbrella allows Pakistan to extract rents from the international community, who underwrite the country because it is "too dangerous to fail."[45]

Given the enduring nature of this elemental Pakistani strategy to prosecute its foreign policy objectives, there are dozens of Islamist militant groups that currently operate within and from the country. Drawing upon the vast descriptive literature about them, these myriad collectives can be typologically understood by evaluating them across several dimensions.[46] One such dimension is the sectarian affiliation of the groups, which is determined by the *maslak* (school of Islamic thought, which derives from the Arabic *salaka*, which means "to walk" or "to walk on a path") that an individual or group embraces. In Pakistan, there are five *masalik* (pl. of *maslak*): four of which are Sunni while the fifth is Shia, which also has various divisions. The four Sunni *masalik* are: Barelvi, Deobandi, Ahl-e-Hadees and Jamaat-e-Islami (JI).

The Barelvi movement began in Bareilly, a small town in Uttar Pradesh in northern India. It coalesced around Ahmed Riza Khan (1856–1921), an important Muslim scholar and Sheikh of the Qadiri order of Sufis. Barelvis, often referred to as Sufis in Pakistan, are associated with traditional devotional practices such as the celebration of *'urs* (death anniversary of Sufi saints) and ritual practices associated with the shrines of Sufi saints. The Deobandi school originated in 1867 at a *madrassah* (religious seminary, pl. *madaris*) in Deoband, Uttar Pradesh. It emerged as a South Asian Muslim religious revival movement that aimed to uplift Muslims by purifying Islamic practices through discouraging mystical beliefs, such as intercession by saints, and propitiation at graves and shrines, among other things. The Ahl-e-Hadees was another reformist movement that originated in South Asia in the 1870s. Influenced by some strands of Arab reform, it antagonized other Muslims in South Asia because they argued that the learned should consult the Quran and *hadees* directly rather than follow the interpretations, rulings and commentaries of the various schools of Islamic law discussed below. They notoriously introduced a controversial and distinctive mode of offering prayers.[47] Finally, JI is regarded as a *maslik* in Pakistan even though it is best understood as mass-based political party.[48]

Most Sunnis in Pakistan follow the Hanafi school of Islamic jurisprudence (*fiqh*). For example, even though Deobandis and Barelvis have many differences, they are both Hanafi. Ahl-e-Hadees, as noted above, rejects all *fiqh*. Ahl-e-Hadees adherents self-identify, and are considered by others, as *ghair-muqallid* (those who do not follow *taqlid*, which is guidance that has been historically given). Ahl-e-Hadees proponents see the various schools of jurisprudence as being tantamount to personality cults surrounding their various founders. As such, they are even more zealous than Deobandis in establishing a singular standard of piety and behavior, and even more unrelenting in extirpating the various customary practices that they understand to be *bid'at*. *Bid'at* literally translates as innovation, but it carries the valence that it is heretical and displeasing to Allah.[49]

All the afore-mentioned groups identify as Sunni despite their differences; in contradistinction to them is the Shia community. The Shia differ from Sunnis in that they believe that upon the death of the prophet Muhammad in 632 CE, Ali bin Abu Talib (his closest living relative) should have been his rightful successor or first *Khaleefa* instead of Abu Bakr, the prophet's associate and advisor. As with Sunnis in Pakistan, there are several sects within Shia Islam. While most Pakistani Shias follow the Twelver (Ithna 'Ashariyya) school of thought, there are also smaller branches of Ismaili Shias and subsects thereof (for example, Khojas and Bohras). The majority of Shia in Pakistan follows the Ja'fari *fiqh*.[50]

In addition to their sectarian background, we can distinguish Pakistan-based militant groups by where they operate (e.g. Afghanistan, India, Pakistan), by the makeup of their cadres (e.g. Arab, Central Asian, Pakistani and ethnic groups thereof), by their objectives (e.g. overthrow of the Pakistan government, seizing Kashmir, supporting the Afghan Taliban, etc.), the kinds of operations they undertake (suicide attacks, high risk missions, etc.), and their relationship with the Pakistani state, among other characteristics.[51] With these considerations in mind, I suggest the following typology of the clusters of Islamist militant groups:

- Al Qaeda (in Pakistan): In the early years after 9/11, most Al Qaeda operatives who were based in Pakistan were largely non-Pakistani. In some measure, this is still true. Al Qaeda cadres and leaders in Pakistan work with and through networks of supportive Pakistani militant groups. They have the strongest ties with the Deobandi groups such as the Pakistani Taliban, JeM, Lashkar-e-Jhangvi (LeJ, Army of Jhangvi), etc. From sanctuaries in the tribal areas as well as key Pakistani cities, Al Qaeda has planned international attacks as well as facilitated attacks within and without Pakistan.[52] In September 2013, Al Qaeda's leader Ayman al Zawahiri announced the establishment of a new branch in South Asia, Al Qaeda Indian Subcontinent (AQIS), ostensibly to compete with the Islamic State-Khorasan.[53] There is no solid evidence that the Pakistani state views Al Qaeda as a strategic partner; on occasion, the Pakistani state has acted vigorously against Al Qaeda despite its obvious failures with respect to Osama bin Laden, whom American forces located and killed in Abbottabad (near the famed Pakistan Military Academy).[54] Gall alleges, albeit based on thin evidence, that the state harbored bin Laden. She argues that because he fathered four children, two of whom were born in Pakistani government hospitals, there must have been official collusion in providing him sanctuary.[55] This sustains suspicion that bin Laden enjoyed state protection, though the highest level of authority for that protection remains unknown.[56] What is undeniable is that the Pakistani state has shown no interest in discerning who enabled bin Laden's stay in Pakistan, which must have required some degree of official sanction. In contrast, it has dedicated resources in tracking down and detaining those Pakistanis, such as Dr. Shakil Afridi, who enabled the Americans to locate and eliminate him.[57]

- Islamic State-Khorasan (IS-K): Prior to al Baghdadi's declaration of an Islamic State in June 2014, hundreds of Pakistanis flocked to Syria and Iraq to engage in sectarian conflict there. In recent years, various Pakistani militant commanders have aligned with IS-K, which is the IS branch active in Afghanistan and Pakistan. IS-K draws its commanders and cadres from Deobandi militant organizations such as LeJ and the Pakistani Taliban, who previously embraced an explicitly sectarian agenda.[58] The Afghan government alleges that Pakistan supports IS in Afghanistan, though it is nearly impossible to evaluate this claim.[59] What is known is that the Pakistani state has done very little to counter IS' presence in Pakistan, and has been loath to concede the organization's presence in the country despite insurmountable evidence.[60]

- Afghan Taliban: The Afghan Taliban is led by Mawlawi Haibatullah Akhundzada, as of June 2018. Akhundzada took the reins of the organization after the United States killed Mullah Akhtar Muhammad Mansour in a drone strike in May 2016. Mansour was the controversial successor to the group's founder, Mullah Omar, who died in Pakistan in 2013.[61] While the Afghan Taliban operates in Afghanistan, they enjoy sanctuary in Pakistan's Balochistan province, parts of the FATA, the Khyber Pakhtunkhwa provinces, and key cities in the Pakistani heartland (for example, Karachi). The Afghan Taliban emerged from Deobandi *madaris* (pl. *madrassah*) in

Pakistan and retains their nearly exclusive ethnic Pashtun and Deobandi sectarian orientation. The Afghan Taliban remains focused on re-establishing their governance role in Afghanistan. To do so, they have waged a sustained insurgency against Afghan and international security forces with extensive assistance from Pakistan.[62] The Taliban is a close ally of the Pakistani state along with allied fighter networks such as the Jalaluddin Haqqani Network.[63]

- Kashmiri *tanzeems* (organizations): Several groups of varying sectarian backgrounds claim to focus their militant efforts upon the liberation of that portion of Kashmir which is governed by India. These ostensibly "Kashmir *tanzeems*" include the JI-backed Hizbul Mujahideen (HM) and related splinter groups such as al Badr; several Deobandi groups (such as JM), Harkat-ul-Jihad-e-Islami (HUJI), and the Ahl-e-Hadees group, LeT, renamed JuD. With the notable exception of HM, most of these groups claim few ethnic Kashmiris and came into being as surrogates of the ISI or were quickly adopted by the ISI upon forming *sui generis*.[64] There has been considerable factionalization among the Deobandi groups, some of which have turned their guns against the state; however, LeT, Jamaat-e-Islami (JeI), HM, and the Afghan Taliban remain its allies.

- "Sectarian groups": In the past, there were several notable Shia militias which targeted Sunnis which enjoyed support from Iran. Since the mid-2000s, especially in areas like the tribal agency of Kurram—where Shia are targeted by Sunni Deobandi militants—Shia militias have formed in small numbers.[65] With these few and notable exceptions, sectarian groups are mostly Sunni—as of June 2018. Those Sunni groups targeting Shia are almost always Deobandi (i.e. Sipah-e-Sahaba-e-Pakistan (SSP) and LeJ, which now operate under the umbrella Ahl-e Sunnat Wal Jamaat (ASWJ)). In addition, there is considerable intra-Sunni violence with Ahl-e-Hadees and Deobandi targeting Barelvis. In recent years, Barelvis too have taken up violence against Deobandis in retaliation.[66] These groups have at times served the interest of the Pakistani state. For example, the LeJ/SSP was one of the first Pakistani organizations to fight in Afghanistan in the early 1990s alongside the Taliban.[67] More generally, these groups benefit from benign neglect.[68]

- The Tehreek-e-Taliban-e-Pakistan (TTP, Pakistani Taliban): Groups self-nominating as the "Pakistani Taliban" appeared in Waziristan as early as 2004 under the leadership of Waziristan-based Deobandi militants who fought with the Afghan Taliban in Afghanistan. By late 2007, several militant commanders organized (at least nominally) under the leadership of

South Waziristan-based Baitullah Mehsud and used the moniker (TPP). There is no serious evidence of coordination among the varied leaders operating under this nom de guerre, and considerable disagreement exists among its local commanders. The TTP, while based in the Pashtun areas of the FATA and Khyber Pakhtunkhwa (KPK), include Pashtuns and Punjabis among their ranks as well as other ethnicities in smaller number. The TTP collaborates with Al Qaeda and has long drawn personnel from the numerous Deobandi militant groups including sectarian and so-called Kashmir-focused groups.[69] The TTP is not a monolithic organization, and some of the commanders who have affiliated with the TTP have actually become state allies, such as the Maulvi Nazir and Baitullah Mehsud factions.[70] Others have defected and joined IS-K or even the IS in Syria and Iraq.[71] On 15 June 2018, the Afghan Ministry of Defense reported that a US drone strike in Kunar (Afghanistan) killed the leader of the TTP, Mullah Fazlullah. In June 2018, the TTP announced that Mufti Noor Wali Mehsud will replace him.[72]

Several refinements of and caveats to this proposed taxonomy are worthy of discussion.[73] For example, Deobandi groups have extensive overlapping membership with one another and with the Deobandi Islamist political party, Jamiat-e-Ulema Islami (JUI), hence a member of JeM may also be a member of ASWJ (or other Deobandi group for that matter) and/or an office holder within the JUI. As is discussed below, in late 2001, several Deobandi groups turned against the Pakistani state following its participation in the US-led global war on terrorism. Former members and breakaway factions of JeM and LeJ, for instance, have collaborated with the TTP to provide suicide bombers and logistical support. These connections with Punjab-based Deobandi groups have permitted the TTP to conduct attacks throughout Pakistan, far beyond the TTP's territorial remit. Both LeT and several Deobandi militant groups have also been operating in Afghanistan against US, NATO and Afghan forces. In contrast, other "Kashmiri groups" are operating under the influence of the Islamist political party JI, such as al Badr and HM, which tend to comprise ethnic Kashmiris and have retained their operational focus upon Kashmir.[74]

There are several factors that distinguish LeT from the myriad other groups operating in and from Pakistan. First, as mentioned above, LeT (along with the JI-based organizations) has never attacked any target within Pakistan. This is further evidence of the tight linkages between it and the Pakistani security establishment. Second, unlike all other groups, the LeT has not experienced significant splits in the organization, in large measure because the ISI has engineered or fomented dissent among the other militant groups to ensure enhanced control over them while working to preclude such ruptures within LeT.[75] In fact, the LeT is the only group that the ISI has permitted to remain intact without significant cleavages at the apex body of decision-makers. (As with all organizations, some discord has been observed among local commanders.) Finally, whereas the state has taken on several of the Deobandi groups (e.g. the TTP, elements of the sectarian groups) and Al Qaeda through inept and, at times, ineffective military operations, it has taken only the most marginal and cosmetic steps against LeT despite receiving significant international pressure to do so. While LeT—along with several other *jihadi* groups—was banned in 2002, all of them regrouped under other names with their financial assets largely intact.[76] JuD escaped a second round of bans in 2003, which were prompted by complaints lodged by the US Ambassador to Pakistan Nancy Powell that these militant outfits had simply reconstituted themselves without any enduring impacts upon their operational capabilities.[77] This enabled JuD to continue to expand its overt as well as covert actions with preferential state treatment.[78] In fact, Pakistan was extremely reluctant to ban JuD after the Mumbai attack and promised to do so only after the United Nations Security Council (UNSC) proscribed the organization and identified its leadership as terrorists; however, in actuality Pakistan did not proscribe JuD or any of its other purportedly philanthropic organizations, such as the FIF.[79] As of 2017, all of these organizations operate openly in Pakistan.

Data and Methods

While in this book I draw upon the extant scholarly literature on the organization, I hope my principle contribution will be the results from my mixed-methods analysis of LeT's extensive publications, which includes books, pamphlets, calendars, and periodicals on wide-ranging topics printed and edited by their exclusive publisher, *Dar-ul-Andlus*. I rely upon two different types of publications for this book. First, I collected the organization's books and pamphlets. While it is preferable to assemble all of LeT's published books from which I could draw a well-characterized sample, this is unfeasible if not impossible. Per force, I adopted a second-best alternative: working from a list of all Dar-ul-Andulus publications available on WorldCat, which is a master catalog of library materials drawn from 16,131 partner institutions in 120 countries, I drew a master sample of publications.[80] Searching on books published by Dar-ul-Andulus, WorldCat lists ninety-six items that were published between 1999 and 2016, including fifty-four books and forty-two non-circulating items such as audio recordings and posters. My long-time collaborator, Safina Ustaad, and I worked through the inter-library loan facilities at Georgetown University and Harvard University to acquire the books (We did not evaluate non-circulating items because they are not available through interlibrary loan.) I augmented this sample of potential candidate works with materials that I had personally collected during many trips to Pakistan between 1995 and 2013.

Ustaad and I next examined the books jointly to determine which ones cast light on the empirical questions posed for this and a related scholarly effort.[81] Specifically, we looked for volumes that delineate what LeT/JuD says it does as an organization, what external and internal political imperatives shape the organization's behavior in and beyond Pakistan, how the organization recruits and retains fighters, and how it cultivates a larger community of support. We also sought volumes that discussed the fighters of LeT, what motivates them, and who are the families that empower and enable them. Once we selected the key books, Ustaad and I perused the volumes and identified key sections for translation. In most cases, Ustaad translated the sections used here except where noted. I provided spot checks on the translations.

A second data source includes nearly one thousand so-called martyr (*shaheed*) biographies that my team and I collected as a part of a quantitative analytical project that I oversaw, along with Don Rassler, for the Combatting Terrorism Center at West Point, as described in Chapter 5.[82] These biographies were assembled from my personal library as well as those of others who provided copies of their collection for this project, such as Mariam Abou Zahab (who sadly passed away in November 2017) and Arif Jamal.[83] Some of these publications were also procured through Georgetown University's inter-library loan service. While the Combatting Terrorism Center effort focused upon a quantitative analysis of these documents, in this volume I use them for both quantitative and qualitative purposes. For the latter, working with my research associate, Ali Hamza, we drew a random sample of 100 biographies for translation. Unless noted elsewhere, Hamza did these translations with oversight from me. (For a note on translations, see the appendix titled 'Notes on Transliteration and Translation.'

Plan of the Book

In many ways, this book is a sequel to my earlier work *Fighting to the End: The Pakistan Army's Way of War*,[84] in which I argued that Pakistan is a revisionist state in Kashmir and seeks to resist India's rise in the region and international system largely for ideological rather than security reasons. Relying upon an analysis of cultural artifacts produced by the Pakistan army, I describe the lineaments of the Pakistan army's strategic culture. I focus upon the army because it is the most important institution in deciding Pakistan's security policies at home and abroad. The army is dedicated to not only protecting Pakistan's territorial borders but its ideological borders as well, which includes promoting the so-called "Two Nation Theory," upon which Pakistan's claim to Kashmir principally rests. To prosecute these policies, the Pakistan army has principally relied upon non-state actors operating under the security of its expanding nuclear-umbrella. This present work reflects upon one of the most important organizations that the army has fostered to prosecute its foreign and domestic security objectives. (My forthcoming book focuses upon the development of Pakistan's nuclear program without which Pakistan could not use militants with such outrageous impunity.) Consequently, parts of this book draws from *Fighting to the End*. I am grateful to Oxford University Press for permitting me to do so.

I have written this book such that the reader can generally read any chapter in any order. Each chapter discusses a specific theme. Chapter 2 provides a brief history of Pakistan's security competition with India in the context of Partition. While India preferred that Partition not happen at all, India emerged as generally satisfied with the territorial status quo. In contrast, Pakistan was deeply aggrieved by Partition, and surfaced from this process as an inherently insecure and unsatisfied state hell-bent upon changing the territorial status quo through force. This chapter condenses and updates Chapters 3–6 from my book, *Fighting to the End: The Pakistan Army's Way of War*, with permission from the publisher.[85]

Chapter 3 describes the co-evolution of Pakistan's non-state actor strategy along with its development of nuclear weapons. Pakistan has used both Islamist and non-Islamist proxies in India since its earliest days, and Islamist and Islamist militant groups to manipulate events in Afghanistan from the mid-to-late-1950s. Pakistan became ever more emboldened in its use of proxy actors when it became an incipient nuclear power, using nuclear weapons to deter India from punishing Pakistan militarily for dispatching terrorists to kill Indians as well as coerce the international community, especially the Americans, to insulate Pakistan from the costs of its actions and remain engaged in various aid programs. This chapter draws upon Chapters 8 and 9 from *Fighting to the End*. As I show here, Pakistan's nuclear assets are a necessary condition that enables Pakistan to use groups like LeT as an instrument of foreign policy. In turn, LeT/JuD has been an active party in promoting the army's security imperatives even going so far as to make detailed pronouncements on nuclear strategy, which is an unusual role for a terrorist organization to take. These pronouncements have no doubt fueled some analysts to mistakenly believe that LeT wants to acquire nuclear assets for its own use, which belies a seriously flawed understanding of the organization and the Pakistani state at whose behest LeT operates.[86]

In Chapter 4, I provide a historical account of LeT's ideological roots as well as its organizational and operational development, including its most recent foray into Pakistani politics despite decades of forswearing direct political participation. Even though Pakistan did not create LeT/JuD or its parent organization MDI, it quickly co-opted it and rendered it the most lethal and loyal proxy in Pakistan's arsenal for managing external threats but also for assisting its military and intelligence agencies domestically.

In Chapter 5, I provide quantitative and qualitative insights about the foot soldiers of the LeT. I draw upon qualitative studies of martyr biographies to demonstrate basic characteristics of LeT fighters who appear in a database which I prepared, along with similar data on the Pakistan army officer corps to demonstrate some of the important similarities between these two fighting forces. From the *shaheed* biographies, I infer qualitative insights about the means with which the LeT recruits family members—particularly mothers—to sustain their various proselytizing and militant operations. These biographies also offer insight into the varied motivations of LeT's martyrs. This chapter takes as its departure point work that I conducted under the auspices of the Combatting Terrorism Center at West Point[87] and published in *The Journal of Strategic Studies*, with permission from the publisher.[88]

In Chapter 6, I exposit what I call the domestic politics of the organization, the second component of the new argument advanced in this volume. As noted earlier, most scholarly and policy analytic work focuses upon the importance of LeT with respect to Pakistan's external goals in India and to some extent Afghanistan; but here I draw upon the organization's varied publications to map out its internal importance to Pakistan. Specifically, while many of Pakistan's numerous Deobandi erstwhile proxies have turned against their patrons, LeT has not. Moreover, LeT vigorously argues against any sort of violence in Pakistan whether sectarian or communal. Instead, it staunchly contends that the only legitimate *jihad* is waged beyond Pakistan's borders. Due to both the domestic and external perquisites that LeT offers Pakistan's military and intelligence agencies, the state has thrown its full support behind the organization to amplify its domestic activities.

In the final chapter, I discuss the implications of my principle argument about the organization's centrality to the army's efforts to further its security goals abroad, while seeking to roll back the blowback from decades of cynically deploying Islamist militants in the service of its foreign policies. I submit that Pakistan will not give up LeT, or other cherished proxies, for that matter, under most conceivable circumstances.

What then can be done to curb LeT's lethality even if the organization cannot easily be extirpated? I engage the leadership decapitation literature along with what I have learned from this exercise to offer some options. Unlike other terrorist groups based in Pakistan, LeT has a very hierarchical structure with a small number of leaders that circulate about the known leadership positions. Saeed's entry into politics under the guise of the MML further entrenches the MML within this shallow bench of leaders. Moreover, many of the latter are close to Hafiz Saeed through extended kinship ties. Reflecting the security it enjoys in Pakistan, it has very little depth of leadership because it has never had to prepare for the contingency of leadership loss, with the exception of their combat commanders in Indian-administered Kashmir who die in the course of engaging Indian forces. I argue that leadership decapitation, under these circumstances, may be the best option to degrade the *quality* of terror that the organization can perpetrate for some time even if such actions do not dampen the *quantity* of terror the organization generates.[89] I then offer broader considerations for the American and Indian governments in overcoming what is essentially a nuclear-coercion strategy by Pakistan.

2

THE GENESIS OF INDO-PAKISTAN
SECURITY COMPETITION[1]

Pakistan's security competition with India originated during the Partition of the Raj. After two world wars, Britain was indebted, war-weary and had little enthusiasm for holding onto colonial India, which had become increasingly difficult to control. There was little public appetite in Britain for resuscitating the waning Empire and key allies such as the United States insisted that London transfer power to the Indians. Great Britain had planned to depart South Asia by June 1948; however, amidst pressures at home and abroad, London resolved to transfer power to the new dominions of Pakistan and India on 14 and 15 August 1947, respectively—almost a year earlier than previously decided. Consequently, the British failed to plan for the Partition and the predictable violence that engulfed north India as millions of Muslims left their homes in what was to become India for Pakistan, while Sikhs and Hindus left their homes in what was to become Pakistan for India. Compounding the problem, the British did not announce the territorial boundaries of the new states until after the transfer of power, which only incentivized further communal predation. With borders uncertain as independence neared, communal militias mobilized to cleanse districts of minorities in the hope of achieving either Muslim majority or non-Muslim majority localities. Sikhs and Hindus attacked Muslims while Muslims attacked Sikhs and Hindus. The brutality of Partition included large-scale rapes, abductions, slaughter, mutilation of corpses, and other atrocities. Hundreds of thousands of people died in the communal butchery before, during, and immediately after Partition. Another twelve million persons were displaced to become refugees in their adoptive countries.[2]

This bloodstained disarticulation of the Raj endowed the emergent states with eidetic notions of nationhood that were diametrically opposed and structurally in conflict with each other.[3] However, while Partition has become less salient in India over time, the gruesome legacy of Partition continues to animate Pakistani security perspectives that are embraced by the military, militant organizations, political parties and ordinary citizenry alike. In part, this is because for many Indians, Partition was an undesired, but essentially finished process. For Pakistan, Partition remains "unfinished business."[4] In considerable measure, the continued importance of Partition in Pakistan's security narratives derives from the unequal experiences of Partition that both new states experienced. Pakistan was the seceding state and, compared to India, the comparatively diminutive Pakistan had fewer resources to manage the myriad problems associated with Partition. Unlike India, which retained most of the colonial governance and administrative infrastructure, Pakistan had to build a state from scratch with severe shortfalls in human, material, and financial resources. Furthermore, Pakistan's leaders were deeply aggrieved about Pakistan's territorial award. These grievances abide after nearly seven decades, and it is a matter of faith amongst Pakistan's civilian and military leaders and the general population alike that the British conspired with India to deprive Pakistan of key Muslim-majority areas in the Punjab and, most importantly, the Muslim-majority princely state of Kashmir. Strangely, many Pakistanis fulminate that Pakistan was entitled to Kashmir, despite the fact there is no legal or historical support for this position. Thus, for most Pakistanis, Partition was and remains an inherently unfair and incomplete process. In fact, Pakistan's previous army chief, Raheel Sharif, while addressing an audience at the Royal United Services Institute in London in October 2015, declared that "Kashmir is an unfinished agenda of Indo-Pak Partition,"[5] a point he reiterated again in January 2017, a few months after his retirement in November 2016.[6] Pakistan's president, Mamnoon Hussain, reiterated this point during a celebration of Pakistan Day when he declared—in front of the service chiefs—that Kashmir is the "unfinished agenda of the sub-continent's partition," and declared Pakistan's unwavering "moral, political and diplomatic support to its Kashmiri brethren."[7]

As I have detailed at length, Pakistan remains committed to rectifying these ostensible iniquities and inequities of Partition.[8] Whereas many countries are resentful about lands they lost, Pakistan nurtures "a sense of bitterness and grievance for territories that have never formed part of its polity."[9] To capture all or portions of Kashmir, Pakistan initiated—and subsequently failed to win—wars in 1947–48, 1965, and 1999, and has sustained an intense proxy war in Kashmir since 1990 in addition to a campaign of sabotage of varying intensity since 1948.[10] Pakistan fought and lost another war with India in 1971 over East Pakistan, which resulted in the emergence of an independent Bangladesh. While that conflict had little to do with Kashmir per se, it continues to animate Pakistan's desire to reciprocate by fomenting separatist movements in India, including in Kashmir.

The Pakistani state long ago developed two dangerous tools to reverse these purported crimes of Partition (see Chapter 3). One is the ever-expanding fleet of Islamist militant groups, as well as non-Islamist groups, that Pakistan deploys in India as well as Afghanistan. The second is a growing arsenal of nuclear weapons, which makes it virtually impossible for India or any other state for that matter to punish Pakistan for using terrorism as a tool of statecraft or compel it to cease doing so. Pakistan acquired a crude nuclear device around 1983–4,[11] after which Pakistan became evermore emboldened in its strategy of sub-conventional warfare as it continued making progress in developing its nuclear deterrent. Under this expanding nuclear umbrella, Pakistan became increasingly confident that India would not risk responding militarily to Pakistan's various terrorist outrages in Kashmir and the rest of India. Equally important, Pakistan became steadily assured that the United States and the international community would intervene to prevent any conflict from escalating to an all-out war, with the always lingering possibility for inadvertent or deliberate escalation to nuclear use.

Finally, Pakistan has long understood that its nuclear deterrent and the attendant fears about the possibility that terrorists will obtain nuclear materials, weapons or knowhow, coerces the United States to eschew severing ties with Pakistan much less impose costly sanctions as it did against Iran for decades. In fact, the more reckless Pakistan behaves through its sponsorship of terrorist groups as well as nuclear proliferation, the greater the American desire both to remain engaged in the country in hopes of using inducements to influence Pakistan's behavior, as well as to use the cover of the embassy and its various missions to deploy covert assets to gather intelligence about Pakistan's program.[12]

Understanding the tortured history of Pakistan's revisionist agenda with respect to India is critical to appreciating the utility of LeT and other militants to Pakistan's deep state. For this reason, this chapter provides a brief history of the independence movement, the inherent communal ideologies that Pakistan's proponents mobilized to achieve an independent state, and a précis of the disastrous Partition process that gave rise to India and Pakistan. Three particular issues remain significant in contemporary Pakistan. First, many Pakistanis continue to pass onto their descendants these tales of communally-motivated murder, rape, and mayhem that accompanied the countries' births. Second, Pakistanis continue to assert that the way in which the British parsed the districts of the Punjab was inherently unfair and prejudicial to Pakistan's interests. Third, Pakistanis believe that the princely state of Kashmir should have gone to Pakistan and that the way in which the British carved up the Punjab enabled India to mobilize troops against Pakistani invaders, thus thwarting Pakistani efforts to secure the state by force.

Next, I discuss the legacy of Partition for Indo-Pakistani security competition generally, as well as the Pakistan army in particular. The Pakistan army aims to secure Pakistan's territorial integrity, wrench Kashmir from India, and protect Pakistan's ideological frontiers. In the service of these goals, the Pakistan army and Pakistan's Inter-Services Intelligence Agency (ISI) have developed a covey of militant groups over the last six decades, which it has used in a variety of ways that include conventional as well as proxy warfare. Therefore, I also provide a brief description of these wars and crises, drawing particular attention to the army's strategy of asymmetric conflict and concomitant utilization of non-state actors or regular troops disguised as non-state actors. I conclude this chapter with a series of implications that this torturous history has, not only for Pakistan's military and intelligence agencies, but also the numerous so-called *jihadi* groups that these organizations have increasingly relied upon in the pursuit of Pakistan's foreign and defense policies.

Summoning A Muslim Zion in South Asia

The Indian National Congress (Congress), founded in 1885, dominated the political scene in pre-Partition British India with an established presence throughout India.[13] Even though the All India Muslim League (League), founded as an explicitly communal party in 1906, was a comparative late comer, it became the Congress' principle oppugner at the all-India level. Congress and the League competed with each other and their deeply entrenched provincial parties as the fate of a united India teetered in the balance of their contest. As Britain's exit became imminent, the League's leadership grew evermore concerned about the security of India's large Muslim minority within a Hindu-dominated India under a Congress-led government.[14] The League's leadership became progressively more disquieted as the Congress appeared to be retreating from its commitment to secular democratic principles and, subsequently, began evaluating options that could best safeguard Muslim communal interests.[15] Muhammad Ali Jinnah was one of the League's most important leaders whom, today, many Pakistanis extol as the founder of the nation and whom they call the *Quaid-i-Azam* (literally Great Leader, often shortened to the *Quaid*).[16]

Jinnah did not embrace the idea of an independent Muslim nation-state until quite late; instead, he sought to protect Muslim communal concerns within a united India.[17] In fact, as late as 1940, Pakistan was not the stated, primary goal of the League. On 23 March 1940, during a meeting of the Muslim League in Lahore, the League demanded that constitutional discussions be reconsidered to account for the League's claim that Indian Muslims constitute a "nation." The League furthered that Muslim-majority provinces in the north-east and north-west should "be grouped to constitute Independent States in which the constituent units... [would] be autonomous and sovereign."[18] The use of the plural "states" remains a subject of debate; some dismiss it as a mistake in diction or dictation, while others, such as latter proponents of an independent Bangladesh, claim that it was literally a demand for multiple states.[19] Oddly, most Pakistanis believe he simply said "state."[20] Pakistanis also believe this speech was the moment when Jinnah and the League officially made the demand for an independent Pakistan. For this reason, Pakistanis refer to this event as the "Pakistan Declaration" and celebrate 23 March 1940 as "Pakistan Day," even though this famous speech was known as the "Lahore Declaration" by Jinnah's contemporaries and furthermore, Jinnah never once uttered the word "Pakistan," nor referred to requisite Partition of the subcontinent.

The demand for these "independent states" was based upon the Two Nation Theory, which Jinnah adumbrated at that meeting:

> Islam and Hinduism are not religions in the strict sense of the word, but are; in fact, different and distinct social orders .... The Hindus and the Muslims belong to two different religious philosophies, social customs, and literatures .... To yoke together two such nations under a single State, one as a numerical minority and the other as a majority, must lead to growing discontent and the final destruction of any fabric that may be so build up for the government of such a state.[21]

While the demand for Pakistan was acute in Muslim-minority areas of north India, elsewhere there was considerably less enthusiasm.[22] In the 1937 elections, the Muslim League suffered a crushing defeat. Jinnah and the Muslim League again vied for "the Muslim vote" in the 1945–46 elections by negotiating deals with provincial power brokers endowed with plush vote banks. To secure this victory, the League promoted a simple, incitive communal message: Muslims, who comprise a separate nation from Hindus, will be unable to live with dignity and security under the tyranny of the Hindu majority and its purported antipathy towards Muslims in a united India.[23] This communal campaign appeal galvanized waves of sanguinary violence that seized the Punjab and Bengal before, during, and after Partition. This ensuing bloodshed validated the League's communal claims that Muslims cannot live safely among Hindus. Jinnah also deliberately kept the notion of Pakistan as vague as possible and for as long as possible to maximize votes for the League and Pakistan—howsoever ideated by the various voters.

The combination worked: The League swept all Muslim seats in the central assembly and secured a majority (three-quarters) of the votes cast by Muslims in the various provincial assembly elections. Jinnah construed this victory as a referendum on the League's demand for an independent Pakistan based on undivided Punjab and Bengal, even though those who voted for the League— and for Pakistan, howsoever imagined—in the 1946 elections did so without truly knowing what borders it would have, what kind of citizenship and governance structures it would embrace, and ultimately, what this Pakistan would be.[24]

The Two Nation concept continued to garner proponents as Indian political leaders either rejected the legitimacy of Pakistan's statehood outright, or niggardly accepted it, fearing that unless they did so the British would either refuse to transfer power or offer the myriad 562 princely states (also called Native States) the option of independence, which would confer upon India its own moth-eaten geography. On several occasions, Indian leaders publicly contended that Pakistan would fail and return to India's fold, which only confirmed the deepest fears of Pakistan's early leaders that India harbored ill will towards Pakistan or even rejected its right to exist.[25] The violence that surrounded Partition and the reluctant acceptance of Pakistan by Indian political leadership contributed to the growing antagonism between the citizens of both states, whose national ideologies stood in clear opposition: Pakistan's national ideology would be premised upon the posited fundamental inability of Hindus and Muslims to coexist; while India purported to embrace the principles of a secular democracy which is multi-ethnic and multi-religious. While Pakistan's early leaders hoped that religion would be the ideological supra-identity that would undermine ethnic identities and aspirations, India's leaders hoped that ethnicity and caste pulls would subsume religious identities.[26]

As soon as Pakistan came into fruition, Jinnah and the League leadership had to contend with a grave set of foundational and existential problems. While the communal appeals of the Two Nation Theory helped secure an independent Pakistan, they posed a serious threat to Pakistan's political unity. After all, prior to Partition, nearly one in three inhabitants of what became Pakistan were non-Muslims.[27] Even after the harrowing population transfers related to Partition, nearly one in four of Pakistan's citizen were non-Muslim. While most of these were Bengali Hindus who were concentrated in East Pakistan, Parsees (Zoroastrians), Christians, and Sikhs also lived in the nascent Pakistan.[28] Ultimately, Pakistan's leaders made little effort to temper the divisive rhetoric that they had deployed to dismantle the subcontinent that was necessary to enable Pakistan's Muslim and non-Muslim citizens to co-exist peacefully within this new nation, encumbered with a precarious political geography and inadequate resources.[29] Consequently, the Two Nation Theory obtains as the bedrock of Pakistani political and ideological identity with the predictable consequences that with each passing year, Pakistan's non-Muslims became ever more marginalized politically, socially and economically.

The Origins of Pakistan's Kashmir Obsession

On 20 February 1947, newly elected Prime Minister Attlee announced that Britain would transfer power to Indians by June 1948. In June 1947, his government passed the Indian Independence Act which called for the formation of Pakistan and India, which would become independent on 14 and 15 August 1947, respectively. Pakistan would be comprised of those provinces of East Bengal and West Punjab, as well as the territories which were included in the province then known as Sind, the Chief Commissioner's Province of British Balochistan and, subject to a referendum, the territories of the Northwest Frontier Province.[30] Note that it made no mention of Kashmir, as Kashmir was one of the afore-noted 562 princely states.

Two specific issues pertaining to Partition are particularly important to understanding the ways in which Pakistan prosecutes its revisionist agenda with respect to India. The first of these issues is the disposition of the princely states from which Pakistan's Kashmir fixation originates. The second relates to the division of the Punjab, which Pakistanis still view in conspiratorial terms because they believe that the way in which the British allocated the Punjab across the two new states enabled India to move its military forces to Kashmir, depriving it of territory it coveted primarily for ideological reasons.[31]

Three Obdurate Princes

Roughly speaking, the Raj included two kinds of territories: those areas which were under British rule, and those 562 so-called "princely states," which were governed by various indigenous rulers (*maharajas, nawabs, nizams, khans*, etc.) in accordance to specific agreements negotiated by these rulers and the relevant British authorities.[32] These princely states accounted for about 41 per cent of the territorial landmass of British South Asia.[33] While these local potentates exercised near-autonomy in their internal affairs, they recognized the paramountcy of the Crown.[34] They posed a fairly serious problem for the future states of India and Pakistan because these princely states were not bound by the Indian Independence Act of 1947, and many of these local sovereigns preferred to retain their quasi-independence rather than join either of the new states.[35] As a consequence of Lord Mountbatten's assiduous efforts, all but three agreed to join Pakistan or India by 15 August 1947.[36] Those that resisted his efforts of suasion were the rulers of Junagadh, Hyderabad, and Kashmir.[37]

Hyderabad, a territory that spanned more than 80,000 square miles, was governed by a Muslim *nizam*, who presided over a majority Hindu population of more than sixteen million. The *nizam* wanted to remain independent, which was untenable for the new Indian state, as the sprawling princely state was deep within and accounted for a considerable percentage of Indian territory. After increasing violence as the Nizam's military forces (*razakars*) fought for independence, India seized full control of the state in a brutal so-called police action in September 1948. According to very conservative estimates, Indian security forces killed between 27,000 and 40,000 persons.[38]

Junagadh's sovereign (referred to as a *nawab*) was a Muslim whose subjects were preponderantly Hindu. Thinking of his own personal equities, he announced his intention to join Pakistan on 14 August 1947[39] even though Junagadh, located on the Kathiawar peninsula in Western India, was surrounded by India (except for its long seacoast on the Arabian Sea). Junagadh became a part of India after Indian forces invaded on 9 November 1947. This status was ratified by a plebiscite in February 1948, in which participants overwhelmingly voted to remain with India.[40] Many Pakistani maps depict

Junagadh as well as Hyderabad as Pakistani territory, even though the latter's ruler never wanted to join Pakistan.

Kashmir, with its five principle regions in its some 84,471 square miles, was more expansive than Hyderabad.[41] While many Pakistanis are wont to depict Kashmir as simply "Muslim" or "Muslim majority," the area's 4 million thinly dispersed residents were quite heterogeneous. In Jammu, which abutted the Punjab, there was a slight Muslim majority (53 per cent) prior to Partition. Partition sparked a wave of panic, which prompted many Muslims to flee, bequeathing to Jammu a majority Hindu population after Partition. The so-called "Vale of Kashmir" was dominated by Muslims. Ladakh lies to the east of the valley and borders Tibet, and was (and remains) populated mostly by Buddhists. The areas of Gilgit and Baltistan, which were west of the valley, were also peopled by a majority of Muslims who were mostly Ismaili Shia and thus distinct from the Sunni Muslims who were the majority in the Vale. Kashmir's potentate was Maharaja Hari Singh, a Hindu who governed the complex polity noted above.[42]

Singh, preferring to remain independent, signed a standstill agreement with Pakistan that obliged Pakistan not to invade.[43] Singh's indecisiveness discomfited India's political leaders, who feared that the longer he dithered, the more likely he would opt to remain independent or, worse, permit Pakistan to enter the state. Pakistan too was unnerved; without Kashmir, Pakistan would remain "incomplete" and the notion of the Two Nation Theory would linger unfulfilled.

Several developments in Kashmir influenced Singh's course of action. Perhaps the most important event that conditioned Singh's options was an invasion of his state by Pakistanis. Troubles for the Maharaja began when some 60,000 veterans of World War II returned to their homes in Poonch (Western Jammu) to find that they had become subjects of Hari Singh of Kashmir, whom they disliked due to his imposition of onerous taxes. These mostly Muslim Poonchis, annoyed with becoming Singh's subjects and out-raged by the communally-motivated murders of Muslims ongoing throughout India, declared their preference for joining Pakistan during a public assembly in August 1947. Singh responded by dispatching his Hindu Dogra troops, who open fired upon the assembled Poonchis. This encounter catalyzed a wider rebellion in Poonch, which drove many Poonchis to Pakistan. Sadar Mohammed Ibrahim Khan, a lawyer and member of the Kashmir state assembly, was one of those who fled to Pakistan. Upon arriving, he met Colonel Akbar Khan of the Pakistan army and solicited his assistance in emancipating Kashmir from Hari Singh.[44]

Colonel Khan, the director of Weapons and Equipment at General Headquarters in Rawalpindi, knew that Pakistan had scant stockpiles of munitions and weapons, owing to the incomplete process of dividing assets between the two armies of India and Pakistan.[45] Nonetheless, he condemned working weaponry and munitions and furtively outfitted the swelling ranks of men who wanted to fight for Kashmir's liberation from Singh. Khan could not approach General Sir Frank Messervy, the British chief of the Pakistan army, because he feared that Messervy would inform Field Marshal Sir Claude Auchinleck, the Supreme Commander India and Pakistan, who oversaw both the Indian and Pakistani armed forces and who was tasked with apportioning elements of the armed forces of British India into those of India and Pakistan. Had Auchinleck come to know of these plans, he would have most certainly recalled the British officers from the Pakistan army, which, given Pakistan's acute officer shortage, would have been a dangerous gamble. As such, Khan worked clandestinely to first arm, and then, organize and train the fighters. Initially unable to use active Pakistani military forces, Khan employed ex-servicemen who had joined the Indian National Army (INA) but had not been re-inducted into service after their release from prison.[46] When Prime Minister Liaquat Ali Khan and Sadar Shaukat Hayat Khan, a minister in the Punjab government, learned of Khan's activities, they strove to ensure that General Messervy remained unaware of the scheme.[47]

To date, Pakistani officials insist that these operations did not involve the support or amenities of the new state of Pakistan.[48] These claims are belied by the evidence gathered by Shuja Nawaz, the brother of a deceased Pakistan army chief who garnered access to the Pakistan army's archive of classified records. In fact, there were multiple sources of state support at the provincial and, increasingly, federal levels.[49] By October 1947, the Pakistan army was deeply apprehensive about Singh's disinclination to join Pakistan. On 23 October 1947, Prime Minister Liaquat Ali Khan sanctioned the dispatch of some 2,000 tribesmen into Kashmir (often called *lashkar*s under the command of Col Akbar Khan, who took the nom de guerre of General Tariq.[50] On the following evening, Nehru apprised Mountbatten of the developments as the tribesmen reached Kashmir via Pakistan military transports. Seeing the invaders, Singh requested India's help to expel them. India agreed to do so, on the condition that Singh sign an instrument of accession which would render Kashmir a formal part of India. India was adamant that it would send troops only to defend sovereign Indian territory. Singh signed the instrument on 26 October, after which Indian troops landed in Srinagar.[51]

The newly formed armies of India and Pakistan fought a limited war for over a year. Nehru sought the intervention of the United Nations, which brokered a ceasefire that came into effect on 31 December 1948. The terms of the ceasefire left about three fifths of Kashmir under Indian control, with the balance of the state under Pakistani administration. According to the United Nations Security Council (UNSC) Resolution 47, passed in 1948, Pakistan was to first withdraw its regular and irregular forces from Kashmir. Following Pakistan's demilitarization, India was to follow suit; however, India was permitted to maintain a minimum force for defensive purposes. Once these two sequential conditions were met, Kashmiris were to decide their future through an impartial plebiscite.[52] Nonetheless, Pakistan never withdrew and the plebiscite never took place. Notably, Pakistan has still not complied with the first requirement despite Pakistan's insistence upon the plebiscite.

This has not deterred Pakistan's civilian and military leadership from making disingenuous pleas to the United Nations to fully implement these resolutions. For example, in August 2016, Pakistan's former Prime Minister Nawaz Sharif called for the implementations of the UN resolutions on Kashmir.[53] Pakistan's former army chief, Raheel Sharif, made similar calls while addressing various audiences[54] and its current army chief reiterated his support for Kashmiri self-determination.[55] Pakistan still aspires to control all of Kashmir in fulfillment of the Two Nation Theory, motivated by an erroneous belief that Pakistan was entitled to Kashmir based upon the state's Muslim majority population composition.[56] As detailed in this volume, Pakistan has fought three wars over Kashmir in 1947–48, 1965, and 1999, and has sustained an intense proxy war since 1989 using Islamist militants such as the Lashkar-e-Tayyaba (LeT).

Rending the Punjab

Pakistan's beliefs about why it did not secure Kashmir are deeply tied to other conspiracies about Partition: namely, that the British purposefully divided the Punjab to facilitate India's capture of Kashmir by force. The Indian Independence Act established separate commissions to Partition the northern state of Punjab and the eastern state of Bengal on "the basis of ascertaining contiguous majority areas of Muslims and non-Muslims." In doing so, they were also supposed to "take into account other factors."[57] After the Bengal and Punjab provincial assemblies voted to divide their provinces respectively on 20 and 23 June 1947, the requisite commissions were established for

Partitioning both. Sir Cyril Radcliffe, who arrived in South Asia for the first time on 8 July 1947, chaired both bodies.[58] Even though the British did not publicize the boundaries until 16 August 1947, a day after the actual transfer of power and Radcliffe's departure from India on 15 August, Lord Mountbatten had obtained the prior assent of the political leaders of erstwhile Pakistan and India to the commissions' decisions.[59]

Both sides honored their agreements and accepted the boundary awards but neither was satisfied: India repined that some of the districts awarded to East Pakistan should have gone to India while Pakistan was piqued because India received seven Muslim-majority *tehsils*[60] in Punjab, including Gurdaspur, Batala, Ajnala, Jullundur, Nakodar, Ferozepur, and Zira, as well as a part of Kasur district. Pakistan, in contrast, received no non-Muslim-majority *tehsil*.[61]

Pakistan was most aggrieved by the division of the district of Gurdaspur, often claiming erroneously that all of Gurdaspur went to India when, in fact, the *tehsil* of Shakergarh went to Pakistan, whereupon it became part of Punjab's Sialkot district.[62] Moreover, Pakistan's public schools, military institutions and media continue assert that the British deliberately awarded "Gurdaspur" to India to influence the eventual territorial disposition of Kashmir[63] even though scholarship decisively disproves this conspiracy.[64] As Ilahi notes, since the *tehsil* of Pathankot had a Hindu majority, it would have gone to India even had the principle of religious affinity been applied without regard to other considerations. Critically, since Pathankot hosted the main road and rail links as well as the only bridge at the time that traversed the Ravi River, India only required this *tehsil* to send ground troops into Kashmir.[65]

Military, Mullah, Militant Nexus: The Army and the Ideology of Pakistan

The multiplicity of Jinnah's explanations permits proponents of one vision or another for Pakistan to pick and choose from his statements in support of their preferred position.[66] Because Jinnah died within a year of independence, he was unable to resolve the competing claims about his actual vision for Pakistan. Consequently, his successors were ambivalent whether they should "take their cue from his independence eve call to keep religion out of politics or to build on the religious sentiment generated during the political bargaining for Pakistan."[67] Pakistan's leaders needed to find some way to manage the inherent contradictions between the clearly communal underpinnings of Pakistan and the imperatives of consolidating a weak state, while contesting the demands and expectations of a multi-ethnic and multi-religious polity.

Pakistan's leaders ultimately chose to erect and promulgate what various civilian and military leaders alike have labeled a "state ideology" based upon Islam and the Two Nation Theory. Shortly after independence, the Islamists demanded an Islamic constitution. Their efforts culminated in the so-called "Objectives Resolution," which Liaquat Ali Khan put before the first constituent assembly in March 1949. This was a contingent event that determined Pakistan's path to becoming an ideologically Islamic state. The Resolution, which became the preamble to the constitution, asserted that:

> Whereas sovereignty over the entire universe belongs to Allah Almighty alone and the authority which He has delegated to the State of Pakistan, through its people for being exercised within the limits prescribed by Him is a sacred trust.
>
> [...] The principles of democracy, freedom, equality, tolerance and social justice as enunciated by Islam shall be fully observed...the Muslims shall be enabled to order their lives in the individual and collective spheres in accordance with the teachings and requirements of Islam as set out in the Holy Quran and the Sunnah.[68]

What has inhibited Pakistan's development into an outright theocracy—e.g. in contrast to neighboring Iran—is the diversity of Pakistan's Islam. In Pakistan, there are five *masalik* (pl. *maslak*, interpretative tradition). In addition to the Shia *maslak* there are four others which are Sunni, including: Jamaat-e-Islami (JI, Islamic Assembly), which is also a political party; Deobandi; Barelvi; and Ahl-e-Hadees. The first three Sunni *masalik* follow the Hanafi school of jurisprudence. While adherents to the Ahl-e-Hadees school (who are sometimes referred to as Salafis) are often conflated with Wahhabis who follow the Hanbali school of jurisprudence, they consider themselves to be *ghair-muqallids* (followers of no path). In addition to this sectarian diversity, the *ulema* (pl. of *alim*, religious scholar) of Pakistan lack a clerical hierarchy of the sort present in Iran, for example. As a consequence of both this variation of interpretative traditions and the non-hierarchical organization of the various clerical groups, the "Objectives Resolution" inadvertently created a permanent role for Pakistan's various competing *ulema* to define who is a Muslim, what creed is most suitable for Pakistan, and thus, to weigh heavily on the status of any given citizen.[69]

Under General Muhammad Ayub Khan (henceforth Ayub), the army expropriated the role of defending Pakistan's ideological frontiers in addition to the country's geographical boundaries.[70] Ayub, who was not personally pious and even evidenced disdain for religious leaders, argued early in his tenure that Pakistan should adopt a modern Islam. Like all army chiefs who followed him, Ayub instrumentalized Islam for his personal governance projects. Ayub sought to forge a robust central government that would be reinforced by Islam and its flagbearers.[71]

Ayub's ideations of the ideology of Pakistan and Pakistani nationalism were informed by "Pan-Islamic aspirations and fear of Hindu and Indian domination."[72] In his autobiography, Ayub explains that Pakistan's most significant security and existential threats derive from India's "inability to reconcile herself to our existence as a sovereign independent State. The Indian attitude can only be explained in pathological terms. The Indian leaders have a deep hatred for the Muslims.... From the beginning, India was determined to make things difficult for us."[73] Elsewhere in his book, he cites India's hegemonic impulses and obdurate inimicality towards Pakistan, as well as the intolerance of the Brahmins (the Hindu priestly caste) as evidence of the mutual incompatibility of India and Pakistan.[74] Ayub believed that if Pakistan's "ideology" failed, then Pakistan itself would fail. After all, could Pakistan truly be different from India if it were denuded of ideological differentiation? It was during Ayub's tenure that "Pakistan began the process of official myth-creation in earnest. A large central bureaucracy was created to manufacture an ideology for Pakistan, one that glorified the army as the state's key institution."[75]

Following the 1971 war when East Pakistan emerged as independent Bangladesh, Zulfiqar Ali Bhutto, the founder of the Pakistan Peoples Party (PPP), became the first civilian chief martial law administrator, commander-in-chief and president (20 December 1971–13 August 1973) and later the prime minister (14 August 1973—5 July 1977). Rather than concluding that Pakistan lost East Pakistan because of West Pakistan's chauvinism, exploitative and extractive policies, and systematic efforts to deprive Bengalis of equal citizenship, Bhutto concluded that the promotion of Islam as a primary identity was the most effective means to unify Pakistan's diverse polity and promote state cohesion amidst revivified ethnic separatist aspiration in Balochistan and Northwest Frontier Province (NWFP). Bhutto propitiated the Arab states of the Persian Gulf for financial, political, diplomatic and religious support. In exchange for their patronage, Bhutto expanded the role of Arabic in the public school curriculum, thereby creating new jobs for those who specialized in Islamic studies. He declared Ahmadis to be non-Muslims to accommodate the long-standing demand of Islamists who consider Ahmadis to be apostates because they do not recognize the chronological finality of the prophet Muhammad (even though they consider themselves to be Muslims). In turn, apostasy is punishable by death in Pakistan and elsewhere.[76] Bhutto enshrined

Islamization within the 1973 constitution, which identified Pakistan an Islamic state for the first time.[77] It should be noted that Pakistan's constitution explicitly disqualifies anyone from holding a seat in the parliament (and thus becoming prime minister) if they do not uphold the "ideology of Pakistan."[78]

While Bhutto firmly entrenched Pakistan on a path of expanding Islamism, General Zia ul Haq pursued these initiatives with even greater verve after he ousted Bhutto in a 1977 coup. General Zia enlarged the role of Sunni Islam within the Pakistani state and polity at the explicit expense of Pakistan's Shia, who comprise between 10 and 15 per cent of Pakistan's population.[79] General Zia ul Haq established several government bodies to institutionalize Sunni interpretations of Islam, strengthened a collective of laws known as "the *Hudood* Ordinances" that prescribed purportedly Islamic punishments, and instituted a system of interest-free banking that was based on a system of sharing profits and losses as well as *zakat*, an Islamic tax.[80] The imposition of *zakat* became a flash point for sectarian discord in Pakistan, which was exacerbated by regional developments such as the Iranian Revolution, the Iran-Iraq War, and the anti-Soviet *jihad*. Despite his commitment to Islamizing Pakistani society, General Zia ul Haq was thwarted by the variation and competition among the differing Islamic schools of thought in Pakistan, because the *ulema* of these schools fundamentally and vigorously disagreed on various points of *shariat*. Consequently, Zia's efforts to impose *shariat* devolved into an inter-sectarian struggle over which kind of Islam would prevail in Pakistan and who would be the custodians of this Islam.[81]

After Zia died in an unexplained airplane crash in 1988, Pakistan returned to an army-controlled democracy. The prime ministership shifted between Benazir Bhutto, Z. A. Bhutto's daughter and leader of the PPP, and Nawaz Sharif, of the Pakistan Muslim League-Nawaz (PML-N). No government served out its full term due to army manipulation.[82] General Pervez Musharraf disrupted this brief interregnum of democracy when he ousted Nawaz Sharif in a bloodless coup in 1999. Like the military dictators before him, Musharraf instrumentalized Islam during his tenure notwithstanding the heavy international criticism of him given his purported secular credentials. As with Zia's government, the *ulema* figured prominently in Musharraf's regime. The Muttahida Majlis-e-Amal (MMA, a bloc of Islamist parties) comprised Musharraf's opposition party of choice at the center and in two of Pakistan's four provinces.

Before resigning as army chief in November 2007, Musharraf promoted Ashfaq Parvez Kayani, who previously served as the chief of ISI, to full

General and made him the Vice Chief of Army Staff and thus, Musharraf's anointed successor as army chief. Kayani, like many army chiefs before him, made ample reference to the so-called ideology of Pakistan and the importance of protecting it. On 14 August 2011, he addressed an audience at Pakistan's Military Academy in Kakul for the annual Azadi Parade (to celebrate independence). Kayani explained that:

> 14th August 1947 was a historic day for the Muslims of the Subcontinent. This day is testimony to the indomitable will of the Muslims to establish a separate homeland under the inspiring leadership of Quaid-i-Azam Muhammad Ali Jinnah. Let us, on this day, humbly thank Allah Almighty [...]. We must stay committed to the ideals of Pakistan and remain ever ready to protect our motherland [...]. The basis of our existence is the 'Ideology of Pakistan.' [...] We have a firm belief that by following the golden principles of Islam, we shall progress and win a respectable place in the comity of nations. We should never forget that Islam is the religion of peace [...] that binds us together and should not in any way divide us.[83]

Raheel Sharif, who became the Pakistan Army chief on 29 November 2013, was initially less loquacious than his predecessor and preferred to maintain a lower profile.[84] At first, he appeared less doctrinaire and less political than Gen. Kayani, at least based upon some of his few public addresses. However, during his oration on *Yom-e-Shuhada* (Martyrs' Day) on 30 April 2014 at General Headquarters in Rawalpindi, he spoke generally about the variety of internal and external threats to the country and the preparedness of the armed forces to contend with them. However, Sharif did not miss an opportunity to wax on about Kashmir. He explained that Kashmir is Pakistan's *sheh rag*, or jugular vein, which subsequent military and civilian leaders have reiterated since.[85] Pakistan's dispute over Kashmir is "nothing less than a struggle for very existence of Pakistan as a viable nation-state."[86] He added that the Kashmir conflict is an international dispute about which there are several standing United Nations resolutions, and that it is only possible to resolve this dispute and establish durable peace if it is resolved per the aspirations of the Kashmiri people.[87]

Hostilites in Kashmir intensified under Raheel Sharif.[88] By summer 2015, he was as pugnacious about the Kashmir issue as Kayani before him. For example, in June 2015, he had abandoned any previous caution and declared that "Pakistan and Kashmir are inseparable," and that "Kashmir is an unfinished agenda of Partition."[89] This is the position that he continued to articulate in domestic and international forums until he retired on 29 November 2016.[90] He continued his sabre-rattling until his last day in office, threatening India with aggressive action and stammering, yet again, that "in South Asia, lasting peace and progress is impossible without solution of the Kashmir issue."[91]

Lieutenant General Qamar Javed Bajwa succeeded Sharif as Pakistan's 16th COAS when Indo-Pakistan ties were intensely fraught, owing to LeT's attack on an Indian army base in Uri and India's much-publicized retaliatory "surgical operation" along the LOC.[92] Bajwa was likely selected for this position because he had extensive experience in managing security along the LOC, was commissioned in the 16 Baloch Regiment, and was an instructor at the Command and Staff College in Quetta, the provincial capital of Balochistan. The controversial so-called China-Pakistan Economic Corridor (CPEC, a corridor for road and rail connectivity, economic zones, and energy production) is also rooted in the north in Gilgit and Baltistan and to Gwadar Port (Balochistan) in the south. Baloch Pakistanis throughout the presumed CPEC route, along with Baloch militants, are very active in opposing this and related projects in the province, because they have been excluded and view the Punjabi-dominated state as colonizers seeking to make them minorities in their own province.[93]

Pakistan Repeatedly Tries to Change Maps through War

Consistent with its enduring rhetoric, Pakistan has prosecuted a relentless security competition with India in an effort to alter the territorial status quo in Kashmir and to retard both India's rise in South Asia and in the international system. Pakistan and India have fought four wars in 1947–48, 1965, 1971, and 1999, and have weathered several crises that attenuated short of war. Pakistan relies upon unconventional warfare to prosecute its conflict with its conventional foe to the east. Either Pakistan's military or its Islamist proxies precipitated nearly all of these conflicts, while Pakistan's insistence upon nonstate actors or military and paramilitary forces disguised as non-state actors is a common element to virtually all of these wars and crises slides.[94]

The first Indo-Pakistan war began in October 1947 as a result of Pakistan's first adventure using non-state actors. Pakistan, anxious because Maharaja Hari Singh desired to remain independent, dispatched thousands of Pakistani tribal *lashkars* (militia members) to invade the princely state of Jammu and Kashmir, despite having signed a standstill agreement which obliged Pakistan not to undertake such an invasion. The invaders enjoyed extensive assistance from Pakistan's new civilian government and elements in the military leadership. The Maharaja, whose own forces were unable to defend against the intruders, sought Indian assistance to repel them. India agreed to do so provided that Singh signed an instrument of accession to India, which he was fully empowered to do under the terms of the British transfer of power. Nehru, concerned about the legitimacy of the accession rather than the legality of it, requested that the Kashmiri nationalist leader Sheikh Abdullah consent to Kashmir's accession, which he did.[95] India airlifted troops to defend what had become Indian territory.[96]

The conflict ended on 1 January 1948 with a United Nations-sponsored ceasefire. The ceasefire line divided the territory into Indian and Pakistani administrative zones, with India retaining the important Muslim-majority valley of Kashmir. However, Pakistan's military likely concluded the efficacy of using non-state actors as a part of its national security strategy. Had it not been for the so-called marauders, Pakistan would have acquired no part of Kashmir.[97]

Pakistan also started the second Indo-Pakistan war of 1965 to alter Kashmir's dispensation. This war had two phases. The first (1964–1965) was comprised of a series of clashes between forward-deployed Pakistani and Indian patrols operating in the Rann of Kutch. While Indian and Pakistani accounts of this conflict differ, there is consensus that India's response to Pakistani incursions was tepid due to the seasonal rains which rendered sustained ground conflict on the marshy terrain arduous and unlikely to lead to a propitious course of action. Pakistan attributed India's feeble response to an aversion to vigorous combat and believed it could behave more aggressively in Kashmir without significant resistance or consequence.[98]

Pakistan commenced the second phase of the conflict in spring 1965 by launching "Operation Gibraltar," which aimed to denervate the Kashmir issue.[99] During "Operation Gibraltar," Pakistan's army mustered and trained several thousand irregular fighters, called *mujahideen*. Estimates of the size of the force range between 3,000 and 30,000 militants.[100] Afterwards, Pakistan followed up with "Operation Grand Slam," during which Pakistani regular forces crossed the cease-fire line to invade Indian-administered Kashmir. Pakistan's civilian leadership was confident that Pakistan could defeat India both due to the latter's lethargic response in the Rann of Kutch and hence, Pakistan's downward assessment of India's capabilities, as well as Pakistan's will to fight after India's demoralizing defeat in its 1962 war with China.[101]

Contrary to Pakistan's expectations, India was prepared and quite willing to fight. India opted to open a new front along the international border and began a major counter-offensive against Lahore and Sialkot, which were and are two major cities in Pakistan's Punjab. With the war approaching a stalemate, the UNSC passed a resolution on 20 September 1965 calling for a cessation of hostilities. India's civilian planners, who had poor information from its military leadership and underestimated its ability, accepted the ceasefire prematurely.[102] While the use of non-state actors did not result in a victory, they diminished the cost of Pakistan's failure in that war. As such, Pakistan would continue using proxy fighters in East Pakistan, Afghanistan, and India.[103]

The 1971 Indo-Pakistan war differed from the previous two because it was not about Kashmir; rather, it stemmed from the civil war that developed in Bengali-dominated East Pakistan. Pakistan's Bengalis were exhausted with decades of economic exploitation and political disenfranchisement. When it became clear that West Pakistan would not let the Awami League enjoy the fruits of their victory, Bengalis launched a series of protests that morphed into an independence movement. Yahya Khan, unable to find a political compromise between the elites in West and East Pakistan, cancelled the convening of the parliament. For Bengalis, this was the final provocation which exposed West Pakistan's undaunted commitment to deprive East Pakistanis of their right to exercise their democratic strength, and they demanded complete independence. On 26 March 1971, Yahya Khan announced that negotiations had failed and banned the Awami League. By the time he made this announcement, the military had already moved into the East to quash the rebellion in a brutal operation known as Operation Searchlight.[104]

Pakistan employed proxies as they had in the previous wars, namely ruffians from the student wing (Islami Jamiat-e-Talaba) of the Jamaat-e-Islami (JeI) and armed militias associated with the JeI, such as al Badr and al Shams. The complicity of the JeI in what was by most accounts genocide in East Pakistan still animates Bangladeshi politics to date. Prime Minister Sheikh Hasina (the autocratic daughter of Mujib and Awami League leader) currently controls Bangladesh. Her government initiated war-crime tribunals in which JeI leaders, their minions, and other political foes of the Awami League are being tried and sentenced to death or long prison sentences.[105]

The civil war between West and East Pakistan formally morphed into the third Indo-Pakistan war on 3 December 1971 with an "Israeli-style pre-emptive air attack by Pakistan on India's northern air bases ... [which] failed miserably on all counts."[106] The war ended on 17 December with the emergence of independent Bangladesh. With its nemesis vivisected, India emerged as the undisputed hegemon of South Asia. The war dealt yet another serious blow to the Two Nation Theory: Bengalis in East Pakistan mobilized along ethnic lines and even resisted West Pakistan's efforts to promote Islam as a supra-identity which would vitiate the salience of ethnic mobilization. While the Pakistan that emerged was more politically coherent and militarily defensible, Pakistan concluded from the war that India could never accept Pakistan and would seek to exploit such fissures in the future, with the aim of further dismembering Pakistan along ethnic lines. As such, Pakistan redoubled its commitment to the Two Nation Theory and implementing political Islam as a tool of nation-building first under Zulfiqar Ali Bhutto, who became Pakistan's chief martial law administrator and president after the war and later the prime minster, and then during the military regime of General Zia ul Haq, after he ousted Bhutto.[107]

The fourth Indo-Pakistan conflict was the Kargil War, which was the first war between India and Pakistan after India's May 1998 nuclear test and Pakistan's reciprocal nuclear tests seventeen days later.[108] Planning for this war was conducted by General Musharraf and three trusted generals. They envisioned taking several high-altitude Indian outposts, which Indians routinely evacuated during the winter and reoccupied in the spring. They had hoped that the operation, to be conducted by paramilitary troops from the Northern Light Infantry (NLI), would give a fillip to militant efforts in Kashmir and rekindle international attention to the dispute.[109] Militarily, Pakistan sought to pose a credible military threat to India, present it with a *fait accompli*, and bring it to the negotiating table from a position of weakness.[110] As the world became aware of the incursion, international opinion unanimously sided with India. To Pakistan's stupefaction, China, too, importuned that Pakistan extract its forces and accede to the status quo.[111] Eventually, Pakistani forces retreated amidst fears of a catastrophic defeat. While Pakistan saw modest success in its secondary goal of keeping the Kashmir dispute in the international eye, it had flatly failed in its first objective, which was to wring any concession from India on Kashmir.

One of the curious aspects of the Kargil war is that while it was fought by paramilitary and regular military forces, Pakistan initially claimed that the invaders were *mujahideen*. This coincided with earlier Indian claims to the same effect. While conducting fieldwork in Pakistan on the Kargil conflict under the auspices of Peter Lavoy, Lt. Gen. (ret.) Chaudry Iftikhar, the former Chief of General Staff of the Army and Defense Secretary to Nawaz Sharif, told our team that during a 17 May 1999 briefing, Pakistan Army officials explained: "To the outside world, the information given will be that *mujahi-*

deen are operating, not the Pakistan army."[112] As I have written previously, one senior retired Pakistan army officer explained that the locally-based NLI was a core component of Pakistan's denial and deception strategy. He, and others interviewed, conceded that these troops were sent across the Line of Control in "mufti" (without their uniforms) with the aim of concealing their NLI affiliation. This contributed to the perception that the intruders were Kashmiri militants, or *mujahideen*. Another component of this denial and deception strategy is that the NLI troops transmitted military communications in Pashto, Balti, Shina, and other local dialects. As hoped, some of these transmissions were "intercepted" by Indian intelligence networks, which lent further credence to Indian analysts who had initially assessed that the intruders were civilian militants, not Pakistani soldiers.[113]

The Pakistan army hoped that the *mujahideen* façade would last long enough to obtain some territorial gains even if eventually the truth would be discerned. However, the Pakistan army was surprised by the subterfuge's success, due in good measure to India's inability to properly identify the intruders.[114] But this success was also due to the crucial role that LeT played in this disinformation campaign. In 2000, while I was conducting fieldwork in Pakistan on the Kargil war for RAND, I found that the LeT was actively promoting in speeches and in their publications the canard that they were involved in the Kargil War. These activities undertaken by LeT helped convince Pakistanis that the army was not involved and that, in fact, the heights grabbed in the Kargil-Dras sector were the glorious accomplishments of the brave *mujahideen* of the LeT. We know beyond a shadow of a doubt that there were no non-state actors involved in Kargil. In fact, the operation was so closely held that even the Director General of the ISI (DGISI) was not involved. The input of the ISI would have been crucial in concerting militants on both sides of the LOC had militants been involved.[115]

The propaganda of the LeT has continued to mislead those scholars who read their publications but who are not familiar with Pakistan's military and intelligence agencies. For example, Samina Yasmeen takes LeT's claims to this effect at face value and devotes an entire chapter in her recent, and otherwise superb, book on LeT to the Kargil war and how LeT's participation in the same transformed the organization.[116] Yasmeen's unfortunate mistake is a clarion call to other scholars that one must use LeT's written materials very carefully while simultaneously engaging the scholarship on Pakistan's military and intelligence agencies. In some cases, these materials can be best understood as a statement of what the organization (and their patrons in uniform) want us to believe rather than a truthful account of what the organization does or believes while in others they represent the intellectual, philosophical, theological or political exposition of the organizations' core beliefs.

Implications of this History

The Two Nation Theory, despite the numerous assaults upon its salience and logic, persists as the founding ideology of the Pakistani state. Pakistan's civilian and military leadership have embraced their respective responsibilities to protect and nurture this ideology. From the army's optic, should it forego this ideology, Pakistan as a state is not worth defending. After all, if Pakistan is not "Muslim," how does it meaningfully differ from India?[117] The army's dogged attention to this ideology of Pakistan has several direct security implications. First, the army constructs its security competition with India in ideological and civilizational terms. The army insists that "Hindu India" is implacably opposed to the Two Nation Theory and, by extension, Pakistan. This allows the army to cultivate and sustain endless support for a conflict among Pakistan's citizenry, who, with few exceptional periods, unstintingly support the army and its characterization of India. Second, because the Two Nation Theory posited an inherent equality between Hindus and Muslims, the army insists that peace with India must be on terms of the Two Nation Theory according to which India—and indeed the international community—recognize Pakistan as India's equal. Third, Pakistan's insistence upon the Two Nation Theory is the fundamental basis of Pakistan's claims to Kashmir. Should Pakistan abandon the Two Nation Theory, there is no other logic to undergird Pakistan's demand that it "free" all of Kashmir from India's grip. Pakistan's inability to do so signifies that the Partition process remains incomplete. To forsake the Two Nation Theory and Kashmir is to accept the permanence of Pakistan's incompleteness. Fourth, the centrality of the Two Nation Theory and the isomorphism of Islam, on one hand, and on the other hand, Pakistan, animates the army's thinking and policies towards India.[118]

Because Pakistan cannot ever win a direct confrontation with India, it has developed dozens of militant organizations since 1947 to deploy in India as well as Afghanistan. Pakistan's acquisition of nuclear weapons since 1980 has permitted Pakistan to expand these operations with ever greater impunity—as I discuss in the following chapter. Much of the language of the Pakistan army with respect to the importance of the Two Nation Theory, their belief that protecting Pakistan is coterminous with Islam, and the need to coerce India to relinquish Kashmir, is used by LeT in their own publications. This reflects the close relationship between the army and the LeT, as I discuss in the following chapters.

3

PAKISTAN'S CREEPING JIHAD AND EXPANDING NUCLEAR UMBRELLA

How is that Pakistan, a country with a shambolic economy and an army that has never won a war, can unremittingly orchestrate a deadly arpeggio of terror against India, a larger and generally better-armed country, without any significant adverse repercussions? Not only has Pakistan deliberately cultivated a menagerie of Islamist militant groups to harass India and Afghanistan since its inception as an independent state in 1947,[1] many of the 9/11 conspirators stayed and enjoyed sanctuary in Pakistan, while—perhaps most egregiously— US forces located and killed Osama bin Laden in the cantonment town of Abbottabad, less than one mile from the prestigious Pakistan Military Academy.[2] Despite what was surely a vertiginous outrage to the United States, Pakistan escaped American wrath unscathed. Understanding how Pakistan has managed to use Islamist (and non-Islamist) proxies with breathtaking impunity requires one to grasp how the state developed its nuclear program precisely to shield it from reprisals for its proxy warfare strategy. In many ways, the history of Pakistan's nuclear program and strategy of proxy warfare are inexorably tied together. This chapter describes this twinned history. Not only does Pakistan's nuclear program constrain India's punitive options, it also keeps in check the options of the international community, which is also coerced by Pakistan's fast expanding arsenal. Punishing Pakistan for using terrorists as an elemental pillar of foreign policy will require not only India but the United States as well to disencumber themselves from Pakistan's nuclear coercion strategy. While not impossible, doing so is politically risky and few policy makers would be willing seriously to contemplate such options. I return to these options in the final chapter of this book.

Pakistan first grasped the utility of proxy actors in 1947, when it mobilized *lashkars* (or tribal militias) from Pakistan's Pashtun areas to invade and seize Kashmir.[3] From 1947 until the mid-1980s, Pakistan supported various kinds of low-level sabotage. Its efforts to spark a wider insurgency in the 1960s failed. Pakistan's opportunity and capabilities to cultivate mayhem dramatically improved in the mid-1980s when Kashmiris in Indian-administered Kashmir began to rebel against New Delhi for an array of excesses including appalling electoral manipulation, malfeasance in managing Kashmiri political expectations, and state-sponsored violence against protestors.[4] While the uprising began indigenously, by the early 1990s Pakistani Islamist militants had taken the helm from the local ethnic Kashmiri insurgents who had initiated this phase of political violence.[5]

While Pakistan is renowned for its efforts to instigate Islamist insurgency and terrorism, it has also supported other militant movements in India. In the mid-1950s, Pakistan (as well as China) backed India's Naga rebels in the northeast and, in the 1960s, Pakistan supported the Mizo rebels, also in India's northeast.[6] From the mid-1970s through the early-1990s, Pakistan also supported the Sikh insurgency in Punjab.[7] Similarly, before and during the 1971 war in East Pakistan, the military relied upon Islamist militants to brutalize ethnic Bengalis in East Pakistan.[8]

To complement and enable its advances at the lower end of the conflict spectrum, Pakistan also innovated at the strategic level through the acquisition of nuclear weapons. We now know that Pakistan had a crude device around 1983–4, if not earlier.[9] Varun Sahni, describing Pakistan's beliefs that its capabilities deterred crises with India in the 1980s, refers to the lingering but indecisive role of nuclear weapons as "nuclear overhang."[10] As Pakistan became increasingly confident of its nuclear capabilities, it was ever more emboldened to use its proxies in India, secure in the belief that India would be unable to punish Pakistan militarily. Consequently, Pakistan's adventurism in India became bolder both through the use of state-sponsored proxies, but also through Pakistani security forces masquerading as militants in the 1999 Kargil War. Until the reciprocal nuclear tests by India and then Pakistan in May 1998, scholars used a term introduced by McGeorge Bundy, "existential deterrence," to describe the deterrence that seemed to exist between India and Pakistan. Given the opacity and uncertainty surrounding the two countries' programs, the mutual deterrence calculation of India and Pakistan did not rest on "relative capabilities and strategic doctrines, but on the shared realization that each side is nuclear-capable, and thus any outbreak of conflict might lead to a nuclear war."[11]

This chapter lays out the dual trajectories of Pakistan's development and deployment of Islamist proxies and nuclear weapons. First, I describe the twinned evolution of Pakistan's non-state actor policy and Pakistan's development of nuclear weapons. Second, I discuss how, due to its ever-expanding nuclear arsenal, Pakistan can prosecute its proxy warfare without penalty in India, and elsewhere. The third section provides an overview of the various militant groups that Pakistan has developed to secure its interests in India and Afghanistan, and discusses the recent problems that Islamabad has encountered in managing this zoo of proliferating and ever-more problematic proxies. Next, I tie these two trajectories together to show how nuclearization has emboldened Pakistan to rely upon this dangerous stable of non-state actors ever more aggressively, even as the threat of full-scale war with India diminishes. I conclude this chapter with a discussion of how Pakistan's policy of *jihad*, under an expanding nuclear umbrella, shapes security dynamics in South Asia.

Twinned Histories of Proxy Warfare and Nuclear Coercion

While Pakistan's use of non-state actors to pursue state goals originated in 1947, its army began formalizing this strategy when US military training began in 1954, when the two countries were formally allied against the purported communist threats posed by China and the Soviet Union.[12] The United States sought to bolster Pakistan's ability to combat communist insurgencies in Asia. However, as Pakistani officers interacted with American trainers and absorbed American doctrinal materials, some officers deduced that their army could initiate and sustain a "peoples' war," perfect the art of infiltration, or develop its own "people's army" as a second line of defense against India.[13] One of the best evidentiary sources to document this doctrinal evolution is Pakistan's own professional military journals.[14]

In 1957, General Headquarters began publishing the *Pakistan Army Journal*. The journal's maiden issue republished an article from the *Australian Army Journal* titled "Guerrilla Warfare" in which the author, Maj. C. H. A. East, argued that successful prosecution of guerrilla warfare requires a careful appraisal of three concepts: terrain, political situation, and national conditions. East believed that mountainous areas (especially those with jungle or forest cover), swampy flat areas, or flat areas with jungle- or forest-cover were most suitable terrains for guerrilla warfare. Guerrilla forces require unstinting support of either their own or an allied government to ensure the requisite logistical support for their activities and they must cultivate the political sympathies of the local civilian population.[15] The most effective means of ensuring control over guerrilla forces is to "provide the trained personnel and organization from the regular army to establish a formal guerrilla organization."[16]

East's suggestions were salient, given Pakistan's foray into non-state actors in 1947. Kashmir's mountainous and heavily wooded terrain seem to typify East's ideal insurgent geography. Politically, guerrilla forces in Kashmir also enjoyed the full support of the Pakistani state. Moreover, Pakistan's civilian and military leadership were persuaded that Kashmiris in Indian-controlled Kashmir would provide fighters, because they believed that they were antagonistic towards their purportedly "Hindu occupier." Finally, the Pakistan army was well positioned to train, organize, and oversee these guerrillas and, in fact, had already been doing so.

Throughout the 1960s, the *Pakistan Army Journal* published several articles that argued for the efficacy of a peoples' army for both defensive and offensive operations against India, the importance of infiltration as a "form of attack," and increasingly, the usefulness of being able to wage peoples' war. El-Edroos argues that infiltration is ideal for Pakistan due to India's presumed conventional superiority.[17] Pakistani defense writers believed that using these methods would better situate Pakistan to defeat India in either conventional or unconventional warfare.[18] Redolent of LeT publications (discussed later in this volume) that argue that every Muslim should prepare for *jihad*, Qazi argues that the Pakistan Army should assume that "every Pakistani is a soldier." This would obviate the need for lavish expenditure on a large peacetime army, and Pakistan's "standing regular army should be just enough to absorb the initial shock of attack and to provide the necessary leadership and training facilities for the citizen army.[19] Echoing the writings of contemporary *jihadi* organizations, citizens must become "soldiers in plain clothes, and the soldiers become citizens in uniform" to prepare Pakistan for a defensive war against the enemy's superior forces.[20]

High profile civilians embraced these views too. Zulfiqar Ali Bhutto, who was a civilian in Ayub Khan's cabinet at the time, strongly supported the Operation Gibraltar misadventure and its reliance upon troops disguised as civilians, which escalated to a general war in 1965. So did Aslam Siddiqi—a civilian bureaucrat in Ayub Khan's National Reconstruction Bureau—who dedicated an entire chapter on *jihad* in his 1964 book, which elucidated the efficacy of a *jihad* waged by the people. Like his contemporary writers in uniform, Siddiqi demanded a *jihad* in which "every able-bodied person is expected to participate. The penalty is rejection by God...."[21] Siddiqi reproved von Clausewitz for his ignorance of the warfare waged by the prophet and his immediate successors, as well as concomitant ignorance "of the power of faith" while historicizing irregular warfare within the military history and tradition of the prophet. Siddiqi asserted that during the prophet's time, Muslims were few in number and thus the prophet was "driven to adopt the technique of irregular warfare."[22] Given Pakistan's various weakness vis-à-vis India, Siddiqi believed that "the best defence" requires "every able-bodied national" to participate, eliminating "the difference between a civilian and a soldier."[23]

After the 1971 war, the Pakistan army was demoralized and held in low esteem by its citizens after effectively losing half the country. The people's ire was compounded when they learned that Pakistan had been defeated despite unremitting state propaganda to the contrary.[24] Z.A. Bhutto, whose Pakistan Peoples Party won the largest share of votes in West Pakistan in the 1970–1 elections, seized the reins of power. He had wanted to pursue a nuclear weapon as early as 1964; however, General Ayub rebuffed him then, arguing that developing a weapon would alienate Pakistan's western allies and furthermore, if necessary, Pakistan could likely "buy a weapon off the shelf somewhere," presumably from one of its Western allies.[25] With his now unchecked authority, Bhutto began actively pursuing a nuclear weapon, hoping to curry favor with the army, diminish the chance of a coup, and consolidate the role of civilian decision-making in security and defense matters.[26] Bhutto tasked A.Q. Khan with the ignominious task of stealing nuclear secrets for his country, and established two rival organizations in the hopes that their competition would hasten Pakistan's acquisition of a nuclear weapon.

In his gasconading death-row autobiography, *If I am Assassinated*, Bhutto professed that the United States facilitated Zia's coup for the sole purpose of denying Pakistan a nuclear future. (I found no evidence to support this claim in any secondary or primary source I have encountered.) According to Bhutto, when he came to power in December 1971, Pakistan's nuclear weapons program was twenty years behind that of the Indians. However, by the time he was deposed, in 1977, Pakistan was on the threshold of possessing a nuclear capability. He prated that while Christian, Jewish, and Hindu civilizations, as well as the Communist powers, had acquired nuclear weapons capabilities, it was he—not the army—who had delivered this capability to all Islamic civilizations.[27]

In early 1979, the United States acquired "unspecified intelligence going back to 1977 on Pakistan's attempts to 'import critical components.'"[28] A cable dated January 1979 reveals Indian assessments that Pakistan could weaponize within two to three months.[29] In February 1979, the United States confronted Zia with photographic intelligence about the nuclear facility at Kahuta, which Zia rubbished as "ridiculous." The US Ambassador to Pakistan, Arthur W. Hummel, warned Zia that the divergence between what Washington was learning about Pakistan's program and Pakistan's official statements increased the likelihood of sanctions under the Symington Act, which prohibits most forms of US assistance to countries that traffic in nuclear enrichment technology or equipment outside of international safeguards.[30] After the Americans failed to persuade Pakistan to abandon its nuclear push through an "audacious buyoff," it learned in March 1979 that Pakistan had acquired critical technologies for its enrichment program.[31] The Department of State assessed that Pakistan was rapidly building a "secret uranium enrichment plant, which by 1983 will begin to yield sufficient quantities of fissile materials to support a nuclear weapons program."[32] When confronted, Zia confirmed the status of the enrichment program, and the United States was left with no option but to apply Symington sanctions in April 1979.

Initially, the Americans did not want this decision to be known publicly; nor did Washington even officially notify Islamabad that the US had terminated aid programs or address the issue of their future continuation.[33] While the Americans sought to keep this matter private, the Indian and British media discovered the extent of Pakistan's progress in reprocessing technology.[34] The Secretary of State Cyrus Vance wrote to President Carter urging him to personally intervene to manage the diplomatic fallout over the imposition of sanctions. In this letter, Vance explained to Carter "India has detailed knowledge of the Pakistani enrichment program, and [Prime Minister Morarji] Desai has written Zia of his concern about Pakistani nuclear activities."[35] American efforts to shield their policy decisions from the media were obviated by India's "persistent efforts to stimulate international public attention to Pakistan's weapons-related programs" by writing editorials and news stories publicizing Pakistan's progress in centrifuge enrichment.[36]

In October 1979, the US Embassy in New Delhi cabled to the Secretary of State to describe a private meeting between (presumably) the US Ambassador and India's Prime Minister Desai. According to a declassified June 1979 cable from the Department of State, the US Secretary of State asked Desai what "he proposed to do about the danger, not only to India but much more widely, should the Pakistanis develop an explosives capability, he said that he proposed to take Zia at his word for now, but if he discovered that Pakistan was ready to test a bomb or if it exploded one, he would act at [once] 'to smash it.'"[37] By June 1979, State reported rumors about a potential nuclear test.[38] Later in December 1985, the US government acquired intelligence intimating that Pakistan, with Chinese assistance, had "produced an atomic weapon in early October [1985]."[39] These American assessments accord with revelations of prominent and knowledgeable Pakistani writers, such as former Foreign Minister Abdul Sattar, who wrote that Pakistan had a nuclear device as early as 1983.[40]

This historical account is important for several reasons. First, it suggests that the Americans and other members of the international community knew about Pakistan's efforts to acquire a nuclear device prior to the Soviet Union's invasion of Afghanistan on Christmas Day 1979. In fact, the April 1979 sanctions delayed American efforts to provide Pakistan security assistance in the immediate wake of the invasion. Second, Pakistani officials made frequent long-winded speeches about the program's progress and defended it publicly and privately.[41] In early 1986, A.Q. Khan declared that Pakistan had a "nuclear weapons capability" and General Zia himself asserted "Pakistan can build a bomb whenever it wishes."[42] The Indians moreover were very much aware of these developments and were publishing copious accounts about them. Thus, it is fair to assume that Pakistani defense writers were aware of these public statements about the progress in Pakistan's nuclear weapons program, even if they were not privy to its classified technical details or the precise date by which Pakistan had a crude nuclear weapon.

Several Pakistan writers began explicitly yoking together Pakistan's burgeoning nuclear arsenal with its well-honed strategy of asymmetric conflict. For example, Lt. Col. Anwari in 1988 asserted that Pakistan must develop nuclear weapons and their means of delivery to prevent India with presenting Pakistan with a *fait accompli*, presumably on Kashmir.[43] Moreover, he argued that "guerrilla warfare" should be part of Pakistan's deterrence package, and that India must be aware of this capability. Many years later in 2000, Maj. Gen. Asif Duraiz Akhtar wrote:

> Nuclear explosions of 1998 have brought a semblance of equilibrium in the region [and have] put the conventional all-out war scenario on the back burner [however]...This situation leaves the room open for low intensity conflict (proxy war) or the war with limited aims restricted to confines of disputed areas e.g. Indian-held Kashmir and Siachin.[44]

Maj. General Shahid Iqbal similarly linked Pakistan's strategic and non-state assets when he observed that "nuclearisation of the Subcontinent has given a shot in the arm to this erstwhile concept of limited war," and predicted that limited war between India and Pakistan will be "intricately intertwined with [the] freedom struggle in Kashmir, the impact of exterior manoeuvre by respective countries, the global interests in the region, the consequent world opinion and the makeup of political forces in the two states."[45] Shahid further observes that Pakistan is positioned to calibrate the tempo of the so-called freedom struggle while India's options are circumscribed by Pakistan's nuclear deterrent observing that "During [the] Kargil conflict, India had its freedom of action drastically curtailed due to [Pakistan's] extant nuclear deterrence." In 2008, Brigadier Shaukat Iqbal also recommended that Pakistan's army employ the intelligence agencies to train and deploy *mujahideen*, but he argues that this kind of asymmetric strategy "requires retention of credible nuclear deterrence throughout."[46] Iqbal unquestionably asserts that Pakistan can use its militant assets *only* in conjunction with a robust nuclear deterrent. As Pakistan's nuclear arsenal continued to expand, increasingly defense analysts put its growing nuclear arsenal in the service of enabling a proxy war to coerce New Delhi regarding Kashmir and to hamstring India's rise in the international system by bogging it down in managing recurrent offensives.

Given this tight association between Pakistan's non-state actor strategy and its nuclear weapons, it should come as no surprise that its non-state actors themselves are vigorous proponents of Pakistan's nuclear arsenal. Recently, Hafiz Saeed's son and likely successor, Talha Hafiz Saeed argued that:

> There are several reasons for which the enemies of Islam see Pakistan as a major threat. First of all, Pakistan is a formidable nuclear power. Celebrated across the Muslim world, its nukes were dubbed as the 'Islamic Bomb' by the West. Moreover, it has developed miniaturized nuclear weapons, usable in conventional battlespace, as part of its full spectrum deterrence doctrine.[47]

Ordinarily, it would be quite unusual to see prominent militant leaders opining on full spectrum deterrence. However, in Pakistan, this is not unusual. Prof. Hafiz A. Rehman Makki, brother-in-law of Hafiz Saeed and a key LeT/JuD leader, called for the need to defend Pakistan's nuclear program at home and abroad.[48] Other militant leaders such as Sami-ul-Haq, who is often considered one of the Taliban's most important "fathers," made similar statements.[49] In fact, JuD publications frequently discuss the importance of nuclear weapons in Pakistan's defense and inveigh on complex matters such as India's bid to join the Nuclear Suppliers Group.[50] As I argue later in this volume, one of the most important roles of JuD public outreach is to create public support for the military's preferred policy whether it's Pakistan's nuclear arsenal or the pursuit of CPEC.

After the 1999 Kargil War, Indian defense planners realized that nuclearization of the sub-continent need not only afford Pakistan with advantages at the lower end of the conflict spectrum. In its immediate aftermath, Indian strategists began arguing that nuclear weapons ensured that the Kargil War remained limited. In this sense, the Pakistani misadventure played to India's advantage: nuclear weapons may also permit India to punish Pakistan for territorial incursions by either state or non-state actors. Furthermore, the presence of nuclear weapons would ensure that the international community would act to constrain the scope and duration of the war, as well as prevent escalation beyond the remit of a limited-aims conflict.[51] This basic notion of limited war gave birth to the concept of "Cold Start," which was bandied about India's defense community after the military crisis following JeM's attack on India's parliament in December 2001.[52] "Cold Start" is an offensive doctrine that called for reorganizing India's offensive capabilities away from its "three large strike corps into eight smaller division-sized 'integrated battle groups' (IBGs) that combine mechanized infantry, artillery, and armor in a manner reminiscent of the Soviet Union's operational maneuver groups."[53] These formations would enable India to make shallow plunges into Pakistani territory before the international community could mobilize to dampen tensions. India could use this seized territory as arbitrage to ensure Pakistan's formal acquiescence to the territorial status quo in Kashmir.[54]

For years, India's civil and military leadership had demurred from confirming or denying these assertions. In fact, there is very little incontrovertible evidence that India has undertaken the various steps to effectuate "Cold Start," whether one looks at defense acquisition, organization of forces, or command structure.[55] However, in early January 2017, India's Army chief, General Bipin Rawat, was the first senior official to publicly confirm the existence of India's so-called Cold Start doctrine.[56] Irrespective of the actual state of Cold Start, from Pakistan's optic, these doctrinal innovations have been real since the media began popularizing the notions. Purportedly out of fear that "Cold Start" would deprive Pakistan of its coveted ability to rely upon non-state actors given the impunity afforded by its nuclear umbrella, Pakistan began aggressively developing tactical nuclear weapons, better known as "battlefield nuclear weapons." (Some analysts believe that Pakistan would have done so anyway but used Cold Start as a convenient excuse to do so.) Astonishingly, this doctrine calls for the use of such weapons on Pakistani territory to first prevent Indian forces from crossing into Pakistan and working their way towards major cities. Should India persist and cross the international border despite this warning burst, Pakistan would use these weapons upon India's forces. Under India's nuclear doctrine, India will retaliate with a retaliatory nuclear strike. Pakistan reckons that India would be unwilling to undertake a course of action with such a gruesome cascade of outcomes. These weapons serve as a risk generation tool to vitiate India's ability to employ its new doctrine.[57]

Zulfiqar Khan, a senior Ministry of Defense analyst, argued in 2011 that inducting tactical nuclear weapons would confer upon Pakistan escalation dominance in a crisis with India, perhaps even allowing Pakistan to deter a crisis in the first place, and—if necessary—wage and win a conflict with India. Given the conventional forces Pakistan confronts, he argues that "Pakistan should focus on maintaining the balance of terror with appropriate strategy against its adversary—India, instead of indulging in conventional forces number game."[58] He argues that "any transparency [in Pakistan's nuclear doctrine] ...would only undermine Pakistan's ability to deter India's calibration of 'Cold Start Strategy' or limited conflict thinking, to its peril."[59] Accordingly, in recent years, Pakistan's military organs have publicly boasted that it has the world's smallest nuclear weapons and that this arsenal will deter any Indian consideration of "Cold Start."[60] In 2011, Pakistan announced that it developed and tested a "Short Range Surface to Surface Multi Tube Ballistic Missile Hatf IX (NASR)".[61] In addition, since the late 1980s, Pakistan has been pursuing an inter-continental ballistic missile (ICBM) with the likely eventual intent of targeting the United States and Israel. Little is known about this program and the progress it has experienced. Press reports suggest that the Pakistanis are working to produce an ICBM with a range of 7,000 km, named Taimur.[62] This would allow it to target Israel but not the United States.

Decades of defense writings intimate a positive correlation between nuclearization of the subcontinent and militarized disputes between India and Pakistan. These writings also demonstrate that nuclearization has enabled Pakistani adventurism—both by deterring India and by forcing the international community to intervene. My earlier examination of Pakistan's literature demonstrates that early concepts of infiltration and guerrilla war continued to evolve along with Pakistan's (and India's) nuclearization. By the twenty-first century, Pakistan defense writers were explicitly discussing Pakistan's ability to prosecute sub-conventional conflict under its nuclear umbrella.[63]

Pakistan's nuclear deterrent facilitates low-intensity conflict and proxy war in two important ways. First, by cultivating ambiguity as to its employment and deployment doctrine and the red lines that would precipitate Pakistan's use of nuclear weapons, Islamabad (or more accurately Rawalpindi) believes that it can deter any militarized Indian response either to territorial incursions by regular or irregular Pakistani troops or significant strikes against Indian interests by Pakistan-supported and/or -based nuclear weapons, and, increasingly, tactical nuclear weapons, India is simply likely to "tolerate" these nuisances rather than risk a full-scale war.[64] Second, nuclear weapons facilitate Pakistan's ability to wage low-intensity conflict by drawing in international actors who work to limit a conflict once it unfolds.[65] Moreover as Pakistan achieves the capability of targeting the United States with its ICBMs, it is certain that Washington will be unable to punish it either. The Pakistan military has concluded that nuclear weapons have "reduced the prospect that India will use force to solve regional problems" and "enhance[d] Pakistan's foreign policy leverage vis-à-vis India and its other neighbors."[66]

Pakistan's battlefield and other nuclear weapons, coupled with its many Islamist militant groups, bestow upon Pakistan another important strategic benefit: these weapons must be forward deployed to be useful. In such a scenario, they may become vulnerable to theft by terrorists, or inadvertent or inaccurate use. These are the United States' core security concerns with respect to Pakistan, which is well known by Pakistan's defense planners. This lethal combination not only coerces the Americans to remain engaged in Pakistan—with an open checkbook deployed—but also ensures a steady supply of resources with which it can continue investing in the very assets that disquiet them the most. Under these circumstances Pakistan has no incentive either to reverse course on nuclear proliferation or take action against its terrorist menagerie.

Jihad in Afghanistan and India Under Expanding Nuclear Umbrella

Pakistan relied upon proxy actors in Afghanistan as well as India long before it acquired a crude nuclear weapons capability in the 1980s. As I have argued previously, as Pakistan's nuclear capability progressed from nuclear overhang to covert capability, and finally, to the overt acquisition of a weapon, Pakistan became ever more risk-acceptant.[67] In other words, as Pakistan made progress at the strategic level, it became ever more emboldened at the sub-conventional level. While Pakistan was endeavoring to acquire a crude nuclear device, it was concurrently running proxy wars in Afghanistan and India's Punjab. By the end of the decade it would add to this portfolio a revivified proxy war in Kashmir. Because LeT's origins lie in the fag-end of the anti-Soviet *jihad*, I discuss both Pakistan's proxy wars in Afghanistan and India in turn.

Pakistan's Jihad in Afghanistan

Pakistan has instrumentalized political Islam in Afghanistan since the 1950s to warp its domestic politics to suit Pakistan's strategic preferences. In recent years, there has been a tendency to reduce Pakistan's apprehensions towards Afghanistan to its suspicions about Indian meddling there, as well as Afghanistan's long-standing relations with India. For example, William Dalrymple writes that "the hostility between India and Pakistan lies at the heart of the current war in Afghanistan."[68] Such assumptions have given rise to notions of a "grand bargain," according to which Washington could force India to make some concession in Kashmir that would persuade Pakistan to ratify the border there. With this enduring threat resolved, Pakistan could stand down its *jihadi* assets in India as well as Afghanistan. Thus, such arguments suggest that peace in Afghanistan must first pass through Kashmir.[69]

This logic is fundamentally flawed because it fails to recognize that Pakistan and Afghanistan have long been at loggerheads since 1947, when Afghanistan initially opposed Pakistan's admission to the United Nations.[70] Pakistan believes that Afghanistan staked out this position with Indian prompting and support, even though there is no evidence that this was the case. Additionally, Afghanistan has long asserted irredentist claims upon vast stretches of Pakistani territory that extend from Balochistan in the south, all the way to the northern arc of the Federally Administered Tribal Areas (FATA) and Khyber Pakhtunkhwa. According to Pakistan, Afghan regular troops and tribesmen attacked its northern border and infiltrated into Pakistan thirty miles northeast of Chaman, Balochistan in September 1950. Pakistan announced that it quickly repelled the invaders after six days of fighting. Later, in 1960 and 1961, Pakistan made similar claims than Afghan regular and irregular forces entered its territory on several occasions. One such skirmish escalated into a major battle when, according to Pakistan, Afghan forces— including tanks—massed on the Afghan side of the border near Pakistan's Bajaur tribal agency.[71]

In the mid-1970s, as Afghanistan's domestic affairs quickly spiralled out of control, so did Pakistan's efforts to manipulate them. When Muhammad

Daoud ousted his cousin, King Zahir Shah, and began imposing Soviet-backed secularization reforms, many Islamists fled to Iran and Pakistan. Daoud threw his support behind the Baloch insurgents who had revolted against the Pakistani state, which internationalized the repression of Zulfiqar Ali Bhutto's government in putting down the rebellion. Daoud also publicized his rejection of the Durand Line and articulated his support for Pashtun nationalism in Pakistan. Bhutto, having weathered the aftermath of the 1971 war when an outside power exploited Pakistan's ethnic conflicts, worried that Afghan interference in Pakistan's ethnic disputes would further endanger the integrity of West Pakistan. To undermine Daoud and punish him for these interventions in Pakistan's internal affairs, Bhutto set up the Afghanistan Inter-Services Intelligence Agency (ISI) cell in 1974 and tasked it with organizing a nascent Islamist resistance in Afghanistan. Zia continued with Bhutto's Afghan policy after seizing power from him in his 1977 coup.[72]

By the time the Soviets had crossed the Amu Darya, Zia's army and the ISI—building off the work initiated by Bhutto—had already organized the most important Islamist militant groups, which would go on to become the workhorses of the anti-Soviet insurgency. Throughout 1978, the ISI and the paramilitary organization, the Frontier Corps, worked to consolidate the more than fifty Afghan resistance militias into some seven major groups. For more than one year after the Russian invasion, Pakistan "continued to support the Afghan resistance...providing it modest assistance out of its own meager resources."[73] Abdul Sattar, who served as Pakistan's Foreign Minister between 1999 and 2002, explained that "the Mujahideen would be fighting also for Pakistan's own security and independence."[74] General Arif, who served as Zia's Vice Chief of Army Staff, similarly recounts that "of her own free will, Pakistan adopted the... option to protect her national interest and to uphold a vital principle" by providing "...covert assistance to the *Mujahideen*."[75] These views of prominent Pakistani civilian and military personalities undermine the more typical Pakistani narrative, which describes the United States luring an unwitting Pakistan into an American-imagined *jihad* and leaving the hapless, under-resourced Pakistani state to manage the fallout of Afghanistan on its own.[76]

While the Soviets and the Americans withdrew from Afghanistan after signing the Geneva Accords in 1988, Pakistan remained engaged. General Zia was furious that the Geneva Accords did not install an Islamist government in Afghanistan. Instead of a *mujahid* who was the international face of Afghanistan's ostensible liberation, the accords emplaced a Russian-backed president, Muhammad Najibullah. Despite Pakistan's strenuous objections and use of all its resources to undermine his government, Najibullah stayed in power until 1992, when the Soviet Union collapsed and its successor state, Russia, could no longer fund his government.

After Najibullah's fall, multifarious militias fought to control Afghanistan. Pakistan was very much a party to the conflict. It supported the faction led by Gulbuddin Hekmatyar, a Pashtun Islamist militant leader from the anti-Soviet *jihad*, in the hopes that he could consolidate a pro-Pakistan regime in Afghanistan. In April 1992, Pakistan used its influence to negotiate the Peshawar Accord with the various warring factions. This agreement aimed to accommodate the various combatting commanders by establishing a system of rotating presidents. The accord broke down after four years when the first president, Burhanuddin Rabbani, refused to step down. The various *mujahideen*-cum-militia commanders destroyed Kabul through their brutal war-mongering. The principal contest was between Hekmatyar and Ahmad Shah Massoud, an ethnic Tajik from the Panjshir valley who served as Rabbani's defense minister. Massoud, Rabbani, and allied fighters (collectively known as the Northern Alliance) were very close to India, and thus considered an enemy alliance by Pakistan. Despite Pakistan's robust support for Hekmatyar, Rabbani clung to power until 1996, when the Taliban captured Kabul and ousted him.[77] During this period, the nascent LeT decided to leave Afghanistan, as its leadership did not support this internecine violence among the various Muslim militia groups.

The Afghan Taliban movement coalesced in 1994 in Kandahar under the leadership of Mullah Omar, a veteran *mujahideen* commander who ran a *madrassah* there. Initially, the movement drew from the tens of thousands of exiled Afghan males living in Pakistan and studying in Deobandi *madaris*. The Taliban won the support of many Afghans by opposing the above-noted commanders who, by the mid-1990s, became known as "warlords" (*jangbazi* in Dari). The principle warlords were organized under the umbrella of the Northern Alliance, led by Ahmad Shah Massoud and Hekmatyar's Hizb-e-Islami (HI). The Taliban took on these warlords and promised to provide Afghans with security, freedom of movement without harassment, and swift justice.[78] Until the Taliban emerged, the ISI continued to support Hekmatyar in hopes that he could forge a stable, pro-Pakistan government in Afghanistan. However, when it became apparent that Hekmatyar was unable to do so, the ISI began betting that the Taliban may service Pakistan's goals more efficaciously.

Maulana Fazlur Rehman's faction of the Jamiat-e-Ulema-e-Islam (JUI), a Pakistani Deobandi political party, facilitated the Taliban's interactions with Pakistan's political establishment of Benazir Bhutto, Z.A. Bhutto's daughter.[79] Pakistan's ISI, army, and even the air force provided the Taliban with extensive covert support, which enabled the Taliban to expand from their stronghold in Kandahar either by defeating or co-opting rival warlords and tribal structures. By 1998, the Taliban held all but the Panjshir Valley, which was still controlled Ahmad Shah Massoud's Northern Alliance. India, Russia, and Iran, among other regional actors, supported Massoud's Northern Alliance as they shared acute unease about the rise of the Taliban.[80] Massoud remained the Taliban's most significant challenger until 9 September 2001, when Al Qaeda assassinated him.[81]

The ISI, working with Deobandi *ulema*, also facilitated the Taliban's rise to power by dispatching fellow Deobandi militant groups to Afghanistan. Purportedly Kashmir-oriented Deobandi groups such as Harkat-ul-Jihad-e-Islami (HUJI), Harkat-ul-Mujahideen (HUM), and Jaish-e-Muhammad (JeM, another Deobandi group derived from personnel from HUJI and HUM), as well as sectarian groups such as Sipah-e-Sahaba-e-Pakistan (SSP), made their way to fight alongside the Taliban. After 1998, when the Taliban had seized control over most of the country, the ISI relocated several Kashmiri training camps in Afghanistan. Under the Taliban's watch, Afghanistan continued to be a source of battle-hardened fighters for operations in Kashmir.

As is well known, Osama bin Laden's ties to Afghanistan and Pakistan span decades. During the anti-Soviet *jihad*, he was a financier and facilitator, making numerous trips to Afghanistan and Pakistan. In 1996, he returned to Afghanistan where he remained until the Americans invaded Afghanistan in October 2001. Upon arriving in Afghanistan again, Mullah Omar requested that bin Laden keep a low profile. Explicitly disobeying this request, in 1998 bin Laden masterminded the attacks on the US embassies in Kenya and Tanzania from Afghanistan. This provoked American retaliatory cruise missile strikes on Al Qaeda camps in Afghanistan. While the American strikes failed to kill any Al Qaeda members of consequence, they did slay several Pakistani militants associated HUJI and HuM along with several ISI officers training their novitiates.[82]

Al Qaeda allies such as JeM conducted numerous attacks in India. In December 2001, JeM assailed India's parliament, bringing India and Pakistan to the brink of war. When the Americans invaded Afghanistan on 7 October, 2001, bin Laden, the Taliban leadership, and their Deobandi collaborators fled to Pakistan's tribal areas abutting Afghanistan. However, they continued to collaborate. Many of the attacks that have taken place in Pakistan since 2001 were imagined by Al Qaeda, but executed by its Pakistani Deobandi "subcontractors," such as Lashkar-e-Jhangvi (LeJ) as well as factions of JeM.[83]

When the Taliban fled Afghanistan, much of its leadership relocated to Quetta in Pakistan's western province of Balochistan, which shares borders with Afghanistan and Iran. Some of the Taliban fighters, along with their associates from Al Qaeda and their allied foreign and Pakistani Deobandi militant groups, went to Pakistan's FATA. With Pakistani support, the Taliban were able to regroup and launch an insurgency inside Afghanistan against the United States, NATO, and Afghan forces from about 2005 onward. Even though Pakistan facilitated the initial ground invasion of Afghanistan and became the principal supply route for war materiel into Afghanistan, Pakistan continued to support the Afghan Taliban by housing and protecting its leadership within Pakistan. Islamabad facilitated Taliban activities in Afghanistan and supported key Islamist allies of the Taliban, such as Jalaluddin Haqqani and his Pakistan-based network, and even Gulbuddin Hekmatyar. In fact, much of the so-called Haqqani network is based in North Waziristan, other agencies of FATA, and large cities such as Islamabad.[84] It has also continued to use LeT, particularly to target Indian assets in Afghanistan.[85]

During the early years of the war, the United States and its allies were not that concerned about Pakistan's continued support to the Taliban. The Americans believed that they had defeated the Taliban (when in fact they had merely routed them). Furthermore, Pakistan was cooperating with the United States on eliminating Al Qaeda's leadership in the country. President Bush and other US officials frequently showered President Musharraf with extravagant praise for his assistance in undermining Al Qaeda in Pakistan. The Americans had also not yet identified the Taliban as the enemy in Afghanistan. By the end of 2007, two things were clear: Afghanistan was in the throes of a full-fledged insurgency, and Pakistan was much to blame for the ability of the Taliban to launch and sustain operations against Afghan and international security forces.[86]

Pakistan's Jihad in India

While Pakistan has used non-state actors to wrest Kashmir from India since independence, between the wars in 1947–48 and 1965, Pakistan employed non-state actors in Kashmir to engage in sabotage and intermittent low level disruption.[87] In the early 1980s, the situation in Indian-administered Kashmir began to churn violently, creating the perfect opportunity for a new phase of Pakistani adventurism there. In 1983, Farooq Abdullah of the National Conference (one of the most venerable of Kashmir's leaders) won the state election and became the Chief Minister. His National Conference handsomely beat the Congress Party, which was then led by Indira Gandhi, who had personally campaigned for the Congress in Kashmir against the National Conference by using explicitly communal calls to secure Hindu votes in the state. Base communal appeals became a staple of Congress's electoral politics.[88] During this period, Gandhi sought to undermine several state governments that were ruled by parties other than Congress or its allies. To counter her efforts to centralize control over these non-Congress states— including Kashmir—the opposition parties organized an anti-Congress conclave that Farooq Abdullah's National Conference joined.[89] As opposition enclaves formed in these states, Gandhi used her power to appoint governors to dislodge popularly elected state governments. In Kashmir, she appointed to the governorship a close confidant, who is known by the monabody Jagmohan. Upon assuming his new post, Jagmohan dismissed the National Conference government on the grounds that it had lost majority support in the state assembly.[90]

Farooq Abdullah's dismissal heralded a new phase of alienation in the valley. Strangely, rather than continuing to fight Congress in coalition with other opposition parties, Abdullah signed a deal with the Congress Party in 1986 under Prime Minister Rajiv Gandhi. (Rajiv Gandhi took the reins of the Congress party after Sikh assassins murdered his mother in 1984 in retaliation for her decision to launch a military assault to oust Sikh militants from the Golden Temple earlier that year.) In 1987, new state elections took place. With the National Conference allied with Congress, a coalition of Muslim groups known as the Muslim United Front (MUF) coalesced around the purported notion of *Kashmiriat* (a pan-Kashmiri national identity). Congress, alarmed as the MUF appeared to surge in popularity, rigged the 1987 elections and even assaulted MUF candidates. It is not clear that MUF had enough votes to expel Farooq Abdullah even though his popularity was in decline. Nonetheless, Congress was very disquieted by the mere possibility that any party other than the National Conference-Congress alliance could muster a plurality—much less a majority—of votes in the valley of Kashmir.[91]

Angry Kashmiris began crossing into the porous, mountainous border into Pakistan where they joined the various militant groups that were forming to fight in Kashmir. The insurgency formally began on 31 July 1988 when the pro-independence organization, the Jammu Kashmir Liberation Front (JKLF), launched an insurrection against Indian rule. The JKLF, which was formed in 1977 in the United Kingdom, was a secular group that sought an independent Kashmir based upon Kashmiri ethnicity rather than Islamist ideology. Pakistan, which was under the rule of Zia ul Haq, moved in to exploit this indigenous rebellion. Pakistan sought to bleed India in Kashmir at little cost to the Pakistani state, and hopefully, loosen India's grip on Kashmir. Pakistan also sought to control the militancy by denying parties that were pro-independence a role in the same. Their efforts succeeded: while the JKLF launched the insurgency, within two years it was marginalized by the pro-Pakistan groups, which were nurtured by the Pakistan army and ISI.

The first of such pro-Pakistan "Kashmiri *tanzeems*" (groups operating in Kashmir) was the Hizbul Mujahideen (HM), which formed in 1989. The HM was essentially the armed wing of the Islamist political party, Jamaat-e-Islami (JeI). Zia ul Haq reposed considerable personal faith in JeI, and relied upon the organization heavily during his military rule. Consistent with Pakistan's preference, HM wanted to unite all of Kashmir under Pakistan's governance and institute an Islamic government in the state. The HM claims to largely recruit Kashmiris.[92] However, a recent quantitative study of HM's slain fighters suggests that while they do recruit more heavily from Indian-administered Kashmir, they also recruit heavily from the Punjab, Khyber Pakhtunkhwa, and even Sindh and Balochistan.[93] Of course, it is entirely possible that HM is recruiting Kashmiris from these other provinces. The ISI tried to persuade JKLF to abandon its aspirations for independence and agree to work to bring Kashmir into Pakistan. However, JKLF balked. Ultimately, the ISI stopped funding the JKLF, worked to undermine the organization, intensified support to the HM, and encouraged the HM to massacre JKLF militants. By 1993, HM emerged as the main Kashmiri militant organization. Soon thereafter in 1994, Yasin Malik, the leader of the most important faction of JKLF, renounced violence upon his release from jail.[94]

While HM was the main group, numerous other groups had also formed with the ISI's patronage. In 1993, the Harkat-ul-Ansar (HuA, also known as HUM) coalesced from two wings of the Harkat-ul-Jihadi-e-Islami (HUJI).[95] After the merger, the ISI directed more support to the organization, which soon became an important conduit for foreign fighters to transition from Afghanistan to Kashmir. Unlike HM, which is tied to JeI, HuA/HUM and HUJI are Deobandi organizations, as noted earlier. Later, on 31 January 2000

Maulana Masood Azhar, with ISI assistance, launched a new Deobandi group known as JeM almost immediately upon being released from an Indian jail. Azhar was released when India agreed to swap several Deobandi terrorists for Indian hostages that Azhar's associates had taken while hijacking an Indian Airlines flight on 31 December 1999.[96]

These varied Deobandi groups have long shared overlapping membership with other Deobandi militant organizations such as the Afghan Taliban, the relatively nascent Pakistan Taliban (discussed below), anti-Shia organizations such as the LeJ/SSP (which are now known by the name Ahl-e-Sunnat Wal Jamaat, or ASWJ), as well as various factions of the Deobandi *ulema* political party, JUI. Recent years have witnessed important shifts in alignment among these varied Deobandi groups. As long as Mullah Omar was alive, Pakistan's Deobandi militants remained allied to the nexus between Omar's Afghan Taliban and Al Qaeda, now under the leadership of Zawahiri. However, with the 2011 killing of Osama bin Laden and the 2015 revelation that Mullah Omar had died in Pakistan in 2013, many of these Deobandi militants—particularly those with a sectarian background—are defecting to the Islamic State.[97]

By the early 1990s, there was a new entrant to the fight in Kashmir: Lashkar-e-Tayyaba. LeT, as well as the various Deobandi militant groups, recruit mainly from Pakistan's Punjab—in addition to other parts of the country—and employ limited numbers of fighters from beyond South Asia. Militants who had fought in Afghanistan began streaming into the Valley after 1992 when the Democratic Republic of Afghanistan fell. Indians refer to these non-Kashmiri fighters and even fighters who were ethnically Kashmiri but Pakistani nationals as "guest militants."[98] By supporting numerous groups, the ISI hoped to ensure that they would all act on behalf of Pakistan's interests (e.g. attaining all of Kashmir for Pakistan). However, this policy also incentivized the groups to compete with each other for resources. To manage this competition, Pakistan helped to form two groups. The first was the All Parties Hurriyat Conference (APHC), which formed in 1993 to serve as umbrella for political parties.[99] The second was the United Jihad Council, which the ISI established in 1994 to serve an omnibus organization for the militant groups.[100]

Pakistan had hoped that it could internationalize the Kashmir conflict much as it did the war in Afghanistan to oust the Soviets. However, by 1995, for all intents and purposes, the insurgency had reached a stalemate. The Pakistan army wanted to revitalize it but no longer believed that HuA/HUM would be able to do it. In 1995, HUM tried to give new life to the insurgency and freed critical HUM leaders such as Masood Azhar and Sheikh Omar by kidnapping several western backpackers in Indian-administered Kashmir. The effort was a fiasco that ended in the deaths of all but one backpacker who escaped in the early days of his captivity. Pakistan along with their proxies appeared the villain in the drawn-out affair.[101] HuA/HUM proved to be a very problematic proxy for Pakistan's army and the ISI, for several reasons. First, the organization's commanders in Kashmir operated with considerable autonomy from both the group's leadership in Pakistan and their ISI handlers. Second, the group was less dependent upon the ISI because it was able to access considerably more resources from outside of Pakistan. Also, it could draw off of the extensive and lucrative Deobandi mosque, as well as *madrassah* infrastructure in Pakistan.[102] Third, because they were Deobandi, they also had ties to the Deobandi political party, JUI, which was a coalition partner of the Benazir Bhutto government following the 1993 elections. With this political patronage and exogenous funding, HuA/HUM could operate even if ISI stopped supporting them financially.[103] For this reason, the army and the ISI shifted course and put their full weight behind LeT. The latter conducted its first operation in Indian-administered Kashmir in 1990.[104] Until the introduction of JeM in 2000, LeT was the unrivalled perpetrator of terror in Kashmir and elsewhere in India.

As I discuss below, LeT draws from the Ahl-e-Hadees interpretative tradition. There are no reliable surveys conducted by the Pakistani government that survey which school of Islam its citizens follow. According to the only available—but unverifiable—estimate, Ahl-e-Hadees has a very small following (4 per cent), which is equivalent to the percentage of non-Muslim minorities of Pakistan. In contrast, about 50 per cent of the population consider themselves to be adherents to the Barelvi interpretative tradition, and 20 per cent associate with the Deobandi school. Shias comprise about 18 per cent, Ismailis 2 per cent and Ahmadis 2 per cent.[105] Not only are adherents of the Ahl-e-Hadees school relatively few in number, they are in considerable disunity compared to the Deobandis. In fact, there are at least seventeen major Ahl-e-Hadees organizations in Pakistan and they are riven with feuds as well as competition for resources and patronage. LeT, in particular, has had serious disagreements with mainstream Ahl-e-Hadees *ulema* over the issue of *jihad*. Taken together, this means that LeT has access to fewer domestic resources than do the Deobandi groups. From the ISI's point of view, these factors mean that LeT is easier to control than its rival organizations, being more dependent on the ISI for the backing it requires to function effectively.[106] So far, the ISI's assessment has proven to be correct.

Conclusions and Implications

Pakistan's reliance upon non-state actors is an enduring part of the country's strategy to secure its foreign policy objectives in the region and beyond. Pakistan has been able to do this with increasing impunity since its acquisition of nuclear capabilities. Prior to doing so, Pakistan's dalliance with proxy warfare in India was relatively restricted. However, by the time it acquired a crude nuclear device in the mid-1980s, Pakistan was contributing to the Sikh insurgency in the Punjab, as well as the insurgency in Afghanistan. By 1990, when Pakistan was finally sanctioned by the United States for acquiring a nuclear weapon, Pakistan added its heavy involvement in the Kashmir insurgency to its portfolio of conflicts. With the nuclear tests of 1998, Pakistan became a de facto nuclear weapon state.

Emboldened by this new status, Pakistan launched the Kargil War of 1999. However, it was only after the tests that Pakistani proxies, such as the LeT and JeM, began undertaking operations beyond Kashmir. In December 2000, LeT attacked an intelligence facility co-located near the Red Fort in New Delhi. In December 2001, JeM attacked the Indian Parliament. Since then there have been dozens of attacks outside of Kashmir and many more within Kashmir conducted by LeT or JeM.[107] Thus Pakistan has been able to expand its proxy war because of its concurrent efforts to expand its nuclear capabilities.

The possession of nuclear weapons does not merely raise the cost of any punitive Indian action in response to Pakistan-sponsored militant attacks; they also motivate the international community to intervene in crises as soon as possible to mitigate the chance of any dispute escalating into a full-blown war. Equally important, Pakistan's nuclear weapons make it virtually impossible for the United States simply to abandon Pakistan to its own devices. Moreover once Pakistan acquires an intercontinental ballistic missile (ICBM) which can target the United States, the latter will have virtually no military means to punish Pakistan for its behavior either without serious potential consequences. Lt Col Anwari, writing in 1988, admits that the warnings (issued by the United States and others) against Pakistan developing a nuclear weapon appear "menacing at the moment." However, "once we do develop the capability it would be very difficult for the major powers to execute these threats." He explains:

In international politics, it is easy for a major power to abandon a weak partner but very difficult to abandon a strong one. Pakistan as a "freelance nuclear power" will be far more important to the interests of these major powers, and contrary to what they may be saying, they would rather keep nuclear Pakistan in their fold than abandon her.[108]

Anwari's contentions have been vindicated over time. Pakistan benefits from the looming prospect that some of these militants may one day acquire nuclear materials, weapons, or know-how, which motivates the international community to remain engaged with Pakistan if for no other reason than to use their embassies to collect information about both the militant milieu and the nuclear program. Thus, nuclear weapons, and the *jihadi* activities they enable, also ensure that the international community cannot easily withdraw from Pakistan taking its checkbook with it.

Even though senior LeT leadership are public figures who routinely call for *jihad* in public rallies and in their diverse publications, there is very little that the United States, much less India, can do about it without serious risk-taking, which most politicians eschew. As I will discuss in subsequent chapters, LeT has a clear utility to the Pakistani state in prosecuting these external goals. However, LeT also is an important strand in Pakistan's efforts to manage the ever-degrading internal security situation of the country. Even though the United States has made various forms of financial assistance conditional upon Pakistan cracking down upon LeT and other "good militants" Pakistan considers its allies, the United States has become accustomed to waiving these sanctions. Simply put: despite Pakistan's ongoing support of numerous Islamist militant groups and its aggressive nuclear proliferation, Washingon and its partners have refused to consider alternative policies that rely less on emoluments and more on punishment no matter how perfidious Pakistan proves to be—over and over again.

While much of this book focuses on Pakistan's use of Islamist militants such as LeT to pursue policies in India, it is important to know that Pakistan has also used various Islamist political and militant organizations and personalities to manipulate events in Afghanistan from as far back as the 1950s. As I detail in the next chapter, LeT's own origins are found in Afghanistan, in the waning years of the so-called *jihad* against the Soviet Union's occupation of Afghanistan. Pakistan's reliance upon non-state actors to prosecute its interests abroad has been a foundational and enduring weapon in the state's armoury.

4

WHAT IS THE LET?

A CRITICAL EXAMINATION

Situating LeT within South Asia's Salafis

The expression "Salafi" derives from the term for the pious forefathers, *al-salaf al-salih*, which harks back to the first three generations of Muslims who had "first-hand experience of the rise of Islam and [who] are regarded as exemplary for the correct way to live for future Muslims."[1] Many security scholars of Pakistan lamentably assume that most Islamist militants in Pakistan are Salafis.[2] This misapprehension likely derives from the Salafi anchoring of major terrorist organizations (*inter alia* Al Qaeda and its various regional factions along with the Islamic State) which garner considerable scholarly and media attention. However, Salafis, known as Ahl-e-Hadees adherents in South Asia, are few in number in Pakistan and elsewhere in South Asia, though they have been active throughout the subcontinent since the nineteenth century.[3] While it is true that there has been some convergence of Salafi theology and Deobandi sectarian ideologies in recent decades, most of the terrorist organizations operating in and from Pakistan are in fact Deobandi in sectarian mooring, which is quite dissimilar from Salafi organizations. These distinctions matter because Pakistan's various militant organizations spend considerable time branding themselves and their ideology as a means of recruiting and raising funds and, as such, the varied militants are often strategic competitors even if they co-operate at tactical and operational levels.

Salafis propound a rigorous doctrine of the oneness of god (*tawheed*). However, this commitment to *tawheed* creates several intractable practical dilemmas. If a believer's ruler does not follow Islam as dictated by Ahl-e-Hadees, should the follower concentrate upon education (*tarbiyat*) and spreading the faith through preaching (*dawah*) to create a purified Muslim society? Alternatively, should the believer rise up against the deviant ruler, using violence if need be? This gives rise to an enduring debate within Salafism: is it "primarily quietist or activist, and to what degree should it be one of these alternatives?"[4] Wagemakers and Mandaville offer a helpful division among contemporary Salafis according to which one group is comprised of quietists or purists who shun political action and focus on education (*tarbiyat*).[5] A second group is Salafi Islamists who do engage in political debates and action. A third is the Salafi *jihadis* who embrace the use of violence to bring about a genuine Islamic government in Muslim countries.

There is often considerable animosity among these groups particularly as we expand our aperture to include Salafis beyond Pakistan. For example, in the scholarly debates among the *ulema* of these groups, they tend to use derogatory labels for each other that draw from early years of Islam. One set of such labels are *Khawarij* (alternatively neo-*Khawarij*), which is in opposition to *Murji'i* (and its variant neo-*Murji'i*), which reflect the differences in opinion concerning the proper course of action towards Muslim leaders who fail to impose *shariat* and the proper conduct of *takfiri* (the practice of declaring a Muslim to be a *kafir*—non-believer—and thus subject to the death penalty). *Khawarij* literally means seceders, derived from the Arabic verb, *kharaja* (to secede or move out), while *Murji'i* literally means one who postpones or defers, derived from *irja'* (to postpone of defer). Quietists may label groups who are cavalier in their application of *takfir* to be *Khawarij* or neo-*Khawarij*, referencing the early frondeurs in Islamic history who believed in violent rebellion against unworthy leaders. In turn, the Salafi jihadists denounce the quietists as *Murji'i* or neo-*Murji'i*, alluding to a defunct group of early Muslims who believed that no matter how horrendous a Muslim leader may be, insurrection is not permitted unless the leader commits *kufr* (an act of unbelief), and therefore meets their rigorous process of evaluating the facts and concomitant evidentiary standards for being declared a *kafir*.

This schism persists across various Salafi revival movements in Pakistan and beyond. LeT/JuD is a hybrid organization: while it is most certainly *jihadi*, its *jihad* focuses upon external enemies—most notably in India, where it seeks to "liberate" Muslims in Kashmir and beyond to establish an Islamic government, as well as in Afghanistan, where it fights what it believes is a foreign occupation by Americans and their Afghan and international allies. However, LeT/JuD is very clear on the issue of revolting against the Pakistan government (whether civilian or military): the *tanzeem* asserts without equivocation that the only permissible means to ameliorate the shortcomings of wayward leadership is education about LeT's interpretation of Islam (*tarbiyat*) and proselytization (*dawah*). The response "does not involve rebellion or processions or protests; on the contrary, in administrative matters, they [leaders] ought to be obeyed, while turning to Allah for help."[6] This philosophy is at the heart of the organization's domestic political utility in Pakistan and explains why the Pakistani state invests so heavily in it and its activities at home and abroad. This likely also explains the deep state's interest in the organization forming the newly-launched political party, the Milli Muslim League (MML).[7]

The Ahl-e-Hadees movement began as a reformist organization in late nineteenth century India, led by several eminent families. Unlike Deobandis or Barelvis, those who ascribe to Ahl-e-Hadees only recognize the Quran and the *hadees* as legal sources and, as such, repudiate the various schools of Islamist jurisprudence (*fiqh*). For this reason, they describe themselves as *ghair-muqallid* (non-conformists). This distinguishes them from Wahhabis, with whom they are frequently conflated, who follow Hanbali *fiqh*. Ahl-e-Hadees adherents are critical of what they refer to as Sufis' "wrongful innovation" and revile the syncretic practices that are common among Sufis and other Pakistani Muslims. Barelvis, in particular, draw the ire of Ahl-e-Hadees because of their emphasis upon saints as intermediaries between man and god, their orientation towards shrines and mystics, their faith in amulets and holy relics, and their often cult-like veneration of the prophet. (This fetishization of the prophet among Barelvis in part explains their propensity towards violence in alleged cases of blasphemy.) Ahl-e-Hadees aims to expunge from Islam any practices, beliefs and customs that may have been derived from Hinduism. For Ahl-e-Hadees, all of these practices comprise *shirk* (sometimes translated as idolatry, but also includes ascribing the attributes of Allah to others). Ahl-e-Hadees followers are also inimical to Deobandis, even though both *masalik* are reformist movements that originated in colonial India during the late nineteenth century. More so than Deobandis, Ahl-e-Hadees proponents believe that their *maslak* alone exemplifies the true and authentic practice of Islam. In contrast to Ahl-e-Hadees, Deobandis are relatively more conciliatory towards Sufis, with whom they share an adherence to the Hanafi *fiqh*.[8]

Ironically, while Ahl-e-Hadees is adamant that it alone practices pure Islam, its communities are very fragmented compared to other *masalik* in Pakistan, which tend to be more coherent and unified. There are some seventeen organizations in Pakistan, of which seven participate in politics (including the newly-formed MML) and three engage in *jihad*, while the remainder focuses upon *dawah* (preaching) and establishing *madaris* (religious seminaries, pl. of *madrassah*). Ahl-e-Hadees organizations in Pakistan are highly competitive, expending much energy on refuting one another's convictions and activities, in addition to challenging the beliefs and actions of other *masalik*. For example, some factions of Ahl-e-Hadees in Pakistan reject participation in politics while others contest elections regularly. Some Ahl-e-Hadees groups advocate *jihad al-nafs* (striving against one's base-self) while others stress *jihad al-sayf* (*jihad* with the sword). Some factions believe that militant *jihad* is *farz-e-ayn* (an individual duty) while others yet believe it to be *farz kifaya* (an obligation that when performed by a few relieves the rest of the community from their obligation).[9]

Kashmiris in Indian-administered Kashmir have traditionally followed Sufi traditions (*tareeqa*); however, owing to the presence of Pakistani militants from Deobandi and Ahl-e-Hadees backgrounds, fewer and fewer Kashmiris embrace the syncretic Sufi practices of their forbearers. While MDI and LeT may be the most well-known Ahl-e-Hadees groups in Pakistan, the largest Ahl-e-Hadees organization in Pakistan is the Markazi Jamiat Ahl-e-Hadees (MJAH). The MJAH participates in politics and has been close to the Pakistan Muslim League. It has several subsidiary organizations, including the Ahl-e-Hadees Youth Force, which has enormous ability to mobilize youth, often for violent ends. For example, they frequently engage in sectarian disputes with Shias and Barelvis and have even taken over Barelvi mosques. Perhaps the most important asset of the MJAH is the network of *madaris* it runs under the Wafaq-ul-Madaris Salafiya, which is the oversite body for these *madaris*.[10] Another MJAH offshoot is the Tehreek-e-Mujahideen, (TeM) which has a training camp near Muzaffarabad in Pakistan-administered Kashmir. In addition to fighting the *kuffars* (non-Muslims generally but Indian forces specifically) in Kashmir, it has also converted Barelvi mosques to that of Ahl-e-Hadees.[11]

While Ahl-e-Hadees *madaris* are relatively few in number, they have expanded quickly: whereas in 1988 there were only 134 Ahl-e-Hadees *madaris*, in 2000, there were 310.[12] In contrast, Deobandi *madaris* are the most numerous. According to data from 2013, there were 14,956 *madaris* in total, of which 404 belonged to Ahl-e-Hadees, 8,353 to Deobandis, 531 to Jamaat-e-Islami (JI), 400 to Shias and 5,268 to Barelvis.[13] Despite the common association between Salafism and "radical extremism," Ahl-e-Hadees *madaris* have long taught Pakistani studies, English, mathematics, and science along with the *Dars-e-Nizami* curriculum for religious education.[14] These organizations are in addition to MDI and LeT, to which I devote the rest of this chapter.

It is important to note that LeT has long been estranged from the mainstream Ahl-e-Hadees *ulema*. The LeT rejects the opinions of Ahl-e-Hadees *ulema* that *jihad* is inappropriate under the prevailing conditions and that non-state actors can wage *jihad*. This means that LeT cannot rely upon Ahl-e-Hadees institutions, such as mosques and *madaris*, for recruitment and support. In contrast to the myriad Deobandi militant groups who enjoy the amenities of Deobandi religious mosques, *madaris* and political institutions (various factions of the Jamiat Ulema-e-Islam, JUI) and thus can exert considerable—if undesirable—autonomy from the ISI, the LeT is relatively more isolated and thus dependent upon the ISI. Whereas the ISI has to manufacture divisions and rivalries to manage the cast of Deobandi militant groups, the LeT has never experienced a significant disunion.[15]

At first blush, one may assume that LeT would have difficulty competing for terrorist manpower given the other, presumably better-resourced, Deobandi terrorist groups that have greater operational freedom from the ISI. In fact, LeT has had little difficulty in recruitment and, based upon data I present below, is poised to select from among the best recruits available. The reason for this is simple: unlike the Deobandi groups which espouse sectarian, anti-state and Afghan-centric causes, LeT's rhetoric and focus upon India has perennial appeal among Pakistanis who, through their education and media exposure, are subjected to repeated and stylized accounts of the unfairness of Partition and the purported injustice that Pakistan does not possess Kashmir in its entirety. (Chapter 2). LeT also has enormous reach into Pakistan through its ostensible philanthropic and educational mobilisation. These activities allow LeT to cultivate popular support, collect donations of cash and goods, groom potential parents to encourage their sons to join LeT, and recruit participants for its militant and preaching missions.

The state and LeT work collaboratively in managing public opinion about issues of mutual concern. For example, whenever the Pakistani state engages in political shenanigans with respect to Indian-administered Kashmir, LeT's leadership is at the forefront of public demonstrations that accompany these theatrical hi-jinks. For example, in August 2016, yet another crisis erupted in Indian-administered Kashmir when young Kashmiris began publicly assembling to protest the killing of a Hizbul Mujahideen (HM) commander, Burhan Wani, by Indian security forces.[16] Dozens of Kashmiris were subsequently killed when Indian security forces fired on protesters over several days, catalyzing a larger opposition movement and corresponding violent crackdowns.[17] Pakistan, wishing to exploit India's grievous mishandling of its domestic affairs, declared 19 August a "black day." Subsequently, Maleeha Lodhi, Pakistan's permanent representative to the United Nations (UN), met with senior UN officials to demand an investigation into the violence in Indian-administered Kashmir.[18] While her request had little impact upon the UN or the international community, it did serve the important domestic function of continually churning popular support for Pakistan's endless quest for Kashmir.

While Pakistan pursued these diplomatic and political actions largely for domestic consumption, Hafiz Saeed launched a complementary "Kashmir Caravan" from Lahore, during which he threatened India with war if it did not accept the demands of Syed Ali Shah Geelani, a prominent Pakistan-backed separatist leader in Indian-administered Kashmir.[19] (The expression, "caravan," is noteworthy because it harkens back to the "caravans of jihad," referenced in the Medinan period of the Quran).[20] After stopping in Islamabad, the "caravan" continued onto Chakothi, a small town in Pakistan-administered Kashmir along the Line of Control. There, Talha Saeed, Hafiz Saeed's son, staged a sit-in demanding that India permit them to deliver relief materials collected under the guise of Falah Insaniat Foundation (FIF, Foundation for Welfare of Humanity), even though it is a terrorist organization proscribed by the UN Security Council (UNSC).[21] Hafiz Saeed took a further step to exert pressure on Pakistan's civilian leadership by filing a petition in the Lahore High Court, insisting that the Sharif government take the matter up at the UNSC. Saeed's petition asserted that India's claim on Kashmir is based upon Maharaja Hari Singh's "very controversial and forced accession" on 26 October 1947. He reiterated Pakistan's well-worn—but disingenuous position—that the fate of Kashmir should be decided through a plebiscite.[22] Saeed's efforts aided the army's other efforts to enervate Sharif's legitimacy.

Sharif has been a thorn in the Pakistan army's side since he forced army chief Jahangir Karamat to resign in 1998 after the general irked Sharif by criticizing Pakistan's incompetent and venal civilian leadership and calling for the "creation of a three-tiered national security council that would include the military, credible advisers and a think tank of experts."[23] The move was unprecedented: no civilian had ever removed an army chief. Usually army chiefs were the ones to oust civilian leaders. Sharif appointed General Pervez Musharraf whom he also tried to oust in October 1999 in part because of his role as prime mover in the Kargil Conflict, the first war between India and Pakistan since both became overt nuclear powers. Sharif announced the ouster of Musharraf while he was on a plane returning from Pakistan from Sri Lanka. Sharif refused to let his plane land which the army, not incorrectly, understood to be an attempt to kill him along with the various civilians on the flight with him. The army swiftly moved into action to oust Sharif and protect its chief. Sharif was exhiled to Saudi Arabia and could not return until a political deal was struck called the National Reconciliation Order of 2007.[24]

Given Sharif's history of confronting the army, it should have surprised no one that his campaign promises of normalizing relations with India, accepting Afghanistan as a neighbor rather than forcing it to become a client, and holding Musharraf accountable for treason would have riled the army by threatening its institutional interests. Given the army's opposition to Sharif, many observers expected the 2013 elections to yield a hung parliament which the army could manipulate as required. However, Sharif surprised most observers when his party won an outright majority in the 2013 elections, which was seen by Pakistanis and international observers alike as a clarion mandate for civilian, democratic governance and a rebuke of the army's incessant meddling in the country's politics. Emboldened by his electoral win, Sharif pursued the afore-noted goals and vigorously sought to ensure that General Pervez Musharraf would stand trial for treason. Consequently, from the first months of Sharif's prime ministership, the army orchestrated various political palavers to undermine his legitimacy and weaken his mandate. The generals finally succeeded in August 2017 when Sharif was forced to resign in what can only be understood as a judicial coup. Sharif stood trial for graft when his family assets were identified in the so-called Panama Papers. Pakistan's Supreme Court did not adjudicate Sharif's guilt or innocence; rather, it ruled that he did not meet the standards of *sadiq aur amin* (honest and righteous) identified—but not defined—in Pakistan's constitution. With this ruling, the army has yet another crude tool to hobble civilians who have the temerity to to challenge the preferences of Pakistan's men on horseback.[25]

While the army has crippled Sharif, it has few appealing alternatives. The Pakistan Peoples Party has failed to muster significant support for Benazir Bhutto's maladroit son and heir-apparent, Bilawal Bhutto. And, prior to the July 2018 elections, about which allegations of electoral rigging have already surfaced, it was unclear whether Imran Khan, the lothario cricketer turned conservative politician, could work with the army to transform his Pakistan Tehreek-e-Insaf party from a personality-cult to a mainstream party. Thus, the army needs all of the political assets its can cultivate. It is in this landscape of poor and poorer choices that Saeed's petition and political party should be understood. Saeed's petition to the Lahore High Court—whether or not it was conceived and midwifed by the army—advanced the army's interests in pressuring Nawaz Sharif to follow the army's diktat on Kashmir and India as both matters are core interests of the army.[26] Moreover, the MML may offer the army a potential ally whose small votebank may be useful in constructing electoral coalitions of the willing or billing in forming a government or loyal opposition in a future election.

The foregoing discussion demonstrates that LeT is not only useful for ginning up support for the deep state's agenda domestically; it also has been useful in ratcheting up pressure on civilian politicians such that they subscribe to and endorse the deep state's preferred course of action. The LeT benefits from the state's political maneuvers while simultaneously advancing the latter's agenda, and LeT's leaders deploy selective retellings of Pakistan's Partition-related history, both to buttress accounts received by Pakistanis in the course of their education and exposure to media, but also to generate support for the organization and its mission.

It is notable that Pakistan's Deobandi militant groups rarely behave in the same synchronized manner as does LeT, even if LeT co-opts Deobandi political leadership onto its political platforms. Equally important, even if these Deobandi militant leaders were to behave in such a manner, Pakistan's media does not amplify such participation as they do on behalf of LeT. Hence they routinely cover LeT's political stunts, interview its leadership, and report on its ostensible philanthropic and relief activities. This synergy between the organization and the state exposes the myriad benefits that LeT enjoys by virtue of being Pakistan's most disciplined proxy.

Early History of MDI, JuD and LeT

Early accounts of LeT's history vary widely.[27] Unfortunately, it is impossible to adjudicate which version—if any—of this history is accurate given that these studies tend to rely upon interviews with militants and Pakistani officials who may not be truthful and/or who may remember events incorrectly. Indeed, scholars who have interviewed LeT militants find that they often disagree with which one another on key dates, pivotal events, and even important personalities involved in the group's history and operations. Pakistani officials, moreover, have their own incentive to dissemble about the role of the state in supporting the organization. Thus, while there is general consensus about the LeT's formation and key personalities involved, there are important differences with respect to when particular events transpired. Accounts will sometimes vary by one year or so and, for this reason, I qualify those dates with "*c*." Unfortunately, I cannot adjudicate which of these divergent accounts is most accurate given the information that is publicly available.

Most scholars begin LeT's history when Zaki-ur-Rehman Lakhvi assembled a small group of Pakistani Ahl-e-Hadees adherents to wage *jihad* against the Soviets in Afghanistan towards the end of that conflict.[28] A year later, in *c.* 1985, Hafiz Muhammad Saeed and Zafar Iqbal, two professors from the Islamic studies department of Lahore Engineering University, formed the JuD. Initially it was a small group that was primarily focused upon *tabligh* (proselytization) or *dawah* (missionary work) and aimed to propagate the tenants of the Ahl-e-Hadees creed. In *c.* 1986, Lakhvi's militia merged with JuD to form the MDI. The MDI had three functions: *jihad*; proselytization of the Ahl-e-Hadees *maslak*, and the creation of a new generation of Muslims committed to their ideology. In total, about seventeen persons helped found the MDI, one of whom was Abdullah Azzam, an associate of Osama bin Laden who was affiliated with the Islamic University of Islamabad and the *Maktab ul Khadamat* (Bureau of Services for Arab *mujahideen*). Azzam was killed in a bomb blast in 1989 in Peshawar.[29]

Within one year of its formation, MDI established its first militant training camp, Muaskar-e-Tayyaba, in the Afghan province of Paktia, which does not border Pakistan. It established another camp, Muaskar-e-Aqsa, in Kunar, which abuts the Pakistani tribal agencies of Bajaur and Mohmand in Pakistan's Federally Administered Tribal Areas (FATA).[30] Kunar is home to numerous Ahl-e-Hadees adherents in Afghanistan, which is uncharacteristic in a country where many Afghans are associated with different Sufi orders (e.g. Naqshabandi). For this reason, Kunar has been an attractive safe haven for Wahhabi Arabs in Afghanistan, despite the fact that Wahhabis are technically distinct from Salafis (the former follow the Hanbali school of *fiqh*, and the latter reject *fiqh* altogether). Pakistan-based analysts note that MDI's training camps were always separate from those of the Taliban, which hosted Deobandi militant groups such as Harkat-ul-Jihad-e-Islami (HUJI) and Harkat ul Mujahideen (HUM). This has led some analysts to contend that MDI/LeT has not had the sustained and organic connections to Al Qaeda as enjoyed by the Deobandi groups, many of which became "outsourcers" for Al Qaeda in Pakistan after 2001.[31] This does not mean that individuals have not left LeT to operate on behalf of Al Qaeda, nor does it mean that LeT has not come under pressure from its members to compete with Al Qaeda, as I discuss later. Whereas Saeed has not condemned Al Qaeda and, in fact, offered funerary prayers for bin Laden, he has opposed the Islamic State, which he called "evil" and has encouraged Pakistanis to shun sectarian violence, consistent with LeT's opposition to violence in Pakistan.[32] While some cadres and even operational planners may have left the organization since 2001, LeT has proven itself to be remarkably resilient and resistant to fissures that have bedeviled many of the other militant groups in Pakistan.

After the Soviets withdrew from Afghanistan, MDI shifted its focus to Indian-administered Kashmir. Hafiz Saeed explained that as soon as the Russian troops left Afghanistan, they distanced themselves "from factional fighting and shifted our focus to occupied Kashmir."[33] After internecine warfare broke out among the different *mujahideen* leaders in Afghanistan after the Soviet withdrawal, Lashkar relocated its training facilities to Pakistan-administered Kashmir. It established numerous camps in the mountains of Pakistan-administered Kashmir, the most important of which are: Bait ul Mujahideen in Muzaffarabad, which received its first trainees in late 1990 or early 1991 and is intended to process and house recruits. This was in addition to four major training camps (*muaskar*): Muaskar-e-Umm ul Qura (in Muzaffarabad), Muaskar-e-Abdullah Bin Massood (also near Muzaffarabad); Muaskar-e-Aqsa (Muzaffarabad); and the Muaskar-e-Tayyaba.[34] It later set up a camp in Sindh called Markaz Mohammad bin Qasim, as noted below, as well as other smaller camps throughout Pakistan. (It should be noted that LeT has taken these various names for its training camps and facilities in Pakistan and Afghanistan from important Quranic battles.) The organization's decision to eschew warlord infighting reflects partly MDI's preference to abjure participating in Muslim-on-Muslim violence. The decision also reflects its belief that Kashmir is the most legitimate open front in the region, and that it entered the fray there before it became Pakistan's proxy of choice.[35]

MDI's headquarters (Markaz) was built on a sprawling, 200-acre campus in Muridke, in Pakistan's Punjab province, thirty kilometers from Lahore. The Punjab, unlike the FATA, is one of the most militarized provinces in Pakistan. Of the nine regular Pakistan Army corps, six are in the Punjab as well as the Army Air Defense Command and Strategic Forces Command, which are treated as corps. The MDI Markaz, which is now the headquarters for JuD, hosts numerous amenities and profit-making activities, including: a *madrassah* (seminary), a large *jamia* mosque, a hospital, a market, a large residential area for scholars and faculty members, a garment factory, an iron factory, a woodwork factory, a stable, a swimming pool, a fish farm, and agricultural tracts.[36] There are various unconfirmed rumors that bin Laden contributed ten million Pakistani rupees to help build the mosque and residential area at the Markaz. There are also rumors that, until 1992, when he was ostensibly "banned" from travelling or staying in Pakistan, bin Laden regularly attended rallies at the Markaz.[37]

On 25 January 1990, MDI staged its first militant mission in Kashmir when its operatives ambushed a jeep that was carrying Indian air force personnel traveling towards Srinagar Airport. One squadron leader and three pilots were killed. While attacks on Indian security forces by Kashmiri militants had become commonplace by 1990, the accuracy of this assault by a hitherto unknown militant group was unprecedented. A leader of the organization, quoted by Azmat Abbas, explained the rationale for this particular target:

> We could have attacked any other military target but chose the Indian Air Force because it was instrumental in flying the Indian army into Kashmir through hundreds of sorties between October 27 and November 17 in 1947. This [attack] was our way of saying that now it was the time for the Indian Air Force to fly their army out of Kashmir.[38]

Whether Indian security personal understood that MDI was drawing from the very earliest days of the Kashmir conflict remains unknown. This explanation is yet another example of how the organization deploys Pakistan's Partition-related grievances to justify its actions, secure popular support, and motivate their cadres.[39]

In the early 1990s, MDI segmented its activities and organizational structure. While MDI continued the mission of proselytization and education, it hived off LeT as a tightly related militant wing of MDI.[40] However, Hafiz Saeed was the leader (*amir*) of both organizations, which attests to the degree to which it was nearly impossible to distinguish MDI and LeT.[41] Hafiz Saeed explained the continuity between the two organizations as follows: "Islam propounds both dawa and jihad. Both are equally important and inseparable. Since our life revolves around Islam, therefore both dawa and jihad are essential; we cannot prefer one over the other."[42]

The ISI had hoped that LeT, with its demonstrable superior capabilities, would intensify the conflict in Kashmir and expand the geographical expanse of the insurgency. In the early 1990s, the ISI and the Pakistan army began providing support to the organization. The army helped to build LeT's military apparatus specifically for use against India as opposed to Afghanistan, Chechnya, or other theatres where LeT activists fought periodically. The Pakistan army helped design the organization's military training regime and has long co-located army and ISI personnel at LeT training bases to help oversee the regimen and to lead the organization's trainers.[43] Pakistan's investments paid off: within a few years LeT became the biggest challenge to the Indian security forces in Kashmir, prior to the introduction of JeM many years later.

In 1999, LeT introduced a new tactic in Indian-administered Kashmir: namely the *fidayeen* attack. By doing so, the LeT and its Pakistani handlers hoped to reverse a three-year decline in militant activity in Indian-administered Kashmir. The first such mission involved two LeT operatives, who attacked the headquarters of the Border Security Force (BSF, an Indian paramilitary organization) in Bandipura with grenades and gunfire. The BSF Deputy Inspector General perished in that attack. These attacks embarrassed Indian security forces and helped to burnish LeT's reputation for being the most formidable of the various militant groups operating in Kashmir.[44] Since then, these kinds of attacks have become a hallmark of LeT's operations.

Many writers have often misconstrued LeT's *fidayeen* assaults as "suicide operations," in which the attacker uses his or her body, deliberately and with premeditation, to deliver explosives to kill and maim others, with the supreme goal of dying in that attack. The success, or lack thereof, of a suicide attack is solely contingent upon the death of the attacker in that operation.[45] LeT does not conduct suicide attacks per se; rather, LeT's *fidayeen* missions are more akin to high-risk missions in which well-trained commandos engage in fierce combat during which dying is preferable to being captured. Hafiz Abdul Rehman Makki, a key LeT leader, explained in the pages of *Mujallah al-Dawah* that the *fidayeen* commanders are killed only by the hands of their attackers, not by their own.[46] Thus, while martyrdom is in some sense the ultimate objective of a LeT *fidayeen* operative, the organization selects missions where there is a possibility—howsoever remote—that the assailants will survive to kill more of the enemy in the future.

In 1998, LeT leaders disclosed to Z. Khan that as a matter of policy, LeT's "soldiers" prefer death to capture, because those who are captured are tortured by Indian authorities. Khalid Walid, a LeT leader, told Khan that they "generally [...] fight until death and do not even surrender at any cost."[47] Therefore, the objective of a LeT *fidayeen* commando is not to commit suicide; rather, he aims to kill as many opponents in as many engagements as possible before perishing in the line of fire and becoming, at last, a *shaheed*. Mansoor Ahmad, who uses the *kuniyat* (nom de guerre) of Abu Hamza, illustrates this concept. He fought in Indian-administered Kashmir continuously for one year. During this time, his group undertook ten, if not more, separate encounters with Indian security forces in which ten of his comrades were killed. Hamza averred his commitment to martyrdom, opining: "I will keep going back to Kashmir... until I too receive *shahadat* [martyrdom]."[48]

Abou Zahab explains that in a typical LeT mission:

> The fighters are well trained and highly motivated and they engage the enemy on its own territory. Small groups of fedayeen...storm a security force camp and kill as many soldiers as possible before taking defensive positions within the camp and engaging security force personnel till they attain martyrdom. Battles often last twenty hours, if not more.[49]

She further explains that these spectacular and well-planned strikes earn the LeT maximum publicity, swell its pool of potential recruits, and expand its base of donations, while also demoralizing the enemy which must resort to heavy fire, destroying their own buildings and causing substantial collateral damage in the process.

Considerable insights about this were garnered from the lone survivor of the November 2008 attack on Mumbai: Ajmal Kasab. Kasab and Muzaffar (an associate of Kasab's who would become his "battle buddy" in the LeT training regime) were first contacted by an elderly man while they were wandering about Lahore as people prepared for the Eid festival. He persuaded them to meet with LeT recruiters at a nearby office after which they left immediately for the Markaz-e-Tayyaba in Muridke for the Daura-e-Suffa, the twenty-one-day introductory course to the LeT. After being converted to LeT's Ahl-e-Hadees creed and learning the ways of the Hadithees, the two met an associate of Zaki ur Rehman Lakhvi, known as Qahafa the Bull. Qahafa was in fact Lakhvi's "number two" who imparted basic battle training to the two boys and thirty others who were in the course. According to Kasab, Qahafa emphasized the difference between suicide attacks and the *fidayeen* mission: Whereas suicide entails killing "oneself in desperation after one fails to achieve that goal which has been set," a *fidayeen* attacker is one who "died trying to achieve a virtuous goal."[50] While LeT's various publications contend that it has only assaulted Indian security forces and related targets, their record demonstrates an absolute willingness to kill civilians in these attacks, as exemplified by the Mumbai outrage among others. In addition to the *fidayeen* mission, the LeT became very adept at making sophisticated improvised explosive devices (IEDs) to target Indian security forces on roadsides and other terrain.[51] Nonetheless, the organization is most famed for its much-feared *fidayeen* missions.

In December 2001, Pakistan banned LeT, along with several other militant groups, after JeM attacked the Indian parliament earlier that month, bringing India and Pakistan close to the brink of war. These bans deceived no one. Pakistan's intelligence agencies alerted the soon-to-be banned organizations of the upcoming proscription, providing them ample time to transfer their assets to new accounts and to reorganize and re-launch under new names. In the case of LeT, Hafiz Saeed announced the organization had been restructured and would operate as JuD, separate from LeT, which would be a strictly Kashmiri organization led by Maula Abdul Wahid al-Kashmiri. Saeed dissolved MDI and replaced it with JuD, which was the name of the original organization he founded in 1985 and which was still registered as a Pakistani charity. He resigned as LeT's *amir* and became the *amir* of JuD which was described as an "organization for the teaching of Islam, politics, [and] social work."[52] According to Yahya Mujahid, "we handed Lashkar-e-Tayyaba over to the Kashmiris in December 2001" to be led by al-Kashmiri.[53] This purported division was merely a reorganization: JuD subsumed the vast majority of LeT's human, financial and material assets, while the organizational nodes and operatives outside of Pakistan continued to serve under the banner of LeT. As further evidence of the organizational continuity between the various groups, Hafiz Saeed, Zafar Iqbal, Hafiz Abdul Rehman Makki and Zaki-ur-Rehman Lakhvi were in charge of the new organization while al-Kashmiri was merely a figurehead.[54] Those who could no longer fight in Kashmir were either retained in so-called reserve forces, or remained active by participating in social-work or preaching under the guise of JuD or other organizations under Saeed, such as the FIF.[55]

By 2005, the organization formally began sanctioning and supporting its cadres going to Afghanistan to fight with the Afghan Taliban where they engaged United States, International Security Assistance Force (ISAF), Afghan, and Indian targets.[56] For example, in 2008, LeT militants aided other insurgents to assail an American base in Wanat, Nuristan.[57] In that attack, insurgents came close to over-running the American base. LeT attacks on Indian targets included the July 2008 car-bombing of the Indian Embassy,[58] a February 2010 *fidayeen* attack on Kabul guesthouses hosting Indians,[59] and the May 2014 attack on the Indian consulate in Herat.[60]

LeT was chary about becoming extensively involved in the Afghanistan insurgency and the degree to which it would be required to work with and through the various Deobandi groups who were at war with the Pakistani state. Ultimately, the organization opted to enter the Afghan insurgency for several reasons. Pakistan was forced to restrict Kashmir operations after the Indian parliament attack and that on Indian military families in Kaluchak (in Kashmir) in May 2002. Under significant US pressure, Musharraf adopted the so-called "moderated *jihad*" strategy (which denied LeT and other *jihadi* groups easy access to this prized theatre of operations).[61] The organization, seeking to retain fighters as well as experienced commanders who were anxious for active combat, found Afghanistan a welcoming theatre. The LeT's donors believed that Afghanistan was a more important objective than Kashmir after the ouster of the Taliban and Al Qaeda and the subsequent occupation of the country by American and ISAF forces. Fourth, under the American security umbrella, India established a robust presence in Afghanistan which was a perennial irritant to Pakistan.[62] Most importantly, the ISI sanctioned the organization's expanded role in Afghanistan where it, along with the Haqqani Network, became Pakistan's most important assets with which it could attack Indian and international military targets in Afghanistan. However, the Afghan theatre is of secondary importance to that of Kashmir, and is a theatre of compulsion rather than a theatre of preference.[63]

The organization came under considerable pressure again in 2007 when some members—including senior leaders—considered dumping "its ISI paymasters, [to] join forces with al Qaeda and shift its theatre of activity from fighting Indian forces in Kashmir to launching the attacks against coalition forces in Afghanistan."[64] In January 2006, Deobandi militants under the leadership of two brothers, Maulana Abdul Aziz and Abdul Rashid Ghazi, took over and fortified the Red Mosque in Islamabad and a nearby women's *madrassah*, which they used as a base for vigilante violence and criminal activities such as violent demonstrations, destruction of property, armed clashes with security forces, and kidnapping. The final straw was their abduction of ostensibly Chinese prostitutes. At long last and under Chinese pressure, the Pakistan armed forces launched Operation Silence in July 2007. During the conflict, more than two hundred people died. Ghazi was killed, and his brother, captured, while trying to abscond in a *burqa*.[65]

David Coleman Headley (also known as Daood Gilani) came to LeT at a propitious moment. He is currently serving a thirty-five year prison sentence for his pivotal role in the Mumbai 2008 attacks. Headley is an American-Pakistani who was an agent of both the ISI and the LeT. He also worked as an informant for the US Drug Enforcement Agency (DEA).[66] Additionally, he tried to secure support from the ISI, LeT, and Al Qaeda to attack a Danish newspaper which published offensive cartoons of prophet Muhammad.[67] After receiving substantial training in spy craft by the ISI, Headley carried out the reconnaissance for the Mumbai mission.[68] Headley encouraged both the ISI and the LeT to attack multiple targets in Mumbai. Lakhvi was worried that the organization would not remain coherent under the varying pressures to join Al Qaeda in Afghanistan or even to fight against Pakistanis, a position the organization abjured from the beginning. Major Iqbal, Headley's handler within the ISI, called him to Lahore explaining that he was "under tremendous pressure" to prevent the Lashkar from fracturing.[69]

Until that point, LeT and the ISI were considering Headley's Mumbai mission but were not convinced by it. Now things had changed. The ISI and LeT were "compelled to consider a spectacular terrorist strike in India" that would "sate the desire of some factions to attack the enemies of Islam—Americans, Israelis and Europeans—as well as India."[70] Headley's Mumbai plan fitted the bill. Pakistan deployed government forces outside LeT's Qadisiya mosque in Lahore and ISI agents "rode shotgun" to protect Hafiz Saeed. Similarly, government forces provided security to the complex at Muridke while "plain-clothed agents, hair cropped, cradling machine guns, patrol[ed] the faux Greek villas of the movement's leaders."[71]

The suggestion to attack Chabad House came from sixteen Indians that LeT had recruited in Mumbai to help develop a list of potential attack sites. A late addition to the target list, it was a Jewish welfare center staffed by an American rabbi. Rather than catering to the needs of Mumbai's Indian Jewish community, Chabad House principally served Israelis—many of whom travel to India after completing their compulsory military service. While the attacks on the Taj, the Trident-Oberoi, and the Chhatrapati Shivaji Terminus (CST) were not controversial within the LeT, attacking Chabad House was widely debated. Some within the old guard objected to its inclusion, noting that it was beyond LeT's brief and would result in the organization becoming the target of global counter-terrorism efforts. However, those who were more swayed by Al Qaeda convinced Lakhvi to push the organization in this new direction.[72] Ironically, while the expansion of the target set beyond Indians caused some analysts to interpret the move as LeT cozying up to Al Qaeda, it was, in fact, a move to prevent such a robust embrace.[73]

Organizational Structure

There is a paucity of verified and current information about JuD's structure in the public domain despite the threat it poses to regional and international security, as well as the extremely public and frequent disporting of its leadership in Pakistan's major and minor cities alike. Even estimates about the organization's strength vary enormously: Sharma and Behera assess that the organization has about 50,000 trained personnel who have undertaken some degree of training at one or more of the organization's five major training camps.[74] This number is a full order of magnitude higher than that of the US Department of State, which conjectures that it "has several thousand members in Azad Kashmir [that part of Kashmir administered by Pakistan], Pakistan; in the southern Jammu, Kashmir, and Doda regions; and in the Kashmir Valley."[75]

Prior to 2001, it was relatively easy to research its departments and concomitant leaders because its website regularly disseminated such information and any changes therein. In subsequent years, it has become increasingly difficult to obtain accurate and timely information about its structure, operations and leadership because of the ever-mounting legal pressure on the organization, its Pakistani state sponsors, its various shell organizations, and its members and leaders. Gone are the days when the organization used its website to boast of its operations in India, and publicize exultant accounts of their militants killed in action in so-called "*shaheed*" biographies. JuD's website, when it can be accessed given that it is frequently de-platformed, instead highlights the group's political objectives, humanitarian outreach, and social work, with no mention of its militant activities.[76] This informational problem is compounded by the fact that LeT frequently moves leaders around from one department to another.[77] Thus, in the text that follows, I discuss key members of the organization and note briefly the various positions they have held, with the caveat that specific details about those individuals and LeT may have changed, or that the initial reports may have been incorrect.

Hafiz Saeed is the amir of JuD and the de facto head of LeT and other related organizations, despite his demurrals to the contrary. To manage JuD/LeT's varied domestic and international activities, JuD maintains several departments including: Department of Education; Department of Publishing under Dar al Andalus (which exclusively publishes the organization's books and pamphlets); Department for the Construction of Mosques and Madrassas; Department of Ulema and Teachers; Department of Preaching and Reform; Department of Resources (fund-raising for *jihad*); Martyrs' Department (providing financial aid to families of slain fighters); Department of External Affairs; Department of Media and Propaganda; Department of Public Relations; Department of Social Welfare; as well as specialized wings for technology, physicians, women, students, farmers and workers. All of these come under the leadership of Saeed.[78] Unfortunately, there is very little information about the current heads of all of these divisions, or even a list of current functional departments. One Pakistani analyst remarked of this impressive and complicated structure: "[the] driving force behind its massive success in recruitment is deceptively simple: using its impressive organizational network, which includes schools, social service groups and religious publications to stir up outrage against the injustices meted to Kashmiri Muslims, the [*tanzeem*] creates a passion for jehad."[79]

The Department of Education is perhaps the most influential and profitable arm. Many of the students from their various educational institutes go on to work with LeT in non-combatant capacities, while a very small percentage end up in the fighting ranks. The *Dawah* school system is their flagship educational enterprise. The first *Dawah* schools opened in 1994 in Lahore and Muridke. By 2001, the organization claimed to have opened some 127 schools with 15,000 students and 800 instructors. In 2008, the Punjab Home Secretary told a US consulate official in Lahore that the organization ran some 173 schools; however, that official reported in a cable that the secretary had "grossly underestimated the number of JuD schools, which could exceed one thousand *madrassahs* in Punjab alone."[80] The official's estimate also conflicts with the organization's own website, which asserts that it has "146 with an amalgamate of 2050 qualified teachers providing exceptional education to 35,215 students throughout the country."[81] *Dawah* schools teach conventional educational subjects (math, sciences, and information technology) as well as the importance of *jihad*. JuD uses cross-subsidization in its financial management by collecting fees assessed from those who can afford to pay, while offering need-based financial assistance to those who cannot.

Given the success of the *Dawah* schools, in 2004 the organization established a small chain of schools called *Taqwa* Model School, the first of which opened in Karachi. It currently has five campuses as well as a model college, all in Karachi. Wilson John reports that the school was set up by Professor Zafar Iqbal—who co-founded LeT with Saeed—and Suhail Fazil Usmani—who was associated with the NED University of Engineering and Technology in Karachi.[82] As is apparent from the chain's website, the classrooms are clean, air-conditioned, and appointed with modern technology. The school claims to enjoin "activity-based learning."[83] The language of instruction is English rather than the country's national language, Urdu. Students are also required to study Arabic. By Pakistani standards, *Taqwa* is very expensive, with high monthly fees that are on par with some of Pakistan's elite private schools.[84] Students are admitted based upon their scores in competitive exams.

According to the principal of one of the schools in a "Video Tour," the chain hopes to address a gap that exists between the school system that produces *maulvis* (religious teachers), and another that produces engineers, doctors, et cetera. *Taqwa* wants to combine both systems under one roof such that if a child becomes an engineer, they will be a Muslim engineer. Islamic subjects, such as *hifz* (memorization of the Quran), are heavily emphasized alongside math, science, and other secular subjects. The school also provides Tae Kwon Do training and a variety of other physical sports to both boys and girls to enhance their physical fitness. Curiously, the school system makes heavy use of television and other technologies that the organization elsewhere proscribes.[85]

The *Taqwa* Model Schools have strict requirements for students' dress, decorum, school attendance, and study habits. It also upholds a similar strict set of expectations of parents. Parents are bluntly advised about their personal behavior and the home environment they keep. They are told to make their home as Islamic as possible and provide a healthy environment for their children inclusive of nutritious food (as opposed to "junk food"), properly lit study areas, and adequate opportunities for sleep.

At first blush the school shows no obvious signs of being connected to JuD/ LeT. However, if one peruses the videos that are posted on the chain's website or on its Facebook page, one sees children engaging in activities with the distinctive black and white flag of LeT in the background. Based upon the organization's own materials, it seems set to compete with some of Pakistan's best private schools.[86]

These schools are distinct from JuD's inventory of *madaris*, for which there is no credible assessment of numbers. *Madaris* fall under the purview of the Department of Construction of *Masjid* and *Madrassas*. Similarly, there is no credible appraisal of the number of mosques (*masajid*, pl. of *masjid*) that the organization has built. This department aims to promulgate JuD's rendering of the Ahl-e-Hadees interpretative tradition through religious teaching and preaching at both *masajid* and *madaris*. These *madaris* aim to produce religious scholars (*ulema*, pl. of *alim*), who then go on to impart this instruction to their own future students in a *madrassah*, in which they may preach to *masjid* congregations.

Through its various educational enterprises, JuD aims to purify Pakistani society of the adverse influences of secular education through the teaching of Quran and *Sunnat*; prepare students to be better Muslims in accordance with Ahl-e-Hadees precepts as interpreted by JuD; identify potential future cadres for its various militant and non-militant functions alike; and impress upon students that *jihad* is an individual obligation incumbent upon all Muslims. JuD purports that all persons should be prepared to wage *jihad*, even if they never are given the opportunity do so.

Nonetheless, military training is generally discrete from these schools.[87] While students may develop an interest in *jihad*, they must be selected for and attend military training, and ultimately win the support of the LeT leadership in order to be dispatched on a mission (discussed in Chapter 5). In fact, most students passing through these schools will never even be considered for combat. Estimates that I derived from my field work in Pakistan over many years suggest that fewer than one in ten will ever actually see combat. The rest will be sent back to their localities, where they are expected to engage in proselytization.[88] Zafar Iqbal, co-founder of MDI and former colleague of Hafiz Saeed at the University of Engineering and Technology (Lahore), summed up the goals of the education department thus: "We will continue to work in the twin fields of education and jihad. Jihad is carried out to establish the system of Allah in the world. But this system cannot be established without education. Therefore, education is equally important."[89]

Dar al Andalus, which published all of the materials used in the later chapters of this volume, is one of the most important organs of the group. Note that while LeT is perhaps the most prolific producer of *jihadi* literature, all of Pakistan's *jihadi* groups do so. Pakistan's active and passive support for these myriad militant organizations has allowed them to cultivate an extremely effective media apparatus that operates in a wide array of print formats (pamphlets, books, posters, poetry, and instructional manuals) as well as on-line resources. These *jihadi* publications operate as would any other media purveyor in Pakistan, and by most reports, are extremely lucrative.[90] Analysts believe that Dar al Andalus offers the widest array of *jihadi* offerings in Pakistan. (The name recalls the period (711–1492 CE) when Andalusia was under Muslim rule.)

The first magazine that the organization launched was *Zarbat-e-Haq* and it first went into press shortly after the creation of MDI. Immediately after *Zarbat-e-Haq* went into circulation, it launched what would become its flagship Urdu monthly magazine, *Mujallah al-Dawah*. Amir Hamza was its editor and Tahir Naqqash and Qazi Kashif Niaz were his assistants; however, Saeed was responsible for overseeing its publication.[91] By the end of the 1990s, *Mujallah al-Dawah* reportedly had a circulation of 100,000.[92] Another important monthly magazine, called *Ghazwa*, has a circulation of about 20,000, and details various of LeT's military exploits as well as reports on other *jihadi* battles elsewhere.[93] This is in addition to an assortment of other weekly and monthly publications that cater to students (*Zarb-e-Tayyaba*), women (*Tayyabaat*), and children, as well as those who are literate in English (*Voice of Islam, Invite*) and Arabic (*al-Ribat*). In fact, they publish about 100 booklets per year in a variety of languages.[94] (N.B.: Several of these publications such as *Mujallah al-Dawah* are not currently being published. When my collaborators made visits to their bookshops in 2013, we were told that the publications had been discontinued. The latest year for which I have issues is 2004.)

Under the banner of FIF, which is a separate organization under its direction rather than a "department," JuD/LeT has established considerable renown in Pakistan and beyond for its medical and relief activities, although the organization also engages in similar activities under the name of JuD. JuD made its debut in these efforts during the 2004/05 Asian Tsunami followed by the calamitous earthquake in Kashmir. However, as I show in Chapter 6, their role has been greatly exaggerated in the domestic and foreign media in part because of the way in which the ISI and related organizations handle journalists to ensure that they covered their relief activities but not those of others.[95] Their branding effort has been so successful that many Pakistanis labor under the delusion that FIF is separate from JuD. In turn, many survey data show that Pakistanis neither believe that JuD is the same organization as LeT nor that JuD has any ties to a terrorist organization. Instead, they believe JuD to be a social welfare organization and, as such, hold it in high regard.[96] The belief that FIF is discrete from LeT/JuD is bolstered by the fact that FIF has its own logo and does not use the black and white sword logo of JuD/LeT. Nor does FIF mention JuD in its materials, even though JuD makes heavy use of FIF in its own publications and social media.

In February 2016, Hafiz Saeed felt the need to address the perception in Pakistan that JuD and FIF are unrelated. He explained to assembled journalists that "the Falah-e-Insaniat Foundation is the reality of Jamat ud Dawah."[97] Saeed, referencing FIF's 2015 Annual Report, averred that FIF had provided free medicines and treatment to over two million Pakistanis in its six FIF hospitals (in Gujranwala, Muridke, Hyderabad, Karachi, and Quetta), 157 dispensaries, and 972 medical camps. FIF, on its webpage and through its social media, claims to provide vaccines, ambulance services, prisoner welfare, and emergency relief efforts in the aftermath of floods, earthquakes, cyclones and the like. In recent years, FIF has also undertaken numerous water-related projects to address the water-deprivation that many Pakistanis suffer.[98] FIF boasts of having conducted relief work in Afghanistan, Kashmir, Indonesia,

Somalia, Nepal, Syria, Gaza and Myanmar.[99] FIF's Twitter feed regularly shows photos of the (likely exaggerated) relief work it is doing for the Rohingya in Myanmar.[100] Notably JuD publications also publicize the plight of the Rohingya and their relief efforts under JuD's banner.[101] How the individuals engaged in these activities received visas for these countries is puzzling, given that the UNSC designated the FIF as a terrorist organization in 2012.[102] As I discuss later in this volume, the state's promotion of JuD as a social welfare organization has helped to persuade ordinary Pakistanis that it is distinct from LeT and its terrorist activities.

FIF, like its parent organization JuD, also does its part to keep the Kashmir problem alive and at the forefront of Pakistani popular discourse, consonant with the preferences of the deep state to which its existence is indebted. During one self-aggrandizing political spectacle in 2016, FIF collected funds to provide food and medical treatment to Kashmiris in Indian-administered Kashmir. They had no reasonable expectation of being allowed to cross the border to dispense the aid, given that FIF is a UNSC-designated terrorist organization associated with LeT. FIF subsequently held a rally in Muzaffarabad in Pakistan-administered Kashmir to protest.[103] India's predictable and justified decision was to deny them entry. While these outreach efforts are effective at winning Pakistani hearts and minds and rebranding the JuD franchise and ultimately advance the standing of the newly launched Milli Muslim League (MML), they are also likely viable recruiting opportunities for cadres and medical service professionals alike for missions in Kashmir and beyond. LeT/JuD also recruited students who excelled in the sciences from its own schools and trained them to work as paramedics with LeT militants in India.[104]

JuD's Department of External Affairs reportedly engages with other so-called *jihadi* organizations in Pakistan and beyond. Rana claims that LeT established close ties with more than a dozen *jihadi* groups in the Middle East, South East Asia, Europe (i.e. Bosnia, Chechnya) and elsewhere.[105] Considerably more is known about the organization's key leadership, in part due to their public profiles and numerous publications. The arrests of various LeT cadres and facilitators have offered important organizational and leadership insights from the interrogations that followed. Unlike other Pakistani terrorist groups which operate in discrete cells, LeT/JuD has a very hierarchical commander-cadre structure. (Prior to the ban in 2001, LeT was formally designated the military wing of MDI, which also had this hierarchical structure.) There is a *shura* (consultative assembly) which is comprised of the various department heads described below. This Pakistan-based body makes major decisions about the group's military and other (missionary, social work, etc.) activities in consultation with the ISI.[106] As noted earlier, Hafiz Saeed is the *amir* of the organization, now operating within Pakistan under the moniker of JuD. For all intents and purposes, he is also the head of LeT, which operates under that name within Kashmir, despite the appointment of a Kashmiri as a figurehead for this role. Saeed continues to address rallies in this capacity, and refers to himself in such terms in his social media and interviews with journalists and scholars. Most importantly, Saeed exercises extremely tight control over the organization and its various elements.

To ensure maximal compliance with his *diktats*, Saeed appoints family members or close associates to key positions who answer directly to him. He is grooming his son-in-law, Hafiz Khalid Waleed, as his successor. Waleed was responsible for planning several attacks in India throughout 2016.[107] The organization of the *jihad* department (led by Abdul Wahid Kashmiri) resembles conventional military organizations, with a supreme commander and deputy, provisional commander, divisional commanders, brigade commanders, and so forth. The chain of command is pyramidal and specialized with specific elements responsible for recruitment, training and the conduct of military operations. Saeed exercises tight command and control over these elements, as well as through the various section heads who report directly to him.[108]

Key Leadership

Saeed's tight top-down control over the organization and emplacement of close associates explains in part why the organization has not experienced the same fissures and subsequent uprisings against the state as various Deobandi organizations—though his nepotism, as noted previously, did cause a serious rift in 2004.[109] Saeed's control over his cadres is also buttressed by ISI's willingness to use violence should LeT cadres disobey either their leaders in LeT or the ISI. During Musharraf's so-called "moderated *jihad*,"[110] LeT cadres who were infiltrating the Line of Control without ISI's permission were arrested upon their return. The cadres courted physical harm to themselves and their loved ones if they disobeyed the ISI's orders. The ISI also pressured the guides, porters, and other support personnel to ensure that militants would per force rely upon the state-provided infrastructure.[111] Thus, ISI pressure, coupled with Saeed's strong personal grip on the organization, has contributed to its discipline, in contrast to the Deobandi militant groups who have proven to be a problem for the Pakistani state.

Zafar Iqbal was one of the co-founders of the outfit in addition to Saeed. He is a senior leader within the organization and, commensurate with his long tenure, has had held numerous posts over the years. According to the UNSC Al-Qaida Sanctions Committee, as of late 2010, Iqbal headed JuD's finance department.[112] Iqbal serves as the head of the organization's education section, in which he has helped to recruit for the organization by developing curricula for the vast body of schools that it runs in Pakistan. In addition, as of 2010, he was also the president of the organization's medical wing, as well as secretary of a university trust that was established for purposes that are not well understood.[113] Meanwhile, Talha Saeed is the Head of the Clerics and Teachers Department, Abdussalam bin Muhammad is the administrator for the organization's *madrassah* network, Saifullah Khalid heads up the Invitation and Reform department, and Muhammad Ashraf heads the Finance Department.[114]

Zaki-ur-Rehman Lakhvi is ostensibly the organization's Chief of Operations. He was one of the original founders of MDI, when he merged his militant group with the organization for *dawah* established by Saeed and Iqbal. Lahkvi was one of the prominent handlers of the terrorists involved in the Mumbai 2008 attacks. Recall also that it was Lakhvi who split briefly with Saeed over his nepotism and formed his own militant group. This rift was mended with likely intercession by the ISI. On 7 December 2008, four days after Indian officials named him as a major suspect in Mumbai attack, Pakistani authorities "arrested" him. His tenure in the Adyala Jail was extremely—if absurdly—permissive. He and six associates had access to several rooms next to the jailer's office. The jailer allowed them to have dozens of visitors a day, a television, mobile phones, and internet access.[115]

According to an Adyala jail official, Lakhvi was allowed to "receive any number of guests, any time of day or night, seven days a week."[116] Visitors were not required to obtain permission or even show their identification. During his time in jail, he was permitted to have conjugal visits with his youngest wife who gave birth to a son while he was ostensibly incarcerated. All in all, Lakhvi maintained operational control of JuD/LeT throughout his detention. He was released on bail in April 2015, when the Pakistanis claimed that there was inadequate evidence to continue holding him.[117] However, it is also likely that the Mumbai attacks gave the organization and the ISI an opportunity to constrain Lakhvi in some measure given his brief—but important—defection in 2004. After all, no other senior JuD/LeT leader involved in the attack (e.g. Sajid Mir) was arrested.

Another founding member is Hafiz Abdul Salam Bhuttavi. On the few occasions when the Pakistani state has detained Saeed, Bhuttavi has stepped in to serve as the acting *amir*. Bhuttavi is one of the organization's preeminent scholars and, in this capacity, has provided instruction to its leaders and cadres alike. Bhuttavi has also issued *fatwas* that authorize the organization's varied military operations, alongside overseeing the organization's *madaris*. He also participated in the preparation of the so-called *fidayeen*, who conducted the November 2008 attack on Mumbai.[118]

Abdul Rehman Makki, who is also Saeed's brother-in-law and the son of one of Saeed's maternal uncles, is the Director of Foreign Affairs. In addition to serving as a central leader in this capacity, he is a prominent ideologue of the organization. Previously, he taught in Medina University in Saudi Arabia. In 2004, he reportedly authored a book describing the important ways in which *fidayeen* missions differ from suicide attacks.[119] Some analysts believe that he is second only to Saeed in the structure.[120] In 2010, the US Department of Treasury reported that he was the head of both the Department of Political Affairs and the Department of Foreign Relations.[121]

Lashkar also has a technology chief, Zarrar Shah. Shah's technical expertise was a key enabler of the Mumbai attacks in 2008. Crucially, Shah set up the complicated internet phone system called Voice Over Internet Protocol (VOIP), based in New Jersey. This system allowed the Pakistan-based operators to direct the actions of their kill teams while watching the spectacle on live television, without being located in Pakistan. The conversations were carried over the Internet as opposed to cell towers, and appeared to be originating in New Jersey and Austria rather than Pakistan.[122] It took Indian, British, and American intelligence a considerable amount of time to discern that the voices commanding the killing were in fact coming from Pakistan. This VOIP mechanism was an important part of Pakistan's plausible deniability that the attack originated somewhere other than Pakistan, and thus mitigated the validity of claims that the attack had the imprimatur of LeT or the ISI. We know from the lone survivor of the attack, Ajmal Kasab, that Shah's skills were very important to the operation in other ways. Sitting in the "media room," which was established on a remote training camp in Pakistan-administered Kashmir, Shah used Google Earth maps to show the attack teams the various routes to their target locations in the Mumbai. He also trained the recruits to use Google Earth and global positioning equipment on their own. Before the attack, Shah set up an electronic control room in a Karachi suburb. It was from this location that Mir, Shah, and others would issue the minute-by-minute instructions for the kill teams once they began their terror operation.[123]

Sajid Mir, who also became notorious with the Mumbai attacks, is the Commander of Overseas Operations. Mir gained notoriety both as one of Headley's key handlers within the LeT but also as the "project manager" for the 2008 Mumbai attack. From his redoubts in Pakistan, he personally directed the killing spree through phone conversations with the attackers.[124] Willie Brigitte, a French terrorist who trained with several LeT recruits from Virginia and worked with Mir, was convinced that Mir was a former Pakistani military officer. Brigitte explained in testimony after his arrest that when recruits travelled with Mir to reach the Lashkar camp, they drove throughout the night past numerous checkpoints that were manned by Pakistani soldiers. Brigitte asserts that these solders were very deferential to the group, likely because of Mir's presence. He also explained that during Mir's visits to the camp to evaluate the recruits' progress under LeT's training regimen, "He was very respected by the instructors who were themselves members of the Pakistan Army but also at the checkpoints where he was well-known."[125] US and French anti-terror officials believe that Mir was a major in the Pakistan army who left the military at an unknown point in time to join the LeT.[126]

Azam Cheema is the commander of the Indian operations branch and intelligence chief. He reports to Lakhvi. The US Department of Treasury, which designated him in 2011, contends that he trained (and may well continue to train) cadres in bomb-making and other skills needed to infiltrate and operate in India. He also provided training to the attackers who carried out the 2008 Mumbai assault. Prior to assuming this position overseeing operations in India, he was the organization's commander for Bahawalpur in Pakistan's Punjab province, from which he hails.[127] Additionally, Cheema runs a small weapons laboratory from his Bahawalpur home and trains new recruits in explosives. He reportedly undertook an intense recruitment drive in Mumbai following the 2002 anti-Muslim pogroms in Gujarat. Indian officials identified Cheema as the main conspirator in the July 2006 serial bombings in Mumbai which killed some 200 people.[128]

LeT has a spokesperson named Muhammad Yahya Mujahid, whom I have met on several occasions. Like Saeed, he is a public figure who meets regularly and freely with domestic and international media, even though the UNSC 1267 Committee (also known as the UNSC Al-Qaida Sanctions Committee) designated him in 2009.[129] The organization also has a spokesperson for international media, Abdullah Muntazer, who also edits JuD's website.[130] Tabish Qayyum has been the organization's Head of Social Media.[131] It is not clear whether he will retain this position after becoming the Information Secretary of the MML in August 2017.

Maulana Amir Hamza is another important leader in the outfit. A veteran of the Afghan *jihad*, he is the head of the publications division and the editor of several JuD periodicals (e.g. the flagship monthly magazine, *Mujallah ad-Dawah*) and books, such as *Torkhum se Kohqaf—Roos ke taaqab mein* (From Torkhum to the Caucasus—Hotly Pursuing Russia); *Shahrae Bahisht* (The Road to Paradise); and *Afghanistan ki chotion par qafila dawato jihad* (On the Mountain Tops of Afghanistan—The Caravans of Call and Jihad). Hamza was instrumental in recruitment and outreach efforts throughout Iran as well as the Central Asian Republics. A talented and charismatic religious preacher, some analysts attribute to him the important growth early in the LeT's development. In some accounts of LeT's history, MDI was formed by Lakhvi and Hamza.[132]

The organization maintains offices in most of the major cities throughout Pakistan. By 2000, it operated more than seventy district offices, although it aspired to have offices in all of Pakistan's 138 districts and tribal areas. After LeT was banned, these offices were converted to JuD offices. A current assessment of JuD's footprint across Pakistan is not available. These offices undertake recruitment as well as funds collection. In addition to offices, which are open to the public, JuD/LeT maintains numerous training camps throughout Pakistan. Within Pakistan, district commanders oversee cadres who are managed at the district level. Throughout Pakistan, the organization maintains training camps and branch offices which facilitate recruitment and fundraising.[133] Within Indian-administered Kashmir, the organization has a Chief Operations Commander for the Valley, led by Hafiz Khalid Waleed, as well as regional division commanders for the Central, North and South Divisions who report to this Chief Operations Commander. There is no information about which parts of Indian-administered Kashmir fall under these commands, and the most recent information about those who hold these posts is from 2005. These commands are further divided into area commands for increasingly smaller geographical areas.[134]

In the last decade, LeT's senior leadership council appointed a commander to oversee operations in Afghanistan, where their cadres tended to fight under the banner of other groups rather than that of LeT. However, developing and retaining operational readiness for the Afghan theatre necessitated that they establish a greater presence in the FATA. This brought them into more frequent contact with those Deobandi fighters who have been at war with the Pakistan state, precipitating friction between the two groups. On occasion, the ISI used LeT/JuD cadres to eliminate some of the FATA-based Deobandi fighters targeting the state. However, operating in Afghanistan also required them to work in partnership with some of these other groups. They have also collaborated to infiltrate fighters into Afghanistan; shared safe houses, weapons, and other resources; conducted joint training; and even occasionally fought together.[135]

Interestingly, these varied leaders are not remote characters who are distant from the cadres and their families. Despite the fact that many have rewards on offer for evidence that can be used in court to show that they are directly involved in terrorism, the organization's own publications report that they are deeply involved with the actual militants and their families, and even participate in funeral prayers to honor their dead. According to various bibliographies of slain fighters published in *Mujallah ad-Dawah*, as well as martyr biographies compiled in a three-volume set of books titled *Ham Ma'en Lashkar-e-Tayyaba Ki* (*We, the Mothers of Lashkar-e-Tayyaba*), Azam Cheema Hafiz Saeed, Zafar Iqbal, Abdul Rehman Makki, and Hafiz Abdul Salam Bhuttavi—among numerous other senior leaders—frequently offer the funerary rights and are intimately involved in selecting or approving a particular individual's despatch into Kashmir or elsewhere in India (author's collection of LeT publications).

Financing the Army of the Pure

While the ISI did not establish the LeT, by the mid-1990s the Pakistani state was heavily supporting the organization. There were several reasons for the ISI's decision to become its most important patron. First, its recruits share linguistic and ethnic ties with the residents of Rajouri and Poonch in Jammu in Indian-Administered Kashmir. This means that LeT activists could operate in these areas with more ease compared to other militant groups the ISI oversees. Second, whereas the insurgency had previously been confined to the Muslim-dominated valley, the ISI had hoped it could expand the scope of the conflict to areas that were more heavily populated by Hindus. By expanding the conflict to these areas, militants could more easily target Hindus, which would sustain the communal nature of the conflict as well as encourage Hindus (especially Kashmiri Pandits) to leave the area, thus increasing the Muslim presence there. In other words, the ISI hoped to replicate some of the ethnic cleansing of Kashmiri Pandits that took place immediately after independence and after the recurrence of violence in the valley in 1990.[136] Third, in contrast to militants from these areas, LeT had fewer compunctions about killing Kashmiri civilians.

Moreover, as discussed in the next chapter, LeT recruits have considerable commonality with Pakistan army personnel. This led the ISI to presume it would be easier to control. Equally important, as discussed elsewhere below, LeT was isolated from mainstream Ahl-e-Hadees institutions in Pakistan and could not readily exploit these institutions for fund raising and recruitment. Presumably, LeT would be more dependent upon the ISI relative to the various Deobandi militant groups which could tap into the extensive Deobandi *madrassah* and mosque infrastructure as well as the various factions of the Deobandi political party, the JUI.[137] This support included extensive mentoring by the Pakistani military and the ISI, which, for most intents and purposes, built up the organization's military capability to deploy against India. By late 2001, LeT—along with HM—were the only *tanzeems* that were under ISI control, as many of the Deobandi groups had begun to factionalize and target the state. These various factions would crystalize under the banner of the TTP by late 2007.[138]

JuD primarily uses its funds for three purposes: *dawah* (preaching), *khidmat* (provision of social services), and *jihad*-related activities (e.g. recruitment, training, and procurement of equipment and weapons). Unfortunately, it is impossible to know with certainty what the total operating budget for JuD is, including how much of it comes directly from the state and how much is derived from its own fundraising and commercial activities. Kambere et al. estimate that LeT's annual operation budget is about US$50 million, of which about US$5.2 million is dedicated to military operations.[139] Sharma suggests that the annual budget may be more US$100 million.[140] With these resources, the group runs numerous training centers in Khyber Pakhtunkhwa province, Sindh, Balochistan, Punjab, and Pakistan-administered Kashmir. It is estimated that the organization spends US$330 on each recruit undertaking the groups' Daura-e-Aam (basic) course and about US$1,700 per cadre enrolled in the Daura-e-Khaas (advanced three-month course).[141]

It is unlikely that the state provides the full operating budget, as the organization has a massive fundraising capability through its domestic and foreign charity solicitations (including on-line adjurations), sales of its numerous publications, and annual collection of sacrificial animal pelts, among other lucrative endeavors which I describe below.[142] As a student in Pakistan and as a once-frequent visitor, I often observed that stores and shops prominently hosted donation boxes for LeT. I also witnessed the varied militant groups setting up booths in high-traffic areas on notable holidays, from which they would sell pictures of weapons printed upon post-cards with inflammatory rhetoric about Kashmir, Israel, and the United States, among other intemperate slogans and incendiary graphics. The organization's specialized wings also have specific fund-raising activities. For example, the farmer's wing collects *ushr*, which is an Islamic land tax that obliges farmers to donate 20 per cent of their harvest or remuneration from that harvest to charity.[143] LeT runs legitimate businesses and factories in addition to its profitable school chains and criminal activities (car theft rings).[144]

During the early 1990s, when the organization garnered little international scrutiny, LeT freely admitted receiving funding from Pakistan's intelligence agencies as well as foreign sources.[145] However, in 1998, Yusuf Taibi—the then head of the Markaz' foreign relations—claimed that "for the last three years, there has been no aid from outside sources...because Arabs have become extremely wary of jihadi organisations. They arrest anyone caught sending funds to such groups."[146] The organization prefers to focus upon its domestic sources of revenue, such as the donations of wealthy businessmen, some of whom reportedly pay "hundreds of thousands of rupees each month, while others make donations in kind. One manufacturer of cereals...sends truckloads of specially formulated cereal for the young recruits receiving military training."[147] One early donor was Abdul Aziz, a well-known "patron of Islamic militant organisations around the globe."[148] In fact, he commissioned a house for himself within the Markaz complex in Muridke. He gave Rs. 10 million to build the Jamia *masjid* (mosque).

As noted, the organization's massive publication wing provides substantial—if unknowable—revenue. These publications also encourage readers to donate to the organization and, of course, consider joining it. Islamic charities such as the al-Harmain Foundation (*Harmain* refers to the holy sites in Mecca and Medina); the al-Rashid Foundation, and the Islamic Relief Organization facilitate donations to the organization (and other terrorist outfits). These purportedly charitable organizations came under intense scrutiny after the events of 2001.[149] Another method is the trust-based *hawala* method, through which a person in one city can transfer money informally to another person in a different city or country with ease. While using *hawalah* (also known as *hundi*) is now illegal in Pakistan, it remains the preferred way of transferring remittances even among persons who have no nefarious intentions.[150]

Another extremely lucrative funding source is the above-noted collection of hides from the vast number of animals that millions of Pakistanis slaughter every year during Eid-al-Azha. The men who join the organization help raise funds by collecting the pelts of animals slaughtered during this holiday. In 2013, Pakistanis sacrificed about 6 million animals including goats, cows, and camels. In that year, an official of FIF told journalists that the revenue from collecting these hides is "second only to Ramadan for our income."[151] In 2013, the organization aimed to collect hides by posting personnel at major intersections in major cities and at JuD mosques. The organization also sells animals for sacrifice which allows families to pool precious resources. Clearly this seems to be a small number of the overall animals that Pakistanis sacrifice. This is likely due to the numerous charitable organizations that are competing for these pelts. However, these skins are valuable items. The sacrificial hides from animals slaughtered over three days account for about half of Pakistan's entire annual tannery requirement, and a single cow-hide can fetch US$50 in Pakistan, or about Rs. 4800.[152] By way of benchmarking, it is useful to note that that in 2012–13, the Pakistani monthly minimum wage was Rs. 8000.[153] In 2010, JuD reported that it collected some 100,000 hides from which it raised about US $1.2 million.[154]

Astonishingly, the Pakistani government provides overt support to the organization even though it has been declared a terrorist organization by the UN and the United States, among other countries. Pakistan's civilian government has also contributed to the organization; in the budget for the fiscal year of 2013–14, the current Pakistan Muslim League-led Punjab State Government published a grant of Rs. 61.35 million for the administration of JuD's training camp at Markaz-e-Tayyaba in Muridke as well as Rs. 350 million for a "knowledge park" at Muridke, among other JuD Punjab-based initiatives. Similarly, in 2009–10, the Pakistani Federal Government gave the organization–after it was declared a terrorist organization by the UN Security Council—more than Rs. 80.2 million purportedly for the administration of JuD facilities. Later, in 2010–11, the organization received two separate grants of Rs 79.8 million for the maintenance of six organizations located at LeT's headquarter in Muridke as well as a special grant of an additional Rs. 3 million for JuD's *Dawah* school system in seven Districts of Punjab.[155] More recently in May 2018, the Punjab government requested at least Rs. 1 billion for managing JuD and FIF properties because "the Federal government had not allocated any amount in this year's budget to run the JuD and FIF properties, taken over by the Punjab government." For this reason, the Punjab government wrote to "the federal finance ministry informing that it needs at least Rs 1 billion for the financial year (2018–19) for the purpose" of managing these assets.[156] This, in addition to unknowable state resources, such as the significant amount of state security provided to the organizations—which includes police protection as well as protection from the military and ISI—ensures the release of any activist who is detained by the police.[157]

Training Soldiers in the Army of the Pure

As noted earlier, LeT/JuD established numerous major camps in addition to Bait ul Mujahideen, most of which are located in Pakistan-administered Kashmir. Muaskar-e-Umm ul Qura, Muaskar-e-Abdullah Bin Massood; Muaskar-e-Aqsa and the Muaskar-e-Tayyaba are in the vicinity of Muzaffarabad while Markaz Mohammad bin Qasim in the Sanghar district of Sindh.[158] In addition, it runs dozens of smaller training facilities that are located throughout Pakistan's four regular provinces and the FATA.[159] There are limited journalist accounts of the amenities at these camps. Husnain visited one of these camps in early 2001, before the events of 9/11, after which such access became more restricted. Husnain describes the facilities he observed as spartan. He visited the largest training camp in Pakistan-administered Kashmir which LeT operated. According to Husnain, the camp is set on a vast mountain clearing overlooking Muzaffarabad. (Training grounds for the other three militant groups are located in what is now called Khyber Pakhtunkhwa province.) Armed men guard the facility round-the-clock. There are only two structures, one an armory, the other a kitchen. Trainees live and sleep in the open, whether in the sweltering summer or the depth of winter. The field is dotted with installations used to teach the fervent young—some no older than fourteen—how to cross a river, climb a mountain, or ambush a military convoy.[160]

Despite these ostensibly rudimentary facilities, the organization has developed a rigorous and well-documented training program with the explicit assistance of the Pakistan army and ISI. Yasmeen observes that it is impossible to discern the precise time when Pakistan military first reached out to the militants who were then associated with MDI. The speed with which MDI became a formidable organization suggests early facilitation by the army and/or the ISI and it would be inconceivable that the organization could have professionalized so rapidly without the ISI's explicit concurrence.[161]

What is known is that the army sends ISI and army personnel to train LeT's trainers; the former also helped develop LeT's training regimen to better position the group to achieve Pakistan's strategic objectives. As noted above, the Pakistan army and the ISI essentially formalized LeT's military training regime and structure in the mid-1990s. Pakistan army and ISI personnel were present in LeT's camps, where they engaged in "train the trainer" activities. In addition, representatives from the Pakistan army and ISI work directly with LeT to plan specific attacks, considering the larger strategic environment and how best to shape it. The army and ISI also depute serving or retired persons to provide continual onsite observation of training activities, to ensure that the organization is resourced adequately. Some of these army personnel have taken early retirement to officially join LeT. Consequently, LeT's cadres and trainers are among the most well-trained and tactically adept in the region.[162] In addition to the army and ISI, LeT has also enjoyed the support of other armed services.[163]

The close interaction between the ISI and LeT leadership is very much evident in the planning and execution of the Mumbai 2008 attack, as we learn from the various statements made by David Coleman Headley during his trial and interrogation.[164] Both the LeT and ISI went over surveillance footage, considered the costs and benefits of certain targets, identified operatives for the mission, and helped them prepare for their deadly tasks. Headley described a two-day meeting at which the various plotters met in Muzaffarabad in 2008. The "guest of honor was the crew-cut, clean-shaven frogman named Abdur Rehman. He gave the Lashkar chiefs technical advice." He also brought a sea chart which he used to describe the roughness of the seas at various times of year. Additionally, Rehman provided guidance in how to check the position of Indian naval assets to prevent a gunfight. This Pakistani Navy frogman helped plan the sea-borne portions of their mission and instructed the operatives about the various landing options along the Mumbai coast and advised them about hijacking an Indian vessel.[165] It is entirely possible that naval personnel advising the operation were on second-ment to the ISI, as all services send personnel to the ISI on rotational basis. Even the ISI chief is seconded from the army to which he returns when his tenure with the ISI is complete. Because the ISI chief answers to the army chief, it is very unlikely that the ISI undertakes operations that undermine army interests. The ISI also recruits civilians for long-term work as well as contractors for short-term assignments.[166]

LeT's training occurs in multiple stages and combines military and guerrilla warfare training along with religious indoctrination and instruction consistent with LeT's interpretation of the Ahl-e-Hadees *maslak*. LeT officials evaluate and assess individuals who are interested in joining the organization for their motivation, aptitude, and skill-set required by the organization for varied missions. As noted previously, that the LeT trains far more people than it will ever deploy to India or to Afghanistan for that matter.[167] An office bearer of LeT, while demurring from revealing the exact number of men it deploys in Kashmir, disclosed that Hafiz Saeed himself "decides how many *mujahideen* should be sent to the valley...The decision depends on the number of deaths that have taken place. It also depends on the requirement and capacity of the organization inside Kashmir to absorb new fighters."[168] This is because the organization hopes that those who study with it will return to their localities and propagate LeT's core teachings and ideological commitments. Indeed, as I describe in subsequent chapters, this is a key component of the organization's "internal *jihad*" within Pakistan.[169]

Official training begins with the twenty-one-day Daura-e-Suffa course. This basic course persuades the person to embrace LeT's interpretation of Ahl-e-Hadees, emphasizes that *jihad* is an individual obligation, and counsels the importance of proselytization and inviting people to join the organization (*tabligh* and *dawah*). This course typically takes place at Muridke. Individuals next continue onto the twenty-one-day long Daura-e-Aam, which is usually conducted in Pakistan-administered Kashmir.[170] This phase of training builds upon Daura-e-Suffa by providing lectures on LeT's ideology and imparting instruction on how to conduct Islamic rituals in the Ahl-e-Hadees manner, among other instructions on doctrinal aspects of LeT's interpretation of the Ahl-e-Hadees tradition. It also offers very basic weapons instruction such as training in light arms, particularly in the use of the Kalashnikov and hand grenades, as well as drills in basic guerrilla warfare tactics.[171] While these are entry points into the *jihad*, these two courses are also open to the public, which advances the organization's *dawah* and *tabligh* mission.[172]

After completing Daura-e-Aam, the recruit is sent back to his home locality or another city selected by the organization, often near his birthplace. The recruit may be expected to work at an LeT office in the area and otherwise become more involved with the organization.[173] LeT personnel closely observe the recruit during this period to discern if he has retrenched from his, often newly acquired, Ahl-e-Hadees commitments. Once home the recruit is expected to engage in *dawah* and *tabligh* with his family and throughout his neighborhood. The organization expects that he will bring friends and family members into the LeT fold. After many months of observation, LeT personnel may select the person for additional training, such as Daura-e-Khaas.[174]

Daura-e-Khaas is LeT's advanced training course, which lasts for three months.[175] Generally, LeT's leaders select only those individuals whom they deem fit for combat in Kashmir or other parts of India for this advanced program. The advanced course covers guerrilla warfare, training in the use of arms and ammunition (e.g. grenades, rocket launchers, mortars, bomb-making), wireless communications, mastering complex terrain, such as climbing mountains and crossing rivers, and ambush and survival techniques.[176] In some cases, persons can enter Daura-e-Khaas without first taking Daura-e-Suffa or Daura-e-Aam.[177] Once a person completes this training, he may or may not be selected for a mission in India. As with other courses, more cadres complete this training than will ever be deployed and they return home and engage in *dawah* and *tabligh*.[178]

LeT leaders may also urge a recruit to undergo additional, focused training such as Daura-e-Ribat (the course on intelligence collection). In fact, LeT has a wide array of highly specialized courses such as maritime training for those who will likely operate at sea, commando training for potential *fidayeen*, sabotage and surveillance, reconnaissance, counter-intelligence, and the use of sophisticated communications platforms, among other specialized training consistent with the mission which the individual will most likely execute.[179]

One *mujahid* enthused upon completing his training that "these courses change your life forever...When you go you are one man and when you return you quite another."[180] Upon completing this training, the fighter will adopt a *kuniyat*. He also undergoes a physical transformation: he will allow his beard to grow as long as possible as he will neither trim nor shave it; he will wear native dress (a long shirt (*kameez*) over baggy trousers (*shalwar*)); and he will wear his *shalwar* such that the hem falls above the ankles.[181] Most trainees will work for the organization in various capacities such as running a local office in its sprawling network across Pakistan, and performing assorted duties such as recruiting and fund-raising. LeT personnel will observe these recruits to ensure that they are continuing to live per LeT's interpretation of Ahl-e-Hadees to prevent recidivism.[182]

As I discuss later in this volume, LeT carefully exploits family bonds during its recruitment, paying particular attention to the mothers of recruits. Young men are given an opportunity to avenge alleged atrocities perpetrated against Muslims in India and elsewhere, and the family garners significant social prestige if their son becomes a *mujahid*. Sons who return from the fight alive as *ghazis* are less revered than those who die in battle and become a *shaheed* (martyr). The organization requests that recruits specifically obtain the blessings of their mothers before being dispatched on a mission.[183] According to relatives, young men who undergo training with LeT seem more mature and serious upon returning. Even after death, LeT aims to remain in contact with the slain fighters' families in hopes that they will remain within the fold of Ahl-e-Hadees.[184] To cultivate the support of individuals and their families, LeT operatives are paid well and, upon dying, the slain fighters' families are compensated in various ways.[185]

The Nascence of the Milli Muslim League

In August 2017, Hafiz Saeed announced the formation of a political party. While he initially said that this party was separate from JuD, he disclosed in early December 2017 that JuD would contest the July 2018 general elections under the MML banner.[186] It is implausible that this development could have occurred without the explicit involvement of the army and the ISI. For example, it is notable that Saeed's announcement came a few weeks after being released from house arrest, roughly coincident with the US Congress' decision, under Pentagon pressure, to largely curtail military assistance and reimbursements to Pakistan contingent upon its efforts to retard the activities of LeT/JuD.[187] This move by the United States reflects both an understanding that Pakistan will not turn on the LeT as well as a significant retrenchment from the Trump's administration's August 2017 bluster about getting tough on Islamabad.[188] Washington has been fairly muted about Saeed's release as well as the new political party. In fact, the American government seemed more interested in managing the fall-out from the August 2017 Trump speech than these developments. When Secretary of Defense Mattis went to Pakistan in early December 2017, he explicitly said that he did not intend to "prod" Pakistan to act offering the milquetoast explanation that he expected to Pakistan to fulfil its promises to combat terrorism, even though Pakistan has failed to honor that promise repeatedly.[189]

As discussed in the introductory chapter, the MML's leadership is closely intertwined with that of JuD and has been explicitly mentored by the military. First and foremost, one of its founding members and current information secretary, Tabish Qayyum has long been cultivated by the deep state, as previously described. In June 2013, he presented a series of workshops in Faislabad, Islamabad and Karachi entitled "Social Media Warfare," which were conducted by a retired Pakistani Army colonel named Nazir Ahmed. Ahmed is a close associate of Saeed and was "arrested" along with Saeed after the December 2008 Mumbai attacks. Subsequently, both were released by Pakistan's courts, citing lack of evidence.[190]

In 2016, Qayyum completed his MA at Pakistan's National Defense University. His thesis exposed the presence of the Islamic State (IS) in Pakistan and available means to defeat it, including creating a larger role for JuD in these efforts. As I detail in subsequent chapters, Qayyum rightly notes in this thesis that the Islamic State declared JuD to be an apostate organization both because JuD firmly rejects IS and due to its sinewy connections with Pakistan's security establishment.[191] Qayyum's writings and his digital footprint are the clearest indicators of the support that the security establishment has given the MML.

What is quite extraordinary is that Saeed has promulgated the MML in a complete reversal of its previous policy of abjuring politics. He has not offered even a modest attempt to explain this about-face. (In fact, no one in the Pakistani media is pressing him to justify this decision.) Instead, the organization seems to be acting as if this is a natural progression for the organization and, in many ways, it is—were it not for the organization's principled stand against electoral politics from the outset. In retrospect it is not hard to find evidence that this progression into formal politics was long in the works. After all, the state has given every kind of support to JuD and FIF, which has enabled the organization to rebrand itself as a domestic provider of public goods going back to its roles in the 2004/05 Asian Tsunami and the 2005 Kashmir earthquake, while LeT remains the name of the organization that conducts militant activities.

The clearest exposition of the MML's aims and goals are found in the October 2017 issue of *Invite*, published by JuD. The MML's stated positions are in complete alignment with that of the deep state. Notably, it is committed to the China-Pakistan Economic Corridor (CPEC)[192] and will work to persuade those Baloch in Balochistan who currently oppose the project to embrace the importance of Chinese projects in the country as critical to securing Pakistan's financial independence.[193] In addition to supporting the strategic alliance with China, it also backs Pakistan's position on the existential nature of the Indian threat, the Pakistan army's role in the Saudi Arabia-led Islamic Military Alliance in Yemen and the army's internal security operations. LeT sees combatting the scourge of *Kharijite*-terrorism (see description of *Khawarij* in the introductory chapter) as having two fronts, military and ideological: whereas the "Pakistani armed forces have been working tirelessly on the military front and have laid great sacrifices to protect Pakistan from the scourge of terrorism. JuD on the other hand has taken up the ideological front."[194] The organization claims that it wants to ensure that both Pakistan's society and state conform to the injunctions of the Quran and *Sunnat*; advance internal security; protect Pakistan's ideological, moral and cultural ethos; inculcate the ideology of Pakistan among the country's citizens; transform Pakistan into a modern Islamic welfare state; promote a "political environment in which all members of the society, especially the lower and the middle class, get complete rights and prepare them for leadership roles;" rehabilitate Pakistan's honor and standing internationally; uphold and preserve the rights of religious minorities and women; sustain the struggle in Kashmir morally and diplomatically; promulgate a foreign policy that promotes the interests of the global Muslim community (*ummat*); and repudiate the murderous doctrine of *takfir* while preparing ordinary Pakistanis to do the same.[195] While I describe these issues at length in Chapter Six, it is important to note here that JuD adamantly opposes IS and those Deobandi militant groups (such as the Pakistani Taliban, Sipah-e-Sahaba-e-Pakistan/Lashkar-e-Jhangvi) who have arrogated to themselves the right to declare Muslims infidels (*takfir*) and the subsequent obligation to kill them. In fact, these groups are responsible for all of the Islamist violence in Pakistan. JuD/LeT has never attacked any group in Pakistan (nor has any group tied with Jamaat-e-Islami either, for that matter). JuD's principled opposition to those groups menacing Pakistan undergirds this organization's profound utility to Pakistan in managing its perilous internal security challenges.

JuD and the MML are exceedingly careful when it comes to Ahmadis, as I discuss in greater length in Chapter 6. In fact, it is very difficult to get the organization to say clearly what it believes about this controversial group. The MML's leadership was irritated when Pakistan's Law Minister Zahid Hamid amended the declaration of faith in the finality of the prophet in the Election Act of 2017 to require a mere affirmation in what he called a regrettable clerical error. The MML and others viewed this as a serious dilution of the standard. Since Ahmadis do not recognize the finality of the prophet, this oath effectively bars Ahmadis from contesting elections. A Barelvi movement and party known as the Tehreek Labbaik Ya Rasool Allah (Movement for the Prophet, TLYR)[196] organized a weeks-long sit-in in November 2017 that concluded only when Hamid acquiesced to their demands and resigned. The protesters believed that the amendment oppugned the prophet and was tantamount to blasphemy. (As noted earlier, Barelvis tend to become extremely agitated if they believe the prophet has been insulted, in part because they venerate him.)

However, unlike the Barelvis who took to raucous mobilization on the street to shut down the government, the MML took a legalistic—if word-splitting—approach to defend the original requirement of taking an oath. Tabish Qayum, writing in the Urdu-language *Daily Khabrain*, focused upon the subtle differences between an oath and a declaration or affirmation:

> Before the amendment people reaffirmed their faith in the finality of the prophethood by saying "I take an oath truthfully" and after the change it was "I affirm truthfully", meaning the difference is between oath and affirm. If both

these words have the same meaning then why was there a need to bring in a change? Where the person has to sign on the form, there too the change has been made from "Statement of Oath" to "Solemn Affirmation". What is the difference between the meaning of oath and affirmation?[197]

He answered this rhetorical question by referencing similar changes that took place in European history to accommodate the concerns of Quakers more than three hundred years ago when Quakers refused to take an oath because, according to them "everyone had a bit of God in them" and, instead offered an affirmation of their belief rather than an oath. He noted similarly that some 200 years ago, the atheists of Scotland opposed taking an oath, citing their disbelief in a god. After citing other such examples that facilitated the separation of church and state, Qayyum asks why there is a need in Pakistan, where the population is 99 per cent Muslim, to switch from an oath to an affirmation? He avers that the ruling party, the PML-N, deliberately sought to attack the founding principles of Pakistan in effort to liberalize the country and garner international support for the agenda to secularize Pakistan and the constitution.[198]

Qayyum is very careful to not even mention the Ahmadis even though this is perhaps the most important community affected by this issue. When I asked him directly for MML's position on Ahmadis, Qayyum responded that "There is a consensus on Ahmadis being a Non-Muslim minority." After all, Pakistan's constitution says as much. However, "They, like any other minority should have right to practice their faith without posing as Muslims or representatives of Islam, which would stand in violation of Pakistan's constitution."[199]

The introduction of the MML also may allow the deep state to manage some of its problems politically. In the run-up to the July 2018 elections, the army had no political party that it could entirely support in the confidence that the party would do its bidding. The army views the two mainstream political parties (the Pakistan Peoples Party (PPP) and the Pakistan Muslim League of Nawaz Sharif (PML-N)) as nemeses while Imran Khan's inability to create a national platform for his Pakistan Tehreek-e-Insaf (PTI), with or without army assistance, was uncertain. Taken together, this suggests that the army developed the MML as a potential tool in engineering civilian political leadership in the forthcoming general elections in 2018 and beyond.[200] While the MML ultimately failed abysmally in the July 2018 elections,[201] the MML well play a future role in subsequent elections.[202] When I asked Qayyum about this he said that it is "Too early to comment on this. We welcome and appreciate all such alliances and parties that are working for a stable, progressive and peaceful Pakistan."[203] As I argue particularly in Chapter 6, the deep state has an abiding interest in encouraging JuD to more firmly ensconce itself in the nation's politics formally and the emergence of the MML will achieve this aim while likely further legitimizing the deep state's use of militant assets in Kashmir and elsewhere.

This gambit on the part of the deep state is not without risks. What should happen if the MML—despite the deep state's most concerted effort—fails to become a viable party with national standing? Given that the MML is essentially now the political wing of the JUD, will the MML's failure mitigate the other myriad amenities that the JuD offers to the state? Will the MML simply join the crowd of religious parties or could the MML be a competitor to or collaborator with the Jamaat-e-Islami, which has long been the political hireling of the army and the ISI at home and abroad. Alternatively, what happens if the organization establishes a grassroots presence throughout Pakistan, as transpired when General Zia ul Haq helped Nawaz Sharif and his Pakistan Muslim League-N to become a party with a national presence and political legitimacy? Presumably the army believes that it can enjoy many years of acquiescent partnership with the MML before it has to consider a serious divergence of interests.

Conclusions and Implications

LeT, originally a fusion of Lakhvi's Ahl-e-Hadees *jihadi* organization with Saeed and Iqbal's MDI, originated in the latter years of the anti-Soviet Afghan war but quickly reoriented away from the Afghan theatre to Kashmir. Pakistan's intelligence and military threw their full weight behind the organization, inclusive of providing direct assistance to establish the training regimen, train the trainers, fund, and most importantly, assist in plotting and executing terrorist attacks. Pakistan had hoped that by introducing this particularly lethal group and its signature *fidayeen* attack mode into Kashmir and the rest of India, it could revivify the conflict and renew international attention to the same. After being banned, LeT operated under the new name of Jamaat-ud-Dawah, and this is the name it continues to use. It has spun off front organizations, such as the FIF, among others, and has spearheaded several issue-specific coalitions with various militant and right of center political groups. The organization has reluctantly undertaken operations in Afghanistan again due to constraints on operating in Kashmir, but Kashmir remains the prized theater. As such, it operates in Afghanistan nowadays due to compulsion rather than preference. Because LeT differs from other Ahl-e-Hadees organizations in Pakistan and cannot rely upon its religious and political institutions, it is more dependent upon the Pakistani state.

Similarly, compared to the various Deobandi militant groups, LeT does not have a ready ideological, political, and doctrinal infrastructure to exploit for fundraising and recruiting. This, coupled with a strict hierarchical structure under Saeed's thumb, has enabled the organization to retain extreme organizational continuity. When there have been minor rifts, they have been quickly repaired, likely with the help of the ISI and Pakistan army. The organization's specific structural features, its reliance upon and compliance with the ISI and the Pakistan military, and its particular lethality make LeT a special asset for the Pakistani state.

LeT is the most coherent Pakistan-backed and -based terrorist organization, and it is the organization over which the deep state has the most control. However, LeT is not free of what economists call "agency problems." Agency problems arise from conflict of interests in an organization when one party (often called the agent) is supposed to act in the interests of another (often called the "principal"). Most terrorist organizations have to manage agency problems, described by Shapiro as the "terrorist's dilemma."[204] First, political and ideological leaders (principals) must delegate duties to various agents (e.g. middle-men, low-level and mid-level operatives, collaborators). These delegated activities may include soliciting funds, recruiting members for the organization or even planning attacks. If all members of the group (principals and agents) are perfectly committed to the same cause, share the same understanding of how to best serve the cause and have access to the same information about how best to secure the organization's goals, then such agency problems do not arise. However, this is never the case no matter how coherent the organization is or how obedient the agents may be.[205] Arguably, the entry of the MML into Pakistani politics will compound these extant agency problems.

One example of LeT's agency problems is the episode of Lakhvi breaking with the organization to set up his own *tanzeem*, due to frustration with Hafiz Saeed's nepotism and concomitant marginalization of him. This was eventually resolved by the ISI. Saeed's detention after the Mumbai 2008 attacks also restricted his freedom of action. Another example is the pressure that the organization endured in the wake of the Lal Masjid fiasco, when some members and leaders believed it should abandon its ISI handlers and join groups targeting the Pakistani state. Other examples include Saeed's reluctant decision to enter the Afghan fray under pressure from his commanders and cadres, as well as the debate within LeT over whether to target Israelis in 2008.

LeT is not like the other groups that Shapiro discusses because LeT enjoys state sanctuaries in Pakistan. The state is not trying to eliminate the organization. In fact, one of the most important goals is not to alienate the state and its patrons therein because access to Pakistan is LeT's most coveted resource. Thus the organization needs to control the level of violence it perpetrates even when its cadres, who do not understand the organization's larger strategic interests, believe that more or different kinds of violence would serve the organization better. The latter overcomes these challenges in several important ways. First, consistent with Shapiro's hypothesis, organizations such as LeT which enjoy relative freedom of operation will have a hierarchical structure. In contrast, organizations without such safe-havens will have a more diffuse and delegated structure because doing so provides more operational security even though it imposes certain kinds of operational inefficiencies. Indeed, LeT is tightly hierarchical, with family and long-standing associates of Hafiz Saeed in charge of key departments and functions. While this organizational structure gives Saeed a strong hold over the organization, it means that if a group's leadership is targeted, it may fundamentally degrade the organization's operational capabilities.

Second, it organizes group activities to make detections of shirking more visible. Once an individual joins the organization, they are under constant surveillance from district-level managers. Similar to Hamas, LeT has an extensive network of providers of nonviolent community outreach. This provides LeT (and Hamas) with ample means to mitigate agency problems by holding potentially problematic personnel to account. Another means to temper agency problems is to encourage intermarriage within the movement. This increases the ad hominem cost of individuals transgressing the preferences of the leadership. Indeed, LeT does this as well.[206]

A third mechanism that is useful in managing agency problems is the rigorous screening that individuals endure as they try to join the organization, obtain ever-more training, and ultimately seek deployment to the battlefield. This is evidenced by the degree of leadership involvement in trainee selection for specific missions, as well as the fact that recruits require specific recommendations from LeT teachers or field monitors to be picked up for additional tutelage.

In conclusion, it should be noted that there is another principal-agent problem, in which the ISI and army are the principal and the LeT is the agent. The ISI manages these problems somewhat differently than does LeT. First, the ISI and the army are deeply embedded within the organization both to ensure that it is resourced adequately, but also to enforce compliance with ISI objectives. This is evidenced by the significant joint planning for the Mumbai 2008 attacks that we observe between LeT leadership and ISI officials (Scott-Clark and Levy 2013).[207] This is further facilitated by the members of LeT, who are, in fact, retired military officers. Finally, as I discuss above, the organization is willing to use violence and the threat of violence to restrain persons who violate the ISI's injunctions.

5

WHO ARE THE SOLDIERS IN THE ARMY
OF THE PURE?

Writers on terrorism generally and Islamist groups in particular frequently adduce that terrorists are poor, uneducated, and/or come from criminal backgrounds. Speaking of Islamist militants, writers have long argued that *madaris* are responsible for producing scores of Muslims ready to kill and die for their faith. Various governmental efforts to counter violent extremism (aka "CVE") tend to focus upon men of military age and often subsume many of the aforenoted assumptions about the deprived backgrounds of persons who join militant groups. Many of these ostensible insights are gleaned from anecdotal accounts of captured or killed militants. Fortunately, for understanding Lashkar-e-Tayyaba, we have a very rich source of data that allows us to glean considerable detail about the persons who fight, and ultimately die, for LeT, namely: the hundreds of biographies of slain LeT militants that are widely available in several LeT publications. In this chapter, I provide quantitative and qualitative insights from 918 posthumous biographies of LeT militants, whom LeT calls *shaheed* (martyrs), assembled and analyzed by a team I oversaw at the Combatting Terrorism Center at West Point.

Contrary to popular belief, these biographies suggest that LeT's slain fighters are among Pakistan's most educated males. While they are not poorly educated relative to the populations from which they are drawn, they are underemployed. However, this may be due to choice rather than compulsion, as I explain herein. While LeT militants are not primarily under-educated *madaris* recruits drawn from Pakistan's most disadvantaged classes, they are more likely than Pakistani males generally to have attended a *madrassah*, perhaps during their recruitment or training phases, as LeT emphasizes religious as much as military training. We also learn about venues of recruitment which include recruitment by another LeT member who may also be a relative. Sometimes the person was self-motivated and deliberately sought out the organization after encountering LeT publications or recordings. Mosques and *madaris* are also venues of recruitment as are LeT's conferences and conventions.

We also learn that families are incredibly important in encouraging their sons to join the organization and ultimately to fight and die in its service. Women—particularly mothers—appear to have an incredibly important role which CVE efforts tend to downplay or dismiss altogether. Many of the fighters' motivations speak to their interests in protecting or caring for their families either through a desire to intercede on their behalf at the time of judgement or an interest in encouraging their families to live their lives with greater adherence to Islam. Many of the fighters indicate that they felt unfulfilled in their lives before enlisting with LeT and said that joining the *tanzeem* gave them a better sense of purpose. In short, these biographies allow us to peer into the lives and decision process of some of the most lethal killers dispatched from Pakistan to India and, to a lesser extent, Afghanistan.

The remainder of this chapter is organized as follows. In the next section, I describe this dataset, and preempt the foregoing analysis with several important data caveats that preclude me from generalizing beyond the individuals in this dataset. In the third section, I present salient descriptive findings from these data, including information about: the recruits' home province or districts; age at time of recruitment; theatres of operations; place and age at death; level of secular and religious education; as well as employment background. In the fourth section, I draw upon qualitative aspects of the biographies to discuss what we learn about the motivations of the fighters. Fifth, I draw upon these biographies and other LeT materials to draw out insights about how the organization cultivates individuals and their families. Here, I discuss the particular attention that the organization pays to women. This focus upon women is relatively rare among militant groups operating in and from Pakistan. I conclude with a discussion of the key implications of this exercise.

Introduction to the Dataset on Slain LeT Activists[1]

The dataset I use here was assembled by a team of analysts with whom I worked at the Combating Terror Center at West Point. It contains biographical information for 918 LeT militants.[2] The team used LeT biographies that were published in four Urdu-language publications issued by Dar-al-Andalus, LeT's singular publisher. We collected 181 biographical records from a three volume book, *Hum Ma'en Lashkar-e-Tayyaba Ki* (We, the Mothers of Lashkar-e-Tayyaba); 14 from *Mujallah Tayyabaat* (Virtuous Women); 696 records from *Mujallah al-Dawah* (The Invitation); and 27 from *Mahanah Zarb-e-Tayyaba* (Strike of the Righteous).[3] All of the LeT militants for whom we have death information died during operations between 1994 and 2007.[4]

There are several important data caveats that must be appreciated because they limit the degree to which I can generalize beyond the individuals in this dataset. First and foremost, these data, like others of its kind, are riven with several kinds of dependent variable selection bias. As a consequence of these selection effects, the militants included in this dataset are likely very different from all of those who have been in LeT, as well as from the pool of persons who wanted to join LeT but who were never selected in the first place. There are several reasons why the individuals in this dataset are not representative of LeT overall or those who seek to join the organization.

First, as I discuss later in this chapter and as previously noted, LeT is highly selective when it comes to providing military training, even though its religious training is made widely available. Since there are more persons who want to join the organization for militant activities than can be deployed, LeT has the luxury of leveraging quality control over those they dispatch to fight.[5] As I discuss in subsequent chapters, doctrinally, LeT believes it is the duty of every Muslim to be militarily prepared for *jihad* irrespective of deployment opportunities.

Second, persons who are selected for combat generally must be successful bureaucratic entrepreneurs. Unlike a conventional military in which a recruit will be deployed in a contingency, irrespective of their preferences for warfighting, in LeT individuals must lobby the organization's leadership to be picked up for additional training, as well as to be dispatched on an external combat mission. While the militant is making his various entreaties to continue his pursuit of *shahadat* (martyrdom), the LeT leadership is continually assessing the person's suitability and fitness for military operations. As I discuss herein, ultimately, LeT senior leadership (*inter alia* Hafiz Saeed, Lakhvi, Bhattavi) often make the final decision to deploy specific fighters for a particular mission.

Third, all persons operating in India must successfully infiltrate there, which is no mean feat given the fortifications along the LOC and international border. Some will infiltrate into India through less direct air, land, or sea routes (e.g. via the Gulf, Nepal, Bangladesh, Sri Lanka, etc.). For those who have gone on multiple operations in India, they may also be required to exfiltrate from India into Pakistan to conduct additional training in Pakistan. They must again cross back into India for subsequent operations. Each round of crossing out of and into India exposes the fighters to heightened risk of death or capture, and thus poses an additional selection effect. Fighters who stay under cover in India for an extended period of time must engage in successful operational security, which entails paying sustained acute detail to their language, dress, food preferences, and other behavioral aspects which could reveal their Pakistani identity. In fact, many will learn Devanagari, the Sanskrit-based script in which Hindi is written, as well as the increasingly Sanskritized vernacular increasingly spoken among Hindi-speaking Hindus. If the recruit is from India, which is still rare, he will first have to exfiltrate from India into Pakistan to undergo training, and will likely be subject to rigorous evaluation and vetting to ensure that the person is not working on behalf of Indian intelligence organizations. Operatives whom the LeT leadership dispatches to Afghanistan face similar constraints, although that border is far more permissive. Afghan National Security Forces are not nearly as prepared to counter infiltration, as the Americans and NATO long withdrew from that mission. Moreover, Punjabis, who are the majority of LeT cadres, are easily distinguished from Afghans by their appearance and language, and few LeT operatives know either of the two principle languages of Afghanistan: Dari and Pashto.[6] Finally, all of those in this dataset were killed in action, mostly in India. This is a further indicator of their quality as combatants. Persons must satisfy all of these operational requirements and aptitude indicators, and successfully die in combat, before appearing in this dataset.

Some militants, such as Ajmal Kasab, are not killed per the mission's requirement, and are taken captive and interrogated. Because survivors provide important information about the organization and its operations to India, the United States, and other interested entities, they are enormous liabilities. Successfully being killed in an operation is perhaps the most important dimension of operational security for LeT. Taken together, these different selection criteria make it very difficult to generalize about fighters beyond the dataset. For this reason, the results that I present here may differ from those obtained by scholars using other qualitative methods (i.e. interviewing small samples of fighters or their families).

A final caveat about these data is that I do not use every detail reported in the militant biographies, because some details are less likely than others to be truthful. While I have no reason to believe that the biographies falsify information about birthplace, education, the kind and level of training received, or basic details of the mission (e.g. where and when it took place), I am sceptical about the numbers of persons killed by the slain militant because such information may be falsified to glorify him. Moreover, I cannot independently confirm such details because the fighters are usually killed during encounters in India. Another challenge is that the actual names of the persons involved are rarely reported in either the Pakistani or Indian press, much less the international press. Finally, many activists use a *kuniyat*, which makes it virtually impossible to cross-check the accounts given in the militant biographies with reports in the Indian or other media. For these reasons, I analyze only those data elements for which there is minimal motivation for falsification.

Characteristics of the Soldiers in the Army of the Pure

The biographies generally provide information about the age of the fighter at the time of recruitment, which averages around seventeen years of age. Biographies also state the militant's home province. The vast majority (89 per cent) of LeT militants in this data set come from Pakistan's Punjab province, with an additional 5 per cent from Sindh, and about 4 per cent from Khyber-Pakhtunkhwa. Smaller numbers of militants originated from areas such as Azad Kashmir (about 1 per cent), while Indian Kashmir, Gilgit-Baltistan and Balochistan each account for about 1 per cent of militants in our sample. Three militants had hometowns in Afghanistan (Nuristan province), two came from Saudi Arabia (one from Mecca), and one was born in Europe, with no other details available. This directly contradicts the *tanzeem*'s claims that LeT mostly draws manpower from Kashmir.[7]

In addition to the province of origin, militant biographies frequently provide information about the district from which they were recruited. The map in Figure 5.1 depicts district-level data on LeT recruitment. Each district is color-coded by the number of militants it produces: more militants originate from areas that either border India or are quite close to India (e.g. Punjab, Sindh, and the Northern Areas) than those areas that are farther away, such as Balochistan. In Table 5.1, I list the top ten LeT militant-producing districts in the data set. Notably, these are all in the Punjab.

Many analysts who have written on LeT have claimed, without solid empirical evidence, that LeT and the Pakistan army recruit from similar locales.[8] In considerable measure, these data substantiate these long-standing assertions. Nonetheless, tables 5.1 and 5.2 demonstrate that Pakistan army recruitment (from 1970–2005) is much more diverse than that of the LeT in our sample. Whereas in Table 5.1, ten districts account for 60 per cent of LeT recruitment, eleven districts account for the same percentage of Pakistan army production (Table 5.2). There is little intersection among the highest producing LeT and Pakistan army districts, even though there is considerable correspondence in general. While the Punjab accounts for all of the highest producing LeT districts, only eight of the highest army officer-producing districts are in the Punjab. In fact, the army data in the highest producing cities—which include Lahore, Sialkot, and Faisalabad—tend to correspond to the presence of large military establishments. To provide a district-level proxy for human capital, I have also-added district average literacy rates for males fifteen years of age and older. In general, the highest producing districts for both the Pakistan army and LeT are well educated, relative to the mean for all Pakistani males overall of 55 per cent, although the army does appear to draw from better-educated districts relative to the LeT.

Figure 5.1: Distribution of LeT militants by District.

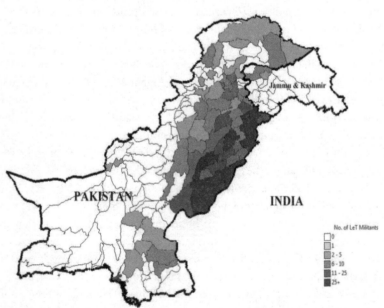

Source: Militant database. Mapped by Sun Lee.

Table 5.1: Top Ten LeT Producing Districts

District Name	State or Province	Number of Militants	Per cent of Total*	District Literacy (Males, 15 yrs. and older) 2010
Gujranwala	Punjab	63	10%	76%
Faisalabad	Punjab	62	10%	70%
Lahore	Punjab	42	7%	79%
Sheikhupura	Punjab	35	5%	67%
Kasur	Punjab	34	5%	64%
Sialkot	Punjab	32	5%	68%
Bahawalnagar	Punjab	31	5%	55%
Bahawalpur	Punjab	31	5%	54%
Khanewal	Punjab	26	4%	65%
Multan	Punjab	26	4%	66%
All Other Districts	–	257	40%	
Missing Data	–	277	–	–
Total	–	916	–	–

Source: LeT data are derived from in-house tabulations of militant data by Anirban Ghosh.

* Excluding militants for whom no district of origin is given. Literacy data are from Pakistan Bureau of Statistics (2011).

The biographies often contain information about the specific places where the militants fought, the locations of their death, and sometimes their age at the time of their demise. The most prevalent fighting front for the militants in this database is Indian Kashmir, even though LeT has gained notoriety for its spectacular operations beyond Kashmir. Of 786 LeT militant biographies that detail where the militant fought, 778 (98.9 per cent) identify Indian Kashmir. Thirty-nine biographies indicate Afghanistan as a battlefield, but even among these militants (who make up 5 per cent of the data); thirty-nine list Indian Kashmir as well. Two individuals list Tajikistan and Bosnia-Chechnya as their fighting fronts. The mean age upon death in our sample was twenty-one years of age. Most of the militants appeared to wait for several years before being deployed; only 5 per cent died within one year of joining the organization. The median length of time between joining and dying was four years.[9]

In many cases (627 in total), we learn something about the training that the militants received. Of the 627 biographies that mentioned militant training, only 5 per cent deployed after completing the basic course (*Daura-e-Aam*). The majority (62 per cent) underwent the advanced *Daura-e-Khaas* and another 12 per cent underwent some other specific training course (i.e. *Daura-e-Saqeela, Daura-e-Abdullah bin Masood*, or *Daura-e-Ribat*, the latter of which provides instruction in intelligence collection) before going to the front.[10] The length of time for these various training types ranges from eighteen days for basic training, to more than four months for some specialized courses. In general, these data suggest that the fighters deploy only after completing several months of training.

Table 5.2: Top Ten Army Officer Producing Districts (1970–2005)

District	Province	No. of Militants	% of Total*	District Literacy (Males, 15 yrs. and older) 2010
Rawalpindi	Punjab	3947	15.25%	86%
Lahore	Punjab	2385	9.21%	79%
Azad Kashmir	Azad Kashmir	1240	4.79%	NA
Karachi	Sind	1112	4.30%	83%
Sargodha	Punjab	1066	4.12%	69%
Chakwal	Punjab	798	3.08%	88%
Gujrat	Punjab	1082	4.18%	76%
Sialkot	Punjab	953	3.68%	68%
Jhelum	Punjab	1000	3.86%	85%
Peshawar	NWFP	882	3.41%	66%
Faisalabad	Punjab	931	3.60%	70%
All Other Districts	–	257	40.53%	–
Total	–	25,889	–	–

Source: Data on Pakistan officer recruitment is from Fair, C. Christine, "Using Manpower Policies to Transform the Force and Society: The Case of the Pakistan Army," *Security Studies*, 23, 1 (2014), pp. 74–112. Literacy data are from Pakistan Bureau of Statistics, Table 2.14(B): Adult Literacy-Population 15 Years and Older, in *Pakistan Social And Living Standards Measurement Survey (PSLM) 2010–11. Provincial/District*, 2011, accessed 1 June 2017. http://www.pbs.gov.pk/content/pakistan-social-and-living-standards-measurement-survey-pslm-2010-11-provincial-district

It is useful to compare this training period to that which Pakistani army enlistees (*jawans*) and officers undergo. Enlisted men, who must have completed the sixth grade to join the army, undergo thirty-six weeks of military training at a regimental center. Prior to this, they may receive supplementary basic education and additional training in Urdu if required. This is also where they may learn, for the first time, how to wear boots or even use an indoor toilet. Enlisted men will typically stay in uniform for fifteen years and undergo regular cycles of military training, as well as take advantage of academic opportunities. Meanwhile, officers are trained at the Pakistan Military Academy over a period of two years. To qualify for the officer corps, they must attain at least twelve years of education and satisfactorily clear a variety of other physical and aptitude assessments. Officers will generally retire between the ages of fifty-two and sixty, depending upon their rank.[11]

Pakistan's army operates on an up or out system, which means that should an officer fail to be promoted, he is expected to retire. It typically takes about ten years to attain the rank of major and fifteen to sixteen years to reach the rank of Lt Colonel.[12] Considering the educational requirement, the length and intensity of training, and the actual time in service, an LeT militant is far more cost effective than his enlisted or officer counterpart in the Pakistan army. Since reservists undergo similar basic training and episodic training cycles, the LeT fighter is also likely less costly than even his reserve analogue. In conventional militaries there are numerous perquisites for the military member and his family inclusive of housing subsidies, medical care, educational assistance and, of course, retirement benefits. In contrast, the tenure of the LeT militant is considerably briefer and his ultimate goal is not to retire with benefits, but to die in combat. Moreover, the benefits that the family of the *shaheed* receives are a fraction of those received by the family members of deceased military personnel. Thus Pakistan's army benefits from working through LeT fighters who have presumably comparable fighting capabilities and human capital endowments as officers or non-commissioned officers, but at a fraction of the life-time costs of those permanently enlisted in the army.

Perhaps the most important contribution of these data is that they continue to provide evidence presented by Fair,[13] Abou Zahab,[14] and Khan[15] that LeT militants are not primarily under-educated *madaris* recruits drawn from Pakistan's most disadvantaged classes, as is often alleged.[16] Many of the biographies provide information about the secular (non-religious education) educational attainment of the fighter. I have produced the summary statistics for education attainment in Table 5.3. As these data show, most militants have at least ten years of education, which is referred to as "matriculate" or "matric" in Pakistan. In contrast, a very small percentage is illiterate at 1.3 per cent, or only primary educated, at 13 per cent. While a tenth-grade education may not seem very impressive, it is striking when compared to the level of attainment of Pakistani males generally or Punjabi males in particular.

Table 5.3: Secular Educational Attainment

Education Level	LeT Militants over 10 yrs.	Pakistani males over 10 yrs.	Pakistani males over 10 yrs. (rural)	Pakistani males over 10 yrs. (urban)	Punjabi males over 10 yrs.	Punjabi males over 10 yrs. (rural)	Punjabi males over 10 yrs. (urban)
Illiterate	1.3%	30.4%	36.4%	19.8%	30.8%	36.0%	21.1%
Primary	12.7%	21.4%	22.4%	19.5%	21.6%	22.5%	20.0%
Middle	21.7%	14.30%	13.6%	15.6%	15.6%	15.5%	16.8%
Matric	44.0%	13.1%	10.8%	17.3%	13.4%	11.1%	17.7%
Intermediate and Above	16.8%	10.9%	6.2%	19.3%	9.3%	5.2%	17.0%

Source: In-house militant data tabulation by Anirban Ghosh, Pakistan Bureau of Statistics, 2010.

To benchmark LeT educational attainment, I assemble comparative educational attainment data, where educational attainment refers to the highest level of schooling a person attained over their lifetime at the time of the survey, using data from the 2009–10 Labour Force Survey conducted by the Pakistan Bureau of Statistics for males over 10 years of age.[17] (Pakistan's Bureau of Statistics did not publish data for this survey before 2001. Arguably, the 2001 data are most comparable to the data presented here.) I compare the LeT militants to all males in Pakistan, as well as to all males in the Punjab and further, by rural and urban places of residence. As the data in Table 5.3 show, whereas very few LeT militants are described as illiterate in their biographies, in 2009 anywhere between one in five and one in three males could not read or write. LeT cadres are more likely to have attained at least a primary school education (five years of schooling) or a middle school education (up to eighth grade) than their Pakistani or Punjabi counterparts, and much more likely than their national or Punjabi peers to be matriculates (up to tenth grade). The LeT militants in our survey are more likely to have an intermediate degree (twelve years of schooling) or above than males in rural areas, and almost as likely to have higher educational attainment as those in urban areas across Pakistan. In general, LeT militants in this sample are more likely to be as educated, if not more so, than Pakistanis or Punjabi males, and are far less likely to be illiterate.

Contemporary discussions of militancy in Pakistan are dominated by the assertion that its *madaris* are a veritable production line for terrorists. These data do not entirely support this contention. Some 284 biographies (31 per cent) provided information about *madrassah* attendance among the LeT fighters. Those data indicate that 56.9 per cent of LeT militants have attended a *madrassah*, with only 4.3 per cent of those having received a *sanad*, a formal degree of religious educational attainment.[18] Given the large amount of missing data for this variable, this finding suggests, but does not prove, that a higher percentage of LeT militants in this sample have spent more time in a *madrassah* than prior studies have indicated. For example, in her groundbreaking study on LeT martyrs, Abou Zahab noted that "the proportion of *madrasah*-educated [LeT] boys is minimal (about 10 per cent), but includes boys who studied in a *madrasah* after studying in an Urdu medium school."[19] Similarly Z. Khan, upon interviewing various LeT office holders, reports that "few of Lashkar's recruits come from a madrassah.... Most are educated at regular schools and some have even attended a college or university."[20] Unfortunately, few biographies (5 per cent) indicate how many years the militants attended a *madrassah*. The average tenure at a religious school turns out to be 2.8 years for this subset of the sample. It is useful to note that, at a minimum, it takes two years of study at a formal *madrassah* that teaches the *Dars-e-Nizami* curriculum to attain the first *sanad*.[21] (A student who completes the entire *Dars-e-Nizami* curriculum will accumulate four *sanads*. The terminal *sanad* confers the status of *alim* (learned, religious scholar) upon the graduate and usually takes eight years or more to complete.) Even though these data on *madrassah* tenure may not be representative of all of the fighters in this database, much less within LeT generally, we can say with certainty that, given the high degree of secular attainment noted above, *madrassah* education must complement, rather than substitute, nonreligious education.

Because LeT has a strong proselytization mission to convert persons from other religious traditions (i.e., Barelvi, Deobandi) to the Ahl-e-Hadees interpretative tradition, it is likely that fighters began their formal religious schooling only after the recruitment process began. The biographies suggest that many militants did not attend a *madrassah* in the beginning of their education as children; rather, they elected to attend later as young adults. This is consistent with a frequent assertion by Hafiz Saeed that he would not put a weapon in the hands of any young recruit who had not first accepted a solid religious grounding, and who was not secure in his faith.[22] Moreover, before recruits could take the *Daura-e-Khaas*, in which they learned weapons training, they had to be model citizens at home where local LeT officials monitored them. The *madaris* mentioned most frequently in this dataset tend to be facilities in Pakistan's Punjab province that are well-known LeT/JuD institutions, including: LeT's main *madrassah* at Muridke, Ma'had al-Ala; Jamia Uloom e-Asria in Jhelum; Jamia Muhammadia in Gujranwala; and Jamia Muhammadia in Okara.[23]

These findings are significant because they suggest that Let fighters are more likely than Pakistanis to attend a *madrassah*. Estimates of *madrassah* attendance vary. The lowest estimate comes from Andrabi et al. who find that less than 1 per cent of all enrolled students attend a *madrassah* on a full-time basis.[24] Cockcroft et al and ASER Pakistan, based upon surveys of school-age children, report that between 2 and 3 per cent of children are enrolled in a *madrassah* either full or part-time.[25] In contrast, Fair reports that 33 per cent of respondents from a nationally representative survey of 3,130 Pakistani adult males between ages eighteen and thirty reported attending a *madrassah* at some point in their lives.[26] All but eleven attended another form of school (public or private) in addition to a *madrassah*. Whether one uses the lower estimate or the higher estimate, LeT fighters in our sample attended a *madrassah* with much higher frequencies than Pakistanis generally.

In about one third of our sample (270), the biographies provide information about the employment of the fighter prior to his death. Aggregating across these varied occupational indicators, we find that the most common occupations include factory worker, farmer, tailor, electrician, and laborer. These occupations tend to suggest that the fighters were poor or lower middle class. This corroborates Abou Zahab's claim that even though "LeT claims that the *mujahidin* are recruited from all social classes, most of them belong to the lower middle class."[27] They also corroborate my previous findings, derived from a 2004 survey that my team fielded among a convenience sample of families who had at least one son killed while fighting for a Pakistani militant organization.[28] Most of those slain fighters died in Indian-administered Kashmir. In that study, we found that the militants in the sample were well educated and not preponderantly educated at a *madrassah*, although one quarter of them were, and nearly one in ten obtained a *sanad*. However, prior to joining the varied militant organizations, most were under-employed. Some 50 per cent of the slain fighters did not work at all prior to joining the organization. One in four worked part time and another one in four worked full time. Taken together, about three-quarters of the sample were either unemployed or under-employed. In contrast, throughout Pakistan between 2002 and 2006, the unemployment rate averaged somewhat below 8 per cent; throughout the 1990s the average unemployment rate was slightly above 5 per cent and for the last half of the 1980s, it was 3.3 per cent.[29] By any measure, the unemployment rate of these males was quite high, particularly given the fact that overall, this was a very well educated sample. These findings also align with those of Haq and Z. Khan.[30]

The problem with such data is that it is impossible to discern the employment preferences of the fighters. We can only observe actual employment or lack thereof. It is tempting to conclude that LeT militants are more likely to be well-educated but under-employed. This interpretation buttresses the argument that individuals with low opportunity costs may be more likely to join terrorist organizations. In turn, that would imply that job creation for educated males may be an important intervention to raise the opportunity cost of participating in terrorist activity and thus motivate some militants to pursue gainful employment outside the militant sector. While this exposition and concomitant public policy proposal is appealing, it is likely to be wrong for the simple reason that it is also possible that the aspiring militant, knowing he sought to join the ranks of a *jihadi* organization, may have deliberately sought flexible employment opportunities such that he could engage in recruitment activities with the militant organization (e.g. attend *tabligh*, socialize and travel with other members, partake of the proselytization (*dawah*) courses) and, eventually, head for pre-conflict training. Recall that the activist may be in his home district for several months or longer between training bouts or eventual selection for a mission. Few professional jobs would permit an individual to come and go consistent with the militant's robust slate of militant-related activities. Incidentally, we observe this in other economic settings. For example, persons seeking government employment, including military service, may defer working altogether or take on temporary work while they await the necessary clearances. For these reasons, we cannot discern whether underemployment prompts individuals to join the group or whether it is symptomatic of the person's preferences to join a militant group instead of full-time employment. Interview-based work confirms this suspicion. Z. Khan interviewed LeT fighters and leadership. He reports that while some are educated and unemployed, others who "are gainfully employed...choose to give up their careers."[31]

Unfortunately, these data provide no insight into the social status of these fighters. This is an important lacuna because researchers who have interviewed fighters have found that while many come from middle class households and abandoned their careers to join the organizations, others come from more austere backgrounds. For example, Z. Khan found that LeT readily embraces men who have "given up a life of crime or quit an addiction to become part of the organization."[32] He interviewed Abu Abdullah who was at the time in charge of the prisoners' welfare office at the Markaz. He had recently been released from prison for murder "when he decided to turn over a new leaf and join the Lashkar. Now on parole, Abdullah is a dedicated Lashkar worker."[33] This anecdote raises numerous questions about the complicity of the Pakistani justice system in letting a convicted murderer out on parole because he has elected to join a militant organization. Khan also reports that other men who came from a background of drug addiction joined LeT and were eventually dispatched to Kashmir, where they died. One particular person was married with three children. For him, his martyrdom seems to have been a form of social rehabilitation and redemption for himself as well as his family, who were no longer stigmatized by his past activities. His wife and children could now boast that he has become a *shaheed* in Kashmir, a coveted status for the family of the slain fighter. Haq also finds that LeT recruits former drug addicts, and notes that while some LeT families are well-off, "the fact remains that it is the poor who have served as the cannon fodder for LeT's jihadi mission."[34]

362 biographies provide details on how LeT uses different means to attract recruits. While most of these biographies indicates only one means of recruitment, there is evidence for about twelve different recruitment paths. About 20 per cent of the fighters in our sample were recruited into LeT by a current member of the organization. An equal number was recruited into LeT when a family member, almost always a brother or the father, facilitated the recruitment. This also overlaps with qualitative studies that emphasize the family nature of this enterprise.[35] Another 16 per cent of the biographies suggest that the person was "self-motivated," most of whom were stirred by LeT's propaganda, including speeches and published writings. Mosques accounted for 9 per cent of the biographies that discuss recruitment modalities, while *madaris* and Islamic study centers accounted for 8 per cent. Another 3 per cent of persons were recruited through a LeT conference, such as the organization's annual convention (*ijtema*).[36] Finally, we also found evidence of cross-over between militant groups. In about 3 per cent of these biographies, persons came into LeT from other militant groups fighting in Kashmir.[37]

Z. Khan found evidence of a different kind of cross-over.[38] He interviewed a twenty-one-year old who joined LeT after attending a public meeting where Major Mast Gul, a fighter associated with a Jamaat-e-Islami (JI, Islamic Assembly) affiliated militant group, addressed the crowd. In other words, he was motivated by this other group but ultimately chose to join LeT. David Hicks, the so-called Australian LeT activist, joined LeT after peripatetically interacting with other militant groups beyond South Asia. He then went to Afghanistan where he allegedly trained in Al Qaeda camps and even met Osama bin Laden. The Northern Alliance captured him and handed him over to the Americans, who remanded him to Guantanamo.[39]

These anecdotes suggest that militant groups confront a few dilemmas. First, they invest resources in branding their name, and engaging in outreach to attract human and other resources. Second, these groups want to recruit persons who are willing to commit violence. But once the person is trained, they are free to join other militant groups.

Conventional militaries face similar challenges. Military services expend considerable advertising and other resources to attract personnel. As one service increases its advertising budget, the others must do the same or lose potential recruits to its rivals, even though all such forces advance shared national interests. There is evidence of cross-over effects in military advertisement as well: when the army reserve advertises, it is also implicitly advertising for the regular army and the army national guard. Similarly, when the navy runs adverts for naval aviation, it is fundamentally promoting military aviation careers which also can be had through service in the air force, army and marines.[40] In other words, the services have difficulty managing their "brand" in their various messaging efforts.[41] Studies in the advertising literature have found that memory recall of an advertisement can be detrimentally influenced when the person is exposed to another, similar advertisement.[42] Equally important, it sometimes happens that an individual may want to become a naval aviator; however, upon trying to join the navy, she finds there is no available slot at that time. This person could wait for a slot to open with the navy, or she can turn to one of the other available services that offer similar opportunities. Once a person is trained in one service, they can leave when their contract expires and join private militias, or even join another service branch. Thus the challenges that LeT and other militant groups face with managing their brand and personnel are not truly distinct from those encountered by traditional military organizations.

The militant biographies, particularly those published in the three-volume set titled *Hum Ma'en Lashkar-e-Tayyaba Ki* (We, the Mothers of Lashkar-e-Tayyaba) and compiled by Umm-e-Hammad, reveal the degree to which recruits must consistently lobby the organization's leadership to receive additional training and/or to be deployed on a mission to fulfill the fighter's goal of fighting and dying in combat. In some cases, a local LeT leader gives a recruit a specific charge, with the explicit warning that his deployment is contingent upon its successful and timely completion. In the biography of Dr Abu Khabib (Mushfiq-ur-Rehman), we learn that he sought permission from Zaki-ur-Rehman Lakhvi to be dispatched to Kashmir. Lakhvi responded that upon successfully wiring the new house of the *mujahideen* within seven days, he would be dispatched into battle. Highly motivated, he completed the task in three days and prepared to depart for Kashmir with a group of fighters.[43] In another illustrative case, Abu al-Hashim Abdul Majeed was anxious to receive permission to taste action and requested permission from Hafiz Saeed. Saeed rebuffed him and told him to focus upon his education instead. Not content with that answer, Majeed began working directly with and accompanying him on various programs. Eventually, Majeed asked his instructor to recommend his deployment, to which Saeed relented. Majeed was dispatched on a mission in which he ultimately died.[44]

Such examples of recruits directly appealing to Saeed or Lakhvi may be atypical, but they occur with adequate frequency in these biographies and as such, merit consideration. Notably, these accounts, published by Jamaat ud

Dawah's (JuD) own publications office, directly refute Pakistan's claims that neither Saeed nor Lakhvi have direct roles in facilitating terrorism in India.

Why They Fight: Motivating the Fighters in the Army of the Pure[45]

One of the perennial questions about organizations like LeT is what drives their combatants to pick up arms and fight under their banner. The hundreds of posthumous martyr biographies consulted for this study provide considerable insight into fighters' motivations. As already noted, I cannot independently confirm the veracity of claims in these biographies. Moreover, LeT ultimately publishes these accounts not for accuracy, but rather, to increase membership of its organization and expand the supply of potential fighters. Thus, it may well be possible that the "battlefield" motivations that I observe here are merely those that the organization projects for perception management. Other "battlefield motivation" projects suffer similar potential distortionary effects of the primary source of information.[46] With that caveat, the biographies usually indicate multiple motivations for the fighter to join the organization and then lobby the organization to be deployed. In this section, I provide a general overview of the kinds of reasons given by the fighter, his family, or fellow colleagues in the *tanzeem*.

On rare occasion, the young man in question exhibited prior violent tendencies that some would associate with sociopathy. For example, the mother of Abu Marsad described him as "a naughty boy since his childhood. He would make strange kinds of mischief at his home. Sometimes, he would kill small animals and use them to scare other children and sometimes use other methods to tease them."[47] Other fighters come from families that had a "*jihadi* mindset" with a long lineage of participation in such conflict[48] or from a family in which another brother already joined the organization.[49] The vast majority of biographies articulate the fighters' desire for martyrdom and the celestial benefits they incur from doing so, such as the *huris* (heavenly maidens), access to paradise after death, and the ability to intercede on behalf of his loved ones at the time of judgement. Many—but by no means all—indicate that the fighter had been spiritually inclined and was moved to sacrifice his life in the way of *jihad* for Allah.

Not all of the fighters described in these works were always pious or interested in *jihad*. Some seemed bored with their lives and sought something that was more meaningful and exciting. Several biographies report that the young men find a new meaning and purpose upon joining the organization, compared to their previous lives characterized by inadequate piety, or imbricated with values they grew to reject. Many of the biographies indicate family reports that their loved ones returned from their training with the *tanzeem* as "transformed," either because they were more serious about life, had abandoned frivolities such as cricket or other leisure activities, or were physically stronger than they were before they left. Many parents remarked that their sons had become men in the course of their training.

Other motivations that fall under this rubric of "higher purpose" include fighters who were disgusted by depravity and decadence, either within their own family or in society at large. Through engaging with JuD, they found a means to effect change, first within themselves, then their family, and ultimately, Pakistani society writ large. Biographies describe the fighters' opinion that "this world does not hold anything exciting for me,"[50] newfound passion for "serving the Mujahideen,"[51] desire for physical transformation,[52] longstanding rejection for the "life of luxury," and desire to "sacrifice himself as a martyr."[53] In some biographies, the recruit seeks to bring his family onto a path of greater piety in conformation to JuD's understanding of a properly "Muslim life" because he is genuinely concerned about their salvation.[54]

Most biographies that I evaluated qualitatively indicate that the fighters drew upon their beliefs about the Kashmir conflict in India. These motivations dwell upon the posited brutality of "Hindu" India, which the fighters, JuD, and the Pakistan government accuse of oppressing Kashmiris and Indian Muslims. And as noted in Chapter 2, while many of these concerns are founded in varying measure, Pakistan has no legitimate claim to Kashmir, and its dispatching of terrorists has hardly advanced the moral standing of Kashmiris' political complaints or the quality of life of Kashmiri Muslims— much less Indian Muslims beyond Kashmir. Such Kashmir-specific motivations, which are pervasive in these biographies, include a desire to protect Kashmiri women whom they believe have been—or will be—raped or harassed, or to avenge the violence already perpetrated against Kashmiri women.[55] They also focus upon what they perceive to be an illegal occupation of Kashmir by India, reflecting the official position advanced by the Pakistani government.[56] The biographies stress the fighters' dedication to fighting the "Hindu" Indian army, and go to great lengths to stress that they do not kill civilians, even though LeT's record belies these claims. In these accounts, the fighters are always battling the Indian army variously described as "Hindu," "infidel," and "oppressor." Some of the biographies cultivate the belief, pervasive among Pakistanis, that Kashmiris welcome their contributions to the battle and actively support their efforts, in contravention to more nuanced scholarly accounts that suggest that while some Kashmiris may do so willingly, others feel like they have little choice in the matter.[57] Other biographies speak about communal issues in India itself rather than simply Kashmir. Some of the biographies mention the destruction of the mosque at Ayodhya in 1992, the 2002 pogrom of Muslims in Gujarat, or the belief that the Indian government and Indians seek to render India a Hindu state, or Hindustan.[58]

Some biographies speak to the larger historical landscape of Muslims in South Asia and beyond. On the most grandiose scale, fighters discuss the historical enslavement of Muslims by non-Muslims throughout the world and the belief that their contributions will aid—in some measure—the awakening of the *ummat*.[59] Some biographies are more regionally focused and draw upon the sub-continent's pre-Partition history. One theme that reoccurs in the biographical accounts of these fighters is the 1024 CE destruction of the iconic Shiva temple in Gujarat by Mahmud of Ghazni, the most prominent ruler of the Ghaznavid dynasty (977–1186 CE). JuD publications and posters frequently assert that it will break India just as Mahmud of Ghazni destroyed the Somnath temple.[60] For Pakistani *jihadis*, this episode is mobilized as an iconic event in the posited Muslim efforts to vanquish polytheism in South Asia. For Hindu nationalists, the destruction of the Somnath Temple and the braggadocious elegies of this feat by Pakistanis and other Muslims is a signifier of Muslim infidelity to the Indian state project, as well as a rallying cry for retribution animating their hostility towards Muslims and the myriad monuments that attest to various Muslims rulers throughout India.[61] That both Hindu and Muslim chauvinists mobilize this history is ironic, given the scholarly consensus that much of the rhetoric surrounding the "Muslim conquest of Hindu South Asia" and the destruction of Somnath are contested.[62] Sometimes the biographies reference fighter outrage over mosques being demolished, Qurans being burned or defiled, and Muslims being harmed or murdered and their property destroyed.[63] Many of these biographies suggest that the fighter believed that he was obliged to fellow Muslims whom he believed were being oppressed or even killed by non-believers, although this sentiment was most acute when discussing Muslims in India in general and in Indian-administered Kashmir in particular.

Given that one of the primary functions of these biographies is as propaganda to recruit other militants, we cannot know whether these posthumous accounts accurately reflect the sentiment and intentions of the fighters, or whether the narrator is adding embellishing with details for rhetorical and recruitment purposes. Nonetheless, these stated motivations tally with the various reasons the organization cites for the necessity of *jihad*. This is a strongly emotive issue because it evokes the brutality that accompanied the Partition of the subcontinent when Muslims raped, murdered, and otherwise brutalized Hindus and Sikhs and when Sikhs and Hindus did the same to Muslims. (Needless to say, LeT's accounts of this period only focus upon the atrocities committed on—rather than by—Muslims.) The Punjab, from which most LeT recruits come, bore the brunt of this violence. While few survivors of Partition are alive today, they passed their stories down to younger generations and the heinous crimes of Partition animate films, poetry, and writing on both sides of the border. In fact, the centrality of Punjab in this sequence of atrocities may well explain why so many so-called Kashmiri militant groups recruit most heavily from that area.

Recruiting the Families of the Fighters: Mothers May Matter Most

LeT, until recently, frequently published biographical accounts of their so-called martyred fighters (*shaheed*). These were variously written by fellow fighters or a family member, and tended to include: testimonies in which one or more family member opines elegiacally about their slain relative; observations from other fighters about the martyr; letters from the fighter while he was deployed; and/or the last will and testament of the fighter. These documents regularly featured commentary from the fighter's family (i.e. parents, siblings, aunts, uncles, cousins), which suggests that LeT believes including them in these accounts is important.

The LeT's focus upon the fighter's family speaks to a larger social strategy by the organization. Not only does it hope to attract the entire family to its movement to promulgate its version of Ahl-e-Hadees dogma, it also aims to expand its pool of potential recruits for militant and other organizational operations. Even after the recruit dies in a mission, LeT remains in contact with the fighter's family to ensure that the family stays within the Ahl-e-Hadees fold.[64] In this sense, LeT is recruiting not just a member or a fighter but the entire immediate and extended family.

Given the frequency with which these issues surrounding approval and blessing arise in these biographies, I infer that the organization both values the idea that families willingly sacrifice their sons and wants to cultivate the belief that LeT values family approval. The organization wants to undermine any suggestion that youths are lured away through deception against their family's wishes. Reportedly, Saeed established a firm policy that requires every candidate for the Kashmir front to obtain explicit consent from the family and to persuade it of the utility of his mission there. This can be achieved most easily if the parents embrace their sons' missions and likely martyrdom in combat. As such, LeT's publications strongly emphasize that such blessings should be granted and provide ample evidence that this permission is, in fact, given in many of the biographies. Though we cannot confirm any of the details in these biographies, whether or not the family actually gave such approval may be less important than the perception that these publications generate that family members—especially mothers—do eventually relent and bless their son's *jihad* irrespective of their purported initial disposition.

An example of such exhortation to parents is in *Tafseer Surah at-Taubah*.[65] Published in both English and Urdu, it is based upon Hafiz Saeed's own *tafseer* (exposition) of the chapter in the Quran titled Surah-at-Tauba. This *surat* details the various *jihads* waged by the prophet after he left Mecca for Medina. In this publication, LeT exposits at length why *jihad* is incumbent upon all Muslims. The volume specifically addresses parents who may oppose their son's participation:

> Remember that the parents, who impede the wish of their youngsters to join Jehad, commit a sin if it is without any formidable reason. The parents ought not stop their children to join Jehad....as ordained by the Holy *Quran*. Question yourself—Do I love Allah and his prophet or the pleasures of the material world?[66]

In another published *shaheed* biography, the mother of "Abu Zubair" readily embraces the fighter's aspiration to become first a *mujahid* and then a *shaheed*. Zubair came to her and shared his disappoinment that others who had completed their training after he completed his own had already embraced martyrdom in Kashmir yet he has not been a given a chance to do so. His mother counselled him to "look for the shortcomings in his character which Allah may not like and that he should make amends,"[67] in hopes that Allah will grant him his wish. Upon receiving permission from LeT's leadership to undertake a mission in Kashmir, he returned home one last time during which his mother not only prayed that Allah would grant her son the blessing of becoming a *shaheed* or *ghazi* (veteran of *jihad*) and protect him from capture or handicap as a result of combat, but also her son's *mujahideen* associates, whom he had brought so she could pray for them as well.[68]

Biographies of slain fighters highlight a particular emphasis upon the role of women in producing fighters through the conjoined processes of birth and nurturing. The mother of Abu Quhafa is another example from martyrdom literature who not only eagerly supported the aspirations of her children, but also buoyed the *jihadi* aspirations of others in myriad ways. We learn from his post-death biography that she herself dispatched her son into the battlefield. When other fighters embraced martyrdom, she would offer support to their mothers. She went door to door to collect supplies for *mujahideen* and she would distribute LeT's periodicals, *Ghazwa* and *Mujhallah ul Dawah*, among the neighbors at her own expense. Her household hosted Ramazan festivities and, at the conclusion of these programs, she lectured guests about the virtues of supporting *jihad* through monetary donations. Leading by example, she would be the first to contribute significant sums to the cause directly to *mujahideen*.[69] When her son was about to go to Kashmir, he asked her for permission to leave. According to his biography, she kissed him on the forehead and asked that Allah guide and help him. She instructed him to "fight those [Hindu] transgressors bravely, and dispatch to hell as many of those enemies of Allah as you can. Do not be cowardly and if it comes to it then take the bullet on your chest because that is what my heart desires."[70] The expression to take (literally "to eat") a bullet on the chest is an expression of utmost bravery in Urdu and occurs frequently in these *shaheed* biographies. Additionally, when her own son was in the Valley, she managed to phone his commander and ask to speak with him. The commander was chary that she may try to lure her son away from the battlefield and asked her why she wanted to speak with him. She replied that she harboured no such thoughts and that she intended to implore her son:

> to kill as many of those animals as possible and to busy himself with killing until the time that his wish for martyrdom is fulfilled. That you should fight with bravery against these transgressors and know that my prayers are with you."[71]

In another biography, the writer describes how the fighter's mother donated gold jewellry to the cause of the *mujahideen* and is "thankful that [her son] received the bullet on his chest as this was her wish as well." The writer enthuses that this mother "continues to invite people to Jihad and that, in this way, she would continue with the mission of her son." The author of the biography addresses the readers directly to explain that it was the *shaheed's* mother who empowered her son to walk the path of *jihad*. The reader also learns that even after losing her son, she is still raising her grandsons to embrace the path of *jihad*. By educating these young soldiers, the biographer tells the reader that "the victory of Islam can be attained quickly." He notes that this is just the story of one mother and posits that if half of Pakistan's mothers imbibed the spirit of *jihad* like her, Kashmir would likely be liberated soon, allowing the organization to move onto other battlefields. He enjoins the reader to pray that this spirit of *jihad* is kindled within the hearts of the mothers of Pakistan.[72]

Similarly, the biographer of another slain fighter named Abu Huzaifa Abdul Waheed remarked upon the fighter's mother and sister that as long as:

> there are such mothers and sisters, who will send their brothers and sons to the battlefield with a smile on their face, then it is only a matter to time before these clouds of cruelty and humiliation will be lifted from upon us.... May Allah give such passion to all the mothers and sisters of the Muslim nation...[73]

This mother, according to the biographer, is the "spiritual daughter of al Khansa."[74] In these biographies, writers favorably compare mothers and other women who enthusiastically encourage their sons and menfolk to embrace *shahadat* to al Khansa (575–645 CE), a female poet who was a contemporary of prophet Muhammad, and is revered both for her poetry but also her sacrifices, which often formed the subject of her writings.[75] A typical example of this comparison is afforded by the biography of Abu Ali Ameer Muavia, who, in his will, writes:

> Dear Mother! You have also been very courageous to let your son die in the path of Islam. Mothers like you are the guardians of Islam. You have proved that mothers like Khansa are alive today and in future will give birth to sons like Ibn-Qasim and Sallah-ud-din to confront pharaohs.[76]

These biographies, as well as LeT's other publications, also frequently accent the difficulty that mothers have in sacrificing their sons to *jihad* and the concomitant need to educate women about the sanctification of *jihad* such that they will sanction their son's participation in it. In another posthumous biography, a mother explains that her son yearned to fight the infidels. One day he returned from college and obtained an LeT pamphlet. This transformed him and he immediately left to train with the organisation. After completing his training, his mother explained that he did everything he could to earn the good will of Allah and of the *mujahideen* he served. She confessed that when he asked her for permission to leave for Kashmir, she repeatedly refused. When she rebuffed his entreaties, he reminded her that when she used to tell him of the atrocities of 1947, he always said that he would avenge those atrocities when he grew up. He told her, "So now let me take my revenge" and held her feet until she relented and gave him permission to serve Allah through *jihad*.[77] (In South Asia, it is a sign of upmost respect to hold or massage the feet of elders.)

The mother of Abu Ayub Ansari was also less enthusiastic initially. Like many mothers we encounter in these *shaheed* biographies, she wanted her son to marry; however, Allah gave her the courage to do the right thing. According to the author of his biography, his mother told his biographer that

> My son Ayub was my favorite child. Since childhood he aspired to be a *mujahid*. My heart sank every time he would ask for my permission to go to Kashmir. He would try to convince me by citing verses from *Quran* telling me how often Allah has commanded us to go for Jihad but I refused to grant him permission. He would threaten me that if I do not give him my permission, then he would go anyway. I used to tell him that I would give permission but not now because I want to get you married first. But he would always reply the he does not want to get married to earthly women, rather he wants to get married to heavenly hoors [celestian maidens]. After his relentless efforts to persuade me, I finally relented and gave him permission to go. My heart was heavy that my son was going away, but then Allah granted my heart peace. And I am thankful to Allah that he gave me courage to return what was rightfully his. I am proud of my son who chose afterlife over this world. May Allah accept the martyrdom of my son. Amen.[78]

The mother of Muhammad Munsha was even more resistant to her son's pleas. His biographer explains that after he decided to take up arms, his mother demurred from granting him permission. He repeatedly and relentlessly insisted that she do so. One day, without her permission, he began preparing for *jihad* and again implored her to bid him goodbye. She said, "No I will not bid you farewell because I know that you will not return." Ultimately, she relented and "gave her permission over the telephone later saying that 'May Allah make you successful and save you from getting arrested.'"[79] The author of the biography asked her whether or not she had any message for other *mujahideen* to which she replied:

> Son, when these people talk against jihad, my heart bleeds. Even after reading eight chapters in *Quran* people still are not clear about how important it is. My message to the *mujahideen* is that they should not let the Kalashnikov of my son fall and continue the struggle.[80]

As we can see, LeT mobilizes—if not outright exploits—women's grief for several ends. First, the organization alleges that if so many women are sacrificing their sons, the cause must be just. Second, it uses the sacrifices and suffering of these mothers to galvanize support beyond LeT's community in an effort to expand its network of supporters. Third, by mobilizing women within and without the organization, LeT aims to diminish parental resistance to their son's decision to join *jihadi* organizations. It is this resistance that the LeT's notable women's wing intends to erode. Haq reports that during her meetings with Jaish-e-Muhammad (JeM) cadres, they complained that many mothers actively opposed their cadres joining the organization. JeM has no comparable women's wing to mitigate this opposition, and LeT is the only *jihadi* organization in Pakistan that has an active women's wing that issues its own publications (e.g. *Mujallah Tayyabaat* or *Journal of Virtuous Women*), holds regular meetings, conducts *dars* (Quran studies), and runs girls *madaris* in villages as well as in lower-class and middle-class urban areas.[81] *Mujallah Tayyabaat* notably publishes letters and short stories by women who long to be a part of the *jihad* but are instructed that their piece of *jihad* is on the domestic front.

LeT women are required to follow strict *purdah*, which includes the wearing of the black *burqa, niqab* (face covering), as well as black socks and gloves. This particular version of veiling—especially the wearing of socks and gloves—is not common in Pakistan or elsewhere in South Asia. This serves as a quasi-marker of identity among LeT women.[82] In addition, LeT women do not permit their family members to watch television, listen to music, take photographs, or engage in rituals that LeT proscribes as un-Islamic. They encourage the males in their family to avoid banking or other financial transactions that involve interest. The ideal LeT woman is informed of political affairs and is vigilant about anything or anyone who attempts to undermine her Muslim identity through fashion, consumerism or the allure of social status. Most of all, she aspires to be a daughter, a sister, or—perhaps most important of all—a mother of *mujahid*.[83]

There is considerable tension in LeT's use of women. On the one hand, LeT encourages women to observe strict *purdah*, but on the other hand, relies upon women to engage in an important set of social and political functions to reach out to other women. A female leader in the wing is able to achieve significant status within the ranks of the organization and enjoy relative freedom of movement because of the legitimacy and presumed piety that her membership in LeT confers upon her. Participation in LeT's women's wing also affords women a socially acceptable public life and an opportunity to leave their homes to participate in LeT's women's *ijtemas* (meetings). Such mobility for women is relatively rare in Pakistan, except for wealthy women who have personal vehicles and thus can travel safely without problematic encounters with unrelated males that may embarrass their families or bring personal disgrace upon the woman. Families without such means may be reluctant to permit their women to move around on foot or public transport unaccompanied for fear they may behave in a manner that will bring shame on her or her family or that men may harass her, for which she will be blamed rather than the ill-behaved male(s) in question.

Perhaps the most well-known member of LeT women's wing is the notorious female propagandist named Umm-e-Hammad. As Haq details, she is a prolific writer of *jihadi* poetry for LeT, as well as the compiler of the three-volume set *Hum Ma'en Lashkar-e-Tayyaba Ki* (We, the Mothers of Lashkar-e-Tayyaba).[84] The first volume was first published in 1998 and republished in 2001. The second and third volumes were published in 2003. In the "Publisher's Note" in the first volume of *Ma'en Lashkar-e-Tayyaba Ki* Muhammad Ramzan Asri of Dar ul Andalus extols the contributions of Umm-e-Hammad and explains the project of the volumes:

> The current publication "We Are the Mothers of Lashkar-e-Tayyaba" is the result of Sister Umm-i-Hammad's tireless efforts and extensive travels. She is a member of our women's wing as well as a mother of martyrs. She has dedicated her family and her life to jihad. Her poetry is popular amongst mujahedeen. Her impassioned words have inspired thousands to abandon their homes for the battlefield where they find themselves at the very gates of paradise.
>
> Umm-i-Hammad has interviewed the mothers, sisters, and relatives and friends of countless martyrs and recorded their sublime emotions in this compilation. Upon reading these biographies one is reminded of the age of the blessed companions (of the prophet) when those who received word of a loved one's martyrdom refused to mourn or lament, but instead celebrated and rejoiced, and offered their consolation and goodwill to the messengers bearing news of the departed.
>
> This book is a testament to the fact that the swelling ranks of martyrs is inspirational in of itself. Every house, clan, and village that loses a member on the battlefield produces many more to take their fallen brother's place. Our volunteers ought to disseminate this publication far and wide so our women are inspired to dispatch their men to the battlefield.[85]

As this note explains, Umm-e-Hammad is herself the mother of multiple martyrs. This gives her considerable credibility among women whom she—and her body of work—hopes to inspire to send their men to fight *jihad*. By extolling Umm-e-Hammad in this way, LeT has conferred to her considerable social status not only as a mother of fallen fighters but also as a key leader in its women league. She also has gravitas among the fighters themselves owing to her poetry, evocative of al Khansa.

Umm-e-Hammad details her own evolution in the preface of the first volume, which she calls a "Memoire." She begins by explaining that she was skeptical of Markaz-ud-Dawah-wal-Irshad (MDI) and suspected that the organization brainwashed Pakistani youth to leave their homes and abandon their studies to "fight in Kashmir only to be slaughtered like lambs for a few riyals and dollars."[86] She was alarmed when her husband began meeting with Hafiz Saeed too frequently, even though the two men had known each other for several years. When her husband expressed concern over the fact that he was raising their children on usurious earnings from the bank, she suspected the "so-called guardians of the Kashmiri jihad" had recruited him.[87] In this way, she builds rapport with other women who may be skeptical of the organization, its intentions and the changes their menfolk may experience once they embrace LeT. In an effort to keep her husband away from *jihad*, she tells her audience that she applied for every loan for which her household qualified in hopes of entrapping her husband in a cycle of endless debt repayment. Remorsefully, she explains that with Satan's help, "while my husband's conscience was weighed down by his usurious earnings, I was trying to protect our future and lifestyle by raising our debts." However, as she explains with relief, Allah foiled her cunning plot when, one morning, her husband handed in his resignation, went straight to the Markaz, and from there, left for LeT's preeminent training center in Afghanistan. Upon learning of this, she was furious and cursed the organization continuously as she made her way to the training camp in Muzaffarabad. Nonetheless, Umm-e-Hammad tells her readers that after spending a few days at the camp where she observed the *mujahideen*'s lifestyle, routine, training, and the passion for their faith, she became deeply ashamed of her own shallowness. She was exposed to the virtues of *jihad* through sermons that instructors gave to fighters. She re-read the various *surats* in the Quran on *jihad* and was reminded of "that radiant period of Islamic history when mothers bore sons like Salahuddin Ayubi, Tariq bin Zayd, Muhammad bin Qasim, and Mahmud Ghaznavi.[88] And thus she took the first step on the path of *jihad* and rued the various ruses she used to prevent her husband from joining *jihad*. Umm-e-Hammad, by explaining her own evolution, hopes to inspire others who resist the virtues of *jihad* to relent and see the truth.

Umm-e-Hammad narrates a similar journey of another recalcitrant mother who, like her, eventually came to see the light with Allah's assistance. When LeT's *mujahideen* arrived at her house to tell her that her son, Abu Sohaib, had been martyred, she asked only one question: "Where did the fatal bullet hit my son?"[89] The *mujahideen* told her that the enemy pumped multiple rounds into his chest. Upon hearing this, she prostrated before Allah in gratitude. However, when her older son, who is now a *ghazi* (living warrior), and younger son joined LeT one after the other, she was profoundly sad. One of her sons had not even graduated the 10th grade while the other hadn't passed his intermediate exams. She wept bitterly and asked Allah to show them the right path. However, Allah showed her the right path, when while weeping and praying, her heart spontaneously whispered, "So, you think your sons will bring you a lot of joy if they pass their B.A and F.A exams, eh? How many years will you live off their earnings? How long do you think you'll live? You fool; they're out there on the battlefield winning palaces in paradise for you by waging jihad in Allah's cause, what more could you want?"[90] Upon having this epiphany, she was at peace and immediately began praying not for their return, but for their martyrdom. Finally, she explains, her prayer was answered. The rest of this volume, as do the other two volumes, depicts similar accounts of mothers whose sons died in the battlefield of *jihad*.

Thus far, this analysis of the LeT *shaheed* biographies has emphasized the important relationship between the mother and the son. Nonetheless, the biographies provide ample evidence that other family members are also important. A typical statement is that afforded by the father of Abu Huzaifa Muhammad Luqman, who recollects his son's obedience and ethical decisions. His father admits that he would frequently concede to his demands and his wish to join the *jihad* was no different, explaining that, "I gave him the permission to fight, and told him to fight with courage. Allah had given him to me, and Allah took him away. The wealth of this world will stay in this world. I pray that Allah accepts our sacrifice and lets us be with Abu Huzaifa in paradise. (Amen)."[91]

In some cases, fathers are also obstinate, as is the case of Abu Saarya Muhammed Tahir. According to his biographer, Um e Abdulrubab, he first underwent training before returning to his home and telling his parents that he wished to achieve martyrdom in the way of *jihad*. At first his mother refused because, in the assessment of the biographer, she did not understand Islam. However, her son was so passionate about becoming a *mujahid* that he would often cry. On the last occasion that he met his mother, he explained to her that it is her love of him that makes her heart weak and thus unable to grant him her blessing for this endeavor. He resolved that he would rebuke her affections. Upon hearing this, she granted her permission by placing her hand on his head. The biographer tells us that her change of heart came about because she was listening to Surah at-Taubah. His father was equally opposed to the idea. According to his mother, he lectured them both on *jihad* and required them to sit *i'tikaaf*. (This refers to a Muslim practice in which a person stays in a mosque for a specified number of days devoting him/herself to worship and demurring from worldly affairs.) According to his mother, "He lobbied his father in every way possible so that he too finally relented to his wishes of fighting Hindus. He went through all this just to secure permission from his father."[92]

Siblings also evidence their support for their brothers who aspire to join the *jihad*. The sister of Ghulam Muhammad said of her deceased sibling that they loved him very much, and that he reciprocated that affection. "But, per Allah's command, we willingly sent our brother to wage Jihad such that he could avenge so many innocent women like us who have been defiled by those infidels [Indian Hindus]. We are very happy that our brother went for such a worthy cause. May Allah accept his sacrifice."[93] Brothers, like sisters, frequently attest to the worthiness of their dead brother's sacrifices and extol their piety and positive influence upon others to become better Muslims. The elder brother of Abu Zeeshan, for example, notes of his deceased sibling that after their father's death, the older brother assumed the family's responsibilities. He remarked upon his brother's death that he was an obedient and good person who never complained about the meagre stipend he received while studying at the seminary. He notes that "when he asked my permission to take up arms, I happily gave him my blessing. Before leaving for Jihad, he made a special visit to say goodbye to me."[94]

In another example, upon receiving the news of her brother's martyrdom, the sister of Abu Umair Shaheed wrote a letter to LeT in which she explains that upon hearing the news of his martyrdom:

> We immediately said praises to Allah because we all happily gave him permission for jihad. May Allah bless our eldest brother because he assumed the burdens of worldly responsibilities thus freeing our brother to go on jihad. It is Allah's blessing that he bestowed upon us the patience and courage to embrace this honor. In this regard, the forbearance of our parents is really exemplary.[95]

Yet another prominent theme that recurs through these publications is the issue of status that the fighter's death bequeaths to the family, particularly their mothers. While being the mother of a *ghazi* accords a significant reputation upon her as a mother of a warrior, the supreme status is to be the mother of a *shaheed*. In the May/July 2000 issue of *Mujallah Tayyabaat*, the author of a particular biography tells his readers about a mother who has recently learned that her second son, Jawad Ahmad Shaheed, has been martyred. The narrator explains that he and a party of *mujahideen* went to console her and to give news of her son's recent martyrdom. He remarks of the mother, Um-e-Hamaad, that

Allah has granted this sister the heart of Jihad, mind of Jihad, tongue of Jihad and the pen of Jihad. Poem and Prose both represent Jihad and Mujahideen. In addition, Allah has granted her the blessing of being a mother of two martyrs. In this respect, she influences both the heart and the mind of everyone. The maternal grandmother was also sitting near Um-e-Hamaad. She has two other martyrs in her family as well hence making this a family of martyrs.[96]

In a biography of Shams-ul-Arifeen written by his mother, she admits that she always envied the mothers of martyrs. However, now that Allah has chosen her for that honor, she is overwhelmed with the amount of respect that people shower upon her for being the mother of a martyr. In this biography, she perorates at length about the importance of women encouraging the men in their lives to embrace *jihad* to exact revenge upon the infidels and redeem Muslims, and she ventilates about the importance of sacrificing their loved ones in the path of *jihad*. She also exhorts Allah to help her husband and children to make amends such that when her martyred son petitions for their salvation on the day of Judgment, her son is not embarrassed.[97]

In another biography of a slain fighter, his sister drafted a lengthy description of her brother's virtues which she concludes with a "plea to all women," in which she tells them that "if you are a mother then educate your son. If you are a wife, then educate your husband. If you are a daughter, then educate your father. And if you are a sister, then educate your brother about the importance of jihad. This will be your success."[98] The sister of a fighter named Asmaar similarly effuses about how blessed she and her sisters are to have the great honor of being the sisters of a martyr.[99] His brother similarly claims that now "we can hold our heads up high because of his honorable sacrifice."[100] The mother of Abu Hafz notes that while she was at first hesitant to give her son permission for *jihad*, she now has "the great honor of being the mother of a martyr," and hopes that other mothers of the true believers will send their sons to fight the infidels everywhere.[101]

Oddly, while the martyrdom biographies are ostensibly intended to demonstrate the families' abnegation and selfless sacrificing of their beloved children, one motivation for this putative sacrifice is decidedly selfish: the family members believe that their martyred relative can take seventy of his relatives with him to heaven. In one martyrdom biography, written by one of the slain combatant's fellow fighters, the biographer explained the fighter has "already left us and is in Allah's heaven where he is lord of seventy-two maidens. And, he will get an entry ticket for seventy of his relatives and his status will be immediately below that of prophets. It is my prayer to Allah that he accepts his martyrdom. Amen."[102] (N.B.: The Urdu actually used the English word "ticket.")

Family members' egotistical preoccupation with their own afterlife is surprisingly recurrent in these biographies. For example, the mother of Abu
Saarya Muhammed Tahir said of her son's death that:

> Every living thing on this planet must die. Death is inevitable. What is wrong
> with joining jihad, particularly when death in jihad is the best death of all. It is
> a step to success both in this life and hereafter. Even if my son had not joined
> jihad he would have died anyways.... And the martyr can take 70 of his relatives
> along to Heaven.[103]

As such, not only do family members seem extremely motivated by this
ostensible reward in the afterlife; in some cases, they actually encourage their
loved ones to become a *shaheed* instead of a *ghazi* (veteran) because of the
status conferred upon the family members as well as this posthumous perqui-
site. The account of the mother of Shams-ul-Arifeen in the latter's death biography typifies this maternal encouragement. In it, the fighter's mother
expresses her "wish that he never returns, that he continues to fight, to fight,
to fight, until he is martyred."[104]

In another biography, the brother of the martyr explained that since love
on earth is ephemeral, "why not love something which both benefits us while
also pleasing Allah. This is why we should sacrifice ourselves in the path of
Allah: we get to heaven ourselves and we can also bring seventy of our relatives
along with us."[105] The brother noted that when they received the news of his
brother's *shahadat*, the family members said "All praises to Allah" and offered
prayers of gratitude.[106]

A martyr's younger sister highlighted a similar version of this in her own
statement about her brother in his biography. According to her:

> If Allah wills, the time of judgment will come. Everyone will be sweating. At that
> time a bleeding martyr will come before Allah. Allah will smile upon him and
> ask why he is in such a state. The martyr will respond that Allah "you understand
> well why I am in this state." Allah will respond "yes you tell the truth. I know all
> what is apparent and what is hidden." Then Allah will tell the martyr "Ask and
> you shall receive." The martyr will then request of Allah "keep your promise and
> take my parents, my siblings and 70 other relatives to Heaven." Then Allah will
> tell him to "go and find them and then lead them to heaven."[107]

The fighters themselves remind family members of this reward as a way of
coercing them to behave in accordance with Ahl-e-Hadees prescriptions for
decorous behavior after their demise. Abu Talha wrote to his sister from the
border with Indian-administered Kashmir ("Occupied Kashmir" or
"*maqbooza* Kashmir" in Pakistani parlance) to explain his mission to her. In

this missive, the fighter explains that his goal is to "liberate the mothers and sisters of Kashmir from the tyrannical rule of these animals, to help those in distress."[108] In this letter, he offers several behaviorial suggestions to her and the rest of the family:

> You people should offer prayers regularly five times a way, and stay away from lies, back biting and fraud. Also steer clear of idle talk and stay away from these useless congregations, instead spend your time in remembering Allah. Recite holy *Quran* in the morning and in the evening and also pray for me and other Mujahideen that Allah grants them determination and makes them successful. Before going to sleep, hold yourself accountable for the deeds of the day if you have pained someone, or if you have called someone bad names or if you have please confirm something over which you had no right. Please convey these thoughts of mine to everyone because these are the things that even the Prophet (PBUH) was very particular about. He would forgive everyone and so should you. Also tell the brothers that they should never usurp someone else's money. Even if you wrongfully take a single rupee, on the day of Judgment this act can drag you to hell for eternity. That is why Allah says all sins can be forgiven but not in which you usurp someone's money. Also offer prayers with patience and by understanding each and every word that you utter during it. And *Quran* says that there ARE bad tidings for those who do not understand the words they offer during their prayers. A lot of people do not know what is the meaning and objective of their prayers, we should focus on what you offer during the prayers and what is right and what is not. If you think my words carry weight then please act upon them. May Allah grant you the courage to act upon this conviction.

> Dear sister, a martyr can recommend 70 people for entry into heaven and if you heed my words then on the Day of Judgment I will recommend you. I miss you and want to meet you, that I shall do on the gates of heaven.[109]

In another example, Abu Ali Shaheed requests his brother to go to Afghanistan with JuD for twenty-one days (implying one of JuD's twenty-one day training programs) such that he can understand the meaning of being an adherent of the Ahl-e-Hadees tradition and improve his knowledge of his faith. He also instructs his sister to observe *purdah* wherever she goes, noting that that this is what garners respect for women. He offers the interesting observation that "one woman may take up to four men along with her to hell."[110]

Such lengthy and intrusive lists of proscribed and prescribed behavior are very common in these biographies. Fighters will often tell the females in their family to observe *purdah* (wearing of veils and traveling outside only with a male relative) and to encourage their children and siblings to embrace the life of *jihad*. Sometimes they will encourage male family members to avoid looking at or harassing women. Family members are generally encouraged to pray and fast and avoid un-Islamic activities such as listening to secular music, watching television, indulging in photos, and they are enjoined to avoid interest and live in a financially responsible way.[111]

Finally, another means through which LeT develops institutional support from the fighters' family is notifying them of fighters' deaths. The accounts of these notifications suggest that they are deeply significant—almost sacred— affairs. In fact, accounts of the commanders going to the family's home to notify them of their loss is highly reminiscent of sober formalities with which conventional militaries notify the families of those slain in warfare. In many of the posthumous martyr biographies, the writers claim that top leaders of LeT deliver the news to the families in person. This is consistent with findings of Abou Zahab and Roy, who report that district officials, along with regional officials and a number of LeT fighters, personally visit the martyr's home to announce and celebrate the news of his auspicious death.[112] Moreover, because the purpose of LeT publishing such accounts is to recruit other families and fighters, whether they are true is less important than that the readers believe them to be true.

In part due to the fighter's last gift to his family and in part due to explicit instructions from LeT, the family members purport not to mourn their lost loved one. One fighter, for example, tells his family members that they will "realise the importance of this sacrifice when, on doomsday, I will make you enter paradise along with seventy other relatives. Please don't mourn my death, because you will receive congratulatory remarks and advise the same to other mothers."[113] Consequently, many of these biographies describe the celebrations that the family holds upon learning of their son's sacrifice. If celebrations are not explicitly mentioned in the biographies, there is frequent mention to the family members serving milk and/or sweets on the occasion of learning of their family member's martyrdom. (In the Punjab, serving milk is an important way of honoring guests. LeT prohibits mourning, citing the occasions when the prophet chided women for lamenting their husbands' death on the battlefield).[114] Sometimes the festivities are characterized as a celebration of their son's marriage to the *huris*, celestial maidens.[115]

For example, in the January 1994 issue of *Mujallah ad-Dawa*, we learn that Azam Cheema and several local LeT officials from Faisalabad went to a local mosque in the hometown of a slain fighter named Iftikhar Ahmed, whose *kuniyat* was Abu Abdullah. Ahmed's mother, upon learning that a group of *mujahideen* were at the mosque, went there herself. Upon seeing the men whom she referred to as "Iftikhar's colleagues," she asked about the well-being of her son. In response, they asked, "Mother! Where did he go?" She responded that he went to occupied Kashmir. One of the *mujahideen* then asked her why he went there and she said he went to "attain martyrdom." At that point, one of the men informed her that her son had achieved martyrdom. To demonstrate the strong support of his mother, the biography states that his mother declared "Praise be to Allah" three times. After wiping her eyes, she went silent and then declared that "you all are my son's friends and have come here with news of his martyrdom." Following her son's wishes, she invited them to the family's home and served them milk.[116]

The family is also instructed to prohibit anyone from coming to the home to condole since lamenting for the martyr will cause him great pain in the afterlife. His brothers are told to join the *jihad* and to "not let my Kalashnikov fall." They are encouraged to avenge the death and defilement of the Muslim women of Kashmir at the hands of non-Muslims. Men are exhorted to maintain long hair and a beard and to wear their *shalwars* (baggy trousers) above their ankles. Women are instructed to observe *purdah* by staying within the *char divari* (four walls of the home), and to embrace the *burqa* along with socks and gloves.[117] During these affairs, the parents of the martyrs are expected to be proud to have been so blessed by Allah with a son who is a martyr. The spectacle successfully achieves the goal of motivating further volunteers to come forward.[118]

Next, LeT reaches out to the family and community from which the fighter hails through the offering of funerary prayers. These prayers are almost always offered in the absence of the body because there is usually no way of retrieving the fighter's remains from where he died. Usually, the bodies are buried in Kashmir (or wherever they died). LeT officials, including high-ranking ones such as Zafar Iqbal, Hafiz Saeed, and Zaki ur Rehman Lakhvi, routinely offer the funerary prayers. Their participation in the event renders it a religiopolitical meeting, rather than a simple opportunity to celebrate the martyrdom of a slain LeT fighter. LeT popularized the *ghaibana namaz-i-janaza*, or funeral prayer for the missing. These ceremonies are typically held in a sports field or some similar location, to accommodate the large crowds that assemble for the occasion.[119] By maintaining contact with the families even after the fighter has died, LeT ensures that the family remains amenable to the organization and the Ahl-e-Hadees ideology. LeT hopes to encourage families to "give" other sons to the *jihad* as well as to present themselves as model LeT families that will inspire others in their social and familial network.

The *shaheed* biographies frequently detail the moving and inspiring nature of the prayers and speeches offered by LeT's luminaries at these events. The biographies often claim that large crowds assemble to hear the allocutions of LeT leaders and commanders as well as the funerary prayers. During these prayers, LeT leaders emphasize the importance of *jihad* and the specific sacrifices of the particular fighter. On these occasions, national as well as local leaders read *jihadi* poems and even sing *jihadi* songs. (In fact, this is an important genre of LeT publications.) On some occasions, the biography indicates that politicians, such as members of the provincial assembly, attend these funerals.[120] Finally, the martyr's will is read aloud by his next of kin. These wills are short and tend to be very similar. They beseech their family members to destroy their television sets and CD players because the music and film accessed through these media reflect the corrosive "Hindu culture" decried by LeT and to follow the sartorial and behavioral prescriptions and proscriptions noted at length above.

The organization also shores up familial support financially. While it is fairly well known that *tanzeems* compensate their fighters' families, there are no reliable data for the amounts received. However, Rana claims that fighters receive a monthly stipend of Rs. 1,500 (USD$25).[121] My previous survey of 141 militant families also found evidence of several kinds of death benefits, including; one time and recurring payouts by Pakistan's intelligence agency, the ISI, as well as various kinds of payments from the *tanzeem* in which the fighter died.[122] These ranged from one-time sums of several thousand rupees, to recurring gifts over several years on occasions such as Eid. Some of the *shaheed* biographies that I use here note that the family receives a payment when their family member dies in combat, although we never learn the amounts. Sometimes the biography makes mention of the stipend in order to demonstrate the morality of the fighter in question. For example, the mother of Abu Sarya explains in his death biography that "when he was offered an honorarium by *Amir* Sahib [his commander], he refused because he was not interested in worldly things. When *Amir* Sahib gave him the stipend, he donated it all to the fund. He instructed his family that even if he is martyred they should not accept the honorarium either."[123]

I have also previously found that in certain cases, families reported that their marital alliances for surviving children had improved: 26 per cent of the sample said that they were able to arrange marriages for their daughters into better families, and 24 per cent said that they were able to arrange marriages for their boys into better families.[124] While these families were able to marry their children into better families ostensibly due to their status as a "*shaheed* family," most reported no such change. And despite these frequent hypergamous marital alliances, most families did not report an increase in dowry obtained for their surviving sons nor did they report a decrease in the dowry that had to pay for their daughters. These survey-based findings buttress the observation of Abou Zahab and Roy, based upon field work, that the "family of a martyr acquires a privileged position, since it receives material benefits and often money."[125]

In many ways, these various LeT efforts to recruit the family and to secure the family's continued support for the organization resemble those that scholars have observed in American street gangs. Levitt and Venkatesh observed that the Chicago drug gang they studied paid substantial sums to the families of slain members, often up to as high as USD$5,000, equivalent to three years' wages.[126] This sum was intended to cover the funeral costs, but also to compensate the family for their loss. Levitt and Venkatesh found that gang leaders believed these payments to be extremely important "both to maintain community support for the gang and, because in the words of one gang leader, 'You got to respect family.'[127] LeT's cultivation of families seems very similar. After all, the organization hopes to continue drawing from the community in general but also the family in particular.

Finally, and perhaps most importantly, fathers and mothers of the martyrs are invited to attend LeT's annual meeting, where more than 100,000 people congregate. (Usually these congregations take place at Muridke but on a few occasions they have been held in Pattoki, also outside of Lahore.) Perhaps the most important illustration of the extent to which LeT goes to cultivate women is the elaborate set of arrangements that take place at LeT's annual meeting. First, LeT provides extensive logistical support to the women who want to attend the conference by providing them free bus transport. In addition, the organization has had to construct separate spaces that were safe and suitable for women and children, because LeT observes *purdah* of the voice—that is women's voices are not to be heard in public.[128] LeT also maintains a trained uniformed cadre of female security agents who are responsible for thoroughly checking the personal belongings of all who arrive in the women's camp, including body searches. Clearly, it would be easier for LeT to simply exclude them. That the organization goes to such lengths to accommodate women underscores the importance the organization ascribes to female participation.

During the annual meeting, women engage in a variety of activities. The mothers of martyrs address the women in attendance about their own losses and impress upon them the importance of giving their sons to *jihad*.

Furthermore, they listen to the speeches of LeT's male leadership, which are piped into their tent through a public address system. During one such meeting in 2002, a recorded speech by Hafiz Saeed was played. (He could not address the meeting in person because he was under detention.) In that speech, he addressed the thousands of women and men at the annual gathering:

> My honorable sisters, you have sacrificed a lot. You have sacrificed your sons for the sake of the deen [faith], and indeed your sacrifices are the most significant for our times. God needs even greater sacrifices. Get ready: prepare this genera-tion. I remember the mother I met in a village when I went to lead the funeral prayer for her martyred son. After the funeral I went to give comfort to the grieving mother, but that elderly woman said to me, "My son became a martyr. I have a younger son who looks like my martyred son. I want the younger one to follow the same path and become a martyr. I am a poor widow; I have done hard labor to bring these sons up. Now I have heard the call of jihad. I have no money to give, but I have this treasure, these sons. Take my second son, and when he is martyred I will have the third one ready." Muslim sisters, you have the greater responsibility in the mission of jihad; men give money, but you give your sons. Your sacrifice, your hard work, is what keeps the jihad going.[129]

Whether or not Hafiz Saeed is recounting a genuine meeting with a widow, the narrative is powerful. After all, in Pakistan, a widow has only her sons to take care of her. That she is willing to give all of her sons to *jihad* is a powerful evocation of sacrifice and a testament to her personal/maternal commitment to protect her fellow Muslims in Kashmir.

Conclusions and Implications

Although LeT purports to be a "Kashmiri *tanzeem*," very few of its recruits actually come from Kashmir; rather, the vast majority of them are Punjabi. In contrast to common perceptions, LeT does not predominantly recruit from Pakistan's seminaries (*madaris*) although LeT's members appear to be more likely to attend a *madrassah* than Pakistani men overall. However, it seems as if their *madrassah* attendance comes later in life relative to those who do so in childhood. Overall, LeT cadres in this dataset are much less likely to be illiter-ate, and much more likely to be substantially better educated than their Pakistani or even Punjabi counterparts. Despite being well-educated, the fighters in this database are more likely to be under-employed or unemployed compared to their peers, and more likely to be employed in jobs for which they are overqualified. Their employment prospects may be an explanatory factor in their recruitment, or these fighters may have employment options that afford them the freedom to engage in LeT-related activities, even if they are over-qualified for such jobs.

LeT aims to recruit not only young men, but entire families. To do so, they cultivate women in particular. The group provides stipends as well as death benefits. It stays in touch with the families after the youth's martyrdom to keep them in the fold of LeT's brand of Ahl-e-Hadees. They invite the fathers and mothers of martyrs to attend the annual *ijtema* (large gathering), where they attest to the heroism of their sons. Families attain within LeT, and society in general, considerable social standing as the family of a martyr. Females in LeT also sustain prestige and political roles that are ordinarily denied to women in Pakistan. Understanding the statuses that families, and women in particular, garner from association with LeT is an important aspect of the organization's operations that remains poorly understood and requires more attention and research.

Unfortunately, most efforts to engage in so-called "countering violent extremism" programmatic activities and research focus upon males of military age. This focus in Pakistan is particularly misplaced. Most empirical research on the determinants of support for Islamist violence in Pakistan (or elsewhere) either excludes gender or merely includes it as a control variable. Scholars who study respondent-level explanations of such support have not made gender the subject of their inquiry. When gender has been examined—either as an independent or control variable—it seems to matter. Shepherd and Fair, using Pew Global Attitudes Survey data from 2002, found that women in Pakistan were more likely to be supportive of suicide attacks than were men.[130] Using data from a nationally representative survey of 907 Pakistani adults, Shapiro and Fair found that women were more supportive of nationalist militant groups; however, gender was insignificant in predicting support for Al Qaeda, the Taliban or the so-called "Kashmiri *tanzeems*."[131] Goldstein, Hamza, and Fair, using a large dataset of 16,279 respondents obtained from a 2011–12 nationally representative survey of Pakistanis, found that while men were much more supportive of the Afghan Taliban than were women, women were more supportive of the Sipah-e-Sahaba-e-Pakistan.[132] Similarly, Littman, Nugent, and Fair used the same dataset but a different empirical approach to find that women were more supportive of Islamist militant groups than were men.[133] This collection of empirical findings—at least for Pakistan—coupled with what we know about how at least this one militant group targets women, strongly suggests that gender should be considered as a crucial factor in fomenting support for and even participation in Islamist militancy.

6

THE DOMESTIC POLITICS OF LET

Most scholars of Lashkar-e-Tayyaba/Jamaat ud Dawah (LeT/JuD) tend to view the *tanzeem* as a proxy militia for the Pakistani army.[1] While the organization certainly performs this role, this narrow understanding undervalues the full scope of activities it performs, alongside the full range of political and social perquisites that the organization affords the Pakistani state, and thus, the importance that the state attaches to it. Presumably, the formation of the Milli Muslim League (MML) will further entrench this alliance between the state and the LeT/JuD.

In this chapter, I demonstrate that LeT/JuD performs a critical role in assisting the deep state to secure its domestic objectives as well as its foreign policies in India and Afghanistan, as previously noted by Tankel, Kapur, and Fair among others.[2] As already demonstrated, like Hamas in Palestine or the Tamil Tigers of Sri Lanka, LeT/JuD provides social services such as, *inter alia*, education, disaster relief, and medical facilities. However, unlike other terrorist groups that behave in this way to win hearts and minds of the populations they claim to represent, LeT/JuD has not contested elections until very recently in August 2017 because it had long rejected democratic governance and claimed to have no interest in governing Pakistan. While the organization argued for the supreme reign of Islam throughout the world for nearly three decades, the organization had been silent about who should govern this ulterior Islamic state. This raises the question: for whom was LeT/JuD winning Pakistani hearts and minds before it launched the MML in August 2017? This also raises the, regrettably unanswerable, question when was the idea of JuD floating a party conceived? One could build an argument, based upon its involvement in social service provision that this was long in making. Alternatively, one could argue that the promulgation of the MML stems from the army's lack of political options after Nawaz Sharif's stunning win in 2013, the army's distaste for the Pakistan Peoples Party and the failure of Imran Khan to become a viable political candidate with national standing. Only time will tell if any of these readings is accurate. However, the launching of the MML is a confirmation of an argument that I have advanced for many years, namely that the JuD is just as important to the deep state for its domestic politics as it is for helping the Pakistani state to secure its objectives in India and Afghanistan.[3]

The domestic politics of LeT/JuD have been neglected by analysts, but as I show here, the organization is an important domestic partner of the deep state. It performs the crucial domestic role of ideologically combatting those Islamist militant groups which are targeting the Pakistani state and its citizenry, such as the various Deobandi groups and the Islamic State Khorasan Province described in the introduction to this volume. Symbiotically, the state provides enormous support to the *tanzeem* and even encourages the domestic and international press to cover the group's varied domestic service provisions. In fact, the state seeks to bolster JuD's public support as a bulwark against international pressure to act against the organization. A recent example of this is afforded by events of late January 2017, when the United States pressured Pakistan to act against the organization. Pakistan announced that it had placed Hafiz Saeed under house arrest. In response, the hashtag "#HafizSaeedServesHumanity" trended on social media, and crowds came out to protest the move ostensibly because of the social work he and his organization delivers.[4]

Another example of such domestic propaganda is provided by a member of the Hindu Panchayat from Thar (in Sindh), who explained that "Saeed may be a terrorist for India or United States of America. However, for the people of Thar, he has proven himself to be a great philanthropist."[5] This domestic work also explains in some measure why the *tanzeem* recruits and trains far more activists than it will ever deploy to the battlefields of India or Afghanistan; instead of fighting *jihad*, these excess militarily-trained cadres are redeployed to the domestic battlefront, where they spread LeT/JuD's message of nonviolence and service within Pakistan. Appreciating this specific function of Let/JuD requires one to pay attention to the ideological moorings of the various militant groups operating in Pakistan. LeT, along with the Jamaat-e-Islami (JI)-associated Hizbul Mujahideen (HM), has never targeted

Pakistanis or the state whereas most Deobandi organizations have. In fact, the domestic groups that have turned against the state are exclusively Deobandi.

These Deobandi terrorist groups commit most of the sectarian and communal attacks in Pakistan. The so-called Pakistani Taliban are Deobandi, and it draws from numerous other Deobandi groups including those that are sectarian (Lashkar-e-Jhangvi (LeJ, Army of Jhangvi)/Sipah-e-Sahaba-e-Pakistan (SSP), Ahl-e Sunnat Wal Jamaat (ASWJ)), allies of the Afghan Taliban, as well as those that the Inter-Services Intelligence (ISI) cultivated for operations in India, such as Jaish-e-Muhammad (JeM), Harkat-ul-Ansar (HuA)/Harkat-ul-Mujahideen (HuM). Pakistan's Deobandi militant groups have long targeted Pakistan's Shia and Ahmadi populations.[6] Deobandi militants also began attacking Sufi shrines in Pakistan in the mid-2000s, as those who frequent them tend to follow the Barelvi school of Islam, which usually includes embracing mysticism, revering saints and venerating their shrines and seeking the living saint (*pir*) of the shrine to intercede on the devotee's behalf with respect to investments, employment prospects, pregnancy, illnesses and the like. Many, if not most Pakistanis are believed to be Barelvi, although there are no reliable data to buttress this perception. Pakistanis generally hold these shrines in high esteem, as these Sufi saints brought Islam to South Asia.[7] Deobandis denounce these mystical practices and beliefs as un-Islamic accretions derived from Hinduism.[8] Deobandi militant groups also attack Pakistan's non-Muslim minorities, such as Christians, Hindus, and Sikhs. The Islamic State has drawn its Pakistani cadres from these Deobandi groups, particularly those Pakistani Taliban commanders who had roots in the anti-Shia groups like LeJ and SSP. While Deobandis perpetrate most terrorist attacks in Pakistan, there are important exceptions. Barelvis, for example, have been often involved in acts of political violence over blasphemy issues in Pakistan because of their extreme reverence for prophet Muhammad.[9] And it was Barelvis who shut down the government in November 2017 over the apparent dilution of the oath that persons must take to contest elections in which they affirm the finality of the prophet.[10] In recent years, minor Shia militias have formed to defend themselves against Deobandi militants in the tribal area of Kurram.[11]

LeT/JuD provides an important ideological competitor to these groups that are killing tens of thousands of Pakistanis, because LeT/JuD vigorously opposes sectarianism and the violence that sectarianism fosters, even if LeT/JuD shares the Deobandi view that these heterodox practices are not acceptable. In October 2015, Hafiz Saeed denounced sectarian violence arguing that "at present, we are at war and we need to maintain unity in our ranks" and declared that the organization will "not accept any action against certain seminaries in the name of war on terror."[12] He also denounced the Islamic State as an "evil" that is spreading throughout the Islamic world. Not only does LeT/JuD reject sectarian conflict, it also rejects the notion of *takfir*, or the process of rendering a Muslim a *kafir* and thus a suitable target for violence. In fact, JuD is so opposed to this concept that it has published an entire volume criticizing *takfir*, titled *Masalah-i-takfir aur is ke usul o zavabit* (The Problem of Takfir and its Terms and Conditions).[13]

JuD also opposes communal violence within Pakistan. Thus, even while JuD denounces Hindus and Christians as polytheists who are worthy targets of *jihad* outside of Pakistan, within Pakistan JuD does not advocate violence against them; rather, their conversion through *dawah*, *tabliqh*, and the provision of relief and public services.[14] Perhaps incongruously, even while declaring that the *jihad* against Hindu India must continue, Hafiz Saeed declared that "his organisation will not allow destruction of Hindu temples and other holy places of non-Muslims in the country."[15]

In this chapter, I first review the most important sources that I mobilize in this analysis to demonstrate JuD's varied arguments for abjuring violence against Pakistanis irrespective of their creed. Next, I describe JuD's beliefs about why it wages *jihad* and the circumstances under which it does so. Following that, I mobilize principal JuD publications to exposit the organization's domestic political role which I submit the Pakistani deep state highly values. I next turn to JuD's views of Christians and Hindus within Pakistan. In the penultimate section, I describe the symbiosis that exists between JuD/LeT and the state, and the efforts that the state has undertaken to bolster its support while protecting it from international demands that Pakistan shut it down. I conclude this chapter with several observations about the ways in which the deep state continues to manage LeJ/JuD as one of several important key militant groups, even though LeT/JuD is its most disciplined *jihadi* organization abroad and a pro-state, quietist organization at home.

Key Sources for this Chapter

Many of LeT/JuD's publications on this subject of appropriate *jihad* tend to reiterate similar messages. To detail JuD's beliefs about how Muslims should interact with other Muslims, I draw upon three particularly important texts. The first is JuD's *minimum opus* titled *Hum Kyon Jihad Kar Rahe Hain*, which translates as "Why We Are Waging Jihad."[16] (This pamphlet has been published many times. I cannot say for certain whether or not the version I have differs from that published in other years.) We know from the preface of this booklet that bin Muhammad drafted an essay by the same title in *Majalla-ul-Dawah* (one of JuD's magazines); however, he does not provide the date of this earlier publication. At the insistence of friends, he tells his readers that he wanted to have this essay published independently of the magazine with important revisions and additions. Notably, he tells us that he appended a speech "Excuses for Waging Jihad" (*"Rah-e-jihad-se faraar ke bahaane"*) which he gave at Muridke on another unspecified occasion. Bin Muhammad wrote this pamphlet in a Socratic style in which a quester first poses a query, which the narrator answers through a combination of a selective recounting of events in the Quran, *Sunnat*, and *hadees* as well as historical and contemporary events that give salience to the textual references that he mobilized. At first blush, the pamphlet addresses the efforts of so-called pious Muslims who refute the necessity of waging *jihad* under various pretenses. However, in advancing these arguments, bin Muhammad makes a very specific case about waging *jihad* beyond Pakistan. In this pamphlet, he identifies specifically who should be the object of *jihad*, and why and—most importantly—who should not be the object of *jihad* and the reasons for their exemptions.

This pamphlet argues that no matter how questionable or even wrong a person's practice of Islam may be, if the individual in question is *kalima-go* (one who has uttered the *kalima* or affirmation that there is no god but Allah and Muhammad is his prophet), he or she are should not be killed. The author argues that anyone who has said the *kalima* will never deny the supreme authority of Allah. Therefore, such persons should be rehabilitated through *dawah* rather than be murdered. This puts the organization in direct opposition to the Deobandi groups and Islamic State which practice *takfir*, and which believe that once one is declared a *kafir*, they are worthy objects of violence.[17] (N.B: Deobandis are not doctrinally *"takfiri,"* although they behave as if they are through their frequent use of declaring persons to be *kuffar* and thus deserving violence or death.)

This raises the interesting question of whether or not Ahmadis are *kalima-go*. Ahmadis continue to endure a campaign of deadly violence against them, mostly perpetrated by Deobandi militant groups as well as individuals motivated by the belief that killing them will confer upon them spiritual rewards to the murderer owing to their *"wajib ul qatal"*[18] status.[19] Despite the widespread antagonism against Ahmadis and the prominent campaign of violence against them, I found no mention of Ahmadis in any of the numerous JuD publications reviewed for this research project. Given JuD's political savvy and the growing salience of this matter in Pakistan's domestic politics, this silence strikes me as strategic rather than accidental. If one assumes that Ahmadis are *kalima-go* and accept the supremacy of Allah, then Ahmadis should not be killed; rather they should be treated as others who behave deviantly in Pakistan, principally through *dawah* and *tabligh*. The problem with Ahmadis is that while they do say the textual-equivalent of *kalima*, when they do so many Pakistanis believe that they are committing an act of apostasy. In fact, Ahmadis are not permitted to use the terms "*namaz*" to describe their prayer, "*masjid*" to describe their place of worship or even the word "*Quran*" to describe their holy book. They do so at the risk of being charged with blasphemy and/or being murdered by vigilantes.[20]

This discontinuity between what Ahmadis say they do and what ordinary Pakistanis believe about their claims opens up an obvious ambiguity about what LeT means when the organization counsels Pakistanis against murdering anyone who claims to be "*kalima-go*." Unfortunately, the organization publicly obfuscates this matter and refuses to clarify this question. I specifically asked JuD spokespersons for clarification on this issue dozens of times over at least two years. On each occasion, the organization deflected my question and refused to answer it. The closest clarification came from Tabish Qayyuum, who was the head of JuD's cyber cell and is now the spokesperson for the MML. Qayyum refused to inveigh upon whether he considered them *kalima-go* or other theological questions; however, citing Pakistan's constitution, he explained that they should be allowed to practice their faith as a non-Muslim minority.[21]

JuD likely prefers this ambiguity because it neither wishes to encourage violence against Ahmadis nor does it wish to incur the wrath of the myriad Pakistanis who believe that Ahmadis are apostates and thus "*wajib ul qatal*." On the one hand, a reasonable Muslim may consider Ahmadis to be *kalima-go* or at least concede that Ahmadis recognize the supremacy of Allah even if they do not share the mainstream view of the ordinal finality of the prophet. On the other hand, such ordinary reasonable Muslims may in fact be offended that Ahmadis could say the *kalima* and engage in other Muslim rituals. It is likely that the organization remains silent on this exigency, preferring this ambiguous situation to prevail, because LeT's leadership likely believe Ahmadis to be *wajib ul qatal*; however, because the *tanzeem* serves at the pleasure of the Pakistani state it must maintain its position of neither committing nor advocating violence against anyone in Pakistan. This is yet another example of how LeT circumscribes its organizational convictions within the hard demands of its sponsors in Pakistan's deep state.

The second important volume that I draw upon is *Difa-i-Jihad* (Defense of Jihad) by Ubaidurrahman Muhammadi (1998).[22] In this book, the editor of Dar-ul-Andulus (Muhammad Saifullah Khalid) offered a publisher's note and Hafiz Saeed himself authored the foreword to the volume. Saeed's imprimatur upon this volume is extremely important because it demonstrates his linkages to JuD's violent mission even though he and Pakistani authorities deny these connections. This volume is structured similarly to *Hum Kyon Jihad Kar Rahain Hain* in that it is generally structured around questions posed by an anonymous inquirer and the answers to those questions are given by a posited, learned *mujahid*. While there is considerable overlap between the texts, they both have distinct focuses as is apparent in the below disquisition.

The third major work from which I draw in this chapter is Rabbani's 2015 book *Masalah-i-takfir aur is ke usul o zavabit* (The Problem of Takfir and its Terms and Conditions), henceforth *Masalah-i-takfir*. This volume must be situated within ongoing and tendentious debates among the various groups of Salafis described in Chapter 4, namely: quietists, Islamists and *jihadis*. Two issues, which generate friction among quietists and *jihadis* in particular, pertain first to the appropriate treatment of Muslim leaders who do not impose *shariat* even when they have the means to do so, and second, to the most punctilious and methodologically rigorous application of *takfir* and those who are qualified to do so. Salafi *jihadis* will denounce those Salafis who are opposed to violent actions against wayward Muslim leaders and/or to those who are highly scrupulous and meticulous in the application of *takfir*. One of the pejorative monikers that *jihadis* will use to denigrate those Salafis who demur violent opposition to leadership and reckless use of *takfir* is the expression *Murji'i*, which references a now defunct sect that is reviled because of its views of *iman* (faith) and *kufr* (unbelief). *Murji'i* are so-called because originally, they applied the notion of *irja'* (postponement) to political conflicts. By the eighth century, they also began applying this concept to people's faith, meaning that they deferred judgement on an individual's *iman*, believing that god alone is fit to judge this matter. Unwilling to pass judgement, the *Murji'i* tended to be loyal to rulers, at least to the extent that they did not support the overthrow of their regimes.[23]

A second controversial matter pertained to how the *Murji'i* conceptualized *iman* (faith) and *kufr* (disbelief). Although there were numerous sub-sects within the *Murji'i*, they generally believed that faith "consisted of belief in the heart and its confirmation by speech of the tongue, thus excluding acts."[24] This was particularly germane when questions arose as to when a person became an unbeliever and when *takfir* of such a person was warranted. In contrast to the *Khawarij*, the *Murji'i* believed that not all major sins warranted excommunicating someone from Islam unless the person verbally confirmed his or her disbelief (*kufr*). Some *Murji'i* extrapolated this reasoning to include acts of *shirk* (polytheism) such as worshipping other gods. Whereas their Sunni contemporaries view such actions as undeniable proof of *kufr*, the *Murji'i* contended that verbal confirmation of *kufr* was required to legitimize *takfir*, even under such extreme cases as committing *shirk*. They also believed that *iman* was an unchangeable quantity: it either existed or did not. A person's actions could not increase or decrease the amount of *iman* he or she possessed.[25]

The *Murji'i* were diametrically opposed to a contemporaneous group, the *Khawarij*, who believed that sinful Muslims were *kuffar* (unbelievers) and expelled them from their community and even fought them. Believing such Muslims to be *kuffar*, they applied passages from the Quran to justify *jihad* against them, including the *Khaleefa* if necessary. (They fought Ali, the Third *Khaleefa*, and assassinated him in 661 CE.) The *Khawarij* believed, in-line with most mainstream *Salafis*, that *iman* consists of three elements: assent of the faith in the heart, verbal confirmation of this faith with the tongue, and corresponding action with the body's limbs. However, the *Khawarij* tended to place more emphasis on acts than do mainstream Sunni Islam generally or Salafis in particular.[26] The conflict between *Khawarij* and *Murji'i* should be apparent: they disagree on what constitutes *iman* and *kufr*. Whereas for *Murji'i*, sinful acts are not necessarily enough to warrant *takfir*, they do warrant *takfir* for *Khawarij*. Another point of serious departure for the two groups is the quality of *iman* itself: whereas *Murji'i* do not permit the possibility that it could increase or decrease, *Khawarij* believe that sinful acts diminished *iman* while good deeds increased it.

In writing and publishing *Masalah-i-takfir* both Rabbani and the editor have several specific motivations. First, as explained by Javed Siddiqui, an editor at Dar-ul-Andulus, the book aims to explain what *takfir* is and how it has been abused in recent years to the severe detriment of Islam and Muslims. Siddiqui writes of the current situation that:

> ... some mischief-makers and those they lead astray sow the seeds of hatred for Islam while pretending to promote it. They declare fellow-Muslims infidels and incite to murder and mayhem. They bring a bad name to all Muslims and present

Islam as terrifying, compassionless, and hateful through their malicious and diabolical approach to religion.

In recent decades, there has been a sharp rise in the scourge of *takfir*, i.e. the declaration of certain Muslims as infidels. A number of Islamic countries have had to deal with a growing misguided population of young and ignorant Muslims who have no exposure to the intricate crafts of religious interpretation; they know little about the ways of the early Muslims, and they interpret Islamic injunctions as they please, thereby leading the masses astray.

The early Muslims and the Hadees compilers have elaborated the principles that govern the sensitive matter of *takfir*. In the light of these principles, a number of important issues involved in *takfir* have already been predetermined i.e. the actions that cause one to exit the realm of Islam, when this person is to be executed, who is to decide the matter, and who is to carry out the conviction.[27]

In the forward to his volume, Rabbani himself argues that this abuse of *takfir* poses an existential threat to the *ummat*. Rabbani opines that:

In modern times, perfidy has taken numerous forms and threatens to destroy the Muslim *ummat*. This poison has entered the bloodstream of society in the form of indecency, sexual freedom, exploitation of women in advertising, gender-bending, soothsayers, and murder and lawlessness. However, the most dangerous and terrifying form of all is *takfir*, the act of declaring Muslims infidels, inciting violence and pillage against them, and then releasing videos of the accused's merciless slaughter in order to terrorize the masses. The young, the ignorant, and the foolish are swept up in this wave of terror. Infidels take full advantage of the situation and employ those who appear to be pious, religious, observant, and God-fearing towards their insidious ends.[28]

While Rabbani and his publishers at Dar-ul-Andulus want to dampen the dangerous enthusiasm for *takfir* against ordinary citizens and rulers alike, there is a second motivation for this book. Namely, Rabbani and Dar-ul-Andulus want to confront those Salafi critics who accuse JuD of being a modern-day *Murji'i* because the *tanzeem* opposes insurrection against Muslim leaders and is extremely judicious about who can be subject to *takfir*, and who is adequately knowledgeable and appropriately trained to make such a grave determination—much less execute the individual in question. Rabbani specifically takes issue with a volume "compiled by an ignorant individual, [which] has been posted to various Ahl-i-Hadith platforms and madrassas" titled *Murji'i-tul-'Asr* (The Murji'i of the Era). Rabbani explains that "Righteous scholars started speaking out against the plague of *takfir*, however a year and a half after our talk in Sialkot, a virtual book titled *Murji'i-tul-'Asr* surfaced on the Internet."[29] Rabbani was concerned with the way in which it promoted *takfir* and how it denounced Salafi scholars who espouse different views on the subject as modern-day *Murji'i*, and he was particularly distressed that his organization, JuD, appeared to be tied to this publication.[30] Thus, Rabbani seeks to clear JuD's name of any association with this publication *Murji'i-tul-'Asr*.

Rabbani also aims to destabilize the linkage between Ahl-e-Hadees scholars and the mis-use of *takfir*. To do so, he begins his volume with an epistolic exchange between Rabbani and a Quranic scholar, Hafiz Salahuddin Yusuf, who was referenced in *Murji'i-tul-'Asr*. The foreword of this volume presents Yusuf's exposition of *takfir*, which forms an important part of JuD's domestic politics. Rabbani is also motivated by his alarm that *takfir* enthusiasts have arrogated to themselves the authority to excommunicate Islamic scholars who reject the claims of ordinary activists to apostatize individuals. Finally, Rabbani also wants to make clear that activists of JuD are not in fact modern-day *Murji'i*s in that they do not oppose all instances of *takfir*; rather, JuD believes that *takfir* must be done in the most scrupulous way possible regarding evidentiary standards articulated for it in the Quran and *Sunnat* and that *takfir* should be carried out exclusively by those who are properly trained and versed in the evidentiary and procedural standards for doing so. This clearly puts JuD in conflict with the Deobandi groups as well as the Islamic State (IS) in Pakistan which have appropriated an unbridled right to excommunicate and execute whoever they deem appropriate objects of such courses of action.

While the above three texts address legitimate targets of *jihad*—all of which reside *beyond* Pakistan—a few texts deal with religious minorities within Pakistan, who are not objects of LeT's *jihad*. Instead, they are targets for conversion. The key text that exposits Lashkar's views of Hindus is *Hindu Customs Among Muslims*.[31] While JuD has published treatises upon Christianity (i.e. al-Rahman and Malakavi's 2007 *Isaiyat?* (What is Christianity?), which is an exposition of the Christian Bible),[32] these texts reveal more about what JuD thinks about Christianity than it does about those Christians who live in Pakistan, among Muslims. One text that does provide such insights into the question at hand is *Shahrah-e-Bahisht* (Highway to Paradise) by Maulana Amir Hamza.[33]

Why Wage Jihad and Under What Circumstances?

Both bin Muhammad's 2004 *Hum Kyon Jihad Kar Rahe Hain* (Why We Are Waging Jihad) and Ubaidurrahman Muhammadi's *Difa-i-Jihad* (Defense of Jihad) from 1998, address those Muslims who reject JuD's claim that *jihad* is appropriate for contemporary circumstances. In *Hum Kyon Jihad Kar Rahe Hain*, Bin Muhammad begins the pamphlet noting that the so-called *jihad* against the Soviets in Afghanistan in the 1980s rekindled the dormant spirit of *jihad* among Muslims in the globally-dispersed *ummat*. This revivified commitment to *jihad* roused the hopes of *jihad* proponents of extirpating *kufr* and upholding Islam. Under such circumstances, battling the disbelievers should have been easy had it not been for those Muslims who proffered multifarious intellectual arguments to delegitimize *jihad* by denouncing it as categorically prohibited by the Quran and *Sunnat* under existing circumstances.

Bin Muhammad bitterly bemoans that these Muslims offer restrictive terms and preconditions for waging *jihad* that simply cannot be met, and accuses them of preferring Muslims to live as slaves under the yoke of nonbelievers. He believes that these "esteemed Muslims who breed doubt and dissonance" have done more to undermine *jihadi* movements globally than have the *kuffar*.[34] Hafiz Saeed, the *amir* of JuD/Let, addresses the problem similarly in the "Publisher's Note" in Ubaidurrahman Muhammadi's *Difa-i-Jihad* when he writes:

> In these trying times, those who are dutiful and fortunate sacrifice their blood, their wealth, and their progeny for the struggle; but then there are those who fall prey to insidious propaganda and skepticism. They give hollow excuses to shirk their obligation. They present fallacious arguments to hinder the struggle. They say jihad in Kashmir goes against shariat. Furthermore, they say there is a lack of resources to combat the disbelievers. They insist it is wiser to focus the struggle against our Muslim leaders than waste time in Kashmir. These people are unconsciously aiding the enemy. Whereas the times call for a concerted effort to unify the Islamic nation to glorify the name of Allah and obliterate the hubris of disbelief; it is time to free the Muslim victims of conniving Hindus, eradicate the Jewish conspiracies against the ummat (Islamic nation), free Bait-ul-Muqaddis (Dome of the Rock) from occupiers, end global Christian domination, and make the true faith overpower all other false ideologies.[35]

Both Muhammadi's *Difa-i-Jihad* and Bin Muhammad's *Hum Kyon Jihad Kar Rahe Hain* contend that Muslims have become divided and weak because they abandoned *jihad*. Muhammadi argues that even though the "world belongs to Allah and his people have the right to rule it," disbelievers control most of the world and where they govern there is "rebellion, chaos, mischief."[36] This can be rectified if Muslims were to govern. For this reason, Muslims must emasculate disbelievers and coerce them until they pay the tribute (*jizya*) readily. Per this argument, "the path of jihad will make the world a peaceful place free of mischief."[37] In addition to this general state of the world is the second concern that when Muslims stopped going on proselytizing tours (*dawah*) and *jihad* missions "to the four corners of the earth," Muslim political and religious power declined and the *ummat* settled into sectarian discord. Muhammadi's *mujahid* explains to his inquirer that "During the reign of the pious caliphs, and many years after, *jihadi* missions were dispatched across the globe; nations fell before the might of Islam by Allah's grace, and the Islamic empire expanded in the east and west;" however, when Muslims ceased these campaigns, "the enemy marched into Muslim territory, stole their lands and subjected them to a bloodbath...Muslims were no longer victorious because their leaders came to love the luxuries of this world and grew to fear glories of death on the battle-field."[38] The *mujahid* narrator proceeds to recount the numerous Muslim empires that succumbed to Buddhists, Hindus, and Europeans, among others. Not only did Muslim empires fall because the leaders of those empires evaded their obligation to wage *jihad*, the world's Muslim population now live as slaves under non-Muslims and engage in sectarian bloodshed. The only way to revivify Muslims' corporate dignity and political power is through *jihad*, which alone will permit Muslims to break the enemy's will. Such an outcome will be propitious for Muslims specifically but also for non-Muslims who will live in a glorious, peaceful order once Muslims govern the earth.

Muhammadi uses an episode from the Afghan *jihad* to illustrate the organization's commitment to avoid fighting with other Muslims irrespective of personal or organizational costs. His posited inquirer asked the *mujahid* why MDI refused to aid Sheikh Jamil-al Rahman's (1939–91) emirate in Kunar, Afghanistan after the Soviet Union withdrew in 1998. During the anti-Soviet *jihad*, many Arab fighters fought under the leadership of Rahman, who had been a member of Gulbuddin Hekmatyar's Hizb-e-Islami (HI). Because of his tutelage of Arab fighters, he received financing from King Fahd of Saudi Arabia. (HI was funded by Pakistan's army and ISI after the Soviets withdrew from Afghanistan, because they adjudged that Hekmatyar could deliver an Afghanistan that would do Islamabad's bidding.) With his funding secure, Rahman left HI in 1986 or 1987 and set up the Jamaat-i-Dawahat-i-al-Quran wa-Sunna-yi-Afghanistan (Society for the Preaching of the Quran and Sunna in Afghanistan). As the name suggests, this party was close to the Ahl-e-Hadees, the *maslak* to which LeT/JuD affiliates. At the end of 1989, with HI his only rival in Kunar, Rahman proclaimed the establishment of an Islamic emirate of Kunar in January 1991. In the spring of 1991, HI lost its main bases in Kunar and its local leader, maulana Faqer Muhammad, was surrounded by Rahman's troops. Rahman, who was in Saudi Arabia, told his troops not to kill him but send him to Peshawar. With the presence of HI extirpated from Kunar, Hekmatyar launched an offensive on Rahman in alliance with several other *mujahideen* groups. Having lost the battle, Rahman fled to Bajour in Pakistan where he was eventually assassinated.[39]

Muhammadi picks up an uncomfortable aspect of this history: Markaz al-Dawah Irshad (MDI, Center for Preaching and Guidance) did not come to Rahman's assistance to defend his emirate even though the MDI was closely aligned ideologically to this emirate and had military camps in Kunar. Per Muhammadi's account, Rahman did not permit his soldiers to fight Hekmatyar's troops "because he despised infighting. Consequently, the people at Kunar did not confront their attackers."[40] Similarly, Muhammadi claims that it was Rahman who refused Zaki-ur-Rehman's assistance because, "after consulting with his comrades the sheikh [Rahman] told Zaki-ur-Rehman that his assistance was neither needed nor appropriate. This message was sent to our training camp Muaskar-e-Tayyaba [in Kunar], which is why our warriors never joined the battle."[41] In this interpretation of events, Sheikh Jamil-al Rahman "sacrificed his life but refused to permit civil war and treachery between Muslim factions."[42] Muhammadi uses this episode as an allegory to contemporary events where conspirators abound who wish to sow discord among different Muslims. Fighting *jihad* against the non-Muslim enemy is one important means of preventing this kind of fratricidal fighting among Muslims.

Considering the various sources of weakness in the *ummat*, Bin Muhammad asserts that *jihad* to fight the infidel is compulsory to achieve eight objectives. Moreover, this *jihad* must be fought until each of these eight objectives are achieved in full. Bin Muhammad does not provide any references from either the Quran, *hadees*, or *Sunnat* to support these eight objectives nor do they not derive logically from the Quranic verses cited in the text immediately preceding the litany of these eight desiderata, which are:

1. End of perfidy (*fitna*): By *fitna*, which has numerous definitions that imply strife or rebellion, the author refers to the ability of disbelievers to inhibit a person from accepting Islam through fear of harm or persecution or their ability to harm Muslims. *Jihad* is compulsory until all obstacles to accepting Islam are categorically eliminated everywhere.

2. Dominance of Islam: *Jihad* against the *kuffar* is compulsory until Islam is accepted and embraced everywhere and the law of Allah reigns supreme.

3. Collection of taxes imposed upon non-Muslims (*jizya*): *Jihad* is compulsory until all *kuffar* pay this tax or convert to Islam.

4. Defending the defenseless: *Jihad is* compulsory if anyone in the world is persecuted. The author implies that only the persecution of Muslims is germane.

5. Avenging Murder: Avenging the murder of a Muslim by the hands of a non-Muslim is compulsory. In contrast, in the event of the murder of a Muslim by a Muslim, religious compassion may prevail and the crime can be punished through paying compensation, or even pardoned.

6. Punishment for breaking a treaty with Muslims: The author implies that this obligation pertains to treaties between Muslims and non-Muslims. The author cites the examples of the prophet signing treaties with the Jewish tribes of Medina. When they broke those treaties, the prophet slaughtered the adult males and seized their women and children as concubines and slaves.

7. Fighting in Self-Defense: When a nation attacks Muslims, *jihad* is compulsory.

8. Freeing land occupied by infidels (*kuffar*): *Jihad* is required to oust the infidels and restore the land to Muslim control.

To demonstrate that the above-noted objectives remain unfulfilled or challenged, Bin Muhammad adumbrates numerous contemporary examples, many of which draw from Pakistan's security competition with India and the stylized version of history that the deep state espouses about the conflict it prosecutes with its neighbour (see Chapter 2). These examples seem calibrated to inflame the sentiments of the reader and curry his or her support for the armed struggle the author prescribes.

To address the first, second, and third conditions conjointly, bin Muhammad adduces that Muslims in Christian lands are persecuted due to their faith. He notes that the global economic market is discordant with Allah's prohibition on usury (interest). He further notes that nowhere do *kuffar* live as "*dhimmis*" (second class citizens), and paying *jizya* to Muslims. *Jizya*, for the author, is important because it demonstrates not only the manifest inferiority of non-Muslims but their acceptance of this diminished status. In fact, bin Mohamad draws upon a contentious issue in Pakistan's own history and its reliance upon loans from the International Monetary Fund, because of which Muslims are paying *jizya* to non-Muslims. *Jihad* therefore is not only necessary to end the humiliation of Muslims but also explicitly to humiliate non-Muslims.

With respect to the fourth condition, he identifies the persecution of innocent Muslims from lands as far flung as the Philippines, Chechnya, Bosnia, numerous states in Russia and China as well as in Kashmir and "Hindustan". The author's use of the word Hindustan, which is multivalent, merits some exposition. Originally it did not have religious connotations; rather, geographic and it referred to the land of the River Indus. Thus "Hindustanis" referred to those people who lived in South Asia because of the prominence of this river in the cultural history and geography of the South Asian subcontinent. Foreign observers would use the expression "Hindustani Muslims" to distinguish Muslims from South Asia from those of the Middle East or other areas. In current Pakistani discourse, the word is often used to denote modern India as the "land of the Hindus." This is most certainly the way in which the author intends to use this word here. The use of "Hindustan" compared to "Pakistan" harkens back to the Two Nation Theory and highlights the inability of Muslims to live fairly under Hindu rule. Note that the author makes a distinction between Kashmir, on the one hand, which under the logic of the Two Nation Theory belongs to Pakistan, and India, on the other, which is tantamount to Hindustan or land of the Hindus. Increasingly, with the ascendance of a militant Hindu nationalist right, activists are embracing the notion of a Hindustan in part because they believe that Hindus are being ousted from their homeland, India. Ajju Chouhan, the leader of the Bajrang Dal which purports to be the foot soldiers in the Hindu nationalist movement, believes that "The time has come for us to take back what's ours, to claim Hindustan for Hindus."[43]

Regarding the fifth objective, bin Muhammad evinces the ongoing requirement to avenge the murder of Muslims by non-Muslims by reverting to Kashmir and "Hindustan." He asks rhetorically how many Muslims have been raped and killed by Hindus in Kashmir. He posits that Pakistanis are responsible for avenging the "murder of five million Muslim deaths in 1947" during Partition. (It should be noted that this figure is absurdly exaggerated, as discussed earlier in this volume.) He asked who will avenge the Muslim women who are giving birth to Hindu and Sikh children, again referring to events in Partition in which Muslim women were abducted and forced into marriages with Sikhs or Hindus. (Recall from earlier chapters of this volume, that Sikhs and Hindus were similarly abducted and forced into marriages with Muslims.)[44]

To establish that non-Muslims continue to dishonor treaties with Muslims, bin Muhammad again deploys an example from Pakistan's specious historical accounts. The author tells his readers that India did not honor a pledge to permit "Kashmiri Muslims" to hold a plebiscite. This example deserves scrutiny regarding peer-reviewed, scholarly history because it is very misleading.

(Whether the author deliberately promulgates this flawed version purposefully or whether the author himself is ignorant cannot be known.) As is well known, in October of 1947, well after the Pakistan-backed tribal invasion began, the Indian Defense Committee resolved that a plebiscite should be held to ascertain public views about Maharaja Hari Singh's accession to India, once the *status quo ante* had been restored. In fact, in November 1947 Nehru had proposed to Jinnah that plebiscites be used to ascertain the wishes of the people whenever a ruler of a princely state belonged to a different community from that of most his subjects. Jinnah objected strenuously. Jinnah wanted to trade Junagardh's accession for that of Kashmir and found the plebiscite option to be undesirable (see Chapter 2). Jinnah also suspected that with Sheikh Abdullah in power in Kashmir and with Indian troops there, the "average Muslim would never have the courage to vote for Pakistan."[45] Lord Mountbatten, the last Viceroy and who was present during this discussion, offered that the United Nations could oversee such a plebiscite. Again, Jinnah demurred proffering that it should be organized by the two governors general: Jinnah from Pakistan and Chakravarti Rajagopalachari from India. In fact, Jinnah was likely gambling that the invasion would succeed despite India's military's intervention. Jinnah expected the Indians to conclude that their position was unsustainable and would accede to his demand to swap Junagadh for Kashmir.

However, Jinnah misread the situation along several dimensions. One, Jinnah erroneously thought this "swapping" outcome would also exempt Hyderabad from a plebiscite, which would strengthen its position of remaining independent. If Jinnah could not obtain Hyderabad for Pakistan, he preferred it remain independent because it would deliver a serious blow to Indian sovereignty and geographical coherence. Second, he underestimated the local anger at Pakistan for the brutality wrought by the Pakistani invaders. Third, Pakistan's military incursion which used irregular and regular forces would not succeed in seizing all of Kashmir for Pakistan, as Jinnah anticipated.[46]

As the military situation stabilized and it became apparent that India would not need to attack Pakistan, India referred the Kashmir dispute to the United Nations under Article 35 of the organization's charter. India claimed that Pakistani nationals attacked the state of Jammu and Kashmir and requested the UN Security Council (UNSC) to take steps to prevent Pakistan from continuing its aggression in the state. Pakistan countermanded that India had "pocketed the accession of Kashmir by fraud and violence" and further accused India of committing genocide of Muslims and belligerence in

Junagadh.[47] Various proposals by the UNSC members were rejected by either or both disputing parties. The resolution that was passed in April 1948 had three components to be overseen by a five-member commission. First, Pakistan was required to "use its best endeavors" to:

(a) To secure the withdrawal from the State of Jammu and Kashmir of tribesmen and Pakistani nationals not normally resident therein who have entered the State for the purposes of fighting, and to prevent any intrusion into the State of such elements and any furnishing of material aid to those fighting in the State;

(b) To make known to all concerned that the measures indicated in this and the following paragraphs provide full freedom to all subjects of the State, regardless of creed, caste, or party, to express their views and to vote on the question of the accession of the State, and that therefore they should co-operate in the maintenance of peace and order.

Once the afore-noted commission was satisfied that Pakistan had complied with the first, necessary but insufficient condition, the resolution said that the government of India "should:"

(a) put into operation in consultation with the Commission a plan for withdrawing their own forces from Jammu and Kashmir and reducing them progressively to the minimum strength required for the support of the civil power in the maintenance of law and order;

(b) Make known that the withdrawal is taking place in stages and announce the completion of each stage; When the Indian forces shall have been reduced to the minimum strength mentioned in (a) above, arrange in consultation with the Commission for the stationing of the remaining forces to be carried out in accordance with the following principles:

(i) That the presence of troops should not afford any intimidation or appearance of intimidation to the inhabitants of the State;

(ii) That as small a number as possible should be retained in forward areas;

(iii) That any reserve of troops which may be included in the total strength should be located within their present base area.[48]

Once these successive requirements were fulfilled to the satisfaction of the commission, India was to permit the conduct of a plebiscite under the auspices of the United Nations. As has been noted previously in the second chapter of this volume, Pakistan never fulfilled the first condition of the resolution.[49]

The empirics of this case resoundingly demonstrate that Pakistan's leadership did not initially embrace the plebiscite. Moreover, Pakistan has stood in enduring historical violation of the first condition that was required to enable the plebiscite, irrespective of how one interprets the impact of Simla upon the modalities of dispute resolution after it came into force in July 1972. Returning to bin Muhammad's claim that India did not honor its "pledge" to let Kashmiri Muslims hold a plebiscite, the assertion is misplaced for several reasons. While Nehru did want to hold a plebiscite, he maintained that it could only happen once law and order had been restored. It never was. In fact, since 1947 Pakistan has continued to militarize the areas of Kashmir under its control thus further undermining the first provision of UNSC 47. India has also continued to militarize Kashmir, but its demilitarization was to follow that of Pakistan and thus cannot be cited as a reasonable impediment to the plebiscite.

Bin Muhammad offers a second example from the early years of the conflict between India and Pakistan as evidence that non-Muslims renege on "treaties" with Muslims to further argue that the sixth condition remains unfulfilled. He posits that "Hindustan" failed to honor the Liaquat-Nehru pact by protecting the lives and property of Muslims and mosques in India. This claim is particularly disingenuous. This pact was penned by Liaquat Ali Khan (Pakistan's first prime minister) and Jawaharlal Nehru (India's first prime minister) in April 1950 in effort resolve an emerging crisis in Bengali-dominant East Pakistan.[50] But as is often the case with JuD materials, the reasons for the accord are not as stated. While the scholarly record of this crisis is contested by all parties, there is general agreement that on 20 December 1949, Pakistani police sought to arrest a communist agent in the East Pakistani town of Khulna, which is in contemporary Bangladesh.[51] While the police failed to capture the suspected agent, they assaulted several Hindus in this Hindu-dominant village. The conflict escalated and two police officers were killed, which precipitated a wider crackdown on Hindus in Khulna and beyond. In turn, many Hindus began fleeing East Pakistan for India. By February 1950, India claimed that some 24,000 Hindus had fled East Pakistan for the Indian state of West Bengal. Indian Hindus in turn began attacking Muslims in India which precipitated further communal clashes within India. With the specter of the Partition-related communal violence looming, Nehru was worried that the Hindu-Muslim discord stemming from Pakistan's treatment of Hindus in East Pakistan would further erode India's social fabric. Ultimately Nehru threatened military force to persuade Liaquat Ali Khan to come to Delhi and find a peaceful way forward in April of 1950.

The ensuing so-called Nehru-Liaquat pact "emphasized the policy of both governments to provide complete equality of citizenship and a full sense of security to minorities."[52] Whereas bin Muhammad implies that India failed to honor its obligations, in fact it was incumbent upon both states to do so. The pact pertained to the crises that precipitated it. It is fair to say that both sides had challenges upholding their obligations then. Taking the longer view of history, India has generally done a better job with respect to its minorities. Constitutionally, India has honored its pledges to ensure that all citizens are equal before the law. However, as painstakingly detailed by Sacchar, Muslims remain one of the most—if not the most—discriminated against minorities in India, facing deprivation of access to education, housing, employment and often the victim of organized communal violence with little recourse.[53] Nonetheless, it cannot be denied that Pakistan's record with respect to non-Muslims is worse in both degree and kind. As is well-known, non-Muslims in Pakistan do not enjoy full and equal rights under Pakistan's constitution. For example, they cannot hold the high offices of president and prime-minister. Non-Muslims, other than Christians, have no marriage law of their own which renders their marriages legally tenuous and intermarriage between Muslims and non-Muslims is not legally recognized.[54] While both Pakistan and India have blasphemy laws on the books, those in Pakistan are used to harass and even murder non-Muslims. Thus, while both Pakistan and India have lamentable records in failing to protect the lives and property of minorities or their houses of worship, Pakistan's record is more sullied in part owing the legal forms of discrimination that exist against non-Muslims.[55]

Turning to the seventh condition for waging *jihad*—fighting in self-defense—Bin Muhammad uses India again as justification for armed struggle. He asserts that Muslims in Kashmir are attacked by a 750,000-strong army, which is likely an exaggeration of the number of Indian security forces in the region. The Indian government refuses to publish official numbers; however, the BBC assesses that there are between "300,000 and half a million Indian troops and police in Jammu and Kashmir."[56] But bin Muhammad also notes the Buddhist attacks on Muslims in Burma as well as "barbaric Serbs, backed by the Christians and communists of the world," who are attacking Muslims in Bosnia.[57] Russian assaults on Chechnya also figure in this discussion. Finally, he turns to Muslim lands that are currently occupied by *kuffar* which includes Andalusia (Spain), all of "Hindustan" (where Muslim sultanates fell to foreigners because Muslims terminated *jihad*), Palestine, as well as numerous other countries (e.g. Bulgaria, Hungary, Cyprus, Sicily, Africa, Russian Turkistan,

Lower Chinese Turkistan, and Kashgar). He tells his readers that "Muslims once ruled the wildernesses of Switzerland and marched up to within 90 kilometers of Paris; today, all this land is occupied by disbelievers."[58]

Defending Jihad against the Myriad Excuses against Jihad

Both bin Muhammad and Muhammad work to establish the salutary benefits of waging *jihad* while also mitigating the arguments against it. One of the most important questions in contemporary discussions about *jihad* is whether armed struggle is *farz-i-ayn* (compulsory for every individual) at present. In bin Muhammad's volume, the ostensible questioner observed that no prophet waged *jihad* with a sword until he began taking practical steps to establish an Islamic state. Since the latter does not exist, how can one assert *jihad* is legitimate, much less compulsory, for every Muslim? The second component of the question is more complex but is at the core of the domestic politics of the organization. The questioner queries if we assume that *jihad* is compulsory to combat the kinds of barbarism and cruelty that we observe in Kashmir and elsewhere, why are we not waging *jihad* in Pakistan to combat the very same ills that exist in our country? After all, if "we strengthen Islam by waging jihad in foreign lands, what good is it if we are hollow from within?"[59]

Bin Muhammad begins by acknowledging the origins of the dilemma motivating this inquiry; namely, that for as long as the prophet lived in Mecca, Allah forbade him from fighting the infidels. It was only when he moved to Medina to set up his Islamic state that Allah gave him permission to fight the infidels who kept harassing him. This distinctive conduct at different points in Muhammad's life, as narrated in the Quran, give rise to the so-called Meccan vs. Medinan debate that motivate foes of militarized *jihad* to say that since the prophet waged *jihad* when he had set up a state in Medina, *jihad* cannot be waged in the absence of such a state or *Khilaafat*. In addressing the concern that *jihad* can only be waged by an Islamic state, he does not deny the observation that the prophet did not wage *jihad* against the disbelievers until he left Mecca and established an Islamic state at Medina. Instead, he points to a variety of Muslim practices that are derived from of the Medinan period (*inter alia zakat*, the ban on usury, call to prayer (*azan*), fasting during the month of Ramazan, and prohibition on temporary marriages, praying, congregational prayers) and contends that, by this reasoning, these cherished practices are not mandated either until the creation of an Islamic state. Of course, he rejects this reasoning and argues that once Islam was revealed in its entirety, its commandments must be obeyed with the exception derived from Surat 2:286 that Allah will not a task a soul beyond its scope. However, this exception cannot be used to excuse oneself from fulfilling certain obligations (i.e. *jihad* and those mentioned above) simply because they were made mandatory in the Medinan period of the Quranic revelations. In fact, in the absence of a *Khaleefa*, *jihad* is blessing that gives hope of restoring the *Khilaafat* and re-establishing an Islamic state.

Muhammadi adopts a similar, but less otiose, line of argumentation. In Muhammadi's volume, his inquisitor, recalling that during the Meccan period the prophet used proselytization to allure his foes to Islam instead of violence to vanquish them, queries whether Markaz ud Dawah is justly waging *jihad*. The *mujahid* responds simply by asking the inquirer whether he follows those commandments revealed during the Meccan period. Naturally, the inquirer responds that he follows Islam in its entirely. The *mujahid* claims that "it makes no sense for us to distinguish between the Meccan and Medinite periods in this day and age since Islam has been revealed in its entirety. We are obligated to follow all the commandments."[60] The *mujahid* narrator proceeds to offer the same examples that bin Muhammad employed as well as additional ones for greater clarity. Muhammadi's explication is simple: if you follow Islam in its entirety, you cannot make foolish distinctions between the Meccan and the Medinan periods and, *jihad*, like these other obligations is binding.

Both bin Muhammad in *Hum Kyon Jihad Kar Rahen Hain* and Muhammadi's *Difa-i-Jihad* tackle several other common arguments that *jihad* is not appropriate for contemporary Muslims. Having established that it is is compulsory even in the absence of an Islamic state, bin Muhammad next addresses the issue of whether *jihad* is *farz-i-ayn* (obligatory for every individual) or *farz-i-kifayah* (compulsory for some members of a community). The latter is compulsory for a certain number of Muslims from a community; however, if the required number of Muslims do not perform the duty then the entire community is responsible for doing so. For tasks that are *farz-i-kifayah*, a certain number of Muslims can perform the duty which releases the rest from having to do so. For acts that are *farz-i-ayn*, every individual is required to do them. An example that clarifies the difference between these two types of obligations is afforded by the funerary prayer and rites. As long as a few Muslims perform them, the rest of the community is relieved of its obligation. However, if no one performs them, then the entire community is responsible. Is *jihad* an obligation like prayer and fasting, which must be done by every

Muslim, or is it an obligation like funerary prayers which, when performed by a few, releases others from their duty?

Here bin Muhammad engages in clever sophistry. Drawing from Surat 9:122, he concedes that not every Muslim is obligated to march into the battlefield. If one contingent fulfills this obligation, the rest of the community is relieved of the obligation. Referencing Surat 4:95, he observes that those who stayed back in their homes were blessed but those who marched into the battlefield were more so. He also references a *hadees* from Abu Huraira, which makes clear that even if a Muslim does not wage *jihad* and decides to stay back at home fulfilling his or her obligations, paradise is not lost.

These examples suggest that *jihad* is *farz-i-kifayah*. Considering these arguments, how can *jihad* be *farz-i-ayn*? Bin Muhammad resolves the conundrum by observing that fighting the infidel is an expansive and expensive operation that cannot be executed without contributions from multiple sections of society which must contribute to the struggle in their own way. Although the most important and preeminent actors are the *mujahideen* who battle the enemy through force, they are not the only ones who fight the enemy. Those who prepare and deliver ammunition to the front lines, those who send food and other supplies and those who protect the homes of the *mujahideen* are also very much a part of the struggle. Moreover, he notes that being ready to be called upon to fulfil this task or inspiring others to participate in *jihad* are all foundational aspects of *jihad*. He mobilizes several *hadiths* to buttress his point that those who help prepare the recruit for his battle for Allah is a part of the fight as are those who care for the soldier's family. Similarly, if one brother becomes a *mujahid* and the other brother stays back to care for the other's business, both are taking part in the war through their different actions. Equally important, he tells his readers that the disbelievers can be fought with one's life, wealth and tongue. One can in fact enjoy the fight and die a martyr simply by intending to so sincerely.

But these arguments are inadequate to make a compelling case that *jihad* is *farz-i-ayn*, when the scripture and *hadees* that he presents clearly suggest otherwise. His innovation is that *jihad* is *farz-i-ayn* only when the *amir* commands everyone to engage in combat, in which case only those who are ordered to stay back are excused from battle but are still considered part of the war. If, on the other hand, the *amir* does not order everyone into the fight, *jihad* is *farz-i-kifayah* because not every Muslim can feasibly join the fight. It is also unwise for all Muslims to enter the battle as no one would be left to manage the Muslim cities and property of Muslims left behind. As noted earlier in this volume, from among all of the recruits that LeT sends to its basic training course *Daura-e-Aam*, fewer than one in ten will be selected for its advanced training course, *Daura-e-Khaas*. Fewer still progress beyond *Daura-e-Khaas* to higher-level courses such as intelligence, driving, and swimming. And even fewer are ultimately sent out on missions in India or elsewhere. JuD dispatches most of the men who receive some degree of training back to their village.[61] In fact, most are dispatched on domestic preaching and recruitment missions and this is by design.

At first blush, this personnel strategy may seem reckless because it is possible that these persons with some degree of training could undertake "lone wolf" operations in Pakistan or elsewhere, causing problems for the organization. After all, one of the virtues of JuD/LeT, from the point of view of the Pakistani deep state, is that it responds to the state's needs as well as its diktats. Arrogating to the *amir* the authority to decide when or if *jihad* is *farz-i-ayn* is one important means through which the *tanzeem* exerts control over the thousands of persons it trains to perpetrate violence. Clearly this system is imperfect: we know that some cadres have been disappointed with the lack of opportunity to participate in *jihad* under JuD/LeT's banner. We also know that some cadres have joined other militant organizations that offer them with greater opportunity to wreak violence. However, these are the exceptions. Indeed, if LeT/JuD did not have the ability to generally control their cadres, the organization would be less appealing to the deep state and the latter would conspire against it, as it has other organizations.[62]

Equally important, if *jihad* refers to a more capacious struggle, which includes the intention of fighting, preparing to fight, weapons training and stockpiling, preparing *mujahideen* for battle, caring for, and protecting the households of the *mujahideen*, or being involved in the war in some way or other, then this *jihad* is *farz-i-ayn*, and no one can escape from this obligation. Indeed, this is precisely the argument advanced by JuD that all persons should be prepared to participate in this struggle in one way or another, pursuant to the judgement of the *amir*. To give further ballast to his logical construction, bin Muhammad draws upon another *hadees* from Abu Hurairah, who reports that the prophet said anyone who dies without having fought in battle and without ever intending to fight in battle has died a hypocrite (*munafiq*). He uses this *hadees* and others to argue that every Muslim is in fact obligated to fight the *kuffar* in some manner or another. If nothing else, every Muslim must at least intend to wage *jihad* and be prepared to do so in the capacity for which they are best suited.

At this point in the essay, bin Muhammad's argument that *jihad* is *farz-i-ayn* rather than *farz-i-kifayah* is still not completely convincing or compelling. Thus, he continues to elaborate this point, noting that some brothers have excused themselves from *jihad*, arguing that *jihad* is in fact *farz-i-kifayah*. Bin Muhammad asserts that this logic is precisely why the Muslim *ummat* stopped fighting *jihad* throughout the world despite being globally humiliated by the *kuffar*. Using this deduction against those who espouse this view, he warrants that until a posited obligation that is putatively *farz-i-kifayah* is satisfied by the mandatory number of able-bodied persons, it is in fact *farz-i-ayn*, just as funerary prayers would be if the requisite numbers of people were not conducting them. Bin Muhammad then returns to the eight objectives noted above and the ostensible proof he marshalled that they remain unfulfilled. He thus deduces that Muslims should stop debating whether *jihad* is *farz-i-kifayah* or *farz-i-ayn*, and embrace the fact that every single able-bodied Muslim is accountable for undertaking *jihad* and the prerequisite training to do so.

Why Not Wage Jihad in Pakistan?

JuD invests considerable space denouncing violence against the Pakistani state and its citizens. The three texts I use here exemplify the kinds of arguments that the organization advances. Both bin Muhammad in *Hum Kyon Kar Rahein Hain* and Muhammadi in *Difa-i-Jihad* assert that *jihad* should not be waged in Pakistan for any reason whatsoever. (Later in this chapter, I turn to the issues JuD perceives with non-Muslims in Pakistan.) Rabbani, in taking on the issue of *takfir*, contends that ordinary persons cannot declare someone to be a *kafir*. He takes great pains to lay out the evidentiary basis and juridical process for doing so and makes it very clear that only qualified Islamic scholars are fit to apostatize someone. Rabbani, like bin Muhammad and Muhammadi, assert that no matter how poorly behaved a Muslim leader may be, the only recourse available to Muslims is teaching and preaching in hopes that the leader will change his or her ways. All three authors affirm that violence is never a legitimate response with which to contend with an illegitimate Muslim leader no matter how dissolute he may be. In this section, I lay out the key arguments advanced by these three authors in these works.

Both bin Muhammad and Muhammadi assert that any argument for *jihad* in Pakistan is a conspiracy, fostered by India or other enemies of Pakistan, to ensnare the country in civil war. (Similarly, Rabbani professes that the evident abuse of *takfir* is essentially a plot by non-Muslims to undermine the *ummat* from within and disgrace Islam and Muslims among non-Muslims.) The writers converge on the notion that there is a global conspiracy to ensnare Muslims throughout the world in a civil war and preclude them from regaining their past glory. JuD's arguments against violence in Pakistan are critical to grasping the *tanzeem*'s domestic utility to the deep state.

In bin Muhammad's treatment, the questioner remarks upon the apparent fact that the rampant cruelty and barbarism that one observes in Kashmir can also be seen in some measure in Pakistan. Why then, he asks, does the *tanzeem* not clean up Pakistan first before taking on external battles? Bin Muhammad's narrator rejects the premise of the question and asserts that the oppression and violence in Kashmir and other non-Muslim countries in fact bear no resemblance to the various injustices that exist in Pakistan. First and foremost, Pakistan was founded on the on the "principle of *La ilaha il la-Allah* (there is no god but Allah) while Hindustan's flag bears the *veer* [spinning] wheel which is a Hindu symbol."[63]

Because Pakistan's leaders are Muslim, Pakistanis can appeal to them to make good on their promises to apply Islam because they do not deny its supremacy. In contrast, India's leaders are self-declared infidels (*kuffar*). Thus, for bin Muhammad, wayward Pakistani leaders are hypocritical Muslims (*kalima-go munafiq*) while India's leaders are nonbelieving infidels (*kuffar*). The author then explains how Muslim hypocrites should be treated versus different kinds of infidels. With respect to the hypocritical Muslims, he turns to the prophet's own deportment and notes that even when some of his contemporaries were at their worst behavior and his companions sought the prophet's permission to kill them, the prophet refused because, if he did so, Muslims and non-Muslims alike would burble that he killed his own followers. The author addresses the situation in Pakistan noting that in the few places in Pakistan where there is unrest, it is between Muslim groups vying for power, rather than between *kuffar* and Muslims. Moreover, bin Muhammad avows that such episodes of sectarian violence within Pakistan are fomented by "Hindustan," where Muslims are subjected to violence for no other reason than simply being Muslim. The claim that India foments domestic violence in Pakistan is important because it contends that its internal security challenges are the direct result of Indian malevolent involvement rather than malfeasance or mismanagement on the part of the state or its various security agencies.[64] Bin Muhammad lectures his questioner, explaining that:

> In Hindustan and Kashmir, Muslims are under attack from the Hindu army. Six hundred and fifty thousand soldiers are stationed in Kashmir. Are there any

Hindu soldiers or foreign soldiers stationed in Pakistan to punish us for being Muslim? Do you not understand the obvious: to free the Muslims caught in the grip of infidels, it is imperative for Muslims to unite, irrespective of their differences? When infidels come to rape and plunder they're not concerned with what school of Islamic jurisprudence you adhere to, or your political affiliation—they won't let you be until you convert to Hinduism.[65]

In this context of purported Indian involvement in stoking violence within Pakistan, the narrator seems to be vexed that the questioner seems unable to discern the difference between oppressing someone because they are Muslim versus more general oppression, and expresses his dismay that a Muslim would see Pakistan and India as equally legitimate for *jihad*.

Like bin Muhammad's assertion in *Difa-i-Jihad* that the Islamic world will experience a political resurgence through waging *jihad*, he maintains that this is also true of Pakistan. He explains to his questioner that it is "it is through jihad against the enemy that we can strengthen ourselves from within."[66] Moreover, *jihad* is waged only by those with a sense of honor. Consequently,

> when Muslim rulers are devoid of honor they cannot stand up to disbelievers. The true Muslim man will always fight infidels because they are infidels, and it is through such a man that Allah will grant the country stability and inner strength. Therefore, make every attempt to continue jihad against infidels and inspire others to fulfill this sacred obligation.[67]

These prescriptions undergird the organization's pivotal role in Pakistan's domestic politics. By waging *jihad* in India—and elsewhere when the *amir* commands it—Pakistanis will abjure fighting each other while at the same time fortifying their country by ridding it of the political ills that plague it. Curiously, this too accords with the army's narrative that the country is weak due to pusillanimous civilians who consistently let the country down.[68]

Consistent with the sub-narrative that Pakistanis must support—rather than undermine or fight—the government, the author ameliorates the questioner's purported reservations about taking assistance from the Pakistani government, which is un-Islamic and even spreads disbelief (*kufr-va-shirk*) in their *jihad* in India and elsewhere.[69] He uses the same approach of positing a query from his questioner, who is really a stand-in for his reader, and proceeds to answer the same. He inquires whether it is more important to wage *jihad* in Kashmir or fight *kufr-va-shirk* in Pakistan. To exposit a response fully, bin Muhammad furnishes a taxonomy of the various kinds of infidels (*kuffar*). There are those *kuffar* who have said the *kalima* (declaration of the one-ness of Allah and the acceptance that Muhammad is his prophet). These are *kalima-go kuffar*, as noted previously. These *kuffar* should be seen and treated very differently from those *kuffar* who have not declared their faith in Islam and who make war on Muslims for no other reason than their Islamic faith. In contrast to these non-believing *kuffar*, *kalima-go kuffar* will not fight with other Muslims because they too embrace Islam. He explains that these *kalima-go kuffar* have simply strayed from the correct path. He expounds:

> We will consider them misguided and misinformed: we will point out to them their pagan ways but we will not war with them because if we wage war against those who declare their faith in Islam, we cannot make war against those who reject Islam.[70]

Thus, the *mujahid* should try to educate the *kalima-go kuffar* rather than fight them, unless they make war on Muslims.

While JuD/LeT believes that those who embrace Sufism should be seen as Muslims who are *kalima-go mashrik*, the organization is not insouciant about the threat that adherents to Sufi mystical traditions pose to the principle of *tawheed*, or one-ness of god. In fact, JuD published an entire volume dedicated to problems posed by the *kalima-go mashrik*, titled eponymously, *Kalima-go mashrik*.[71] The volume focuses upon the importance of *tawheed* as a fundamental pillar of Islam and the requirement to extirpate *shirk* from its roots. In this context, *shirk* specifically means ascribing the attributes of Allah to others. Organizations like JuD/LeT which reflect upon the importance of *tawheed* take considerable umbrage at several Sufi practices and beliefs. For example, they have a cult-like veneration of the prophet, which *tawheed* proponents view as tantamount to *shirk* because their devotion to the prophet is redolent of worship, which should be reserved for Allah alone. For this reason, *mashrik* (one who commits *shirk*) is often translated as "polytheist." (The plural of *mashrik* is *mashrikeen*.) Followers of Sufi traditions, as noted above, will also seek the blessings of saints and intercession in personal and spiritual affairs, and Sufi *pirs* will distribute blessings or amulets in exchange for remuneration. JuD/LeT believes that those who follow these mystical practices verge on equating others alongside Allah, which is a form of *shirk*.

In *Kalima-go mashrik*, Rabbani is less forgiving than bin Muhammad when it comes to Sufis, because they promulgate misinformation about the oneness of Allah. Rabbani encourages his readers to continue the tradition of the prophets by opposing the spread of *shirk*. In the preface to the book, Muhammad Saifullah Khalid, the editor of Dar-ul-Andulus, writes that *Iblees* (a name for the devil) will continue to test Muslims with the temptations of *shirk* because he:

does not derive as much pleasure from the sins of Jews and their ilk as he does from sins committed by Muslims. It is highly unfortunate that nowadays, Muslims often stray from the right path and tread the road of *shirk* showed to them by Iblees. It is evident that this angers god. Muslims have engaged in such activities to such an extent that it is now impossible to differentiate them from ordinary infidels. The selfish and uneducated Sufi clergy has played a big role in spreading this faithlessness. They have misled the populous in the pursuit of satiating their greed. For the sake of a few pennies, they have turned the attention of Muslims from the kaaba (house of god) to their shrines. Rather than focusing on god, they have turned their efforts towards the pleasures of this world resulting in their losing their way as well as the populous.[72]

Whereas bin Muhammad uses the *kalima* as a means of distinguishing those who accept the supremacy of Allah from those who do not, Rabbani focuses upon the inadequacy of stating the *kalima* as a measure of being a proper Muslim in the eyes of Allah. He explains that *kalima* is premised on the negation of equating anyone with Allah and the derivative profession of belief in Allah's supremacy. Thus, the *kalima* is first and foremost the rejection of worship of false deities followed by submission to Allah. (In fact, the word "Muslim" literally means "one who has submitted," with the implication that they have submitted to Allah.) If one utters the *kalima* but continues to worship those other than Allah—as Sufi mystics purportedly do—they will still be seen as sinners in the eyes of Allah. Rabbani mobilizes arguments in the Quran and *Sunnat* to argue against the practice of *shirk* as evidenced by those polytheists (*mashrikeen*) who worship saints, martyrs, *Jinns*, angels and other deities alongside Allah. In *Kalima-go kuffar*, Rabbani challenges other practices, which he believes to be accretions from Hinduism, as discussed below.

Bin Muhammad concedes that the capacious definition of a Muslim that he offers, which includes "grave worshipers" (which refers indirectly to *Sufis*) and "those who ridicule the companions of the prophet" (which refers obliquely to Shia), will not please everyone. Indeed, Deobandi militants hold these very kinds of Muslims to be worthy of death, as noted above.[73] Bin Muhammad asserts that his organization (JuD/LeT) rejects this kind of thinking and believes that it is wrong to make enemies of those who bear allegiance to the prophet despite sectarian differences. While he has no doubts that anyone who prays to anyone other than Allah (a reference to *Sufis*) are acting like polytheists, if they say the *kalima* and do not deny the truth of the Quran, they must be treated differently than those who do not accept Islam.[74] He explains that the organization believes that it is categorically wrong to take up arms against those who have declared their faith to be

Islam even if they are infidels as noted above. Instead, he says that Muslims are obliged to guide them.

Muhammadi also cites other episodes from the *hadees* and *Sunnat* to make the uncomplicated case that "we are at war with the rulers of Hind, in the hope of either dying in the course of our struggle, or surviving to celebrate our redemption from hell, Allah-willing."[75] Muhammadi's inquirer in *Difa-i-Jihad* perseveres in asserting that the *hadees* commands Muslims to help both the oppressor and the oppressed of Pakistan, since they are nearer to Pakistanis than those in Kashmir and thus Pakistanis should first fight oppression in Pakistan. His *mujahid* interlocutor rebuffs him tersely:

> Brother, the point to note here is this: on one side we have oppressive and cruel disbelieving Hindu rulers, and on the other side, we have oppressive and cruel Muslim rulers. Which of the two sides is more threatening? Which side should be engaged militarily and which one deserves to be forgiven and corrected?[76]

The proper response, he further argues, is to invite Muslim rulers to fight the disbelievers through *dawah*. This is the desired means through which the *tanzeem* should encourage Muslim leaders to aid oppressed Muslims.

Muhammadi also takes up the specific issue of fighting Pakistani politicians and government officials. It is worth recalling that when this volume was published, in 1998, Pakistan had experienced a decade of political convulsions. The government was either in the hands of Prime Minister Benazir Bhutto of the Pakistan Peoples Party (PPP) or Nawaz Sharif of the Pakistan Muslim League-Nawaz (PML-N). Neither government served out their complete term due to ineptitude and corruption and military intervention to prorogue their governments. The army has long fostered the narrative that civilians are the root of Pakistan's governance problems, and few Pakistanis reject this argument in exchange for the alternate view that democracy in Pakistan is weak and underdeveloped due to the army's policy of "democracy interruptus."[77] However, this does not mean that the army wanted people to engage in deadly violence to protest government officials. By 1999, the government would again be in the hands of a military strongman. General Musharraf, who seized power in October 1999 in a coup against Nawaz Sharif, became the country's fourth and longest-serving dictator. In this context, the inquirer in *Difa-i-Jihad*, implores to the *mujahid* that:

> Jihad is urgently needed in Pakistan because of rampant corruption in the country. District Superintendent of Police are corrupt, Senior Superintendent of Police rely on extortion, and even Inspectors General of Police are busy greasing their palms. Every level of our administration, from the lowest rung of the reg-

istrar to the commissioner at the top of the pyramid, is run by corrupt officials. Even our judiciary has been taken over by unscrupulous individuals. It seems our armed forces, too, have been infiltrated by enemy agents. For the past fifty years, politicians have been lying to the people while milking the country's resources dry. It seems odd that in this situation you would leave your oppressed countrymen at the mercy of such traitors to wage jihad in a distant land.[78]

The *mujahid* explains to him that Islam prescribes specific punishments for different kinds of crimes. For example, a thief and a person who accepts bribes are not treated equally in the distribution of punishments. Similarly, if a Muslim commits a crime he will be punished accordingly but he cannot be declared a disbeliever and consequently killed.[79] This is an incredibly important claim because it undermines the concept of *takfir*. The *mujahid* and the inquirer next have an exchange in which both agree that those "who oppose the jihad in Kashmir would rather mujahideen abandon their war against Hindu soldiers and wage their jihad in Pakistan against the administration, the judiciary, the politicians, and the armed forces" because they believe that "jihad must first be waged against the oppressive rulers of Pakistan before it is taken abroad."[80]

The *mujahid*, however, counsels the inquirer that corrupt Pakistanis should be dealt with through education and proselytization (*dawah*). He explains that MDI is fulfilling its domestic obligation by proselytizing to local leaders and congregations. They are present in offices, schools, colleges, and university campuses across Pakistan. He claims that the organization engages the armed forces, the administration, and the judiciary. He claims that they urge politicians to replace the democratic system with a *Khilaafat*, and join the dual process of proselytizing and waging *jihad*. But the inquirer is indefatigable. He continues asserting that while Hindus are oppressing Muslims in Kashmir, in Pakistan "grave-worshipping [referring to adherents to Sufi sects] leaders are busy oppressing Muslims. Does it make any sense to help distant victims as opposed to the ones in your own backyard?"[81] The *mujahid* repeats his position that there is a fundamental difference between Muslim oppressors and nonbelieving oppressors. "A Muslim, no matter how depraved, must be dealt with according to his crime, while a disbeliever must be fought as an obligation to Allah."[82] The *mujahid* then turns to the prophet's life for guidance in this specific case. He offers the same example that bin Muhammad did when the prophet refused to let his companions kill those hypocrites among his followers who were conspiring to harm the nascent Muslim community, fearing that people would lament that the prophet killed his own.

The *mujahid* offers another example of the instrumentality of not killing Muslims, no matter how far they transgress. He draws upon the seventh-century Battle of Khandaq (the Battle of the Trenches), in which the pagans of Mecca were the foreign army, and the Jews of Banu Quraiza were the internal foe. There was a third enemy: those hypocrites within the Muslim camp. The Prophet first defeated the pagans because they were the external enemy. After all, it would be imprudent to cause discord from your own camp before taking on the foreign foe. After dispatching with the pagans, he beheaded seven hundred Jews and distributed their wealth as war booty. However, he spared the hypocrites, arguing that they were now rendered harmless because there was no one left with whom they could conspire, but also because they professed to be Muslims. The *mujahid* observes from this episode that Muslims must "unite against the disbelievers and resolutely march upon the enemy. We must resolve our internal conflicts through mutual understanding, dialogue, and preaching, and we must avoid rebellion and civil war at all cost."[83] When the inquirer is still in disbelief that it is forbidden to battle those within Pakistan who exploit the poor, the *mujahid* reiterates his basic argument that *jihad* cannot be waged against a fellow Muslim; rather, the *mujahideen* must "preach more effectively to make the rulers change their ways. In this regard, Markaz-ud-Dawah wal-Irshad is performing its obligation to some extent but institutionalized proselytizing needs to be bolstered much more."[84]

With respect to the appropriate treatment of wayward Muslims generally and morally flawed Muslim leaders, Rabbani, in *Masalah-i-takfir*, comes to similar conclusions but from a different evidentiary basis and line of argumentation that specifically aims to denounce the use of *takfir*. Rabbani cites the opinions of religious scholars and jurists to conclude that the practice of *takfir* requires the utmost caution and restraint, and in fact, should be outright avoided. He observes that presently:

> The *ummat* produces a steady flow of ignorant men who recklessly go around branding people from all walks of life such as politicians, soldiers, security forces, teachers, doctors, engineers, judges, lawyers, as infidels, thereby unleashing a wave of terror and mayhem.[85]

He believes that this is due to involvement of Jews, Christians, Hindus, and other infidels who conspire against Muslims to sow discord. He alleges that young, impressionable, and foolish men are lured by the wealth offered by the enemies of Islam and willingly act as their agents to humiliate the *ummat*. Such agents of the *kuffar* infiltrated mosques, schools, and religious institutions, and threaten everyone with the scourge of *takfir*.

Rabbani's approach to destabilizing the legitimacy of *takfiris* rests on two key arguments. First, they do so out of their abject ignorance about the complexity and difficulty of accurately denouncing a Muslim as a *kafir*, and the commensurate requirement that only learned scholars can do this in a procedurally sound way. Second, those engaging in *takfir* are agents of Islam's enemies. In Pakistan, where the government and civil discourse against Hindus, Jews, and Christians (often called the "Brahmannic-Talmudic-Crusader alliance") is pervasive and toxic, this second argument likely has more heft than simply repudiating *takfiris* as ignorant buffoons murdering people for their provincial and wrong-headed beliefs. In his own foreword, Rabbani explains the contemporary dilemma with *takfir*, which has not only precipitated countless loss of lives in Pakistan but throughout the Muslim world. He laments that:

> It is tragic the way people who have no understanding of the intricacies of faith-based jurisprudence, let alone a working knowledge of the basic principles of ritual and literal hygiene, are appointed to important positions. Many so-called *muftis* [one who issues *fatwas*] fall in this category, whereas accusing a Muslim of apostasy is serious business that has nothing to do with personal objectives, opinions, suspicion, doubt, religious identity, sectarian affiliation, etc. Such an accusation requires concrete evidence scrutinized in the light of the Quran and Sunnah without the slightest room for any kind of doubt.[86]

Rabbani articulates the view of JuD that ordinary persons cannot declare someone to be a *kafir*; rather the person who does so must have "mastered the Quran and Sunnah with an expert working knowledge of Sharia-based injunctions, objectives, and principles, and a clear understanding of how these are to be applied to daily life, and enough compassion to accommodate the general public's ignorance and misdemeanours."[87] The person who does so can have no trace of extremism because excommunicating a Muslim can have grievous ramifications. Rabbani continues to argue that the worst of the lot arrogate to themselves the delicate matter of issuing *fatwas* and apostatizing Muslims, with the potentially ensanguined consequence of threatening their life as well as their property. Rabbani repeatedly stresses the fact that there is an "extensive process of analysis and interpretation before a religious scholar can even think of declaring a Muslim an infidel; in fact, as much as possible, they are keen on correcting a Muslim's *kufr* statement instead of banishing him from Islam altogether."[88]

In Rabbani's interpretation of the Quran and *Sunnat*, declaring "someone an infidel without rigorously applying the principles of the *Quran* and *Sunnat* is nothing short of murder."[89] To buttress his view, Rabbani cites Qazi

Muhammad bin Abdullah al-Shawkani, who maintains that it is simply not permissible for any genuinely faithful Muslim to excommunicate a Muslim unless the "evidence is clearer than the midday sun." Moreover, anyone who "refers to his brother as 'infidel' ought to know that one of the two is going to be at a severe loss," implying that any false accusation will revert to the accuser.[90]

In his letter to Sheikh Hafiz Salahuddin Yusuf, Rabbani explains that a book titled, *Marji'i-tul-'Asr*, has been "compiled by an ignorant individual" and posted to numerous Ahl-e-Hadees platforms, which asserts as fact that many Pakistani Islamic scholars view the current leadership of the country as heretical.[91] Rabbani explains to the Sheikh Yusuf that this view has been attributed to him and his scholarship. Given Rabbani's dubiety that Yusuf, whom Rabbani seems to respect considerably, said this, he wants Yusuf to correct the record. To do so, Rabbani asked the respected Sheikh three questions in hopes that he will reply to each, namely:

1. Do you actually believe that Pakistani leaders, as well as leaders of other Muslim countries, are heretics and infidels?
2. As heretics and infidels do they deserve to be executed?
3. What is your opinion about the scholars who declare these leaders sinful, insidious, and insincere, but refuse to declare them infidels?[92]

Rabbani explains that "the people behind this publication start off by declaring individuals to be infidels, then they go on to spread terror across the land through violence. One hopes you will offer a detailed response by way of guiding the Muslim ummat."[93]

While the Sheikh's response does not follow the three questions directly, he does answer Rabbani comprehensively. He begins by noting that the Quran and *hadees* offer warnings of eternal damnation for both, but the specific warnings about the kinds of actions that Muslims and non-Muslims commit are not the equivalent; notably: while Muslims are warned of a temporary punishment, infidels are condemned eternally. The Sheikh argues that considerable confusion arises because the same words are used to describe the sins of both Muslims and non-Muslims. For example, in the Quran the words for debauchery is the same for both Muslims and infidels who sin; however, a Muslim cannot be declared an infidel simply because he has sinned even though Allah has used these terms for infidels and polytheists as well. Whereas Rabbani laments that many ignorant youth have taken up the practice of *takfir* due to a conspiracy of Muslim's existential foes, the Sheikh attributes the *takfiri* menace to ignorance.

Addressing the first question, albeit indirectly, the Sheikh observes that even if one accepts the position of extremists who use the deadly tool of *takfir*, the question lingers about how Muslims should live. He notes that most Muslims do not actually live per the revelations in the Quran. He observes that the "majority of Muslims completely ignore the laws of inheritance, particularly in how they filch women of their rightful share. Should all those who ignore this law be declared infidels and sent to hell or should we let Allah decide their fate?"[94] He believes that the same argument applies to the case of Muslim rulers behaving un-Islamically. It is Allah who should judge these rulers in the afterlife. Muslims can criticize these rulers but they have no authority to assess their faith. Moreover, doing so would serve no positive purpose but would sow discord and disability throughout the country. The Sheikh worries that if "we start accusing and trying every other person for being an infidel, it's not difficult to imagine the kind of havoc this will cause."[95] It is precisely because of this potential for violent mayhem that *shariat* (Islamic law) insists that "if the leaders of a Muslim population defy Allah's commands and are cruel and oppressive, the common folk are to endure the injustice without rebelling."[96] Thus, he concludes that while Pakistan's current leadership is culpable for not applying Islamic laws despite having the resources and authority to do so, and though they are equally guilty of leading the masses away from Islam, "their reckoning is with Allah and it is not for us to declare them worthy of death."[97]

It is only when these wayward Muslim leaders encourage *kufr* that action is required. However, he also argues that the act of explicitly encouraging *kufr* is not the same as mere moral shortcomings. While he eschews giving examples of what would constitute such a breech, unfortunately, from either the contemporary era or the past, he explains that "it is only when someone explicitly states that they do not believe in the finality of the prophet, or rejects the Quran, prayer, and fasting altogether, that they can be called an infidel and exiled from the realm of Islam."[98] This is perhaps the most direct statement that the organization makes in all of the literature reviewed for this volume that has direct bearing for the Ahmadi question in Pakistan. While Ahmadis do not reject the Quran, prayer or fasting (although they are not permitted to call these actions by their rightful names), they do reject the ordinal finality of the prophet and recognize a living, contemporary prophet. Thus, while the volume does not mention Ahmadis explicitly, this statement suggests that they should be consider *kuffar*.

The Sheikh avers that it is incumbent upon "every Muslim to make whatever effort possible within his capacity to protest against these un-Islamic steps [of declaring wayward Muslims to be a *kafir*]" and work to guide those who have gone astray. Thus, while Pakistani leaders deserve criticism for their actions, they should be counselled "in the spirit of good will and in the tradition of the wise and noble but beyond that, guidance is in the hands of Allah."[99] Since such a solution has been offered to Muslims who seek some recourse for their leaders' shortcoming, there should be no insubordination, processions or protests. Instead, in administrative matters, Pakistanis are to obey their leaders while turning to Allah for help. To emphasize the point that to do otherwise is un-Islamic, the Sheikh observes that such shenanigans is a western democratic practice that should be eschewed by Pakistanis because peace and stability demand that the state be shielded from mavericks and rebels. Without irony, he explains that this subservience "is preserved in certain monarchies, which is why they experience relative peace and stability... However, wherever democracy has taken root, the stability of the state is in serious jeopardy. Consequently, most local resources are expended on managing political unrest that has eroded peace and stability."[100] The Sheikh laments these states of affairs and hopes for a time when the "masses could be freed from the snare of Western democracy so they may set up an indigenous system of government informed by Islamic injunctions."[101]

Challenging the claim that JuD is a modern-day *Murji'i* organization, Rabbani again mobilizes Shokani, who acknowledges that Allah's command that when "*kufr* is exposed it must be rigorously interpreted until one's heart is satisfied and one's conscience is clear"; however, "even the mere performance of a *kufr* act isn't admissible as evidence when the accused has made no attempt to escape to infidel lands, and neither can a Muslim be trusted if he testifies but does not fully comprehend his testimony."[102] Shokani further notes that "when there is no other way to interpret (an act) and there is no other path left to take in light of the aforementioned hadith, then it is mandatory that the hadith be upheld exactly as they were revealed" and excommunicate the individual in question.[103]

Rabbani uses the words of Imam Ghazali to make clear JuD's reticence in using *takfir*. According to Ghazali, *takfir* should be avoided as much as possible because it is wrong to "deny the right to life and property to those who pray facing the Ka'ba and say 'there is no god but Allah and Muhammad is His Messenger.' The blood of an innocent Muslim is more important than the extermination of a thousand infidels."[104] As noted above, Rabbani is also deeply worried that *takfir* enthusiasts will target him and similar scholars. His fear is justified. In fact, Sadeeqo and Narugi do just that in a pro-Al Qaeda book that focuses on discounting Rabbani's moderate stance on when, how, and under what circumstances *takfiri* may be employed. It should be noted in Pakistan that there have been numerous assassinations of religious leaders who disagree with various militants' violent agenda, and thus, his concern is not merely rhetorical or reputational.[105]

It is useful to deliberate upon these passages from the three authors. Pakistanis, whose practice of Islam is discordant with that of the Ahl-e-Hadees tradition as embraced by LeT/JuD, can be considered *kalima-go munafiq* (Muslims who are hypocrites), *kalima-go mashrik* (Muslims who commit idolatry), and those who are *kalima-go kuffar* (infidels in practice but who have accepted Islam as their faith). Unlike the Deobandi organizations which argue that *munafiqeen* (pl of *munafiq*), *mashrikeen* (pl of *mashrik*), and *kuffar* should be killed, LeT/JuD argues that they should be educated and rehabilitated. Bin Muhammad's solution to the sectarian violence and other forms of political oppression and corruption that have gripped Pakistan is to begin fighting the infidels abroad. He explains at length:

> Do you not know the only way to end infighting and oppression in Pakistan is to begin fighting infidels? If we do not fight infidels, we will never stop fighting amongst ourselves, neither will we stop oppressing one another.

> One hopes you see the difference between waging jihad against fellow Muslims in Pakistan (where we live, by Allah's grace, in peace) and waging jihad against Hindus in Hindustan (where Muslims are slaughtered for being Muslims; where we have yet to settle the scores of 1947 and 1971).

> I am deeply saddened when a Muslim brother declares Pakistan and Hindustan equally legitimate for jihad. These are precisely the kinds of things Hindus want Muslims to think and say. May Allah grant all brothers wisdom.[106]

This is an incredibly important message in Pakistan and LeT/JuD is the only organization in Pakistan making this claim. As noted elsewhere in this volume, Deobandi militant groups (inter alia Pakistani Taliban, Sipah-e-Sahaba-e-Pakistan (SSP), LeJ) are responsible for most of the violence in Pakistan. In fact, JuD's discipline at home in promoting security and reliable *jihadi* activities abroad is encapsulated by Muhammadi, who simply asserts that "Instead of rebelling against our own Muslim rulers, we battle oppressive, cruel, disbelieving Hindu rulers," citing a saying of prophet Muhammad who said:

> There are two groups in my *ummat* Allah has protected from hell-fire: one group comprises those who will jihad against Hind, and the second comprises those who will join forces with Jesus, the son of Mary (to war against Dajjal, the anti-Christ).[107]

It is in the supreme interest of the state to support this group and its message of non-violence within Pakistan while directing violent action outside Pakistan in the service of the state's security interests.

Muslims among Non-Muslims in Pakistan[108]

In recent years, Pakistan's Sindh province has been an important area of recruitment and prosyltization for JuD. Sindh is Pakistan's second most populated province with about fifty-one million people,[109] although this number is contested and impossible to verify since Pakistan has not conducted a census and published its results since 1998.[110] (The Pakistan Bureau of Statistics may release results from the ongoing census in late 2018.) Sindh is also where nearly 94 per cent of Pakistan's nearly 800,000 Hindus reside. A mere 4 per cent live in the Punjab and smaller numbers yet in Balochistan and Khyber-Pakhtunkhwa.[111] The *tanzeem's* principle tools to secure conversions are provision of social services, medical care and disaster relief work provided through JuD as well as its dedicated humanitarian relief arm, the FIF. In Sindh, JuD's medical teams have provided relief to Hindu-dominated areas of Sindh plagued by preventable child deaths.[112] JuD also took advantage of floods in 2011 to provide relief to Hindu-affected areas during which they provided tents and food and ample proselytization.[113] FIF has been active in efforts to ameliorate the ongoing draught in Sindh by digging wells and installing hand pumps and by "helping the poor and marginalised sections of Hindu minority with economic incentives… facilitating admission of Hindu children into Madrasas without converting them to Islam… [and is] opening new seminaries for the purpose."[114] The FIF boasted about imparting Islamic education at a relief camp in Badin (in Sindh) which housed about 2,000 persons who were displaced from the 2011 floods in Sindh. An FIF volume explained that "We have taught them namaaz [Islamic prayer[, as well as the required prayers to recite before and after a meal. Even the Hindus sit in the session."[115]

In contrast to JuD, which works through these softer means to convert Sindh's Hindus, others have more draconian methods such as kidnapping Hindu girls and forcing them to convert and marry local Muslims. About 1,000—mostly Hindu but some Christian—girls are abducted and forcibly converted and married every year.[116] This provoked the Sindh government to attempt to pass a bill against activities. However, religious groups such as JuD opposed this measure arguing that it was part of a conspiracy to make Pakistan a secular country. Hafiz Saeed said of the measure that "We will not remain silent on this controversial law."[117] The religious groups succeeded in squashing the measure.

Pakistan's Christian population constitutes about 1.6 per cent of the country's burgeoning population of over 201 million.[118] More than 80 per cent of Pakistan's Christians are concentrated in the Punjab and Islamabad, with smaller populations in the other provinces and tribal areas. The *tanzeem* has made fewer public overtures towards Pakistan's Punjab-based Christian community. However, when it has spoken it has done so in defense of the community even though its publications revile Christians elsewhere. For example, in 2013 when a Pakistani Taliban faction, the Jandullah Group, dispatched suicide bombers to attack Christians praying in their church in Peshawar, Hafiz Saeed made Pakistani headlines by accusing India of conducting the suicide attack and generally spreading extremism and terrorism inside Pakistan. While denouncing India, he also declared that the "Whole nation should support Christian community at this time and steps should be taken to stop such incidents."[119]

While JuD believes that conversion will ultimately address the "problem" of Hindus and Christians living in Pakistan, what is more difficult to fix is the case of Muslims who have adopted both Hindu and Christian practices. Eradicating these vestigial influences from Hinduism and recrudescent practices from Christianity may be considerably more difficult because now "it is difficult to tell a Muslim from a Hindu."[120] Bin Muhammad concedes that because Hindus are the ancestors of most Pakistani Muslims, "some of these accretions are historically understandable even if they are detestable."[121] After establishing the fundamentally base and vile nature of Hindus and the redeeming capacity of kindness and generosity towards them, he turns to the project of this volume: educating Muslims about the Hindu practices they have embraced such that they can expunge them. The continued influence of Hinduism's polytheism upon Pakistani Islam is a particular affront to JuD because of its commitment to *tawheed*.

Bin Muhammad observes similarities between the ways in which Hindus pray and remember their gods and the ways in which Pakistan Muslims do the same. First, the author reflects upon a practice called "*sandhia*" according to which Hindus shut their eyes and nose while remembering their three most important gods.[122] In the morning, they offer *sandhia* facing the east. At noon and in the evening, they raise their hands and face the west while doing so. Sufis similarly close their eyes and hold their breath while remembering Allah. He denounces the way some Muslims revere mystical leaders as

being analogous to Hindus' reverence for their pantheon of deities. He cata-
logues a host of mostly Sufi practices that mirror those of Hindus, such as
chanting, using rosaries, seeking intervention from functionaries at shrines,
pilgrimages to shrines, astrology, spiritual healing, the use of talismans and
the like. He laments that Muslims have appropriated several social and customary practices from Hindus such as bowing deeply and touching the feet,
upon greeting elders or social superiors even though the prophet has forbidden kneeling or bowing for humans as such demonstration of respect is
reserved for Allah alone.

Bin Muhammad next turns his focus upon a "clutch of certain un-Islamic
rituals and customs," pertaining to birth, death, marriage as well as a cluster of
"social rituals."[123] The author observes the complex marriage rituals currently
practiced by many Muslims despite the various ways in which they clash with
Islamic modes of matrimony. First, the spouses must be well-versed in Islam.
There should be no restrictions based upon caste or clan. He excoriates families who delay the marriage of their daughters and enjoins them to marry them
off as soon they are "adult, healthy and marriageable."[124] He criticizes the
elaborate meals served by the families of the bride and groom, which are
extremely costly. First, he notes the common "wrong practice of enjoying din-
ner at the bride's house" in which hundreds of persons from the groom's side
expect a thriftless meal from the girl's side. This he contends is a Hindu practice that still lingers among Muslims. Instead, the meal that is authorized is
called "*walima*" and it is from the groom's side as a token of appreciation after
the couple have met in isolation. Similarly, he depreciates the practice of
dowry, which is another Hindu custom according to which the family of the
bride grants improvident sums of money to the groom's family as a condition
of marriage. The author observes that the family of girls find it very difficult
financially to marry them off when one combines the expenses of the meals
and the dowry as a consequence of which "many a girl stale themselves away
in wait for formidable dowry but they die maiden."[125]

In fact, according to bin Mohammad, per Allah's command, the groom is
to incur all marriage expenses, offer *mehr* (the sum a groom promises to give
his wife in their marriage contract), pay for the *walima* meal, and arrange a
decent home for his new family as well as food and medical treatment for his
bride. He deplores the fact that while Hindus cannot countenance the remar-
riage of a female widow and thus condemn them to *sati* (immolation on her
husband's funeral pyre), celibacy, or single motherhood, Islam exhorts its
adherents to "marry away widows as early as possible. Islam wishes to see a

widow re-settled in society soon after the demise of her husband."[126] The reason for making this argument in the context of this Lashkar volume is practical: "A true believer never hesitates from participating in Jehad. He has the assurance that in case of his martyrdom, some of his Mujahid fellows would marry his wife and his family would get instant support. The recent Jehad-e-Kashmir gives us many such examples."[127] This ultimately is why the author believes it is so important that Muslims be true Muslims and wrest themselves from the weight of their inherited Hindu cultures. If Muslims followed these above-noted Hindu customs, "would a wife easily let her husband go for jehad? She has been living under the awe that after his death, nobody is there to take care of her."[128] She asks herself why she would even consider sending him off to participate in *jihad*. Instead, the author encourages Muslims to arrange for the marriage of widows as well as divorcees.

The author also encourages polygamy *in lieu* of the more typical Pakistani practice of monogamous marriage. The author disparages such contentment with one marriage. He explains:

> This is no manliness. Look, if a person dies, his brother should come forward to marry his *bhabi* [sister in law] who has become a widow. A real uncle can be a kind and caring guardian for his orphan nephews and nieces.[129]

To buttress this point, bin Muhammad cites the prophet's marriage to a widow and his care of her children because her deceased husband had been very helpful to him. The author encourages Muslim men to contract more marriages in an effort to grow the Muslim population, which will preclude the Hindus' ability to combat them. The author informs his readers that non-Muslims fear the *ummat's* fecundity because it enables JuD's twinned missions of *dawah* and *jihad*. In fact, the *kuffar* have "declared it a more dangerous bomb than the Atom-bomb."[130]

Christians Among Muslims[131]

In Maulana Amir Hamza's *Shahrah-e-Bahisht* (Highway to Paradise), we learn that JuD harbors very similar concerns about Christians in Pakistan as it does about Hindus: Pakistani Muslims ape their customs.[132] He lambastes Christians for having a polytheistic philosophy, which likely refers the "Holy Trinity" or "god, the son and the holy ghost," and other Christian beliefs that equate divine status to Jesus which should, in JuD's world, only be reserved for god. While he has no use for this theosophical point of view, he is discomfited that Muslims in Pakistan also go "overboard in praising the Prophet."[133] In a sense, he is using Christian practice and belief as a mirror with which he demonstrates to Pakistani Muslims that they too have analogues in their beliefs and practices. He explicitly draws a parallel from the Christian reference to the "god, the son and the holy ghost" to those Sufi Muslims who refer to their prophet as god's light or even god himself. Whereas Christians have made three into one, Muslims made two into one. He notes that Muslim hymns, like Christian hymns, elide the distinction between the prophet and Allah just as Christian hymns elide the difference between their god and Jesus. Given JuD's firm commitment to *tawheed*, this is an example of *shirk*. He notes that JuD is not opposed to devotional songs *per se*, as long as they do not abrogate the strict injunctions of monotheism.

Hamza criticizes the degree to which the Muslim celebration of *Eid Milad-ul-Nabi*, which commemorates Muhammad's birth, resembles the Christian Christmas holiday, which marks the birth of Jesus. To emphasize how disconcerting this is, he draws from a popular *hadees*, narrated by Abu Sa'eed al-Khudri and compiled in Sahih Bukhari and Sahih Muslim, that the prophet said: "You will certainly follow the ways of those who came before you hand span by hand span, cubit by cubit, to the extent that if they entered the hole of a lizard, you will enter it too." We said: "O Messenger of Allah, (do you mean) the Jews and the Christians?" He said: "Who else?"[134] He wonders, with fear and anxiety, whether Muslims will follow Jews, "who invoked Allah's wrath," or Christians, "who went astray."

Friends with Benefits: Symbiosis with the Deep State

As this chapter has described, JuD wants to pacify Pakistan by discouraging sectarian and communal violence and purify Pakistani society (and Muslim societies in general) by purging it of any Hindu and Christian accretions.[135] JuD has built an enormous infrastructure, mentioned above, to spread these various messages. The *tanzeem* has established a network of more than 2,000 recruitment centers and developed a network of schools (not *madaris*) throughout Pakistan. To spread its message, LeT/JuD trains far more cadres than it will ever need on the military battlefield because it deploys these cadres to the domestic battlefield. Individuals who have trained with LeT garner considerable social cachet upon return, which they can in turn leverage while performing the *dawah* work that they are expected to carry out upon returning home. Cadres who return to their localities after doing some degree of LeT training are well-positioned with their newfound *mujahid* status to provide counter-arguments to the deadly Deobandi militant organizations which are competing for militant man-power as well as for physical, financial, political, and other support from ordi-nary Pakistanis. These LeT-trained missionaries also help recruit others who are willing to train with them, as well as spread the organization's version of Salafi Islam. Because these *dawah* activities are tremendously important for the Pakistani state as well, the state provides ample support to this organization's domestic work as well its military persons.

In fact, once one appreciates the domestic political role of this organization, it becomes clear that the Pakistani state has tremendous self-interest in buttres-sing the domestic role of JuD as well as its foreign operations. For these reasons, the Pakistani state has supported JuD in particular as the "charitable arm" of the organization as well as the Falah Insaniat Foundation (FIF), which is JuD's offi-cial disaster relief arm.[136] During disasters (e.g. the Kashmir earthquake of 2005 and monsoon-related floods of 2010), the state actively promoted JuD and FIF and worked to ensure that the domestic and international media covered their activities. Their objective was to ensure that the organizations would receive accolades, even though their actual roles were quite modest.

For example, during the 2005 7.6-magnitude earthquake which killed as many as 75,000 people in Kashmir and Khyber Pakhtunkhwa, Pakistani and international news sources claimed JuD and other such banned outfits were leading the relief effort, including the deployment and use of tactical x-ray and surgical equipment.[137] However, the data tell a very different story. Das and Andrabi surveyed 28,297 households in 126 villages in the earthquake-affected regions. Among other important questions, they asked respondents which groups were involved in providing relief. More than one quarter of the households reported that an international organization directly aided them. Another 7 per cent of the households identified legitimate Islamic charities (i.e. not affiliated with militant organizations in any way) such as Islamic Relief. In stark contrast, a mere 268 households out of 28,297 (about 1 per cent) recalled groups tied to Islamist militancy (e.g. LeT/JuD, JeM, HM) being involved in relief efforts. Equally important, while LeT/JuD man-aged to visit twenty-six villages, the vast majority of the households reporting contact with the organization was located near its extant infrastructure in Kashmir. In other words, LeT/JuD activists were engaged in relief efforts largely where the organization had infrastructure in place. After the initial advantage afforded by LeT's proximity to parts of the quake-affected area, they were squeezed out as international and national organizations mobilized. Within six weeks, it was the Pakistani army which did the heavy lifting in terms of relief work.[138]

A similar set of events played out during the 2010 monsoon-related flood that left more than one fifth of Pakistan's landmass, the equivalent to the entire United States eastern seaboard, under water. More than twenty million Pakistanis were affected, which is about the entire population of Syria and more than twice that of Israel's population of 7.6 million. As with the 2005 earthquake, international and Pakistani media accounts asserted that militant organizations were stepping in to fill the void left by an inefficacious state and moribund international agencies.[139] However, the reportage over-stated the actual assistance provided by militant organizations. During a November 2010 presentation on Pakistan's floods at Georgetown University, Pakistan's then-ambassador to the United States, Husain Haqqani, noted that a mere twenty-nine camps were run by militant groups compared to more than 5,000 camps run by the government.[140] How is it that international and Pakistani media were led to misreport the role of these organizations in these events? The explanation is straightforward: Pakistan's ISI, Inter-Services Public Relations (ISPR), and Ministry of Information have an extensive role in orchestrating the coverage of both domestic and international media. They do so by facilitating transport to sites of particular interest and thus help target the coverage and, particularly with respect to domestic media, direct reportage by coercing or co-opting Pakistani reporters and news houses.[141] Pakistan's media management efforts are deliberately intended to exaggerate the humanitarian role of these organizations, with the explicit intention of generating support for them domestically and abroad. Pakistan's political as well as military leadership then uses the domestic support that the deep state cultivates to argue that it cannot restrict the organization without facing a massive backlash.

Media exaggerations notwithstanding, it is also true that in recent years, LeT and the Pakistani state have focused increasing attention upon the FIF. In September 2013, the Awaran district of Balochistan was devastated by an earthquake. The government barred international relief organizations from providing assistance, citing fears that ethnic Baloch insurgents might harm them.[142] With other competitors removed, FIF, with its Punjabi roots and Islamist militant ties, was at the forefront of relief. FIF's relief activities were well reported in Pakistan's print and televised media, and covered extensively in social media run by JuD. Baloch nationalists, who have been waging a secular, ethno-nationalist conflict against the Pakistani state and who nurse deep antagonism towards Punjabis because they believe them to be colonizing Balochistan, were outraged by FIF's presence. They interpreted this move as a state-sponsored ruse to embed "jihadi agents" in the area and "inculcate religious extremism to counter secular Baloch nationalism." The spokesperson for a Baloch nationalist organization (BSO-Azad) explained that "the Pakistani government deliberately barred secular aid organizations from participating in relief operations and allowed the FIF to partake relief activities, in line with Pakistan army's counter-insurgency operations." Moreover, the government awarded FIF health and education projects in numerous localities in Awaraan such as Awaraan City, Labach, Dalbidi, Ziaratdan, Malaar and Gishkor.[143]

These skeptical Baloch nationalists are almost certainly correct in their assessment. A perusal of FIF's own accounts demonstrates a growing involvement in Balochistan under its own banner and that of its parent JuD. The clearest exposition for this expanded involvement in the insurgency-torn province is offered by Hafiz Saeed himself, who explained that his organization will demonstrate that the "government needs JuD's ideology to resolve the issues of Balochistan."[144] FIF's chairman, Hafiz Abdur Rauf, echoed Saeed's confidence noting that grievances motivating the Baloch insurgency can "only be resolved by JuD" because "JuD will minimise the differences between the people."[145] JuD is an important ally of the Pakistani state in Balochistan. First, Pakistanis widely believe that India, Afghanistan, and even the United States are behind the secular, ethno-nationalist insurgency. Second, the Baloch insurgents claim to be secular and oppose—if are not outright hostile—to Islamism and to the state's efforts to mobilize Islam as the national ideology. (Although recent evidence suggests that Baloch themselves may not have the same views as the militants who claim to act on their behalf.)[146] Third, Balochistan has also witnessed sanguinary sectarian violence against the ethnic Hazaras perpetrated by Deobandi, anti-Shia militias such as LeJ. As will be explained, JuD discourages sectarian outbursts. Thus, JuD is quite correct that if it can propagate its ideology successfully throughout the province, many of the problems of Balochistan can be mitigated principally by vitiating the ethno-nationalist character of the Baloch grievances and by tempering Deobandi sectarianism in the province.

The above examples of JuD providing an effective ideological countermeasure to dangerous domestic ideologies demonstrate at least partially why the state is so committed to this organization in addition to its external utility. The state's sponsorship of JuD's domestic *dawah* and humanitarian activities also allows the latter to operate, cultivate popular support, proselytize the Ahl-e-Hadees creed, raise funds, and recruit potential militants even in the face of diminishing opportunities for militant activities over the last decade. By encouraging this bourgeoning domestic infrastructure, the state benefits from the diffusion of a state-friendly Islamism within Pakistan; additionally, the state has a ready infrastructure for militant activities in Afghanistan and India that it can scale up or down per the prevailing circumstances and needs of the state. By domestically rebranding the organization, the state also cultivates deep public support for the organization, which the state can then mobilize to resist any international or even domestic pressure to shut down JuD or FIF, both of which are designated terrorist organizations.

The domestic state-sponsored re-branding of LeT, from a militant organization to one that is principally a humanitarian organization, has been very successful. In 2011, I, along with Jacob N. Shapiro and Neil Malhotra, fielded a nation-wide face-to-face survey among 16,279 respondents.[147] We wanted to know what services and activities Pakistanis ascribed to Pakistani militant groups, including JuD. We interspersed questions about militant groups (JuD, Sipah-e-Sahaba and the Afghan Taliban) with an important Muslim relief organization (Islamic Relief), a Pakistani development NGO (Agha Khan), and a proselytization group (Tablighi Jamaat). First, we asked respondents whether they had heard of each group. If respondents were familiar with a particular organization, we then posed a battery of questions to elucidate which services and activities respondents believed each performed.

We found that despite the massive boost from Pakistani media, fewer than 40 per cent of respondents had heard of JuD. It should be noted that this is substantially greater than those who knew of Islamic Relief, and comparable to the share who knew of Agha Khan. (There may be greater public awareness than this metric suggests. It is a well-known problem of such surveys that respondents may be wary of admitting to knowledge of such controversial groups.) Among those who conceded knowledge of JuD and the other organizations, about one half believe that JuD provides social services, provides burial assistance to the poor, and helps internally displaced persons—with somewhat more respondents believing that JuD builds religious schools. Nearly 60 per cent believed that JuD publishes books and magazines (which it does in copious quantities) and propagates Islam (which it also does). This is in addition to about 70 per cent who also believe JuD "trains activists to help oppressed Muslims through Jihad." In several respects, JuD's public profile seems closer to the Agha Khan's than the other militant groups included in the survey.[148]

Conclusions and Implications

Returning to the question posed at the beginning of this chapter, for whom has LeT/JuD been winning Pakistani hearts and minds? LeT/JuD is the only organization with a nation-wide presence that opposes the Deobandi militant agenda of violence against Muslims and non-Muslims alike. As shown in this chapter, JuD/LeT firmly opposes violence against Muslims based upon their sectarian background and argues strenuously that Muslims who are engaged in heterodoxic practices should be subjected to *dawah* and *tabligh* (instruction about the true practice of Islam and proselytization) rather than to violence. The *tanzeem* makes the clear argument that *jihad* against the external foe is the only way to save Pakistan from within, but also is the only means by which the global *ummat* can restore its past glory. Because of the organization's salutary domestic role in promoting domestic tranquility and controlled violence against Pakistan's external enemies—especially in India and Afghanistan—the Pakistani state provides many forms of support to LeT/JuD and works to bolster the image of the organization among Pakistanis as a bulwark against any pressure to act against the organization. Given this history of collaboration with the deep state, the recent launch of the MML is a natural extension of the organization's collaboration with the state to combat the Islamist violence menacing Pakistan and its people.

This does not mean that the deep state has abandoned all hope for the Deobandi militants it has nurtured over many decades; far from it. In recent years, the deep state has continued to re-invest in Jaish-e-Muhammad (JeM) under the leadership of Masood Azhar after the organization split in late 2001, as described earlier. As I have described previously, despite the pressure from JeM commanders and members alike to defect at the end of 2001, Masood Azhar remained loyal to the deep state and reported the defections within JeM to the ISI.[149] In doing so, he demonstrated his value to the ISI. The rump of the organization he founded launched attacks under the name of Jamaat ul Furqan and initiated a series of deadly suicide strikes against military targets, including Musharraf himself.[150] This was the opening salvo in a realignment of militant groups that would eventually congeal into the network of militants that would operate under the banner of the Tehreek-e-Taliban-e-Pakistan (TTP or Pakistani Taliban) in 2007.[151]

Even though the JeM is explicitly proscribed by the United States and the UNSC, among other entities, Pakistan continues protecting the organization and its leader, Azhar. China has effectively placed technical holds upon efforts of the National Security Council to designate Azhar under the auspices of the UNSC 1267 Sanctioning Committee.[152] With firm state support, Azhar freely operates in his home town of Bahawalpur in Southern Punjab and in early 2017 had become extremely active in public events throughout Pakistan.

Despite being technically proscribed even in Pakistan, the organization has expanded in recent years. Since at least 2010 if not earlier, Pakistan's ISI has been resurrecting the Jaish under Azhar's leadership as a part of its strategy to rehabilitate those assets who defected to the Pakistani Taliban.[153] By 2013, I learned during fieldwork in both Pakistan and Afghanistan that Pakistan had resolved to take the Pakistani Taliban seriously, partly due to international pressure and partly due to domestic imperatives. After numerous months of incessant warning, Pakistan's military formally commenced a selective campaign against those militants in the tribal areas attacking them in June 2014 under the operational name of Zarb-e-Azb (strike of the sword of the prophet) after relocating valuable militant assets to safe house in Kurram and elsewhere.[154] Prior to the onset of these operations, Pakistan's military and intelligence agencies sought to persuade elements of the TTP to abandon the fight against Pakistan. Some rejoined the fight in Afghanistan to help the Taliban, some returned to the ranks of JeM to kill Indians. And according to Carlotta Gall of the *New York Times*, Pakistan seems to have been "with Qatar, and perhaps others, to move international Sunni jihadists (including 300 Pakistanis) from Pakistan's tribal areas, where they were no longer needed, to new battlefields in Syria."[155]

Revitalising the JeM was a cornerstone of Pakistan's strategy of managing its own internal security challenges as well as a cornerstone of its policy of terrorism backed by nuclear blackmail to achieve its ideological objectives in Kashmir. In 2015, individuals from international organizations tasked with monitoring these groups told me that since 2014, JeM activists have long been poised for infiltration into India along the Line of Control in Kashmir. By the end of 2016, JeM had become extremely active in Kashmir with no sign of relenting and a concomitant recruitment drive in Pakistan.[156] With JeM rehabilitated, the deep state will be able to replicate the success it had after JeM was founded in late 2001, when it could pit JeM and LeT in a bloody competition or even rely upon JeM while it reels in LeT/JuD for foreign operations while encouraging its domestic activities. Thus, while JuD/LeT is an important asset to the deep state, its handlers are always wary of being over reliant upon one proxy irrespective of the numerous benefits it confers.

7

DEALING WITH LET AND ESCAPING PAKISTAN'S NUCLEAR COERCION

Lashkar-e-Tayyaba (LeT) is Pakistan's most useful proxy because it is both a useful ally in managing Pakistan's domestic insecurity as well as a faithful executioner abroad. Through its various front organizations, such as Jamaat ud Dawah (JuD) and Falah Insaniat Foundation (FIF), it has cultivated considerable support amongst Pakistanis through which the state resists international pressure to act against the *tanzeem*. With the formation of the Milli Muslim League (MML), the JuD's normalization as a part of quotidian Pakistani politics is complete. Presumably the deep state will facilitate its electoral success as it has other preferred religious parties in the past through active support of the party and electoral malfeasance where needed and possible.[1] As discussed in Chapter 3, Pakistan's army is forging ahead with a rapid and reckless expansion of its nuclear weapons program, inclusive of tactical nuclear weapons and their delivery devices. Because of this, Pakistan confronts virtually no pressure to abandon its prized policy of using proxy warfare under its ever-expanding nuclear umbrella. The United States has been reticent to use coercive policies because it has long feared that Pakistan is too dangerous to fail and thus demurs from taking actions that may be destabilizing. The American nightmare is a Pakistani army that is in disarray; unable to exert control over its nuclear assets, materials and/or technical knowledge; and thereby non-state actors acquire a nuclear device or radioactive materials with or without the acquiescence of the army. Motivated by this worst-case scenario, American policy-makers have avoided steps that they assess would push Pakistan to the brink of collapse and actions that would deny American officials (including spies) knowledge of and influence over important decisions that Pakistan makes.

Given these realities and the risk aversion of policy-makers in both capitals, what options exist for the United States and India to deal with LeT specifically, or more generally, the problem of Pakistan's reliance upon terrorism as a key foreign policy tool? Admittedly, the options are few and not without risk. In this chapter, I lay out three broad sets of options: maintain the status quo; manage the narrow problem of LeT through enhanced counter-terrorism efforts and leadership decapitation; and develop a new complement of compellent policies to undermine Pakistan's heretofore successful nuclear coercion strategy. India cannot compel Pakistan to cease and desist from using terrorism as a tool of policy on its own; rather, the United States will have to assume the heaviest burden in this effort. However, there is important—if limited—space for Indian action even if the United States, per its historical record, declines to pursue this course of action.

Option 1. Maintain the Status Quo: American Cupidity and Indian "Strategic Restraint"

Both the United States and India, which are the most important countries for this particular problem set, have responded with unusual insouciance to the various barbarities of LeT and other Pakistani militant groups. China, which also plays an important role in shaping Pakistan's behavior, has been an active abetter because it views Pakistan's proxies as a bigger hazard to India than to its own interests (e.g. its own Islamist militant movement the Uigher East Turkestan Islamic Movement (ETIM) based in Xinxiang which has long collaborated with Pakistan's Deobandi militant groups, Al Qaeda, and the Taliban among others) and because it believes it can pressure Pakistan to crush ETIM activists in Pakistan when its own interests are imperiled. From Beijing's optic, Pakistan's Islamist proxies are a relatively low-cost means of managing its own security competition with India while sustaining its strategic relationship with Pakistan at a price point that is manageable.[2]

The United States generally responds to Pakistan by brandishing threats that it must "do more" to eliminate LeT and other India-focused groups on its soil, but in practical terms it had done little to coerce Pakistan to do so. In fact, even after the most grisly acts of Pakistan-sponsored LeT terrorism, the

United States has continued providing strategic weapons systems to Pakistan and retained the "Major Non-NATO Ally Status," as well as lavish economic and other support to Pakistan's military and other institutions. Between fiscal years 2002 and 2017, the United States has provided Pakistan with $11.1 billion in economic assistance, $8.3 billion in security assistance, in addition to another $14.6 billion in lucrative "reimbursements" under the Coalition Support Fund (CSF) program.[3] The CSF program essentially pays Pakistan to do what sovereign states are required to do, which both distorts Pakistan's incentives to act against terrorists operating on its territory, while vitiating the importance of United Nations Security Council (UNSC) Resolution 1373 (adopted in 2001) which obliges all states to undertake actions to prevent and undermine the ability of terrorist groups to use their soil to organize, train, raise funds and recruit and engage in other activities required to carry out attacks.

Astonishingly the United States has even actively sought to shield Pakistan from the consequences of its behavior under UNSC Resolution 1373, which is a Chapter VII resolution that considers major terrorist events as a threat to international security and carries the possibility of a forceful response by the UN and/or member-states. However, even after the November 2008 terrorist attack in Mumbai and the subsequent revelations that the attack had state sponsorship, the United States—along with China—actively shielded Pakistan from any debate over sanctions—much less other more forceful responses—at the United Nations.[4]

More recently, the United States has even relaxed its pressure on Pakistan with respect to the Lashkar-e-Tayyaba, despite Pakistan's ongoing flouting of all UNSC resolutions and US designations about the group and its leadership inclusive of the formation of the MML. In November 2017, Defense Secretary Mattis pressured the US Congress to dilute conditionalities on CSF. The Department of Defense Appropriations Act for FY2014 rendered CSF payments contingent upon the Secretary of Defense, in coordination with the Secretary of State, certifying to the US Congress that Pakistan is "cooperating with the United States in counterterrorism efforts against the Haqqani Network, the Quetta Shura Taliban, Lashkar e-Tayyiba, Jaish-e-Mohammed, Al Qaeda, and other domestic and foreign terrorist organizations," among other requirements.[5] In 2017, the Department of Defense prevailed upon Congress successfully to have that provision removed.[6] This is just the most recent effort to find ways of not holding Pakistan accountable for its continued pervasive and even ostentatious support for a group that the United States, the United Nations Security Council and others have declared to be a terrorist organization and its prominent members to be designated as terrorists.[7] This set of behaviors underscores the bizarre consistency of US policy towards Pakistan, which treats Pakistan more like an ally when its behavior is more congruent to that of an enemy.

India, for its part, has been no more assertive than the United States even though its interests are more directly impinged upon than those of the United States. India has tended to use what some Indian security elites refer to as "strategic restraint," which has typically involved not responding to any particular act of Pakistan-sponsored terrorism with military force. (The more recent approach of so-called "surgical strikes" has been rare and it is too early to ascertain its results.)[8] Proponents of strategic restraint argue that India should avoid a major conflict with Pakistan because such a conflict may retard India's capacity to focus upon its economic growth and its concomitant ability to invest in its massive military modernization. Pakistan's behavior is also self-marginalizing, as it degrades Pakistan's standing in the comity of nations while also undermining its integrity due to the blow-back of domestic terrorism that its policy of proxies has spawned. Some analysts contemn this notion of "strategic restraint," and assert that India is simply making a virtue out of a necessity because India lacks the military capabilities to punish Pakistan while retaining escalation dominance.[9] Whether one accepts that strategic restraint is the preferred option of a policy choice or a merely exigent outcome is immaterial, especially if one accepts the premise that LeT does not pose an existential risk to India much less the United States.

And indeed, it would be hard to argue that LeT does pose such a threat—at least numerically. As noted in the introduction, LeT has carried out 205 attacks between 1 April 1999 and 19 December 2016, accounting for some 1,191 deaths and 2,411 injuries.[10] In contrast, some 400 Indians die each day in road accidents. This equates to one Indian death every 3.6 minutes.[11] (Fewer people than this died during India's most devastating terrorist attack in 1993, when 257 people perished in Mumbai).[12] On a per capita basis, the United States fares no better with about ninety persons dying daily in motor vehicle accidents.[13] According to the Global Terrorism Database, between 17 June 1984 and 15 December 2016, there have been 2,758 acts of terrorism which claimed the lives of 3,422 and injured 17,396, most of which are due to the catastrophic attacks on 9/11. During that same period of time, over 880,000 people died from vehicle accidents. Most terrorist attacks in the United States result in very few casualties. In fact, the average over this period is 3.5 killed per attack.[14] In contrast to the episodic and rare terror events, car accidents are daily massacres for both countries.

Of course, car accidents are random events while terrorist acts are not. Polities do not typically blame their politicians for automobile fatalities, but they do hold their governments accountable for terrorism because of the public belief that it is the government's duty to protect them from such threats. Indians certainly believe that terrorism is important. A recent Pew survey found that 61 per cent of Indians believed that LeT is a "serious threat," compared to 61 per cent who said the same thing about India's communist-inspired Naxalites, and 42 and 74 per cent who identified China and Pakistan respectively as a "serious threat."[15] Unfortunately, Pew did not ask Indians to rank these concerns alongside other issues such as the economy, global warming, corruption, and so forth. However, Pew did ask Indians to assess the importance of other issues such as terrorism in general, the state of schools, air pollution, and so forth. As the results in Table 7.1 show, while 85 per cent said that "terrorism" was a "very big problem," comparable percentages indicated the same for "rising prices," and "employment opportunities." By all accounts, Indians believe that terrorism generally is a pressing issue and that LeT specifically is a major threat.

Despite Indians acknowledging LeT, terrorism, and Pakistan as important issues, these concerns have not been pressing electoral issues. Perhaps one of the reasons for Indian voters' apparent indifference to this matter is that Pakistan-backed Islamist terrorism usually happens in in India's cities, or in remote Kashmir, while most of India's voting public are rural voters who are less affected by Pakistan-sponsored violence. For better or for worse, terrorism has not been a driving political issue in elections at the national or subnational level, which means that policy-makers will address more rewarding concerns at the ballot box.[16] American voters, of course, are more concerned about other security and economic matters and could scarcely be bothered about LeT—even if they know what the group is. Most voters are similarly disinterested in US policy towards Pakistan, if they are even aware of what that policy is and what Pakistan does to undermine US interests.

If one discounts the loss of lives and simply focuses upon the economic picture, "strategic restraint" has paid dividends.[17] With a steadily growing economy, India has enjoyed an average of 7.2 per cent growth in GDP between 2001 and 2016. In contrast, Pakistan's growth in GDP over the same period has been a more meagre 4 per cent.[18] This has allowed India to make enormous investments in defense while keeping the percentage of defense spending well below 3 per cent of GDP since 2003.[19] In contrast, Pakistan has spent between 3 and 4 per cent of its GDP and still cannot match India's absolute investments in defense due to its much smaller economy.[20]

Whether India is making a strategic decision or simply making a virtue out of inability to act otherwise, India is essentially accepting that many hundreds—if not thousands—of Indians will die in the policy-relevant future as a transaction cost of avoiding conflict with Pakistan and focusing on economic growth. While such a trade-off seems distasteful once articulated, it is not irrational to argue for the overall net national benefits that will accrue from this policy. On the other hand, even if India were to undertake the reforms in intelligence and policing, and develop the requisite conventional, strategic defense assets, and corresponding doctrines to punish Pakistan—the financial and political costs will likely be great and unlikely to fructify over the policy-relevant future.[21] And, despite these investments, success cannot be assured. After all, even the best defenses cannot stop all terrorist groups from infiltrating and murdering Indians.

The United States too believes that its policies towards Pakistan has had some rewards. While most American policy-makers understand Pakistan's duplicity in the war on terrorism, they are grateful that Pakistan has continued to grant the United States and NATO access to Pakistani soil and air lines of communication to move war materiel as well as supplies for the Afghan National Security Forces. American officials with whom I have interacted over the past decade have also expressed satisfaction that Pakistan is allowing the United States to continue eliminating their terrorists through US drone operations. American officials have generally understood the negative role that Pakistan has played in Afghanistan; however, there are few options to resupply the effort without a massive re-optimization of US policy towards Iran, that would permit movement of goods into Afghanistan to move from Iran's port of Chabahar.[22]

Given these ostensible benefits of the status quo, maintaining the current course is all the more appealing to both Washington and New Delhi given that there is no real public pressure in either India or the United States to do something more meaningful to punish Pakistan for any given terrorist outrage much less enact policies to deter future ones. However, the costs of the current American and Indian decisions to not punish Pakistan for using its terrorists under the secure safety of its nuclear umbrella is terrifyingly simple: the Pakistani state continues to dispatch LeT and its other proxies continue to kill at will, ever emboldened by its increasing confidence that both India and the United States are deterred by a combination of its nuclear arsenal, fears that Pakistan is too dangerous to fail, and its strategic utility to the United States in trying (but failing) to shape the outcome in Afghanistan. Worse yet, the United States further rewards Pakistan for its use of terrorism when it encourages India and Pakistan to "resolve their differences through negotiation," because such proclamations legitimize Pakistan's claims when it fact its claims to Kashmir have no historical, legal or moral legitimacy.[23] As a consequence of these American and Indian inactions, Pakistan continues to conclude that it can use proxies with complete impunity. It will become increasingly difficult to mobilize the court of world opinion when such violence has become normalized as part of the sub-continent's status quo. In some measure, this is exactly what has happened.

Table 7.1: Indian Attitudes Towards Various Social Problems

Q: "Now I am going to read you a list of things that may be problems in our country. As I read each one, please tell me if you think it is a very big problem, a moderately big problem, a small problem or not a problem at all."

	Very big problem	Moderately big problem	Small problem	Not a problem at all	DK/ Refused	Total
Crime	93	6	1	0	1	100
Corrupt officials	86	11	1	0	2	100
Poor quality school	77	17	3	1	2	100
Air pollution	74	19	4	1	2	100
Health care	68	24	5	1	1	100
Gap between rich and poor	74	20	4	1	1	100
Corrupt business people	74	19	4	1	2	100
Lack of employment opportunities	87	10	1	1	2	100
Rising prices	87	10	1	0	1	100
Terrorism	85	9	3	0	4	100
Communal relations	59	29	6	1	5	100
Situation in Kashmir	68	20	4	1	6	100
Lack of access to clean toilets	72	21	4	2	2	100

Source: Pew Research Center, "Topline Results: Spring 2015 Survey-September 17, 2015 Release," accessed 1 July 2017. http://www.pewglobal.org/2015/09/17/methodology-14/

Option 2. Leadership Decapitation: What Happens if LeT Heads Roll?

If the human costs and/or political optics of the status quo are no longer tenable, and forging a sweeping set of new policies to help a risk-averse United States and/or equally risk-averse India escape Pakistan's coercion strategy is deemed too risky, is it possible narrowly to counter the threat of LeT? As the research presented here makes clear, LeT's organizational structure is hierarchical, moving a relatively small cadre of tested and increasingly senescent leaders who rotate around locations that are linked to Hafiz Saeed through familial or social ties. Drawing from the work of Shapiro, the LeT opts for this organizational structure because it best allows them to overcome the principal-agent problems discussed in Chapter 4. However this organization structure renders the *tanzeem* highly vulnerable to leadership decapitation.[24] In contrast, the Pakistani Taliban opts for a diffuse network structure because Pakistan and the United States are targeting them. This networked structure protects the organization from catastrophic leadership decapitation and protects other cells when one cell becomes compromised; however, more operational security comes at the cost of the recurring challenge of principal-agent problems.[25] The vulnerability of Hafiz Saeed should increase as he becomes more involved with the MML.

Clearly, LeT—and its managers in the Inter-Services Intelligence (ISI) and Pakistan army—do not anticipate any meaningful threat to its prized proxy. This raises the question of whether or not leadership decapitation is a meaningful route to pursue. As Abrahms and Jochen Mierau note, "the intent of decapitation is to reduce the threat of militant groups by degrading their leaderships."[26] Given that many countries have employed this tactic (or some would say, strategy) against militant groups, several scholars have sought to determine whether targeted killing is effective. Despite the proliferation of quantitative studies, the varied results are inconclusive and often yield contradictory results. While Johnston and Price have found, in their respective studies, that leadership targeting is effective in degrading the organizations in question,[27] Jaeger and Paserman, Jordan, Mannes, as well as Smith and Walsh conclude from their analyses that it is ineffective.[28]

The reasons for these varying results are due to, *inter alia*, the nature of the datasets employed and the biases that inhere in their collection and coding methods with which the datasets were produced; the ways in which scholars instrument for and proxy organizational attributes;[29] the ways in which scholars define and measure "effective," as well as the general problem with so-called "large n" studies that fail to capture complex facets of organizational structure and function as how scholars use sub-optimal proxies for these organizational features.[30] Yet another problem with these studies is that they cannot examine what happens when the senior leadership is targeted because most such leadership targeting has been conducted against the mid-level leaders of terrorist/insurgent groups. While these persons may have specialized skills that are highly valuable to their groups, they are not apex leaders.[31] Taken together, these empirical studies cast little light on what would happen if LeT's leadership were eliminated.

However, there are some studies that do offer germane insights into the question at hand. First, there is a consensus that states should not pursue leadership decapitation if it intends to negotiate with a group because those leaders are best placed to control violence. Removing them expands the opportunity spaces for spoilers to act without senior leadership exerting control over them.[32] However, under no foreseeable circumstances will either the United States or India ever negotiate with LeT. LeT, after all, is but a proxy of Pakistan that acts on the state's behest.

Studies by Long as well as Abrahms and Mierau offer some insights into what LeT may do after a series of successful leadership strikes. Long, drawing from his recent qualitative study of leadership decapitation in Iraq and Afghanistan, finds that "hierarchical groups that are well institutionalized are extraordinarily resistant to leadership targeting, both at the senior and middle levels."[33] This contradicts the findings of Price, who found that such groups are in fact susceptible to such leadership attacks.[34] LeT has the various characteristics of being "well-institutionalized" in that it has a defined hierarchy, which in principle ensures: clear lines of succession following the removal of a leader; functional specialization, which facilitates more efficient organization function and facilitates leadership replacement; and bureaucratic processes and standard operating procedures which afford clear and consistent processes, including personnel management.[35]

However, neither Long's study nor that of Price is appropriate in this context. Long examines the effects of leadership targeting against Al Qaeda in Iraq (AQI) and the Afghan Taliban, also a Pakistan proxy. He found that both of these groups institutionalized in the targeting campaigns early on because their leaders were being eliminated. In other words, this was an adaptive strategy that ensured institutional survival. LeT has long-since been institutionalized; however, no LeT senior leader has been targeted for elimination. Unlike AQI and the Afghan Taliban, LeT is not practiced in the art of replenishing its leadership ranks after devastating strikes against them. Moreover, Hafiz

Saeed has deliberately opted to move the same persons around the various leadership roles as if in a macabre game of "musical chairs;" except no chair is ever eliminated. This raises serious questions whether LeT would respond in the same way as the Afghan Taliban. This also suggests that a splendid first strike that removes operational and apex leadership, as well as key handlers in the Army and intelligence agencies, nearly simultaneously would be optimally effective in degrading the organization's efficacy. Eliminating multiple targets within a short period is as likely as winning a massive windfall in a lottery.

We can likely infer from this literature, and common sense, that such target-ing will not destroy the organization. After all, the LeT is a functional arm of Pakistan's military and intelligence agency and it will regrow the organization as required or spawn an entirely new proxy *tanzeem*. But is it possible that the organization's ability to conduct high-quality terror will be degraded? Using different methods and case studies, both Abrahms and Mierau, as well as Long, concluded that leadership decapitation is disruptive because it takes time to replace eliminated leaders. Leaders are not interchangeable, and some are better in some functions than others. Leadership targeting also forces the organization to focus efforts on avoiding decapitation. Some organizations are so affected by such targeting campaigns that they engage in target substitution by switching from hardened (military) targets to softer (civilian) targets.

It is not a foregone conclusion that the quantity of LeT terror attacks will diminish. However, it seems quite likely that the quality of those attacks will decline.[36] This will likely impose adverse political consequences for LeT and their handlers in the Pakistan army and ISI while conferring positive political effects for India's political leadership. (American voters are unlikely to be ter-ribly moved by a splendid first strike on LeT's leadership.) Ideally, this should be accompanied with a serious information offensive that communicates to Pakistanis that LeT is not merely a social service provider; rather a trained militia that murders civilians as well as security forces. This information offen-sive may be useful in mobilizing Pakistani popular support for its elimination because surveys have shown that Pakistanis are less supportive of *tanzeem*s if they believe they kill civilians.[37]

Having laid out what we can glean from the scholarly work on leadership decapitation and the varied expected outcomes, it is far from obvious whether the United States or India has the capacity to actually eliminate key LeT lead-ers, given that they rarely leave Pakistan (except for Hajj and Umra in Saudi Arabia), enjoy multiple layers of security provided by the provincial and fed-eral government as well as their own resources, and usually move about in highly congested urban areas where the collateral damage from such attacks would be high. Moreover, Americans are not likely to support any ground operation that imperils their own forces given the relative sensitivity to combat fatalities and the lack of salience of LeT to American voters.[38] Indians, on the other hand, seem less sensitive to such fatalities.

Option 3. Escaping Pakistan's Coercion Strategy[39]

As detailed in Chapter 3, it is Pakistan's nuclear arsenal that endows Pakistan with near absolute impunity to use terrorists as tools of foreign policy. Nuclear weapons protect Pakistan in several ways. First, they generate risk to deter India from undertaking punitive military steps to punish it for any particular terrorist outrage. Second, early in a crisis, Pakistan's nuclear weapons draw in the international community to put pressure on India to not escalate. The United States in particular fears that any crisis could evolve into a full-fledged war with the potential for deliberate or inadvertent use of nuclear weapons. Third, by fostering the specter of nuclear weapons and materials or technical information falling into the hands of terrorists, Pakistan ensures that the United States will be indisposed towards sanctioning Pakistan or prosecuting any policy that could imperil (if even remotely) its economic or political survivability. For this reason, the United States encourages the International Monetary Fund (IMF) to continue bailing out Pakistan, even though it has a consistent track record of reneging on its own commitments to undertake economic reforms.[40] Taken together, Pakistan's nuclear arsenal shields itself from the consequences of its own behavior. As Pakistan rushes to acquire battlefield nuclear weapons, its nuclear coercion of India and the United States becomes even more efficacious.

Escaping this coercion loop means different things for the United States and India. For one thing, India is unlikely to be able to do so on its own. For the United States, it will require dramatically refashioning its understanding of US-Pakistan relations historically, accepting that over time Pakistan has often behaved more like an adversary than an ally, and embracing the sobering reality that while the United States has recoiled from imposing meaningful penalties because it anticipates that its financial allurements would buy influence over and/or insights into Pakistan's nuclear program, Washington has failed to acquire either. In the meantime, Pakistan has continued investing in the very assets—nuclear weapons and terrorists—that most perturb Americans while receiving US military and economic assistance. If Washington were to finally accede to the demands of these bitter realities and opt for a new approach, what kind of policies could the United States enact to put an end to Pakistan's license to use terrorism? There are at least three core components required of such a policy.

First, the United States essentially needs to call Pakistan's nuclear bluff that it is "too dangerous to fail." Rather than continuing to shoulder the impossible responsibility of policing Pakistan's potential proliferation, the United States needs to remand responsibility for securing Pakistan's nuclear materials to the Pakistani state itself. Washington should make it clear to Islamabad that Pakistan will be held responsible should non-state actors acquire its materials. The international community is in a good position to identify a putative Pakistani role because Pakistan's "nuclear signature" is now well known thanks to the revelations afforded by investigation of the A.Q. Khan network.[41] The United States should also make it clear that should the Pakistani state engage in first use of nuclear weapons on an adversary, that adversary will not be on its own in retaliating against Pakistan. The United States should consider undertaking countermeasures to subvert Pakistan's program, as it did with Iran, and even consider imposing the kinds of sanctions that crippled Iran and brought it to the negotiating table. Pakistan is not, has not been, and will not be a responsible nuclear state if left to its own devices. To continue entertaining this after Pakistan forthrightly rejected the possibility of a conditions-based civilian nuclear deal is rank fatuity.[42]

Second, the United States should stop incentivizing Pakistan to continue producing the "good jihadi assets" it wants to use in Afghanistan and India, while fighting "terrorists of the Pakistani state." Under the Coalition Support Fund (CSF) program, which actually reimburses Pakistan for its expenses in fighting its war on terrorism, Pakistan remains relevant as long as it has terrorists to fight.[43] Pakistan is engaging in simple asset banking: as long as Pakistan has terrorists to kill, it remains relevant to the United States. Instead of continuing to incentivize the security establishment to groom more terrorists, the United States should devise incentives for Pakistan to abandon Islamist terrorists as tools of foreign policy altogether.

How can the United States do this? As a preliminary matter, it should cease providing CSF funds to Pakistan immediately. This program perverts Pakistan's incentives to eliminate terrorist operating on its soil while eviscerating the significance and materiality of United Nations Security Council (UNSC) Resolution 1373 (adopted in 2001) which obliges all states to undertake actions to prevent and undermine the ability of terrorist groups to use their soil to organize, train, raise funds, and recruit and engage in other activities required to carry out attacks. This is a Chapter VII resolution which considers major terrorist events as a threat to international security and carries the possibility of a forceful response by the UN and/or member-states.[44]

Washington should also refrain from supplying Pakistan with strategic weapon systems even if Pakistan offers to purchase them with its so-called sovereign funds. Instead, it should continue providing those platforms which have proven utility in counterterror and counterinsurgency operations, but which confer little or no significant advantage in fighting India. (Pakistan has long sought assistance from the United States by feigning alignment with US goals for the main purpose of acquiring military assistance to upgrade its forces' ability to fight India.)[45] The United States should continue to provide training to Pakistan's military in these areas as well those that align with the imperatives of domestic security (e.g. natural disaster relief and other humanitarian relief operations). It should also be willing to afford police and counterinsurgency training to Pakistan's domestic security forces, and other forms of assistance to Pakistan's shambolic justice system, should Pakistan permit the United States to so.[46] Washington should also immediately revoke the "Major Non-NATO Ally" status that President Bush conferred upon Pakistan in 2004. Per the legislation that defines this status, it is a "designation given by the US government to exceptionally close allies who have strong strategic working relationships with American forces but are not members of the North Atlantic Treaty Organization."[47]

Furthermore, to alter the incentives that Pakistan confronts, the United States should state—first, privately to Pakistan's political and military leadership, and if need be, publicly—that it will declare Pakistan to be a state sponsor of terror because of the preponderance of supporting evidence for doing so. Such a declaration will impose sweeping and devastating sanctions against Pakistan. To pre-empt such an outcome, the United States should provide a time-line of concrete steps that Pakistan must take against the various militant groups it now supports, including LeT, the first of which includes ceasing active support for these groups and constricting their space for operations and recruitment. Ultimately, Washington should demand the elimination of the remnants of these militant groups. Even if Pakistan were willing to do so, the United States must concede that this will be a long-term project akin to any other disarmament, demobilization, and reintegration program. After all, Pakistan has trained tens of thousands of militants, if not more. However, there should be no economic support to Pakistan for these efforts as long as it continues to actively raise, nurture, support, and deploy so-called *jihadis* in pursuit of state goals.

If Pakistan does not respond to these measures, the United States should devise a suite of negative inducements and the concomitant political will to employ them. For example, in addition to declaring Pakistan to be a state sponsor of terrorism, Washington should target specific individuals who are providing material support to terrorist groups and individuals through international prosecution, Department of Treasury designation and seizure of accounts, and visa denials. Pakistan's civilian and military personalities enjoy coming to the United States for medical treatment, vacations and for their children's education. These privileges should be sharply curbed for any person found to be supporting terrorist groups. These targeted sanctions may be more effective because they are aimed to affect those who enact these noxious policies rather than the population more generally. The United States should work with its allies to ensure that its other partners follow suit. (China and Saudi Arabia would most certainly refuse and even object to such measures. However, neither China nor Saudi Arabia are as coveted destinations as is the United States and its western partners.) The United States should be less concerned about "lost access and influence" than about coercing Pakistan to abandon the most dangerous policies that it currently pursues with lucrative American subsidies.

Even if the US government cannot fathom such a course of coercion, the United States can curb Pakistan's appetite for terrorist misadventures by depriving it of the principal benefit it derives: international attention to its pet cause, Kashmir. Recent administration statements that reiterate support for India and Pakistan to achieve "peaceful resolution of outstanding issues, including Kashmir" reward Pakistan for its malfeasance while treating India as an equal party to the crime. India is, in fact, a victim of Pakistani terrorism. Not only does this language gratuitously reward Pakistan for its use of terrorism in Kashmir, it is also historically ill-informed and dangerously misguided, as detailed in Chapter 2. When the United States acknowledges Kashmir as a disputed area, it either demonstrates an enormous historical ignorance of the issues, or an effort to placate Pakistan at the costs of facts, law, and history. Worse yet, it rewards Pakistan for its continued use of terrorism in Kashmir and elsewhere in India. Consistent with historical facts, the United States should refuse to interject any mention of Kashmir in its various statements with and about Pakistan. Equally, it should abjure making any statements encouraging India to engage with Pakistan on the subject. Pakistan craves such language because it legitimizes Pakistan's contention that it is seeking peace from India, which obstructs its efforts. While it would be preferable if the United States adopted strong language placing the onus on the conflict firmly upon Pakistan, a middle ground may be found simply by omitting such language altogether. The Pakistan government is highly sensitive to such omissions and will understand the intent that such an omission conveys. Such signaling would also advance US interests in discouraging Pakistani terrorism in some measure by depriving Pakistan of this much sought-after benefit.

Along similar lines, when Pakistan-based terrorist organizations attack India, the United States should abandon its usual practice of encouraging India publicly to observe restraint and offering the usual bromidic calls for the both sides to continue dialogue. Such language imposes a false equivalence on India, the victim, and Pakistan, the perpetrator. Most importantly, such language rewards Pakistan for using terrorism, because such language legitimizes Pakistan's claim that it is an admissible claimant in the dispute when it fact it is not, as discussed in Chapter 2. In fact, the US government should seriously consider re-evaluating its official position on Kashmir as "disputed" altogether and work to formally readjust the various, now obsolete, UN Security Council resolutions on Kashmir, given that Pakistan has been the primary impediment to their implementation.

What does such a shift in US policy mean for India? India ultimately faces the same task as the United States: reducing the benefits which Pakistan enjoys from using its proxies while raising the costs of using them. India, like the United States, essentially rewards Pakistan principally by being willing to engage Pakistan in a composite dialogue that includes Kashmir. Unfortunately, these dialogues are never likely to fructify because the Pakistan army will always be a spoiler of even the most well-intended peace overture from Pakistan's beleaguered and besieged civilians. Once one realizes this, one must confront the very real question of the ultimate objective of this dialogue because dialogue with Pakistan cannot produce peace.[48] Worse, any dialogue with Pakistan on outstanding disputes reaffirms the Pakistani deep state's contention to its yoked citizens and wearied international community that there is, in fact, a legitimate territorial dispute. Unfortunately, following serious ostensible breakthroughs between India and Pakistan's civilians, the army often undertakes violent overtures to undermine those efforts. The most dramatic illustration of this spoiler role of the army is from 1999. In that year, Prime Ministers Nawaz Sharif and Atal Bihari Vajpayee celebrated the so-called "Lahore Declaration," which was the most important rapprochement effort in years. In response, Pakistan's Army Chief Pervez Musharraf launched the Kargil operation to undermine it.[49] Thus, not only are such talks unproductive with respect to securing peace, in the near term, they frequently invite violence upon Indians.

Instead, India would be better served by intently focusing diplomatic and political resources upon Pakistan's support for terrorist organizations in international fora and galvanizing the emergence of an international consensus in support of India's position. The principle means to do this is UN Security Council Resolution 1267, which designates specific persons who provide material support to terrorist groups and individuals.[50] These designations are crucial: once an individual is so designated, the organization cannot work through this person. Because terrorist groups often work through legitimate businesses, legitimate businesses will not be willing to engage persons so designated. China will likely rebuff any move to designate Pakistan's prized proxies because China is Pakistan's surrogate at the UNSC. For this reason, India should reach out to its allies to pressure China and hold it accountable for carrying water for Pakistan's terrorist assets. The United States should also support India in these efforts if it is serious about the strategic importance of the US-Indian partnership. While China has vigorously defended against such measures in the past, it should be acknowledged that even China is growing increasingly dismayed about the international opprobrium heaped upon it for defending Pakistan's imprudence. As past efforts have demonstrated, continued pressure at the UN can motivate China to agree to new designations. Recall that initially, China refused to permit designation of JuD, but relented after the 2008 Mumbai attacks.[51]

Short of a decisive, brief war to destroy the Pakistan army—which is likely beyond India's capabilities at present—India has other limited options. First, India may consider declaring Pakistan a state sponsor of terrorism. Arguably, if India wants other capitals to do this, it should lead by example. New Delhi can revoke Pakistan's "Most Favored Nation" status, which was granted in 1996 and never reciprocated. While the financial penalty will be relatively small, the diplomatic significance may be notable. India can downgrade the status of the Pakistan High Commission and its own embassy in Islamabad. It can oust the ambassador as well as the ISI chief in New Delhi, who is the defense attaché. While these characters will be replaced by other cogs in the deep state's wheel, the message will be clear.

There has been discussion of reneging from the Indus Water Treaty. While this sounds like an act short of declaring war, in fact, it will be an opening salvo in a likely conflict as it will threaten Pakistan's core interest: the survival of the state itself. Moreover, India will likely draw international opprobrium, as such a move will harm ordinary Pakistanis as well as the deep state. Instead, India may evaluate options on the lower end of the conflict spectrum. There is surprisingly little public debate about sub-conventional deterrence. After all, if nuclear weapons provide Pakistan with immunity for its follies, do India's own nuclear weapons not afford India the same impunity? There are numerous fault lines that India could exploit if it were willing to forgo its aversion to such actions. Limited air strikes from Indian airspace on Pakistani camps with precision-guided munitions may be an option. However, Pakistan has competent air defenses and may well shoot down Indian aircraft flying sorties in its own airspace. India will need to be prepared for escalation, and make it clear to the United States and the international community that its interests are best served by pressing Pakistan to accept loss of terrorist camps as a price of terrorism.

Over the longer run, India may be best-served by some variant of "Cold Start," discussed in Chapter 3. Pakistan can brandish threats to use its battle-field nuclear weapons. However, simple math reveals that Pakistan's threats are hollow. India will survive any nuclear exchange despite grievous loss of life and damage to key cities. Pakistan will cease to exist as a political entity in its current form. Moreover, India is not likely to be left responding to Pakistan's first use on its own. Ideally, the United States would declare as much.

Finally, while India should certainly consider a more punitive set of policies as noted above, India alone cannot compel Pakistan to quit the terrorism habit. As I have argued, only the United States has the ability if not the willingness to do so.

There Are No Good Options. Just "Less Bad" Options

There are several counter-arguments to what I am proposing here, all of which are specious. First, there are those who note that the American decision to cease aid in 1990 failed to prevent Pakistan from testing nuclear weapons in 1998 and even enabled the rise of the Taliban. This is flawed history. As discussed in Chapter 3, Pakistan developed a crude nuclear weapon by 1984. Moreover, nothing in the cut-off required the United States to outsource its Afghanistan policies to Pakistan, which chose to support Islamist groups including the Afghan Taliban to secure its strategic interests there. Second, Pakistan is not likely to fail. In fact, Pakistan is one of the most stable of instable states. It survived the 1971 war, in which it lost half of its population and 14 per cent of its territory, yet still manages to prosecute its territorial revisionism vis-à-vis India. It has survived cataclysmic natural disasters and managed to survive the avarice and mendacity of its own leadership. Third, there are those who say Pakistan will not continue fighting the terrorists unless the United States pays it to do so. This too is likely wrong. The terrorists Pakistan is killing are Pakistan's terrorists. Pakistan will continue fighting them for reasons of its own. And it does not fight the groups that the United States or India consider to be terrorists, except when some of their members very rarely defect and target the Pakistani state.

Finally, there are those in the US government—especially in the US Congress—who are exceedingly risk averse. They would rather maintain the status quo with the full knowledge that the United States is not getting value for its investments than risk a new and untested approach. Unfortunately, this risk aversion to a radically different approach to Pakistan and the dogged adherence to decades of failed policies has made Pakistan more dangerous to itself, its neighbors, and American interests by, in essence, politically rewarding and bankrolling Pakistan's twinned expansion of its nuclear and *jihadi* arsenals. The time to change course is long overdue. Even if the withdrawal of US resources does not alter Pakistan's behavior, at least the United States would not be subsidizing the undermining of its own most delicately constructed policies. Equally important, it would not be materially contributing to Pakistan's ability to wage war against India, which the United States identified long ago as its most important ally in managing the security of South Asia.

APPENDIX 1

NOTES ON TRANSLITERATION AND TRANSLATION

Due to its nature and content, I make copious use of non-English words throughout the book. I made several decisions about how to treat these foreign words that merit brief explanation. First, I preferred to use the simplest and, where applicable, most common English transliteration over the use of orthographic rules. By way of example, I use *jihad* instead of *jihād* for "جهاد." In doing so, I privileged simplicity and accessibility to readers over orthographic rigor.

Second and more substantively, the orthographic rules for Arabic and Urdu vary. LeT publishes in Urdu, Arabic and English. Except where LeT makes an explicit effort to use an Arabic spelling in the original, I opted for the Urdu variant. This distinction is important because there are both differences in pronunciation, and in some cases, orthography and transliteration as well. One common class of words involves the Arabic character "ة." When a word from Arabic is brought into Urdu, the character is usually rendered into the Urdu character "ت," which is pronounced as a "t." This occurs frequently for words that recur in this book. For example, a very common word is "شریعة," which is pronounced as *shari'ah* in Arabic with the """ (ع) indicating a glottal stop. However, in Urdu this word is written as "شریعت" and pronounced as *shariat*, omitting the glottal stop which is not used in colloquial Urdu. Another common word that occurs in the Urdu source materials that I use in this book is the Arabic-origin word for prayer, "صلاة," pronounced as *salaah* in Arabic. In Urdu it is rendered "صلات" and pronounced as *salaat*. (It should be noted that very few people use the word *salaat* for prayer in Pakistan, as most Pakistanis still prefer the Persian-origin word *namaz* (نماز) despite the

215

ongoing Arabization of Urdu consistent with the growing importance of Saudi Arabia as a source of religious authority. The word for education or training offers yet another example of this type. Arabic speakers will spell the word "تربية" as pronounce it as *tarbiya*, while Urdu speakers will spell it "تربیت" and pronounce it as *tarbiyat*. In some cases, the organization prefers to use the Arabic spelling (i.e. Jamaat ud Dawah instead of Jamaat ud Dawat). In those cases, I will use the Arabic transliteration consistent the organization's own revealed preferences.

Another character that introduces differences in pronunciation (but not orthography) is "ض," which is pronounced as a "d" in many Arabic dialects but as a "z" in Urdu. Thus, the common word "رمضان" is often transliterated as *Ramadan* in Arabic but as *Ramazan* in Urdu. A third character that is written identically in both Urdu and Arabic but pronounced differently is "ث," which is pronounced similarly to the consonantal cluster "th" in Arabic but as a sibilant "s" in Urdu. Therefore, common word "حدیث" is pronounced as *hadeeth* in Arabic but as *hadees* in Urdu.

Finally, one transliterates some Arabic and Urdu words differently because the same word is pronounced otherwise despite being written identically. Perhaps the most common example of this difference is in the word *jihad*. While Arabic speakers will often pronounce this word as *jehad*, with the "e" taking on a sound similar to that in the English word "egg," and the "a" taking on the sound of the vowel in the English word "had." In contrast, Urdu speakers tend to pronounce it as *jihad*, with the "i" taking on the sound similar to the "i" in "it," and the "a" taking on the sound of the vowel in the English word "odd." As noted above, I prefer to use the most common transliteration where possible instead of using formal diacritics. This has some import for how vowels are written and pronounced. If I were to transliterate "مجاهدین" formally I would do so as *mujāhidīn*, to indicate the long "i" sound in the word. However, I have opted instead to use *mujahideen*. (I do not use the other common variant *mujahidin* because it introduces confusion about the correct pronunciation.) In all cases, unless I am quoting an Arabic source or citing a text with a different spelling or quoting text with an alternate, I use the simplest transliteration of the Urdu variant throughout.

In addition to these transliteration choices, I also tend to use the appropriate Arabic or Persian plurals rather than Anglicized plurals. For example, the word for religious seminary is *madrassah*. I use the Persian plural for this word, *madaris*, rather than *madrassahs*. Similarly, I use *mujahideen*, as the plural for *mujahid* instead of *mujahids*, unless I am quoting a work that uses this word.

APPENDIX 1

The transliteration of individuals' names rendered similar choices. I use the transliteration employed by the author in question when they write in English. When the author has no history of writing in English, I apply the same rules as above selecting the easiest translations: Rabani is preferred to Rabaani. I have made no effort to standardize spellings even for names that are pronounced identically but have different spellings (i.e. Ahmad vs. Ahmed or Muhammad vs. Mohammed). The only exception to this rule is that I have standardized the spelling of Muhammad when referring to the Muslim prophet, unless I am quoting an English source that uses a different spelling.

As a non-theist, I do not capitalize the words for "god," "gods," "prophet," "goddesses" and the like unless they are used as a proper noun. So while I will use the expression "the Prophet Muhammad" (with a definite article) I will not generally capitalize the word "prophet" unless I am quoting another author who does. Similarly, Allah is a specific name for a god and thus I will capitalize that word as I would *Kali* or *Ram*, which are proper names referring to a specific (Hindu) goddess and god respectively.[1]

Finally, all foreign words are italicized throughout. While my choices may not please linguistic or orthographic purists or theists for that matter, I believe this approach will make the text more accessible to a wider array of audiences from other disciplines, who are less preoccupied with such matters. In Appendix 3, I have placed a glossary of these non-English words for the reader's convenience and ready reference.

APPENDIX 2

LIST OF ACRONYMS

Acronym	Name and Translation
ASWJ	Ahl-e-Sunnat Wal Jamaat (الجماعة و السنة أهل).
APHC	All Parties Hurriyat Conference.
FATA	Federally Administered Tribal Areas.
FIF	Falah Insaniat Foundation (فلاح انسانیت فاونڈیشن), Foundation for Welfare of Humanity.
FTO	Foreign Terrorist Organization.
HuA	Harkat-ul-Ansar. A militant group whose name translates as "Movement of the Helpers of the Prophet."
HUJI	Harkat-ul-Jihad-e-Islami. A militant group whose name translates as "Movement for Islamic Jihad."
HUM	Harkat-ul-Mujahideen. A militant group whose name translates as "Movement of the Holy Warriors."
HI	Hizb-e-Islami. A militant group whose name translates as "Partisans of Islam."
HM	Hizbul Mujahideen.
IJT	Islami Jamiat-e-Talaba.
IKK	Idara Khidmat-e-Khalq (اداره خدمت خلق), Organization for Humanitarian Assistance.
ISAF	International Security Assistance Force.
JeM	Jaish-e-Muhammad.
JuD	Jamaat ud Dawah (جماعة الدعوة), Organization for Preaching.
JI	Jamaat-e-Islami (جماعتِ اسلامی), Islamic Assembly.

JuF	Jamaat-ul-Furqan (جماعت الفرقان),The Assembly of Those who Can Distinguish Between Good and Evil.
JUI	Jamiat Ulema-e-Islam (جميعت علمائے اسلام), Assembly of Islamic Clergy.
LeJ	Lashkar-e-Jhangvi (لشـکر جھنگـوى), Army of Jhangvi.
LeT	Lashkar-e-Tayyaba (لشـکر طبه), Army of the Pure.
MDI	Markaz al-Dawah Irshad (مرکز دعوة وإرشـاد), Center for Preaching and Guidance.
MJAH	Markazi Jamiat Ahl-e-Hadees.
MUF	Muslim United Front.
SSP	Sipah-e-Sahaba-e-Pakistan (SSP).
TNSM	Tehreek-e-Nifaz Shariat-e-Muhammadi.
TTP	Tehreek-e-Taliban-e-Pakistan, Taliban Movement of Pakistan.
UNSC	United Nations Security Council.

APPENDIX 3

GLOSSARY OF NON-ENGLISH WORDS

Word	Translation
Al-salaf al-salih السلف الصالح	The pious forefathers or predecessors, referencing the first three generations of Muslims which include the prophet Muhammad, his companions or Sahabah, and their successors the Tabi'un, as well as their successors, the Taba Tabi'in.
Alim عام, sing. of *ulema* علماء	Scholar in Islamic law and theology.
Amir أَمِير	Leader.
As-salaam-alaikum السلام عليكم	Peace be upon you, a salutation used among Muslims.
Bahishti darvaza بہشتی دروازہ	Door to paradise.
Bid'at بدعت	Unlawful innovation.
Caliph خِلافة	Person considered to be the successor to prophet Muhammad.
Char divari چار دیواری	Lit. "four walls," used to refer to practice of women remaining in seclusion, see *purdah*.
Dehej दहेज in Hindi, دهیج in Urdu	Amount of cash, durable goods, land or other valuables that the bride's family gives to the groom's

221

	family as a condition of marriage. This is a very different concept from the Muslim practice of *mehr*.
Dars درس	Study, course of study.
Dawah دعوة	Preaching.
Devar ڈیوار	Husband's younger brother.
Farz kifaya فرض كفاية	An obligation that when performed by a few relieves the rest of the community from their obligation.
Farz-e-ayn فرض عين	An individual duty.
Fidayeen فِدائيِن	Persons willing to sacrifice their lives in a military operation, typically used by *jihadi* organizations.
Fiqh فقه	Islamic jurisprudence.
Fitna فتنة	Civil strife, sedition.
Ghaibana namaz-i-janaza غائبانه نمازِ جنازه	Funerary prayer offered in absentia of deceased.
Ghair-muqallid غير مقلد	Non-conformists, those who accept no school of Islamic jurisprudence.
Ghazi غازى	Veteran of a *jihad*.
Ghazwa غزوة	Battles or military expeditions, often referring to those battles in which the Muslim prophet participated.
Ghazwa-e-hind غزوه ہند	A battle to establish Islamic rule declared by the prophet, and the battle-cry of LeT/JuD.
Hafiz حافظ	One who has memorized the Quran.
Hawalah حواله	Informal, trust-based money transfer system also known as *hundi* ھنڈی.
Hifz حفظ, as in *hifz-e-quran* حفظ قرآن	Memorization, often used as short hand for the Hifz-e-Quran course in which students learn to recite the entire Quran from memory.
Hudood حدود	Literally meaning "limits" or "restrictions." Usually refers to punishments purportedly fixed and mandated by Allah e.g. whipping, stoning, amputation, etc.
Hundi ھنڈی	Informal, trust-based money transfer system.
Huri حورى	Celestial maidens available to Muslim men in the paradisiacal afterlife. This noun is always used in the plural.
Iblees إِبلِيس	Name for the devil.

Ijtema اجتماع — Large gathering.

Iman اِیمان — Faith.

I'tikaaf اعتکاف — A Muslim practice in which a person stays in a mosque for a prescribed number of days devoting him/herself to worship and demurring from worldy affairs, frequently during Ramadan when he/she is fasting.

Irja' إرجاء — Lit. "to postpone." In this volume it refers to the practice of deferring *takfir*, or the process of declaring a Muslim to be an apostate.

Jamaat جماعتِ — Assembly.

Jangbazi جنگ بازی — Warlords in Dari.

Jawan جوان — Young man, often used to describe enlisted men in the army.

Jihad جهاد — Lit. "a struggle." In the context of LeT publications, it usually refers to armed conflict in the way of Allah, or "holy war."

Jihad al-nafs جهاد النفس — Striving against one's base self.

Jihad al-sayf جهاد السیف — *Jihad* with the sword.

Jizya جزیة — Yearly, per capita tax levied on non-Muslims by Islamic states.

Kafir کافر, sing. of *kuffar* کفّار — Disbeliever in Islam.

Kameez کمیز — Long, loose-fitting shirt worn by men and women often over baggy trousers gathered with a draw-string called a *shalwar* شلوار.

Kalima کلمة — The affirmation that there is no god other than Allah and Mohammad is his prophet.

Kalima-go کلمة گو — One who has uttered the *kalima* or one who has affirmed that there is no god but Allah and Mohammad is his prophet.

Kalima-go kuffar کلمة گو کفّار — One who has uttered the *kalima* but who otherwise behaves like a non-Muslim.

Kalima-go mashrik کلمة گو مشرک — One who has uttered the *kalima* but who has committed a serious sin, such as polytheism.

Kashmir Pakistan ban jaega کشمیر پاکستان بن جائے گا — A slogan raised by Pakistanis which means "Kashmir will become Pakistan."

Khairun Nas خير الناس   An LeT splinter that briefly existed under the leadership of Lakhvi. It translates as "Good People."

Khan خان   An honorific title used to refer to landowners or other tribal notables.

Khidmat خدمت   Provision of social services.

Khaleefa خَليفة   Person considered to be the successor to prophet
in Arabic, خليفه in Urdu   Mohammad.

Khilaafat خِلافة   Area in which a *khaleef* or Caliph resides.
in Arabic, خلافت in Urdu

Kuffar   see *kafir*

Kufr كفر   Disbelief in Islam.

Kufr-va-shirk كفر و شرک   Apostasy and polytheism.

Kuniya كنيۃ in Arabic,   The name under which a *mujahid* fights, *nom de*
kuniyat كنيت in Urdu   *guerre.*

Madrassah مدرسه, sing.   Religious school/seminary.
of *madaris* مدارس

Maharaja ماهاراجا   Great ruler.

Masjid مسجد, sing. of   Mosque.
masajid مساجد

Mashrik مشرک, sing. of   One who commits *shirk*. Often translated as
mashrakin مشركين   "polytheist."

Maslak مسلک, sing. of   Lit. "a path." Used frequently to refer to a sectarian
masalik مسالک   tradition of Islam.

Maulvi مولوی   Religious scholar.

Mehr مہر   Mandatory payment in money, home, land, jewellery or other goods that must be paid by the groom to the bride at the time of marriage which becomes her legal property. The precise amount of *mehr* is specified in the marriage contract, called *nikah-namah* نكاح نامه, which is signed by both spouses.

Mo-e-muqadis   Lit. "sacred hair," a relic of the prophet's hair in the
مو مقدس   Hazratbal Shrine.

Mudeer مدير   Director, editor.

Mujahid مجاہد, sing. of   One who struggles in the way of Allah. In LeT
mujahideen مجاہدين   materials this usually refers to a combatant in a "holy war."

Munafiq منافق, sing. of   A Muslim who spreads discord in the community.
munafiqin منافقين   Often translated as "hypocrite."

Murtad مرتد	An apostate. Apostasy carries the death penalty.
Naib amir نائب امیر	Deputy leader.
Namaz نماز	Prayer.
Nawab نواب	Honorific title for reigning Mughal emperor.
Nizam نظام	Title for sovereign of Indian state.
Pir پیر	Lit. "older person, elder." Usually refers to a Sufi spiritual leader.
Purdah پرده	Lit. "curtain." It refers to the practice of women concealing themselves either by veiling when in public or remaining within their homes. Synonymous with "*char divari*."
Raja راجا	Princely ruler in South Asia.
Sakhi Sarwar سخی سرور	Sufi saint.
Salaat صلات	Prayer.
Salaka سالکه	To travel or walk on a path.
Sanad سند	Credential, a certificate of achievement from a religious seminary.
Shahadat شهادت	The act of giving testimony. The word is more generally used for martyrdom.
Shaheed شهید	Lit. "a witness"; the word is often used to describe a martyr or one who dies fulfilling a religious commandment. In practice, the term "*shaheed*" is used for most kinds of death.
Shalwar شلوار	Baggy trousers, worn by men and women, that are gathered with a drawstring and often worn under a long, loose-fitting shirt called a *kameez* کمیز.
Shariat شریعت	Islamic canonical law.
Sheh rag شاه رگ	Jugular vein.
Sheikh شیخ	Honorific title afforded to Muslim men; women are referred to as *Sheikha*.
Shirk شرک	To ascribe to others the attributes of Allah, often translated as "polytheism."
Shura شورا	Consultative assembly.
Sunnat سنت	Verbally transmitted record of the deeds and sayings of the Muslim prophet Mohammad.
Surah سورة	The term used to describe a chapter in the Quran.
Tabligh تبلیغ	Proselytization.
Tafsir تفسیر	Exegesis.

Tayyaba طیبه   Righteous men.

Tayyabaat طیبات, fem. pl.   Virtuous women.
of *tayyaba* طیبه

Tanzeem تنظیم   Organization.

Takfiri تکفیری   One who declares a fellow Muslim to be a disbeliever, *kafir*.

Taqlid تَقْلید   Lit. "to follow." In Islamic legal lexicon it suggests following an Islamic scholar who can interpret *Shariat* Islamic law.

Tarbiyat تربیت   Teaching.

Tareeqa طریقه   Way, manner.

Tasbeeh تسبیح   Rosary beads used by Muslims.

Tawheed توحید   Oneness.

Tehreek تحریک   Movement.

Tehsil تحصیل   Administrative division.

Ummat أمت   The entire global community of Muslims, held together by their shared faith.

'*Urs* عرس   A celebration of the death anniversary of a Sufi saint in South Asia. It is usually held at the saint's *dargah* shrine or tomb.

Ushr عُشر   Islamic land tax.

Wa-alaikum-salaam   Peace unto you as well. Typically said in response
وعلیکم السلام   to As-salaam-alaikum السلام_علیکم.

Wahdat-ul-wajood   Unity of being.
وحدة الوجود

Wajib ul qatal   Worthy of being killed; one who kills such a person
واجب القتل   will receive divine rewards.

Ya ali madad یا علی مدد   "Ali help me." Often used as a salutation.

Zarb-e-azb ضربِ عضب   Lit. "a sharp and cutting blow." It refers to the strike of the prophet's sword.

Zakat زکاة in Arabic,   Almsgiving in Islam, treated as a tax.
زکات in Urdu

Zamindar زمیندار   Landowner.

NOTES

1. INTRODUCTION

1. Rabasa, Angel et al., *The Lessons of Mumbai*, Santa Monica: RAND Corporation, 2009.
2. "Global Terrorism Database," *National Consortium for the Study of Terrorism and Responses to Terrorism*, accessed 11 June 2018. https://www.start.umd.edu/gtd/.
3. Rassler, Don, C. Christine Fair, Anirban Gosh, and Nadia Shoeb, "The Fighters of Lashkar-e-Taiba: Recruitment, Training, Deployment and Death," *West Point Combating Terrorism Center*, April 2013, accessed 11 June 2018.
4. See Fair, C. Christine, "Antecedents and Implications of the November 2008 Lashkar-e-Taiba Attack Upon Mumbai," testimony presented before the House Homeland Security Committee, Subcommittee on Transportation Security and Infrastructure Protection, 11 March 2009, accessed 11 June 2018. https://www.rand.org/pubs/testimonies/CT320.readonline.html; and Rabasa et al., The Lessons of Mumbai.
5. See Rabasa et al., *The Lessons of Mumbai;* and Fair, C. Christine, "Antecedents and Implications of the November 2008 Lashkar-e-Taiba Attack Upon Mumbai."
6. See Tankel, Stephen, *Storming the World Stage: The Story of Lashkar-e-Taiba*, London: Hurst, 2011; and Jamal, Arif, *Call for Transnational Jihad: Lashkar-e-Taiba 1985–2014*, East Brunswick: Avant Garde Books LLC, 2014.
7. See Waze, Sachin and Shirish Thorat, *The Scout: The Definitive Account of David Headley and the Mumbai Attacks*, New Delhi: Bloomsbury, 2016; and Unnithan, Sandeep, *Black Tornado: The Three Sieges of Mumbai 26/11*, Noida: HarperCollins India, 2015; and Sanghvi, Vir, *26/11 The Attack on Mumbai*, New Delhi: Penguin, 2009; and Scott-Clark, Cathy and Adrian Levy, *The Siege: 68 Hours Inside the Taj Hotel*, New York: Penguin, 2013; and Rotella, Sebastian, "Pakistan and the Mumbai attacks: The Untold Story," *ProPublica*, 26 Jan. 2011, accessed 11 June 2018. https://www.propublica.org/article/pakistan-and-the-mumbai-attacks-the-untold-story; and Rotella, Sebastian, "Four Alleged Masterminds of 2008 Mumbai Attacks Are Indicted in Chicago," *ProPublica*, 25 April 2011, accessed 11 June 2018. https://www.propublica.org/article/four-alleged-masterminds-of-2008-mumbai-attacks-are-indicted-in-chicago; and Rotella, Sebastian, "Mumbai Case Offers Rare Picture of Ties Between Pakistan's Intelligence Service,

Militants," *ProPublica*, 2 May 2011, accessed 11 June 2018. https://www.propublica. org/article/mumbai-case-offers-rare-picture-of-ties-between-pakistans-intelligence-serv; and Rotella, Sebastian, "Chicago Terrorism Trial: What we learned, and Didn't, About Pakistan's Terror Connections," *ProPublica*, 9 June 2011, accessed 11 June 2018. http:// www.propublica.org/article/chicago-terrorism-trial-what-we-learned-and-didnt; and Rotella, Sebastian, "The Man Behind Mumbai," *ProPublica*, 13 November 2010, accessed 11 June 2018. https://www.propublica.org/article/the-man-behind-mumbai.

8. Mannes, Aaron, John. P. Dickerson, Amy Silva, Jana Shakarian, and V.S. Subrahmanian, "A Brief History of LeT," in *Computational Analysis of Terrorist Groups: Lashkar-e-Taiba*, New York: Springer, 2013, pp. 23–68.

9. See Abou Zahab, Mariam, "The Regional Dimension of Sectarian Conflicts in Pakistan," in *Pakistan: Nationalism Without a Nation?* (ed.) Christophe Jaffrelot, London: Zed Books, 2002, pp. 115–28; and Haq, Farhat, "Militarism and Motherhood: The Women of the Lashkar-i-Tayyaba in Pakistan," *Signs*, 32, 4 (Summer 2007), pp. 1023–1046.; and Fair, C. Christine, "Lashkar-e-Tayiba and the Pakistani State," *Survival*, 53 (2011), pp. 1–23. It turns out that another author, Samina Yasmeen, was working on their literature simultaneous with this effort. See Yasmeen, Samina, *Jihad and Dawah*, London: Hurst & Co., 2017.

10. I first made this argument in 2011. See Fair, C. Christine, "Lashkar-e-Tayiba and the Pakistani State," Survival, 53 (August 2011), pp. 1–23. I expand upon this in Fair, C. Christine, "Jamaat-ud-Dawa: Converting Kuffar at Home, Killing Them Abroad," *Current Trends in Islamist Ideology*, Vol. 22, forthcoming 2017. See also Qayyum, Tabish. "The ISIS' Footprint in Pakistan: Myth or Reality," accessed 11 June 2018. https://www.academia.edu/31628011/The_ISIS_Footprint_in_Pakistan_Myth_or_Reality.

11. Fair, C. Christine. "The Only Enemy Pakistan's Army Can Beat Is Its Own Democracy," Foreign Policy, 9 August 2017, accessed 11 June 2018. http://foreignpolicy.com/2017/08/09/the-only-enemy-pakistans-army-can-beat-is-its-own-democracy/.

12. Asif Shahzad, "Pakistan army pushed political role for militant-linked groups," *Reuters*, 15 September 2017. accessed 20 November 2017. https://www.reuters.com/article/us-pakistan-politics-militants/pakistan-army-pushed-political-role-for-militant-linked-groups-idUSKCN1BR02F; "Jamaatud Dawa enters political arena, launches Milli Muslim League party," *The Dawn*, 8 August 2017, accessed 11 June 2018. https://www.dawn.com/news/1350202. The party's key leadership have undergone training by the army. For example, the party's information secretary, Tabish Qayyum, completed his MA at Pakistan's National Defense University in the Department of International Relations, Faculty of Contemporary Studies in 2016. See Qayyum, "The ISIS' Footprint in Pakistan."

13. See Sikand, Yoginder, "The Islamist Militancy in Kashmir: The Case of the Lashkar-e-Taiba," in *The Practice of War: Production, Reproduction and Communication of Armed Violence*, (ed.) Aparna Rao et al., New York: Berghahn Books, 2007, pp. 215–238; and Abou Zahab, Mariam, "I Shall be Waiting at the Door of Paradise: The Pakistani Martyrs of the Lashkar-e-Taiba (Army of the Pure)," in *The Practice of War: Production,*

Reproduction and Communication of Armed Violence (ed.) Aparna Rao et al., New York: Berghahn Books, 2007, pp. 133–158; and Shafqat, Saeed, "From Official Islam to Islamism: The Rise of Dawat-ul-Irshad and Lashkar-e-Taiba," *Pakistan: Nationalism without a Nation*, (ed.) Christophe Jaffrelot, London: Zed Books, 2002, pp. 131–147; and Khan, Zaigham, "Allah's Army," *The Herald Annual* (Jan. 1998), pp. 123–130.

14. See Fair, C. Christine, *The Counterterror Coalitions: Cooperation with Pakistan and India*, Santa Monica, CA: RAND; and Chalk, Peter and C. Christine Fair, "Lashkar-e-Tayyiba leads the Kashmiri insurgency," *Jane's Intelligence Review*, 14, 10 (Dec. 2002), pp: 1–5.

15. "US embassy cables: Lashkar-e-Taiba terrorists raise funds in Saudi Arabia," *The Guardian*, 10 August 2009, accessed 11 June 2018. https://www.theguardian.com/world/us-embassy-cables-documents/220186

16. Tankel, Stephen, "Lashkar-e-Taiba: Past Operations and Future Prospects," *New America Foundation*, National Security Studies Program Policy Paper, April 2011.

17. See US Department of Treasury, "Recent OFAC Actions," 27 April 2006, accessed 11 June 2018. https://www.treasury.gov/resource-center/sanctions/OFAC-Enforcement/Pages/20060427.aspx.

18. Author's field work, Dec./Jan. 2004.

19. US Department of State, 'Addition of Aliases Jamaat-Ud-Dawa and Idara Khidmat-E-Khalq to the Specially Designated Global Terrorist Designation of Lashkhar-E-Tayyiba,' 28 April 2006, accessed 19 June 2017, https://2001-2009.state.gov/r/pa/prs/ps/2006/65401.htm.

20. See US Department of State, "Secretary of State's Terrorist Designation of Falah-i-Insaniat Foundation," 24 November 2010, accessed 11 June 2018. https://www.state.gov/j/ct/rls/other/des/266648.htm; and United Nations, "Security Council Al-Qaida Sanctions Committee Adds Four Names to Its Sanctions List, Amends One Entry," 14 March 2012m accessed 11 June 2018, http://www.un.org/press/en/2012/sc10578.doc.htm.

21. Fair, C. Christine and Ali Hamza, "The Foreign Policy Essay: Whether or Not Pakistan Will Join the War in Yemen May Depend on a Group You've Probably Never Heard Of," *Lawfare*, 12 April 2015, accessed 11 June 2018. https://www.lawfareblog.com/foreign-policy-essay-whether-or-not-pakistan-will-join-war-yemen-may-depend-group-youve-probably.

22. Mannes et al., "A Brief History of LeT," pp. 23–68.

23. Tankel, *Storming the World Stage*.

24. "Hafiz Saeed's JuD Launches Political Party in Pakistan," *The Quint*, 8 August 2017, accessed 6 September 2017. https://www.thequint.com/news/hafiz-saaed-jud-launches-political-party.

25. Fair, C. Christine. "The Only Enemy Pakistan's Army Can Beat Is Its Own Democracy," *Foreign Policy*, 9 August 2017, accessed 11 June 2018. http://foreignpolicy.com/2017/08/09/the-only-enemy-pakistans-army-can-beat-is-its-own-democracy/.

26. "A-120 by-polls: JUD fields candidate," *The Nation*, 13 August 2017, accessed 11 June 2018. http://nation.com.pk/national/13-Aug-2017/na-120-by-polls-jud-fields-candidate.

27. Shahid. Kunwar Khuldune. "A Win for All: Pakistan's NA-120 By-Election," The Diplomat, 21 September 2017, accessed 11 June 2018. https://thediplomat.com/2017/09/a-win-for-all-pakistans-na-120-by-election/.

28. Ahmad, Jibran, "Imran Khan's PTI retains seat in by-election, but new religious parties gain," Reuters.com, 27 October 17, accessed 11 June 2018 https://www.reuters.com/article/us-pakistan-politics-election/imran-khans-pti-retains-seat-in-by-election-but-new-religious-parties-gain-idUSKBN1CW0W2.

29. Shahid, Kunwar Khuldune. "India dictating terms to Pakistan' claims Jamaaat ud Dawa," Asia Times, 24 November 2017, accessed 11 June 2018. http://www.atimes.com/article/india-dictating-terms-pakistan-claims-jamaaat-ud-dawa/.

30. "Hafiz Saeed's JuD to contest 2018 Pakistan general elections," Economic Times, 3 Dec., accessed 11 June 2018. https://m.economictimes.com/news/international/world-news/hafiz-saeed-to-contest-pakistan-general-elections-next-year/amp_article-show/61897257.cms.

31. Musharraf did not consult the MML before making this peculiar announcement. See "Musharraf may ally with Hafiz Saeed for 2018 polls," 4 Dec. 2017, accessed 11 June 2018. https://timesofindia.indiatimes.com/world/pakistan/musharraf-may-ally-with-hafiz-saeed-for-2018-polls/articleshowprint/61914511.cms.

32. Abdullah Niazi, "MML scores two big victories ahead of NA-4 by-polls," Pakistan Today, 24 October 2017. Accessed 2 June 2018. https://www.pakistantoday.com.pk/2017/10/24/mml-scores-two-big-victories-ahead-of-na-4-by-polls/;"MML allowed to be enlisted as political party," Business Recorder, 9 March, 2018. Accessed 2 June 2018. https://fp.brecorder.com/2018/03/20180309350162/.

33. Jamal, Umair. "What Is Behind the Political "Mainstreaming of Jamaat-ud-Dawa in Pakistan?," The Diplomat, 8 August 2017,. http://thediplomat.com/2017/08/what-is-behind-the-political-mainstreaming-of-jamaat-ud-dawa-in-pakistan/; Barker, Memphis. "Pakistan Is Inviting Its Favorite Jihadis Into Parliament," Foreign Policy, 4 October 2017, accessed 11 June 2018. http://foreignpolicy.com/2017/10/04/pakistan-is-inviting-its-favorite-jihadis-into-parliament/.

34. "Pakistan varsity trained students to support LeT via social media," Hindustan Times, 28 November, 2015, accessed 11 June 2018. http://www.hindustantimes.com/world/pakistan-varsity-trained-students-to-support-let-via-social-media/story-tNKCjqQOb-DmyGrUW35F7jJ.html. See also "Pakistan trained people to use social media for JuD, LeT propaganda," Economic Times, 27 November 2015, accessed 11 June 2018. https://economictimes.indiatimes.com/news/defence/pakistan-trained-people-to-use-social-media-for-jud-let-propaganda/articleshow/49946412.cms.

35. See Qayyum, Tabish. "The ISIS' Footprint in Pakistan: Myth or Reality," accessed 11 June 2018. https://www.academia.edu/31628011/The_ISIS_Footprint_in_Pakistan_Myth_or_Reality.

36. "Aims and Objectives: Milli Muslim League," Invite, Issue No. 7 (October 2017) pp. 12–13.

37. In recent decades, the concept of the "deep state," has become increasingly popular in scholarly writings as well as news accounts. The phrase originated in the 1990s in the

context of Turkey's politics, but it has increasingly been mobilized in treatments of authoritarian and illiberal regimes. In the specific case of Pakistan, Ayoob (2004) appears to be among the first to have used it to describe the dominance of Pakistan's security structure and institutions (armed forces and intelligence agencies) over the state and society and the existential threats that these institutions cultivate to justify their pre-eminence in domestic affairs. (Ayoob, Mohammed. "Political Islam: Image and Reality." *World Policy Journal* 21, no. 3 (2004): 1–14.). Ayesha Siddiqa (2007) built upon this concept of dominance by the military establishment and its intelligence agencies by focusing upon their vast business interests and their need to secure them. This overdeveloped security apparatus dominates Pakistan's society by working with and through allies to ensure that its preeminence in decision-making directly and indirectly. This notion of the over-developed and over-bearing military dominating and controlling the state to secure its corporate interests is generally referred to as the "deep state." Siddiqa, Ayesha. 2007. *Military, Inc.* London: Pluto Press.

38. "Hafiz Saeed's JuD Launches Political Party in Pakistan."
39. During the month of November 2017, I corresponded with the MML leadership and posed several questions. Despite their initial willingness to engage, they ignored all of my questions.
40. See, *inter alia*, Chakraborty, Angshukanta, "Indian Army normalised war crime by awarding officer who used a Kashmiri as human shield," 23 May 2017, accessed 11 June 2018. https://www.dailyo.in/politics/kashmir-indian-army-nitin-leetul-gogoi-award-farooq-ahmad-dhar/story/1/17367.html; "50% human rights violation complaints between 2012–2016 are from Jammu and Kashmir: RTI query," *First Post*, 17 July 2017, accessed 11 June 2018. http://www.firstpost.com/india/50-human-rights-violation-complaints-between-2012-2016-are-from-jammu-and-kashmir-rti-query-3823919.html; US Department of State, "India 2016 Human Rights Report," 3 March 2017, accessed 11 June 2018. https://www.state.gov/documents/organization/265748.pdf.
41. Kambere, Geoffrey et al., "The Financing of Lashkar-e-Taiba," *CTX Journal*, 1, 1 (2011), accessed 11 June 2018. https://globalecco.org/ctx-v1n1/lashkar-e-taiba.
42. See Kambere, "The Financing of Lashkar-e-Taiba;" and Rana, Muhammad *Amir, The A to Z of Jehadi Organizations in Pakistan*, translated by Saba Ansari, Lahore: Mashal, 2004.
43. "Defence budget set at Rs920.2bn for FY2017–18," *The Dawn*, 26 May 2017, accessed 11 June 2018, https://www.dawn.com/news/1335574.
44. Burki, Shahid Javed, *Kashmir: A Problem in Search of a Solution*, Washington, D.C.: United States Institute of Peace, 2007, accessed 11 June 2018. https://www.usip.org/publications/2007/03/kashmir-problem-search-solution.
45. Fair, C. Christine, *Fighting to the End: The Pakistan Army's Way of War*, New York: Oxford University Press, 2014; Kapur, Paul, *Jihad as Grand Strategy: Islamist Militancy, National Security, and the Pakistani State*, New York: Oxford University Press, 2016.
46. See Fair, C. Christine, "Militant Recruitment in Pakistan," pp. 489–504; and Fair, C. Christine, "The Militant Challenge in Pakistan," *Asia Policy*, 11 (Jan. 2011), pp. 105–

137; and Mir, *Amir, True Face of the Jehadis*, Lahore: Mashal, 2004; and Howenstein, Nicholas, "The Jihadi Terrain in Pakistan: An Introduction to the Sunni Jihadi Groups in Pakistan and Kashmir," University of Bradford, Pakistan Studies Research Unit, 1 (2008), accessed 11 June 2018. https://bradscholars.brad.ac.uk/handle/10454/2224; and Jamal, Arif, *Shadow War: The Untold Story of Jihad in Kashmir*, New York: Melville, 2009; and Qazi, Shehzad H., "Rebels of the Frontier: Origins, Organisation, and Recruitment of the Pakistani Taliban," *Small Wars and Insurgencies*, 22, 4 (2011), pp. 574–602; and Zaidi, Syed Manzar Abbas, "The Taliban Organisation in Pakistan," *The RUSI Journal*, 154, 5 (2009), pp. 40–47; and Rana, *The A to Z of Jehadi Organizations*.

47. See Abou Zahab, Mariam, "Salafism in Pakistan: The Ahl-e Hadith Movement," in *Global Salafism: Islam's New Religious Movement*, (ed.) Roel Meijer, London: Hurst, 2009, pp. 126–139; and Metcalf, Barbara, *Islamic Contestations: Essays on Muslims in India and Pakistan*, New Delhi: Oxford University Press, 2004; Philippon, Alix. "The Role of Sufism in the Identity Construction, Mobilization and Political Activism of the Barelwi Movement in Pakistan." PARTECIPAZIONE E CONFLITTO7.1 (2014): 152–169.

48. Nasr, Vali R., *Islamic Leviathan: Islam and the Making of State Power*, Oxford: Oxford University Press, 2001.

49. Ahl-e-Hadees followers are frequently confused with Wahhabis; however, Wahhabis follow the Hanbali school of jurisprudence. See Abou Zahab, Mariam, "Salafism in Pakistan: The Ahl-e Hadith Movement," in *Global Salafism: Islam's New Religious Movement*, (ed.) Roel Meijer, London: Hurst, 2009, pp. 126–139; and Metcalf, Barbara, *Islamic Contestations: Essays on Muslims in India and Pakistan*, New Delhi: Oxford University Press, 2004.

50. Fuchs, Simon Wolfgang, "Third Wave Shiism: Sayyid "Arif Husain al-Husaini and the Islamic Revolution in Pakistan," *Journal of the Royal Asiatic Society*, 24, 3 (July 2014), pp. 493–510.

51. See Staniland, Paul, "Militias, Ideology, and the State," *Journal of Conflict Resolution* 59, 5 (2015), pp. 770–793; and Tankel, Stephen, "Beyond the Double Game: Lessons from Pakistan's Approach to Islamist Militancy," *Journal of Strategic Studies*, 24 July 2016, accessed 11 June 2018. http://www.tandfonline.com/doi/full/10.1080/01402 390.2016.1174114.

52. See "Al-Qaeda "rebuilding" in Pakistan," BBC, 12 Jan. 2007, accessed 11 June 2018. http://news.bbc.co.uk/2/hi/south_asia/6254375.stm; and Kronstadt, K. Alan, "US-Pakistan Relations," Washington D.C.: Congressional Research Service, 2012, accessed 11 June 2018. https://fas.org/sgp/crs/row/R41832.pdf.

53. See Bennett, Elizabeth, "A Comeback for al-Qaeda in the Indian Subcontinent?," *Foreign Policy Journal*, 12 May 2015, accessed 11 June 2018. https://www.foreignpolicyjournal.com/2015/05/12/a-comeback-for-al-qaeda-in-the-indian-subcontinent/; and Roggio, Bill, "Pakistani Taliban emir for Bajaur joins Islamic State," *Long War Journal*, 2 February 2015, accessed 11 June 2018. http://www.longwarjournal.org/archives/2015/02/pakistani_taliban_em.php.

54. Abbottabad Commission, *Abbottabad Commission Report*, 4 Jan. 2013, accessed 11 June 2018. http://www.aljazeera.com/indepth/spotlight/binladenfiles/

55. Gall, Carlotta, *The Wrong Enemy: America in Afghanistan, 2001–2014*, New York: Houghton Mifflin Harcourt, 2014.

56. Brummit, Chris and Zarar Khan, "1 Year on from OBL raid, no answers from Pakistan," *US News and World Report*, 1 May 2012, accessed 11 June 2018. https://www.usnews.com/news/world/articles/2012/05/01/1-year-on-from-obl-raid-no-answers-from-pakistan.

57. "Shakil Afridi: Doctor who helped CIA catch Bin Laden 'can be released very soon' after Pakistan prison move," *The Independent*, 28 April 2019, accessed 3 June 2018. https://www.independent.co.uk/news/world/asia/bin-laden-doctor-shakil-afridi-pakistan-prison-released-cia-a8327231.html.

58. See Rassler, Don, "Situating The Emergence of The Islamic State Of Khorasan," *CTC Sentinel*, 8, 3 (March 2015), pp. 7–11; and Haq, Riazul, "In rare admission, Pakistan recognises growing presence of Islamic State," *Express Tribune*, 10 February 2016, accessed 3 June 2018. https://tribune.com.pk/story/1043735/in-rare-admission-pakistan-recognises-growing-presence-of-islamic-state/.

59. Tanzeem, Ayesha, "Afghanistan Implies Pakistan Supporting IS Militants," *VOA News*, 29 June 2016, accessed 11 June 2018. http://www.voanews.com/a/afghanistan-pakistan-islamic-state/3397298.html.

60. Zahid, Farha, "Growing Evidence of Islamic State in Pakistan," *Terrorism Monitor*, 14, 3 (2016), accessed 11 June 2018. https://jamestown.org/program/growing-evidence-of-islamic-state-in-pakistan/.

61. See "Mullah Omar: Taliban leader 'died in Pakistan in 2013,'" *BBC*, 29 July 2015," accessed 11 June 2018. http://www.bbc.com/news/world-asia-33703097; and Popalzai, Masoud, Euan McKirdy, Tim Lister and Tim Hume, "Taliban's new leader 'natural choice' to unite group, say analysts," CNN.com, 25 May 2016, accessed 11 June 2018. http://www.cnn.com/2016/05/25/middleeast/new-taliban-leader-announced/

62. Giustozzi, Antonio, *Koran Kalashnikov and Laptop: The Neo-Taliban Insurgency in Afghanistan, 2002–2007*, London: Hurst, 2009.

63. Brown, Vahid and Don Rassler, *The Haqqani Nexus and the Evolution of al-Qa'ida*, West Point, NY: Combating Terrorism Center, 2011.

64. See Fair, C. Christine, "Militant Recruitment in Pakistan," pp. 489–504; and Fair, C. Christine, "The Militant Challenge," pp. 105–137.

65. Rehman, Zia Ur. "The battle for Kurram." *The Friday Times*, 24, 3 (2012), accessed 11 June 2018. http://www.thefridaytimes.com/beta2/tft/article.php?issue=20120302&page=3.

66. See Khan, Ismail, "The Assertion of Barelvi Extremism," *Current Trends in Islamist Ideology*, 12 (2011), pp. 51–72; and Zaman, Muhammad Qasim, "Sectarianism in Pakistan: The Radicalization of Shi'i and Sunni Identities," *Modern Asian Studies*, 32, 3 (1998), pp. 689–716; and International Crisis Group, "The State of Sectarianism in Pakistan," 18 April 2005, accessed 11 June 2018. https://www.crisisgroup.org/asia/south-asia/pakistan/state-sectarianism-pakistan; and Nasr, Vali R., "International

Politics, Domestic Imperatives, and Identity Mobilization: Sectarianism in Pakistan, 1979–1998," *Comparative Politics*, 32, 2 (2000), pp. 170–191; and Jamal, Arif, "Sufi Militants Struggle with Deobandi Jihadists in Pakistan," *Terrorism Monitor*, 9, 8, 24 February 2011, accessed 11 June 2018. https://jamestown.org/program/sufi-militants-struggle-with-deobandi-jihadists-in-pakistan/.

67. Abou Zahab, "The Regional Dimension of Sectarian Conflicts," pp. 115–28.

68. Staniland, "Militias, Ideology, and the State," pp. 770–793.

69. See Qazi, "Rebels of the Frontier," pp. 574–602; and Zaidi, "The Taliban Organisation in Pakistan," pp. 40–47.

70. Fair, C. Christine and Seth G. Jones, "Pakistan's War Within," *Survival*, 51 (Jan. 2010), pp. 161–188.

71. Roggio, "Pakistani Taliban emir for Bajaur joins Islamic State."

72. "Pakistan Taliban chief Mullah Fazlullah 'killed in drone attack,'" *Al Jazeera*, 15 June 2018, accessed 21 June 2018, https://www.aljazeera.com/news/2018/06/pakistani-taliban-chief-mullah-fazlullah-killed-drone-strike-180615094513389.html; Khattak, Daud, "Who Will Be the Next Leader of the Pakistani Taliban?," *The Diplomat*, 19 June 2018, accessed 21 June 2018, https://thediplomat.com/2018/06/who-will-be-the-next-leader-of-the-pakistani-taliban/.

73. Staniland, Paul, "Militias, Ideology, and the State," *Journal of Conflict Resolution* Vol. 59, No. 5 (August 2015), pp. 770–793; Tankel, Stephen, "Beyond the Double Game: Lessons from Pakistan's Approach to Islamist Militancy," Journal of Strategic Studies, published online 16 June 2016, accessed 27 November 2017. http://www.tandfonline.com/doi/abs/10.1080/01402390.2016.1174114.

74. Fair, C. Christine, "Antecedents and Implications of the November 2008 Lashkar-e-Taiba Attack Upon Mumbai," testimony presented before the House Homeland Security Committee, Subcommittee on Transportation Security and Infrastructure Protection on 11 March 2009.

75. Tankel, *Storming the World Stage*.

76. Cohen, Stephen P., *The Idea of Pakistan*, Washington DC: Brookings Institution Press, 2004.

77. Rashid, Ahmed, *Descent into Chaos*, New York: Viking, 2008, pp. 230.

78. Tankel, *Storming the World Stage*.

79. Solomon, Jay. "U.N. Security Council Sanctions Lashkar Members," *Wall Street Journal*, 10 Dec. 2008, accessed 11 June 2018. http://online.wsj.com/article/SB12289533 2614496341.html.

80. "About," *Online Computer Library Center*, accessed 11 June 2018. https://www.oclc.org/en/about.html.

81. Ustaad, Safina and C. Christine Fair, *A Call to War*, New Delhi: Oxford University Press, forthcoming 2018.

82. Rassler, Don, C. Christine Fair, Anirban Gosh, and Nadia Shoeb, "The Fighters of Lashkar-e-Taiba: Recruitment, Training, Deployment and Death," *West Point Combating Terrorism Center*, April 2013, accessed 11 June 2018.

83. I am deeply touched and even inspired that Mariam still answered important questions

about LeT and other Pakistani groups even though she was gravely ill. I miss her profoundly.

84. Fair, *Fighting to the End.*
85. Ibid.
86. "Lashkar-e-Taiba, Jamat-ud-Dawa trying to acquire weapons of mass destruction: Book," *Economic Times,* 29 June 2014, accessed 11 June 2018. http://ecoti.in/PDI6hY.
87. See Rassler et al, "The Fighters of Lashkar-e-Taiba."
88. Fair, C. Christine, "Lashkar-e-Tayiba and the Pakistani State," *Survival,* 53 (August 2011), pp. 1–23; Fair, C. Christine, "Insights from a Database of Lashkar-e-Taiba and Hizb-ul-Mujahideen Militants," *Journal of Strategic Studies,* 37, 2 (2014), pp. 259–290.
89. Benmelech, Efraim, Claude Berrebi, and Esteban F. Klor, "Economic conditions and the quality of suicide terrorism," *The Journal of Politics* 74, 1 (2012), pp. 113–128.

2. THE GENESIS OF INDO-PAKISTAN SECURITY COMPETITION

1. This chapter summarizes several chapters from Fair, C. Christine, *Fighting to the End,* particularly chs Three ("Born and Insecure State") and Four ("The Army's Defense of Pakistan's Ideological Frontiers.")
2. Brass, Paul R., "The Partition of India and retributive genocide in the Punjab, 1946–47: Means, methods, and purposes," *Journal of Genocide Research,* 5, 1 (2003), pp. 71–101.
3. Khan, Yasmeen, *The Great Partition: The Making of India and Pakistan,* New Haven: Yale University Press, 2007.
4. Fair, *Fighting to the End;* Tellis, Ashley J. "Stability in South Asia," RAND Documented Briefing, 1997, accessed 11 June 2018. https://www.rand.org/pubs/documented_briefings/DB185.html.
5. Haider, Mateen, "Pakistan and Kashmir are inseparable: General Raheel Sharif," *Dawn,* 3 June 2015, accessed 11 June 2018. https://www.dawn.com/news/1185928.
6. Rana, Shahbaz. "Kashmir is last unfinished agenda of partition: Raheel, Express Tribune, 20 January 2017, accessed 11 June 2018. https://tribune.com.pk/story/1301258/kashmir-last-unfinished-agenda-partition-raheel/.
7. "Pakistan's nuclear, conventional capabilities meant for global, regional peace: President," Associated Press of Pakistan, 23 March 2017, accessed 7 Sept. 2017. https://www.app.com.pk/pakistans-nuclear-conventional-capabilities-meant-for-global-regional-peace-president/.
8. Fair, *Fighting to the End.*
9. Tinker, Hugh, "Pressure, Persuasion, Decision: Factors in the Partition of the Punjab, August 1947," *Journal of Asian Studies,* 36, 4 (1977), pp. 695–704.
10. Swami, Praveen, *India, Pakistan and the Secret Jihad: The Covert War in Kashmir, 1947–2005,* London: Routledge, 2007.
11. As early as 1984, Pakistan had a "large bomb that could be delivered ... by a C-130." Khan, Feroz, *Eating Grass: The Making of the Pakistani Bomb,* Stanford, CA: Stanford University Press, 2012, p. 189. This assessment roughly coincides with earlier state-

ments by Abdul Sattar, a former foreign minister, who claimed that Pakistan developed nuclear devices as early as 1983. Sattar, Abdul, *Pakistan's Foreign Policy 1947–2005*, Karachi: Oxford University Press, 2007. For more details, see Fair, C. Christine, "Pakistan's Nuclear Program: Laying the Groundwork for Impunity," in *Routledge Handbook of Asian Security Studies* (2nd edition), Joseph Liow, Andrew Scobell and Sumit Ganguly (eds), Abingdon: Routledge, 2017: 126–139.

12. Fair, *Fighting to the End*.

13. Greenberg, Michael, "India's Independence and the War," *Pacific Affairs*, 15 (June 1942), pp. 164–187.

14. According to the 1941 census, there are 94.5 million Muslims (24.3 per cent of the total population) and 270.2 million Hindus (69.5 per cent of the total population). All other religious groups were below 3 per cent of the population. See Davis, Kingsley, "India and Pakistan: The Demography of Partition," *Pacific Affairs*, 22, 3 (1949), pp. 254–264; and Moore, R. J., "Jinnah and the Pakistan Demand," *Modern Asian Studies*, 17, 4 (1983), pp. 529–561.

15. Riaz, Ali, "Nations, Nation-State and Politics of Muslim Identity in South Asia," *Comparative Studies of South Asia, Africa and the Middle East*, 22, 2 (2002), pp. 53–58.

16. Jinnah was the leader of the Muslim League from 1913 until Pakistan's independence on 14 August 1947. He became Pakistan's first Governor General from 14 August 1947 until his death on 11 Sept. 1947. Jinnah was a Twelver Shia, having converted from the Ismaili sect. As Pakistan continues to be riven with sectarian tendencies, some Pakistanis are uncomfortable with his Shia identity. For a discussion of this, see Ahmed, Khaled, "Was Jinnah a Shia or a Sunni," *The Friday Times*, 22, 45 (Dec. 2010), accessed 11 June 2018. http://www.thefridaytimes.com/24122010/page27.shtml.

17. Even the word "Pakistan" (which translates literally as "Land of the Pure") came into use some 27 years later, in 1933. The word "Pakistan'" is a somewhat contrived acronym coined by Chaudhury Rahmat Ali, founder of the Pakistan National Movement, while he was a student at Cambridge. As he explained in his pamphlet "Now or Never," by "PAKISTAN" its proponents "mean the five Northern units of India viz: Punjab, North-West Frontier Province (Afghan Province), Kashmir, Sind, and Baluchistan." Thus P is for Punjab; A is for Afghan Province, K is for Kashmir, S is for Sindh and "Tan" is for Balochistan. See Ali, Chaudhury Rahmat, *Now or Never*, Pakistan National Movement, 1933, accessed 11 June 2018. http://www.columbia.edu/itc/mealac/pritchett/00islamlinks/txt_rahmatali_1933.html; Jaffrelot, Christophe, "Nationalism without a Nation: Pakistan Searching for an Identity," in *Pakistan: Nationalism without a Nation?*, pp. 7–47; and Moore, "Jinnah and the Pakistan Demand," pp. 529–561.

18. "Address by Quaid-i-Azam Mohammad Ali Jinnah at Lahore Session of Muslim League," March 1940, Islamabad: Directorate of Films and Publishing, Ministry of Information and Broadcasting, Government of Pakistan, Islamabad, 1983, pp. 5–23, accessed 11 June 2018. http://www.columbia.edu/itc/mealac/pritchett/00islamlinks/txt_jinnah_lahore_1940.html.

19. Ali, Rabia Umar, *Empire in Retreat: The Story of India's Partition*, Karachi: Oxford University Press, 2012.

20. An excellent recent example of popular discourse around this day is from a 2012 article published in *The News*, a right of center paper that tends to support the government. The author explains the significance of this day to readers in the following words: "The people of Pakistan celebrate the 23 March, every year, with great zeal and enthusiasm, to commemorate the most outstanding achievement of the Muslims of South Asia who passed the historic 'Pakistan Resolution' on this day at Lahore in 1940. Seventy-one years ago, on 23 March 1940, at Muslim League's 27th session, under Quaid-e-Azam Muhammad Ali Jinnah's dynamic leadership, Mr A.K. Fazl-ul-Haq moved a resolution and demanded a separate sovereign state for the Muslims in the North West and Eastern Zones of the sub-continent, where they were in majority." See Malik, Jawayria. "23rd March: A day to remember," *Yes Urdu*, 19 March 2015, accessed 11 June 2018. http://en.yesurdu.com/international/europe/23rd-march-a-day-to-remember-jawayria-malik/.

21. Jaffrelot, "Nationalism without a Nation," p. 12.

22. See Talbot, Ian A., "The 1946 Punjab Elections," *Modern Asian Studies*, 14, 1 (1980), pp. 65–91; and Jalal, Ayesha, *The State of Martial Rule: The Origins of Pakistan's Political Economy of Defence*, Cambridge: Cambridge University Press, 1990.; and Jaffrelot, Christophe, "India and Pakistan: Interpreting the Divergence of Two Political Trajectories," *Cambridge Review of International Affairs*, 15, 2 (2002), pp. 251–267; and Jaffrelot, "Nationalism without a Nation," pp. 7–47.

23. Jalal, *The State of Martial Rule*, p. 20; and Khan, The Great Partition.

24. Haqqani, Husain, *Pakistan: Between Mosque and Military*, Washington, D.C.: Carnegie Endowment for International Peace, 2005.

25. See Cohen, Stephen P., *The Idea of Pakistan*, Washington DC: Brookings Institution Press, 2004; and Haqqani, *Pakistan*.

26. Wilkinson, Steven I., *Army and Nation: The Military and Indian Democracy since Independence*. Cambridge: Harvard University Press, 2015.

27. Spate, O.H.K., "The Partition of India and the Prospects of Pakistan," *American Geographical Society*, 38, 1 (Jan. 1948), pp. 5–29.

28. Davis, "India and Pakistan," pp. 254–264.

29. Haqqani, *Pakistan*, pp. 12–23.

30. "Indian Independence Act of 1947," 1947, accessed 11 June 2018. http://www.legislation.gov.uk/ukpga/1947/30/pdfs/ukpga_19470030_en.pdf.

31. Fair, *Fighting to the End*.

32. The British coined the appellation "prince" to describe a diverse array of greater and lesser Indian *rajas, khans, nawabs, nizams* (among other local titles) who were dependent upon larger states as well as large landowners, often referred to as *zamindars*.

33. See Guha, Ramachandra, *India After Gandhi: The History of the World's Largest Democracy*, London: MacMillan, 2007; and Ramusack, Barbara N., *The Indian Princes and their States*, Cambridge: Cambridge University Press, 2003.

34. British paramountcy was represented by the viceroy or crown representative, the political department, and Britain's various local agents. Until the 20th century, the foreign department was responsible both for foreign affairs and relations with the princely

states. However, by 1914, a dedicated political department had been formed within the foreign and political department to manage relations with the states. See Kooiman, Dick, "Communalism and Indian Princely States: A Comparison with British India," *Economic and Political Weekly*," 30, 26 August 1995, pp. 2123–2133.

35. Copland, Ian, "The Princely States, the Muslim League, and the Partition of India in 1947," *The International History Review*, 13, 1 (Feb. 1991), pp. 38–69.

36. Guha, *India After Gandhi*.

37. Copland, "The Princely States," pp. 38–69

38. Purushotham, Sunil, "Internal Violence: The 'Police Action' in Hyderabad," *Comparative Studies in Society and History*, 57, 2 (2015), pp. 435–466.

39. Pakistan was not initially enthusiastic about this accession because of Junagadh's large Hindu population and did not respond to his announcement for weeks. Pakistan finally assented to Junagadh's accession on 13 Sept. Guha speculates that Pakistan ultimately accepted Junagadh's accession with the intention of leveraging it with India to obtain Kashmir, which was the most important princely state for Pakistan given its commitment to the Two Nation Theory. See Guha, *India After Gandhi*, p. 50.

40. Noorani, A.G., "Of Jinnah and Junagadh," *Jinnah Papers: Pakistan: Pangs of Birth 15 August–30 Sept. 1947*, Oxford University Press, 2001, accessed 11 June 2018. http://www.frontline.in/static/html/fl1821/18210760.htm. See also Raghavan, Srinath, *War and Peace in Modern India*, New Delhi: Permanent Black, 2010.

41. Guha, *India After Gandhi*.

42. Ibid.

43. Nawaz, Shuja. "The First Kashmir War Revisited," India Review, Vol. 7, No. 2 (2008): 115–154.

44. See Nawaz, "The First Kashmir War Revisited."

45. See Khan's own account in Khan, Akbar, *Raiders in Kashmir*, Karachi: Pak Publishers Ltd., 1970.

46. Cohen, Stephen P., "Subhas Chandra Bose and the Indian National Army," *Pacific Affairs*, 36, 4 (1963), pp. 411–429.

47. Nawaz, Shuja, "The First Kashmir War Revisited."

48. The Pakistani government sustains a variety of fictions at the website of its permanent representation to the United Nations. See "Kashmir-The History," available at http://www.pakun.org/kashmir/history.php, accessed 11 June 2018.

49. Nawaz, "The First Kashmir War Revisited."

50. Ibid.

51. Whitehead, *Mission in Kashmir;* Ganguly, Sumit, *Conflict Unending: India-Pakistan Tensions Since 1947*, New Delhi: Oxford University Press, 2001; Raghavan, *War and Peace in Modern India*.

52. United Nations Security Council, "United Nations Security Council Resolution 47: The India-Pakistan Question," 1964, http://www.un.org/en/sc/documents/resolutions/1948.shtml, last accessed 11 June 2018.

53. "Nawaz draws UN attention towards Indian atrocities in Kashmir," *Daily Times (Pakistan)*, 9 August 2016, accessed 11 June 2018. http://dailytimes.com.pk/pakistan/09-Aug-16/nawaz-draws-un-attention-towards-indian-atrocities-in-kashmir.

54. Panda, Ankit, "Pakistan Army Chief: Kashmir and Pakistan "Inseparable"," *The Diplomat*, 4 June 2015, accessed 11 June 2018. http://thediplomat.com/2015/06/pakistan-army-chief-kashmir-and-pakistan-inseparable/.

55. "Army reiterates support for right to self-determination for Kashmiris across LOC," *The Dawn*, 10 June 2017, accessed 11 June 2018. https://www.dawn.com/news/1338673.

56. As I show in Fair, *Fighting to the End*, Pakistan's arguments about acquiring Kashmir are not primarily about security.

57. Ali, Chaudri M., *Emergence of Pakistan Hardcover*, New York: Columbia University Press, 1967, pp. 204–205. Also see "Indian Independence Act of 1947," 1947, accessed 11 June 2018. http://www.legislation.gov.uk/ukpga/1947/30/pdfs/ukpga_19470030_en.pdf.

58. See Wirsing, Robert G., *India, Pakistan, and the Kashmir Dispute*, New York: Saint Martin's Press, 1998; and Khan, *The Great Partition*.

59. Guha, *India After Gandhi*.

60. The district is a unit of administration below the province while a tehsil is subunit of a district.

61. See Wirsing, *India, Pakistan, and the Kashmir Dispute*; and Khan, *The Great Partition;* and Ilahi, Shereen, "The Radcliffe Boundary Commission and the Fate of Kashmir," *India Review*, 2, 1 (2003), pp. 77–102; and Tinker, "Pressure, Persuasion, Decision," pp. 695–704.

62. Typifying this characterization, Pervez Iqbal Cheema—an influential Pakistani scholar who has directed one of Pakistan's premier think tanks and who now holds a post at Pakistan's National Defense University—contends that "The loss of Gurdaspur District was viewed as a major blow because it meant something much more than a simple award of additional territory to India. This was a decision which not only linked Kashmir to India but also facilitated India's forcible occupation of the State at a later stage. The district of Gurdaspur consisted of four *tehsils* (sub divisions), Gurdaspur, Batala, Shakergarh and Pathankot. Apart from Pathankot which had a Hindu majority, all the others were Muslim majority tehsils. If the principle of religious affinity had been applied, then the whole district should have been awarded to Pakistan. Radcliffe decided to allot three-fourths of the district to India giving an access to the State of Jammu and Kashmir." Cheema, Pervaiz Iqbal, "The Politics of the Punjab Boundary Award," *Heidelberg Papers in South Asian and Comparative Politics*, 1 (2000), p. 8, accessed 11 June 2018. http://www.ub.uni-heidelberg.de/archiv/4006

63. See Cheema, "The Politics of the Punjab Boundary Award;" and Ahmad, Qazi Shakil, "Pakistan-India Relations: Some Geostrategic Considerations," *Pakistan Horizon*, 57, 3 (2004), pp. 13–19; and Ahmad, Aftab, "At the Time of Independence," *The Express Tribune*, 12 August 2014, accessed 11 June 2018. https://tribune.com.pk/story/747233/at-the-time-of-independence/.

64. Ilahi, "The Radcliffe Boundary Commission."

65. Ibid.

66. Shaikh, Farzana, *Making Sense of Pakistan*, London: Hurst, 2009.

67. Haqqani, *Pakistan: Between Mosque and Military*, p. 13.

68. "Objectives Resolution Text," in "Constitution of Pakistan," accessed 11 June 2018. http://www.pakistani.org/pakistan/constitution/annex_objres.html. Minority legislators were very disturbed by this. They argued for a secular constitution fearing, perspicaciously, that they would become the objects of persecution and discrimination. They argued for an amendment that would replace "Muslims shall be enabled to order their lives...in accordance with the teachings and requirements of Islam" with "Muslims and non-Muslims shall be *equally* enabled to order their lives in accordance with their respective religions." See "Objective Resolution Text" and Shaikh, *Making Sense of Pakistan*.

69. Haqqani, *Pakistan;* "Nasr, Vali R., "International Politics, Domestic Imperatives, and Identity Mobilization: Sectarianism in Pakistan, 1979–1998," *Comparative Politics*, 32, 2 (2000), pp. 170–191.

70. General Ayub became the first Pakistani army chief on 17 Jan. 1951, following the departure of the outgoing British army chief, General Sir Douglas Gracey.

71. See Khan, Mohammad Ayub (Gen.), "Pakistan Perspective," *Foreign Affairs*, 38 (July 1960), pp. 547–556; and Khan, Mohammad Ayub (Gen.), *Friends Not Masters*, Islamabad: Mr. Books, 2006 (First published in 1967).

72. Haqqani, *Pakistan*, p. 42.

73. Khan, *Friends Not Masters*, p. 135.

74. Khan, *Friends Not Masters*.

75. Cohen, *The Idea of Pakistan*, p. 67.

76. The Ahmadis view themselves as Muslims. The Ahmadi movement began at the end of the 19th Century in British India with charismatic reformer Mirza Ghulam Ahmad (1835–1908) who claimed to be the messiah. Because this claim contradicts the essential Islamic tenet of the finality of prophet Muhammad, other Muslims denounce Ahmadis as apostates in Pakistan and beyond.

77. Nasr, Vali R., *Islamic Leviathan: Islam and the Making of State Power*, Oxford: Oxford University Press, 2001; Haqqani, *Pakistan*.

78. See specifically Articles 62 and 63 in "Chapter 2: Majlis-e-Shoora (Parliament)," n.d., accessed 11 June 2018. http://www.pakistani.org/pakistan/constitution/part3.ch2.html.

79. *Central Intelligence Agency World Fact Book*, 30 August 2017, accessed 11 June 2018. https://www.cia.gov/library/publications/the-world-factbook/geos/pk.html. For alternative estimates see Fair, C. Christine, Neil Malhotra, Jacob N. Shapiro, "Islam, Militancy, and Politics in Pakistan: Insights from a National Sample," *Terrorism and Political Violence*, 22, 4 (Sept. 2010), pp. 495–521.

80. See Rizvi, Hassan Askari, *Military, State and Society in Pakistan*, London: Palgrave, 2000; and Nasr, *Islamic Leviathan*.

81. Cohen, *The Idea of Pakistan*.

82. See Shah, Aqil, *The Army and Democracy: Military Politics in Pakistan*, Cambridge: Harvard University Press, 2014; and Shah, Aqil, "Pakistan's 'Armored' Democracy," *Journal of Democracy*, 14, 4 (2003), pp. 26–40.

83. "COAS address on the occasion of Azadi Parade 2011 at PMA Kakul," YouTube video, 5:26, posted by "mrdanish1996," 13 August 2011, accessed 11 June 2018. http://www.youtube.com/watch?v=CuzYxuSXZh8.

84. Hussain, Shaiq, "Pakistan has a new, little-known military commander," *The Washington Post*, 27 Nov. 2013, accessed 11 June 2018. https://www.washingtonpost.com/world/pakistan-has-a-new-little-known-military-commander/2013/11/27/acce6802-579c-11e3-bdbf-097ab2a3dc2b_story.html?utm_term=.6b216f56f9ff.

85. Benazir Bhutto, for example, said that "Kashmir is Pakistan's jugular vein and we will not allow our jugular vein to be trampled under the feet of repression. God willing, the day is not far off when Kashmir will be with us." De Bergh Robinson, commenting upon this formulation of Kashmir as Pakistan's jugular vein under Indian threat and the related formulation that "Kashmir Pakistan banega" (Kashmir will become Pakistan) that the Kashmir dispute is seen as "nothing less than a struggle for very existence of Pakistan as a viable nation-state." See "COAS General Raheel Sharif Speech on Youm-e-Shuhada," 30 April 2014, accessed 11 June 2018. https://www.pakistanarmy.gov.pk/awpreview/pDetails.aspx?pType=PressRelease&pID=216; Behuria, Ashok, "India-Pakistan Relations and the Kashmir Issue (1947–2009)," in *South Asian Security: 21ˢᵗ Century Discourses* (ed.) Sagarika Dutt and Alok Bansal, Abingdon: Routledge, 2012, pp. 65–82.

86. Robinson, Cabeiri deBergh, *Body of Victims, Body of Warrior: Refugee Families and the Making of Kashmir Jihadists*, Berkeley: University of California Press, 2013, p. 56.

87. "COAS General Raheel Sharif Speech on Youm-e-Shuhada."

88. See "Pak Trying to Push Terrorists into J&K: Rajnath," *The Tribune (India)*, 2 Jan. 2015, accessed 11 June 2018. http://www.tribuneindia.com/news/nation/pak-trying-to-push-terrorists-into-j-k-rajnath/25390.html; and Ul-Hassan, Manzoor, "347 violent incidents along LoC in JK in 2013: Report," *Rising Kashmir*, 20 Feb. 2014, accessed 11 June 2018. http://www.risingkashmir.com/news/347-violent-incidents-along-loc-in-jk-in-2013-report.

89. Haider, "Pakistan and Kashmir."

90. See Sharif, Raheel, "COAS Defense Day Speech," 6 Sept. 2015, accessed 11 June 2018. https://www.ispr.gov.pk/front/main.asp?o=t-press_release&date=2015/9/6; and Hussain, Sajjad, "Kashmir unfinished agenda of Partition, says Pakistan army chief," *LiveMint*, 3 October 2015, accessed 11 June 2018. http://www.livemint.com/Politics/FTbFjetzbLqYXgqQWy8PSM/Kashmir-unfinished-agenda-of-Partition-says-Pakistan-army-c.html.

91. "Pakistan's outgoing army chief sends warning to India over Kashmir," *Reuters*, 29 Nov. 2016, accessed 11 June 2018. http://indianexpress.com/article/world/world-news/pakistan-raheel-sharif-general-qamar-javed-bajwa-kashmir-4401365/.

92. See Joshi, Shashank, "Everything that we know about India's cross-LoC strikes before Uri," *Scroll.in*, 5 Oct. 2016, accessed 11 June 2018. https://scroll.in/article/818324/everything-that-we-know-about-indias-cross-loc-strikes-before-uri; and Swami, Praveen," Surgical strikes: Bodies taken away on trucks, loud explosions, eyewitnesses

give graphic details," *Indian Express*, 7 Oct. 2016, accessed 11 June 2018. http://indianexpress.com/article/india/india-news-india/pakistan-border-terror-camps-surgical-strikes-kashmir-loc-indian-army-jihadist-3065975/.

93. Foizee, Bahauddin, "The Real Reason Bajwa Was Appointed Pakistan's Chief of Army Staff," *The Diplomat*, 21 Dec. 2016, accessed 11 June 2018. http://thediplomat.com/2016/12/the-real-reason-bajwa-was-appointed-pakistans-chief-of-army-staff/; Fair, C. Christine, "Pakistan has a New General: Policy Implications," *Journal of South Asian and Middle Eastern Studies*, Vol. 40, No. 4 (2017): 82–98.

94. Ganguly, Sumit, *Conflict Unending: India-Pakistan Tensions Since 1947*, New Delhi: Oxford University Press, 2001; Chari, P.R., Pervaiz Iqbal Cheema, and Stephen Cohen, *Four Crises and a Peace Process*, Washington DC: Brookings Institution Press, 2001.

95. See Nawaz, Shuja, *Crossed Swords: Pakistan, Its Army and the Wars Within*, New York: Oxford University Press, 2008; Nawaz, "The First Kashmir War Revisited;" Whitehead, *A Mission in Kashmir;* Ganguly, *Conflict Unending*; and Khan, *Raiders in Kashmir.*

96. There is some debate about whether the Indian government had a signed copy of the instrument of accession in New Delhi before it began airlifting troops. See Whitehead, A Mission in Kashmir.

97. Fair, *Fighting to the End;* Wirsing, Robert G., *India, Pakistan, and the Kashmir Dispute*, New York: Saint Martin's Press, 1998.

98. Khan, Gul Hassan (Lt. Gen.), *Memoirs*, Karachi: Oxford University Press, 1993; Chari et al., *Four Crises and a Peace Process.*

99. Notably, Operation Gibraltar was named after the early eighth-century battle led by General Tariq Bin Ziyad (the Islamic conqueror of Visigoth Hispania) in which he established a beach head at Gibraltar. Gibraltar is derived from the Arabic "Jabel al Tariq" (or Rock of Tariq). See Khan, Gul Hassan (Lt. Gen.), *Memoirs*, Karachi: Oxford University Press, 1993.

100. Nawaz, *Crossed Swords.*

101. See Nawaz, *Crossed Swords;* and Ganguly, *Conflict Unending.*

102. Raghavan, Srinath, "Civil–Military Relations in India: The China Crisis and After," *The Journal of Strategic Studies*, 32 (2009), pp. 149–175.

103. See Bass, Gary J., *The Blood Telegram: Nixon, Kissinger, and a Forgotten Genocide.* New York: Alfred A. Knopf, 2013; Hussain, Rizwan. *Pakistan and the Emergence of Islamic Militancy in Afghanistan.* Burlington: Ashgate, 2005; Fair, *Fighting to the End.*

104. Bass, The Blood Telegram.

105. Sen, J., "The Trial of Errors In Bangladesh: The International Crimes (Tribunals) Act And The 1971 War Crimes Trial', *Harvard Asia Quarterly*, 14, 3 (2012), pp. 33–43.

106. Ganguly, *Conflict Unending*, p. 67.

107. Fair, *Fighting to the End.*

108. Tellis, Ashley J., C. Christine Fair, and Jamison Jo Medby, *Limited Conflicts Under the Nuclear Umbrella-Indian and Pakistani Lessons from the Kargil Crisis*, Santa Monica: RAND, 2001.

109. See Qadir, Shaukat, "An Analysis of the Kargil Conflict of 1999," *RUSI Journal*, 147, 2 (2002), pp. 24–30; and Lavoy, Peter R., "Introduction," in *Asymmetric Warfare in South Asia: The Causes and Consequences of Kargil*, (ed.) Peter R. Lavoy, Cambridge: Cambridge University Press, 2009, pp. 2–38.

110. Qadir, "An Analysis of the Kargil Conflict;" and Tellis et al., *Limited Conflicts*; and Lavoy, "Introduction," pp. 2–38.

111. Tellis et al., *Limited Conflicts*.

112. Lt. Gen. (ret.) Chaudry Iftikhar interview, 19 Jan. 2003. See Fair, C. Christine, "Militants in the Kargil Conflict: Myths, Realities, and Impacts, in *Asymmetric Warfare in South Asia*, p. 233.

113. Fair, "Militants in the Kargil Conflict."

114. See discussion in V. P. Malik, *Kargil: From Surprise to Victory* (New Delhi: HarperCollins, 2006), pp. 42–46, 82–83, 92–97, 110.

115. Fair, "Militants in the Kargil Conflict;" Qadir, "An Analysis of the Kargil Conflict;" and Tellis et al., *Limited Conflicts*.

116. Khan, Yasmeen. *Jihad and Dawah: Evolving Narratives of Lashkar-e-Taiba and Jamat ud Dawa*. London: Hurst, 2017.

117. Fair, *Fighting to the End*.

118. Fair, *Fighting to the End;* Tellis, Ashley J. 1997. *Stability in South Asia*. Santa Monica, CA: RAND.

3. PAKISTAN'S CREEPING JIHAD AND EXPANDING NUCLEAR UMBRELLA

1. Swami, Praveen, India, Pakistan and the Secret Jihad: The Covert War in Kashmir, 1947–2005, London: Routledge, 2007.

2. Meacher, Michael. "The Pakistan Connection," *The Guardian*, 21 July 2004, accessed 11 June 2018. https://www.theguardian.com/world/2004/jul/22/usa.september11; Lister, Tim. "Abbottabad—The military town where bin Laden hid in plain sight," *CNN. com*, 2 May 2011., accessed 11 June 2018. http://www.cnn.com/2011/WORLD/asiapcf/05/02/bin.laden.abbottabad/index.html.

3. See Nawaz, Shuja, *Crossed Swords: Pakistan, Its Army and the Wars Within*, New York: Oxford University Press, 2008; and Nawaz, Shuja, "The First Kashmir War Revisited," *India Review* 7 (April 2008), pp. 115–154.

4. See Ganguly, Sumit, *The Crisis in Kashmir: Portents of War, Hopes of Peace*, Cambridge: Cambridge University Press, 1997; and Varshney, Ashutosh, "India, Pakistan, and Kashmir: Antinomies of Nationalism," *Asian Survey*, 31, 11 (1991), pp. 997–1019.

5. Ganguly, *The Crisis in Kashmir;* Varshney, "India, Pakistan, and Kashmir.

6. Chadha, Vivek, "India's Counterinsurgency Campaign in Mizoram, in *India and Counterinsurgency: Lessons Learned*, ed. Sumit Ganguly and David E. Fidler, London: Routledge, 2009, pp. 28–44.

7. Fair, C. Christine, *Urban Battle Fields of South Asia: Lessons Learned from Sri Lanka, India and Pakistan*, Santa Monica, CA: RAND, 2004.

8. See Haqqani, Husain, *Pakistan: Between Mosque and Military*, Washington, D.C.: Carnegie Endowment for International Peace, 2005; and Hussain, Rizwan, *Pakistan and the Emergence of Islamic Militancy in Afghanistan*, Burlington: Ashgate, 2005; and Rubin, Barnett R., *The Fragmentation of Afghanistan*, New Haven: Yale University Press, 2002.

9. See Bhutto, Zulfiqar Ali, *If I Am Assassinated*, New Delhi: Vikas Publishing House Pvt. Ltd., 1979; and Khan, Feroz (Brig. Retd), *Eating Grass: The Making of the Pakistani Bomb*, Stanford, CA: Stanford University Press, 2012; and Sattar, Abdul, *Pakistan's Foreign Policy 1947–2005*, Karachi: Oxford University Press, 2007.

10. Sahni, Varun. 2009. A Dangerous Exercise: Brasstacks as non-nuclear near war. In *Nuclear Proliferation in South Asia: Crisis Behavior and the Bomb*, ed. Sumit Ganguly and S. Paul Kapur, 12–35. New York: Routledge, p. 22.

11. Kumar, Arvind, "Theories of Deterrence and Nuclear Deterrence in the Subcontinent," in *The India-Pakistan Nuclear Relationship: Theories of Deterrence and International Relations*, (ed.) E. Sridharan, New Delhi: Routledge, 2007, pp. 239–265.

12. As I explain in *Fighting to the End*, even though the defense pacts also applied to China, Pakistan was largely exempted from participating in any US effort to contain Chinese communism.

13. See Fair, *Fighting to the End*; Cohen, Stephen P., *The Idea of Pakistan*, Washington DC: Brookings Institution Press, 2004.

14. Fair, *Fighting to the End*.

15. East, C.H.A. (Maj.), "Guerrilla Warfare," *Pakistan Army Journal*, 1, 4 (1958), pp. 57–66.

16. East, "Guerrilla Warfare."

17. El-Edroos, S.A. (Maj.), "Infiltration-A form of attack," *Pakistan Army Journal*, 3, 2 (1961): pp. 3–15.

18. See El-Edroos, "Infiltration—A form of attack'; and El-Edroos, S.A. (Lt. Col.), "General Vo Nguyen Giap and the Viet Nam People's Army," *Pakistan Army Journal*, 6, 1 (1964), pp. 10–17; and El-Edroos, S.A. (Maj.), "Mao Tse-Tung and the Chinese People's Liberation Army (1927–1964)," *Pakistan Army Journal* 6, 2 (1964), pp. 8–28; and Shafi, Mohammad (Maj.), "The Effectiveness of Guerrilla Warfare," *Pakistan Army Journal*, 5, 1, pp. 4–11, 1963; and Akram, Muhammad (Lt. Col.), "Dien Bien Phu," *Pakistan Army Journal*, 13, 2 (1971), pp. 29–37; and Siddiqi, Aslam, *A Path for Pakistan*, Karachi: Pakistan Publishing House, 1964; and Qazi, Shamsul Haq (Lt. Col.), "A Case for Citizen Army," *Pakistan Army Journal* 6 (June 1964): pp. 18–25.

19. Qazi, "A Case for Citizen Army," pp. 18–25.

20. Qazi, "A Case for Citizen Army", pp. 18–25.

21. Siddiqi, *A Path for Pakistan*.

22. Siddiqi, *A Path for Pakistan*.

23. Siddiqi, *A Path for Pakistan*.

24. Nawaz, *Crossed Swords: Pakistan*.

25. "Statement of the Prime Minister of Pakistan regarding the Indian nuclear explosions," 19 May 1974, *Pakistan Horizon*, Vol. 27, No. 2 (Second Quarter, 1974), pp. 115–164.

26. Fair, *Fighting to the End*.

27. Khan, Feroz (Brig. Retd.), *Eating Grass: The Making of the Pakistani Bomb*, Stanford, CA: Stanford University Press, 2012 offers the richest and most detailed accounts of Pakistan's nuclear program from its inception under Bhutto to the present. Ironically, while F. Khan seeks to undermine the popular contention that Pakistan acquired its nuclear program through theft and espionage, the details he provides of the extensive transfers of material and assistance from China among other sources undermine this contention mightily. See also Bhutto, *If I Am Assassinated*.

28. "The United States and Pakistan's Quest for the Bomb: National Security Archive Electronic Briefing Book No. 333," *National Security Archive*, 21 Dec. 2010, accessed 11 June 2018. http://nsarchive.gwu.edu/nukevault/ebb333/.

29. US Department of State, "Department of State cable 22212 to Embassy New Delhi: Ad Hoc Scientific Committee and Related Topics," 27 Jan. 1978, accessed 11 June 2018. http://nsarchive.gwu.edu/nukevault/ebb333/doc24.pdf.

30. The Symington Amendment was adopted in 1976 to amend the Arms Export Control Act, which was previously known as Section 669 of the Foreign Assistance Act of 1961. This legislation prohibits US assistance to any country that is found to be trafficking in either nuclear enrichment technology or equipment. In contrast to Pakistani arguments that this legislation was promulgated to punish Pakistan, it was actually enacted in response to the Indian test in 1974. See US Department of State, "Presidential Review Committee [Sic] Meeting," 9 March 1979, 1 June 2017. http://nsarchive.gwu.edu/nukevault/ebb333/doc29.pdf; and "Herbert J. Hansell through Lucy Wilson Benson to Mr. Newsom: Pakistan and the Symington Amendment," 17 March 1979, accessed 11 June 2018; and Hathaway, Robert M., "Confrontation and Retreat: The US Congress and the South Asian Nuclear Tests," *Arms Control Today*, 2 Jan. 2000, accessed 11 June 2018. https://www.armscontrol.org/act/2000_01–02/rhjf00; and Salik, Naeem (Brig. Retd.), *The Genesis of South Asia Nuclear Deterrence: Pakistan's Perspective*, Karachi: Oxford University Press, 2009.

31. See US Department of State, "Steve Oxman to Warren Christopher, enclosing memorandum from Harold Saunders and Thomas Pickering through Mr. Newsom and Mrs. Benson to the Secretary: A Strategy for Pakistan," 5 March 1979, accessed 11 June 2018; and "The United States and Pakistan's Quest for the Bomb: National Security Archive Electronic Briefing Book No. 333," *National Security Archive*, 21 Dec. 2010, accessed 11 June 2018. http://nsarchive.gwu.edu/nukevault/ebb333/ http://nsarchive.gwu.edu/nukevault/ebb333/doc28.pdf.

32. US Department of State, "Ambassador Pickering, Paul Kreisberg, and Jack Miklos through Mr. Newsom and Mrs. Benson to the Secretary: Presidential Letter to President Zia on Nuclear Issues," 21 March 1979, accessed 11 June 2018. http://nsarchive.gwu.edu/nukevault/ebb333/doc31.pdf.

33. See US Department of State, "Herbert J. Hansell through Lucy Wilson Benson to Mr. Newsom;" and US Department of State, "Ambassador Pickering, Paul Kreisberg, and Jack Miklos through Mr. Newsom and Mrs. Benson to the Secretary."

34. See US Department of State, "Ambassador Pickering, Paul Kreisberg, and Jack Miklos through Mr. Newsom and Mrs. Benson to the Secretary;" and US Department of State,

"Steve Oxman to Warren Christopher, enclosing memorandum from Harold Saunders and Thomas Pickering through Mr. Newsom and Mrs. Benson to the Secretary: A Strategy for Pakistan," 5 March 1979, accessed 11 June 2018. http://nsarchive.gwu.edu/nukevault/ebb333/doc28.pdf.

35. US Department of State, "Ambassador Pickering, Paul Kreisberg, and Jack Miklos through Mr. Newsom and Mrs. Benson to the Secretary."

36. US Department of State, "Anthony Lake, Harold Saunders, and Thomas Pickering through Mr. Newsom and Mrs. Benson to the Deputy Secretary: PRC Paper on South Asia," and "Interagency Working Group Paper: South Asian Nuclear and Security Problems, Analysis of Possible Elements in a US Strategy," 23 March 1979, accessed 11 June 2018. http://nsarchive.gwu.edu/nukevault/ebb333/doc32a.pdf

37. US Department of State, "US embassy New Delhi cable 9979: India and the Pakistan Nuclear Problem," 7 June 1979, accessed 11 June 2018. http://nsarchive.gwu.edu/nukevault/ebb333/doc35b.pdf.

38. US Department of State, "Gerard C. Smith, Special Representative of the President for Non-Proliferation Matters, to the President: Nonproliferation in South Asia," 8 June 1979, accessed 11 June 2018.

39. National Security Archive, "The United States and Pakistan's Quest for the Bomb: National Security Archive Electronic Briefing Book No. 333," 21 Dec. 2010, accessed 11 June 2018. http://nsarchive.gwu.edu/nukevault/ebb333/.

40. Sattar, Abdul, *Pakistan's Foreign Policy 1947–2005*, Karachi: Oxford University Press, 2007.

41. US Department of State, "US Embassy Paris cable 24312 to State Department, "French Go Public (Partly) on Reprocessing Issue with Pakistan,"' 3 August 1978, accessed 11 June 2018. http://nsarchive.gwu.edu/nukevault/ebb333/doc10.pdf; and US Department of State, "State Department cable 205550 to Embassy Islamabad, "Discussion between Under Secretary Newsom and Pakistan's Minister of State for Foreign Affairs Agha Shahi on the Reprocessing Issue,"' 14 August 1978, accessed 11 June 2018. http://nsarchive.gwu.edu/nukevault/ebb333/doc13.pdf.

42. US Department of State, "US Embassy Paris cable 24312."

43. Anwari, Masood Navid (Lt. Col.), "Deterrence—Hope or Reality," Pakistan Army Journal, 29 (March 1988), pp. 45–53."

44. Akhtar, Asif Duraiz (Maj. Gen.), "Nation Building," Pakistan Army Green Book: Role of Pakistan Army in Nation Building, Rawalpindi: Pakistan Army Headquarters, 2000, p. 1.

45. Iqbal, Shahid (Maj. Gen.), "Doctrinal Aspects of Limited War and Its Applicability in the Region," in *Pakistan Army Green Book 2004: Limited War*, Rawalpindi: Pakistan Army General Head, 2004, pp. 83.

46. Iqbal, "Doctrinal Aspects of Limited War and Its Applicability in the Region," p. 83.

47. Saeed, Talha Hafiz. "DPC—Countering the War on Pakistan," *Invite*, August 2016, p. 18.

48. Makki explained that "Another very dangerous aspect of friendship with India is the question concerning the purpose of Pakistan's nuclear technology. If India is not our

enemy, then why do we need a nuclear bomb? Then this is an 'Islamic bomb' and must be eliminated. How will Pakistan defend its nuclear program internationally? India is our enemy. Enmity is due to the Kashmir issue. This must be very clearly broadcasted." Makki, A. Rehman, "Moving Forward on Kashmir: Articulating a Compelling State Policy & Narrative," *Invite*, July 2017, p. 33.

49. Sami-ul-Haq, Maulana. "Difa-e-Pakistan Council Countering the War on Pakistan," *Invite*, August 2016, p. 10.

50. For example, Mohsin, Tufail. "India's Perpetual Humiliation," *Inspire*, March 2017, pp. 18–19. *Inspire* is one of JuD's most recent magazines, launched in August 2016.

51. Tellis, Ashley J., C. Christine Fair, and Jamison Jo Medby, *Limited Conflicts Under the Nuclear Umbrella-Indian and Pakistani Lessons from the Kargil Crisis*, Santa Monica: RAND, 2001.

52. See Ladwig, Walter, "A Cold Start for Hot Wars? The Indian Army's New Limited War Doctrine," *International Security*, 32, 3 (2007), pp. 158–190; and Perkovich, George and Toby Dalton, *Not War, Not Peace? Motivating Pakistan to Prevent Cross-Border Terrorism*, New Delhi: Oxford University Press, 2016.

53. Ladwig, "A Cold Start for Hot Wars?"

54. Ibid.

55. Perkovich, George and Toby Dalton, *Not War, Not Peace? Motivating Pakistan to Prevent Cross-Border Terrorism*, New Delhi: Oxford University Press, 2016.

56. Shukla, Ajai, "Why General Bipin Rawat Acknowledged the Cold Start Doctrine," *The Wire*, 20 Jan. 2017, accessed 11 June 2018. https://thewire.in/101586/cold-start-pakistan-doctrine/.

57. See Khan, Feroz and Nick M. Masellis, *US-Pakistan strategic partnership: A Track II dialogue*, Jan. 2012, Center on Contemporary Conflict, US Naval Postgraduate School, accessed 11 June 2018. https://www.hsdl.org/?view&did=709607; and Sankaran, Jaganath, "Destroying Pakistan to Deter India? The Problem with Pakistan's Battlefield Nukes," *Bulletin of the Atomic Scientists*, 70, 4 (2014), pp. 74–84.

58. Khan, Zulfiqar, "Tactical Nuclear Weapons and Pakistan's Option of Offensive-Deterrence," in *Nuclear Pakistan: Strategic Dimensions*, (ed.) Zulfiqar Khan, Karachi: Oxford University Press, 2011, p. 7.

59. Khan, "Tactical Nuclear Weapons."

60. "A Conversation with Gen. Khalid Kidwai," transcript, Carnegie Endowment for International Peace, 23 March 2015, accessed 11 June 2018. http://carnegieendowment.org/files/03-230315carnegieKIDWAI.pdf.

61. See Kristensen, Hans M. and Robert S. Norris, "Pakistani Nuclear Forces," and Inter Services Public Relations, *Press Release No. PR94/2011*, 19 April 2011, accessed 11 June 2018. http://www.ispr.gov.pk/front/main.asp?o=t-press_release&id=1721.

62. Arms Control Association, "Factsheets and Brief: Arms Control and Proliferation Profile: Pakistan," updated April 2017, accessed 11 June 2018. https://www.armscontrol.org/factsheets/pakistanprofile.

63. See Fair, *Fighting to the End;* Kapur, *Dangerous Deterrent*.

64. Khan, Zulfiqar, "Tactical Nuclear Weapons."

65. See Tellis, Ashley J., C. Christine Fair, and Jamison Jo Medby, *Limited Conflicts Under the Nuclear Umbrella*; and Lavoy, Peter R., "Pakistan's Nuclear Doctrine," in *Prospects for Peace in South Asia*, edited Rafiq Dossani and Henry Rowan, Stanford, CA: Stanford University Press, 2005, pp. 280–300.

66. Cheema, Zafar Iqbal, "Pakistan's Nuclear Use Doctrine and Command and Control," in *Planning the Unthinkable: How New Powers will Use Nuclear, Biological, and Chemical Weapons*, Lavoy, Peter, Scott D. Sagan and James J. Wirtz (eds), Ithaca, NY: Cornell University Press, 2000, pp. 180.

67. See Fair, *Fighting to the End*; and Kapur, Paul S., *Dangerous Deterrent: Nuclear Weapons Proliferation and Conflict in South Asia*, Stanford, CA: Stanford University Press, 2007.

68. See Dalrymple, William, "A Deadly Triangle: Afghanistan, Pakistan, and India," *The Brookings Essay*, 25 June 2013, accessed 11 June 2018. http://csweb.brookings.edu/content/research/essays/2013/deadly-triangle-afghanistan-pakistan-india-c.html; and Ahmed, Zahid Shahab and Stuti Bhatnagar, "Pakistan-Afghanistan Relations and the Indian Factor," *Pakistan Horizon*, 60, 2, (April 2007), pp. 159–174; and Ali, Shazad, "India: Jostling for geopolitical control in Afghanistan," *Open Security*, 27 March 2014, accessed 11 June 2018. https://www.opendemocracy.net/opensecurity/shazad-ali/india-jostling-for-geopolitical-control-in-afghanistan.

69. Rubin, Barnett R., and Ahmed Rashid, "From Great Game to Grand Bargain," *Foreign Affairs* (Nov./Dec. 2008), accessed 11 June 2018. https://www.foreignaffairs.com/articles/2008–11–01/great-game-grand-bargain.

70. Fair, C. Christine, "Pakistan's Deadly Grip on Afghanistan," *Curretn History*, 116, 789, pp. 136–141.

71. See Gartenstein-Ross, Daveed and Tara Vassefi, "The Forgotten History of Afghanistan-Pakistan Relations," *Yale Journal of International Affairs*, 7, 1 (2012), pp. 38–45; and Fair, C. Christine, 2017. "Pakistan's Deadly Grip on Afghanistan," *Current History*, 116, 789 (April 2017), pp. 136–141.

72. See Hasan, Khurshid, "Pakistan-Afghanistan Relations," *Asian Survey*, 2, 7 (1962), pp. 14–24; and Arif, Khalid Mahmud (Gen.), *Working with Zia: Pakistan Power Politics, 1977–1988*, New York: Oxford University Press, 1995; and Khan, Feisal, "Why Borrow Trouble for Yourself and Lend It to Neighbors? Understanding the Historical Roots of Pakistan's Afghan Policy," *Asian Affairs: An American Review*, 37, 4 (2010), pp. 171–189.

73. Sattar, Abdul, *Pakistan's Foreign Policy 1947–2005*, Karachi: Oxford University Press, 2007, p. 159.

74. Ibid., p. 157.

75. Arif, *Working with Zia*, p. 314.

76. See Ahmad, Manzoor, "Implications of the War on Terror for Khyber Pakhtunkhwa, Pakistan," *Journal of Critical Globalisation Studies*, 3 (2010), pp. 102–112; and Hussain, Touqir, "US-Pakistan Engagement: The War on Terrorism and Beyond," *United States Institute for Peace*, 10 July 2005, accessed 11 June 2018. http://www.usip.org/publications/us-pakistan-engagement-the-war-terrorism-and-beyond.

77. See Hussain, *Pakistan and the Emergence*; and Rubin, *The Fragmentation of Afghanistan*.

78. See Johnson, Thomas H. and M. Chris Mason, "Understanding the Taliban and Insurgency in Afghanistan," *Orbis*, 51, 1 (2007), pp. 71–89; and Sinno, Abdulkader, "Explaining the Taliban's Ability to Mobilize the Pashtuns," in *The Taliban and the Crisis of Afghanistan*, Robert D. Crews and Amin Tarzi (eds), Cambridge: Harvard University Press, 2008, pp. 59–89.

79. Rehman, who was an important political partner of B. Bhutto during her second term as prime minister, coordinated the interactions between the Taliban's leadership and her Minister for the Interior, Nasirullah Babar. (Babar forged Pakistan's Afghan policy during Z.A. Bhutto's tenure.) Bhutto's ostensible secular credentials notwithstanding, Pakistan began furnishing logistical and military support as well as other amenities to the Taliban.

80. See Johnson, Thomas H. and M. Chris Mason, "Understanding the Taliban and Insurgency in Afghanistan;" and Sinno, "Explaining the Taliban's Ability to Mobilize the Pashtuns."

81. Fair, C. Christine, "India and Iran: New Delhi's Balancing Act," *The Washington Quarterly*, 30 (Summer 2007), pp. 145–159.

82. See Abou Zahab, Mariam, "The Regional Dimension of Sectarian Conflicts in Pakistan," in *Pakistan: Nationalism Without a Nation?*, Christophe Jaffrelot (ed.), pp. 115–28; and Abou Zahab, Mariam, and Olivier Roy, *Islamist Networks: The Afghan-Pakistan Connection*, London: C. Hurst and Co., 2004.

83. Fair, C. Christine, "Militant Recruitment in Pakistan: Implications for Al-Qa'ida and Other Organizations," *Studies in Conflict and Terrorism*, 27, 6 (Nov./Dec. 2004), pp. 489–504.

84. See Brown, Vahid, and Don Rassler, *The Haqqani Nexus and the Evolution of al-Qa'ida*, West Point, NY: Combating Terrorism Center, 2011; and Jones, Seth G., "The Rise of Afghanistan's Insurgency: State Failure and Jihad," *International Security*, 32, 4 (2008), pp. 7–40.

85. Tankel, *Storming the World Stage*.

86. See Jones, "The Rise of Afghanistan's Insurgency;" and Gall, Carlotta, *The Wrong Enemy: America in Afghanistan, 2001–2014*, New York: Houghton Mifflin Harcourt, 2014.

87. Swami, Praveen, *India, Pakistan and the Secret Jihad: The Covert War in Kashmir, 1947–2005*, London: Routledge, 2007.

88. Varshney, "India, Pakistan, and Kashmir," pp. 997–1019.

89. Ibid.

90. Contrary to standard procedure, Jagmohan did not give the Chief Minister an opportunity to test his majority in the lower house; rather, Jagmohan provided Farooq Abdullah with a list of persons who defected from his party. See Varshney, "India, Pakistan, and Kashmir," pp. 997–1019.

91. See Ganguly, Sumit, "The Crisis of Indian Secularism," *Journal of Democracy*, 14, 4 (2003), pp. 11–25; and Varshney, "India, Pakistan, and Kashmir," pp. 997–1019.

92. See Fair, "Militant Recruitment in Pakistan', and Tankel, Stephen, *Storming the World Stage*.

93. Fair, C. Christine, "Insights from a Database of Lashkar-e-Taiba and Hizb-ul-Mujahideen Militants," *Journal of Strategic Studies*, 37, 2 (2014), pp. 259–290.

94. See Evans, A., "The Kashmir insurgency;" and Ganguly, "The Crisis of Indian Secularism;" Jamal, Arif, *Shadow War: The Untold Story of Jihad in Kashmir*, New York: Melville House, 2009; and Tankel, *Storming the World Stage;* and Varshney, "India, Pakistan, and Kashmir," pp. 997–1019.

95. In 1997, after the US government banned HuA, the group changed its name back to HuM to escape sanctions. While it continued to act in Kashmir, the organization was also back in Afghanistan helping the Taliban. HuJi also re-emerged and deepened its involvement in Afghanistan. See Tankel, *Storming the World Stage*.

96. "Kashmiri, Freed After Hijacking, Is Still Militant," *New York Times*, 6 Jan. 2000, accessed 11 June 2018. http://www.nytimes.com/2000/01/06/world/kashmiri-freed-after-hijacking-is-still-militant.html.

97. See Nazish, Kirin, "The Islamic State Is Spreading Into Pakistan," *The New Republic*, 23 Sept. 2014, accessed 11 June 2018. https://newrepublic.com/article/119535/isis-pakistan-islamic-state-distributing-flags-and-flyers; Fair, C. Christine, "Is Pakistan in ISIS' Crosshairs?," *Boston Review*, 16 Oct. 2014, accessed 11 June 2018. https://bostonreview.net/world/c-christine-fair-isis-pakistan-militant-foreign-policy; and Jamal, Umair, "The Islamic State Threat Is Real in Pakistan," *The Diplomat*, 18 Feb. 2016, accessed 11 June 2018. http://thediplomat.com/2016/02/the-islamic-state-threat-is-real-in-pakistan.

98. Evans, "The Kashmir insurgency."

99. Blank, Jonah, "Kashmir: All tactics, No strategy," *India Review*, 2, 3 (2003), pp. 181–202.

100. Schofield, Victoria, "Kashmiri Separatism and Pakistan in the Current Global Environment," *Contemporary South Asia*," 16, 1 (2008), pp. 83–92.

101. Levy, Adrian and Cathy Scott-Clark. *The Meadow*, London: Harper Collins, 2012. See also Daulat, A.S., and Aditya Sinha, *Kashmir: The Vajpayee Years*, Noida: Harper Collins India, 2015.

102. Fair, C. Christine. *The Madrassah Challenge: Militancy and Religious Education in Pakistan*, Washington, D.C.: United States Institute of Peace, 2008.

103. Tankel, *Storming the World Stage*.

104. Abbas, Azmat, "In God We Trust," *The Herald (Pakistan)* (Jan. 2002), pp. 45–49.

105. "Barelvi Islam," *Global Security*, accessed 11 June 2018. http://www.globalsecurity.org/military/intro/islam-barelvi.htm.

106. See Abou Zahab, Mariam, "Salafism in Pakistan: The Ahl-e Hadith Movement," in *Global Salafism* (ed.) Roel Meijer (ed.), pp. 126–139; and Popovic, Milos, "The Perils of Weak Organization: Explaining Loyalty and Defection of Militant Organizations Toward Pakistan," *Studies In Conflict & Terrorism* 38, 11 (2015), pp. 919–937.

107. Bora, Kukil. "Major Terrorist Attacks in India Over The Last 20 Years: A Timeline," *International Business Times*, 13 Dec. 2014, accessed 11 June 2018. http://www.ibtimes.com/major-terrorist-attacks-india-over-last-20-years-timeline-1752731.

108. Anwari, "Deterrence."

4. WHAT IS THE LET? A CRITICAL EXAMINATION

1. Meijer, Roel, *Global Salafism*, p. 3.
2. See Ceccoli, Stephen and Ron Gelleny, Karl Kaltenthaler, William J. Miller, "The Sources of Pakistani Attitudes toward Religiously Motivated Terrorism," *Studies in Conflict & Terrorism*, 33, 9 (2010), pp. 815–835; and Siddiqa, Ayesha, "Jihadism in Pakistan: The Expanding Frontier," *Journal of International Affairs*, 63, 1 (2009), pp. 57–71; and Paul, T.V., *The Warrior State: Pakistan in the Contemporary World*, New York: Oxford University Press, 2014.
3. Abou Zahab, Mariam, "Salafism in Pakistan: The Ahl-e Hadith Movement," in Meijer, Roel, *Global Salafism*, pp. 126–139; Metcalf, Barbara. "Islam and power in colonial India: the making and unmaking of a Muslim princess." *The American Historical Review*, 116.1 (2011), pp. 1–30.
4. Meijer, *Global Salafism*, p. 9.
5. See Wagemakers, Joas, ""Seceders" and "Postponers"? An Analysis of the "Khawarij" and "Murji'a" Labels in Polemical Debates between Quietist and Jihadi-Salafis," *Contextualising Jihadi Thought* (ed.) Jeevan Deol and Zaheer Kazmi, London: Hurst, 2012, pp-145–164; and Mandaville, Peter, *Global Political Islam*, Abingdon: Routledge, 2007.
6. Rabbani, Abul Hassan Mubbashir Ahmed, *Masalah-yi takfir aur is ke usul o zavabit* (The Problem of Takfir and its Principles and Regulations), trans Safina Ustaad, Lahore: Dar-ul-Andulus, 2015, pp. 32.
7. Fair, C. Christine, "The Milli Muslim League: The Domestic Politics of Pakistan's Lashkar-e-Taiba," Current Trends in Islamist Ideology, 7 May 2018, accessed 11 June 2018. https://www.hudson.org/research/14305-the-milli-muslim-league-the-domestic-politics-of-pakistan-s-lashkar-e-taiba.
8. See Abou Zahab, "Salafism in Pakistan;" and Meijer, *Global Salafism*.
9. Abou Zahab, "Salafism in Pakistan."
10. Fair, C. Christine, *The Madrassah Challenge: Militancy and Religious Education in Pakistan*, Washington, D.C.: United States Institute of Peace, 2008.
11. Abou Zahab, "Salafism in Pakistan."
12. Ibid.
13. Butt, Intzar Hussain and Tahir Mahmood Butt, "Sectarian Divisions of Pakistani Society: Role of Madrassa and Politics," *Middle-East Journal of Scientific Research*, 19, 3 (2014), pp. 196–201.
14. Abou Zahab, "Salafism in Pakistan' and Fair, *The Madrassah Challenge*.
15. See Fair, C. Christine, "Leader-Led Jihad in Pakistan: The Case of Lashkar-e-Taiba," in *The Evolution of the Global Terrorist Threat: From 9/11 to Osama bin Laden's Death*, Bruce Hoffman and Fernando Reinares (eds), New York: Columbia University Press, 2014, pp. 571–599; and Fair, C. Christine, "Lashkar-e-Tayiba and the Pakistani State," *Survival*, 53 (August 2011), pp. 1–23; and Popovic, Milos, "The Perils of Weak Organization: Explaining Loyalty and Defection of Militant Organizations Toward Pakistan," *Studies In Conflict & Terrorism* 38, 11 (2015), pp. 919–937; and Tankel,

Stephen, *Storming the World Stage*; and Tankel, Stephen, "Beyond the Double Game: Lessons from Pakistan's Approach to Islamist Militancy," *Journal of Strategic Studies*, 24 July 2016, accessed 11 June 2018. http://www.tandfonline.com/doi/full/10.1080/01402390.2016.1174114.

16. Devadas, David, "Death of Burhan Wani and what it means to Hizbul Mujahideen, Kashmir," *FirstPost.com*, 9 July 2016, accessed 11 June 2018. http://www.firstpost.com/india/burhan-wani-militancys-poster-boy-is-dead-and-the-army-is-ready-for-more-battles-in-kashmir-2882806.html.

17. Ehsan, Mir and Bashaarat Masood, "Kashmir unrest: Five killed in fresh Valley firing, toll 65; curfew, restrictions tightened," *The Indian Express*, 17 August 2016, accessed 11 June 2018.

18. Lodhi is widely viewed among Pakistanis who are critical of the army's dominance over the state's foreign affairs as one of the army's "favourite spin doctors" and even served an unofficial envoy between Pakistan's army chief and the Obama administration. See Sultania, Devyani, "Pak to observe July 19 as 'Black Day' against Kashmir violence, demands UN probe," *International Business Times*, 15 July 2016, accessed 11 June 2018. http://www.ibtimes.co.in/pak-observe-july-19-black-day-against-kashmir-violence-demands-un-probe-686816.

19. Goshal, Arkadev, "Hafiz Saeed threatens war against India if Geelani's Kashmir solution not accepted," *International Business Times*, 22 July 2016, accessed 11 June 2018. http://www.ibtimes.co.in/lashkar-e-taiba-chief-hafiz-saeed-says-he-coming-india-after-phone-call-sister-asiya-andrabi-687565.

20. Azzam, Abdullah, "Join the Caravan', English translation, accessed 11 June 2018. http://english.religion.info/2002/02/01/document-join-the-caravan/.

21. "JuD caravan led by Hafiz Saeed's son stopped near LoC," *The Times of India*, 2 August 2016, accessed 11 June 2018. http://timesofindia.indiatimes.com/world/JuD-caravan-led-by-Hafiz-Saeeds-son-stopped-near-LoC/articleshow/53510300.cms.

22. "Jamaat-ud-Dawah chief Hafiz Saeed files petition over taking up Kashmir issue at UNSC," *The Indian Express*, 12 August 2016, accessed 11 June 2018. http://indianexpress.com/article/india/india-news-india/jamaat-ud-dawah-chief-hafiz-saeed-files-petition-over-taking-up-kashmir-issue-at-unsc-2971450/.

23. McGirk, Tim, "The General Speaks Out," *Time*, 19 Oct. 199, accessed 11 June 2018. http://content.time.com/time/world/article/0,8599,2054276,00.html.

24. Kronstadt, K. Alan. Pakistan's Political Crises. Congressional Research Service, 2008, accessed 10 June 2018. https://fas.org/sgp/crs/row/RL34240.pdf.

25. Shaikh, Farzana, "Judiciary's Coup," *The Indian Express*, 1 July 2017, accessed 10 June 2018. http://indianexpress.com/article/opinion/columns/nawaz-sharif-pakistan-panama-papers-supreme-court-judiciarys-coup-4776279/; Fair, C. Christine. "The Only Enemy Pakistan's Army Can Beat Is Its Own Democracy," Foreign Policy, 9 Aug. 2017, accessed 11 June 2018. http://foreignpolicy.com/2017/08/09/the-only-enemy-pakistans-army-can-beat-is-its-own-democracy/.

26. Fair, C. Christine, *Fighting to the End*.

27. See Yasmeen, Samina, *Jihad and Dawah: Evolving Narratives of Lashkar-e-Taiba and*

Jamat ud Dawah, London: Hurst, 2017; Sikand, Yoginder, "The Islamist Militancy in Kashmir: The Case of the Lashkar-e-Taiba," in *The Practice of War: Production, Reproduction and Communication of Armed Violence*, Aparna Rao et al. (eds), New York: Berghahn Books, 2007, pp. 215–238; and Abou Zahab, Mariam, "I Shall be Waiting at the Door of Paradise: The Pakistani Martyrs of the Lashkar-e-Taiba (Army of the Pure)," in *The Practice of War*, pp. 133–158; and Abou Zahab, "Salafism in Pakistan;" and Shafqat, Saeed, "From Official Islam to Islamism: The Rise of Dawat-ul-Irshad and Lashkar-e-Taiba," *Pakistan: Nationalism without a Nation*, pp. 131–147; and Tankel, *Storming the World Stage;* and Tankel, Stephen, "Beyond the Double Game;" and Jamal, Arif, *Call For Transnational Jihad: Lashkar-e-Taiba 1985–2014*, East Brunswick: AvantGarde Books LLC., 2014.

28. The Geneva Accord which brought the conflict to a close was signed in 1988. See Tankel, *Storming the World Stage* and "Lashkar-e-Taiba: Past Operations and Future Prospects."

29. See Khan, Zaigham, "Allah's Army," *The Herald Annual* (Jan. 1998), pp. 123–130. Yasmeen's timeline is somewhat different. She says that linkages between JuD and Lakhvi's militia happened in 1995. See Yasmeen, *Jihad and Dawah*.

30. See Sikand, Yoginder, "The Islamist Militancy in Kashmir: The Case of the Lashkar-e-Taiba," in *The Practice of War*, pp. 215–238; and Abou Zahab, "I Shall be Waiting at the Door of Paradise;" and Shafqat, "From Official Islam to Islamism."

31. See Bearak, Barry, "After the Attacks: In Pakistan; Estimates Of Toll In Afghan Missile Strike Reach As High As 50," *The New York Times*, 23 August 1998, accessed 11 June 2018. http://www.nytimes.com/1998/08/23/world/after-attacks-pakistan-estimates-toll-afghan-missile-strike-reach-high-50.html; and Filkins, Dexter, "'All of Us Were Innocent,' Says Survivor of US Attack on Camp," *The Los Angeles Times*, 24 August 1998, accessed 11 June 2018. http://articles.latimes.com/1998/aug/24/news/mn-16045.

32. See Taseer, Aatish, "Pakistan's rogue army runs a shattered state," *Financial Times*, 5 May 2011, accessed 11 June 2018. https://www.ft.com/content/ed7622b4–773e-11e0-aed6-00144feabdc0.

33. Abbas, Azmat, "In God We Trust," *The Herald (Pakistan)* (Jan. 2002), pp. 45–49.

34. Abbas, "In God We Trust;" Rana, Muhammad *Amir, The A to Z of Jehadi Organizations in Pakistan*, trans Saba Ansari, Lahore: Mashal, 2004; Yasmeen, *Jihad and Dawah*.

35. Tankel, "Lashkar-e-Taiba: Past Operations and Future Prospects."

36. Khan, "Allah's Army."

37. See Fouda, Yosri and Nick Fielding, *Capture or Kill: The Pursuit of the 9/11 Masterminds and the Killing of Osama bin Laden*, New York: Arcade Publishing, 2012; and John, Wilson, *Caliphate's Soldiers: The Lashkar-e-Tayyeba's Long War*, New Delhi: Amaryllis and the ORF, 2011.

38. Abbas, "In God We Trust."

39. Ibid.

40. See Tankel, *Storming the World Stage*, which says that this happened in 1990; and the other sources which suggest it happened later in 1993: "Hafiz Saeed asks govt to curb

foreign bid to bolster IS in Pakistan," *Indian Express*, 17 Oct. 2015, accessed 11 June 2018. http://indianexpress.com/article/world/world-news/hafiz-saeed-asks-govt-to-curb-foreign-bid-to-bolster-is-in-pakistan/; and Sikand, "The Islamist Militancy in Kashmir," and Abou Zahab, "I Shall be Waiting' and "Salafism in Pakistan;" and Shafqat, "From Official Islam to Islamism."

41. Tankel, "Lashkar-e-Taiba: Past Operations and Future Prospects."

42. Cited in Tankel, *Storming the World Stage.*

43. See Tankel, *Storming the World Stage* and "Lashkar-e-Taiba: Past Operations and Future Prospects;" and Scott-Clark, Cathy and Adrian Levy, *The Siege: 68 Hours Inside the Taj Hotel*, New York: Penguin, 2013.

44. Mannes, Aaron, John. P. Dickerson, Amy Sliva, Jana Shakarian, and V.S. Subrahmanian, "A Brief History of LeT," in *Computational Analysis of Terrorist Groups: Lashkar-e-Taiba*, New York: Springer, 2013, pp. 23–68.

45. Moghadam, Assaf, "Defining Suicide Terrorism," in *Root Causes of Suicide Terrorism: The Globalization of Martyrdom*, Ami Pedahzur (ed.), New York: Routledge, 2006, pp. 13–24.

46. Rana, *The A to Z of Jehadi Organizations in Pakistan.*

47. Khan, "Allah's Army."

48. Ibid.

49. Abou Zahab, "I Shall be Waiting at the Door of Paradise."

50. Scott-Clark and Levy, *The Siege*, pp. 106–107.

51. Chalk, Peter and C. Christine Fair, "Lashkar-e-Tayyiba leads the Kashmiri insurgency," *Jane's Intelligence Review*, 14, 10 (Dec. 2002), pp: 1–5.

52. Tankel, *Storming the World Stage*, p. 116.

53. Ibid.

54. See Tankel, *Storming the World Stage*; and Noonan, Sean, and Scott Steward, "The Evolution of a Pakistani Militant Network," *Stratfor*, 15 Sept. 2011, accessed 11 June 2018. https://www.stratfor.com/weekly/evolution-pakistani-militant-network.

55. Tankel, *Storming the World Stage.*

56. Author work with the UN Assistance Mission to Afghanistan between June and Oct. 2007.

57. Subrahmanian et al, *Computational Analysis of Terrorist Groups.*

58. "2008 Indian embassy attack in Kabul sanctioned by ISI, new book claims," *The Times of India*, 23 March 23 2014, accessed 11 June 2018. http://timesofindia.indiatimes.com/india/2008-Indian-embassy-attack-in-Kabul-sanctioned-by-ISI-new-book-claims/articleshow/32545791.cms.

59. Mazzetti, Mark, "A Shooting in Pakistan Reveals Fraying Alliance," *The New York Times*, 12 March 2011, accessed 11 June 2018. http://www.nytimes.com/2011/03/13/weekinreview/13lashkar.html. Accessed June 1, 2017.

60. "LeT Responsible for Attack at Indian Consulate in Herat: US," *The Times of India*, 25 June 2014, accessed 11 June 2018. http://timesofindia.indiatimes.com/world/us/LeT-responsible-for-attack-at-Indian-Consulate-in-Herat-US/articleshow/37205339.cms. See also American Foreign Policy Council, "Lashkar-e-Taiba," in *The World*

Almanac of Islamism, Rowman and Littlefield Publishers, 2011; and Tankel, *Storming the World Stage*; Brulliard, Karin. "Afghan Intelligence Ties Pakistani Group Lashkar-i-Taiba to Recent Kabul Attack," *The Washington Post*, 3 March 2010, accessed 11 June 2018. http://www.washingtonpost.com/wp-dyn/content/article/2010/03/02/AR2010030202427.html; and Swami, Praveen, "Kabul Attack: US Warning was accurate," *The Hindu*, 3 August 2008, accessed 11 June 2018. http://www.thehindu.com/todays-paper/Kabul-attack-US-warning-was-accurate/article15271791.ece.

61. Fair, C. Christine and Peter Chalk. *Fortifying Pakistan: The Role of US Internal Security Assistance*, Washington, D.C.: United States Institute of Peace, 2006."

62. See Fair, "India and Iran: New Delhi's Balancing Act," *The Washington Quarterly*, 30 (Summer 2007), pp. 145–159; and Tankel, *Storming the World Stage*.

63. Author work in Afghanistan in 2007 with the U.N. Assistance Mission to Afghanistan; See also American Foreign Policy Council, "Lashkar-e-Taiba," in *The World Almanac of Islamism*, Rowman and Littlefield Publishers, 2011; and Tankel, *Storming the World Stage*; Brulliard, "Afghan Intelligence;" and Swami, "Kabul Attack."

64. Scott-Clark and Levy, "*The Siege*," p. 52.

65. Pardesi, Manjeet, "The Battle for the Soul of Pakistan at Islamabad's Red Mosque," in *Treading on Hallowed Ground: Counterinsurgency Operations in Sacred Spaces*, C. Christine Fair and Sumit Ganguly (eds), New York: Oxford University Press, 2008, pp. 88–116.

66. Rotella, Sebastian, "Four Disturbing Questions about the Mumbai Terror Attack," *ProPublica*, 22 Feb. 2013, accessed 11 June 2018. https://www.propublica.org/article/four-disturbing-questions-about-the-mumbai-terror-attack.

67. "Mumbai Case Offers Rare Picture of Ties Between Pakistan's Intelligence Service, Militants," ProPublica, 2 May 2011, accessed 11 June 2018. https://www.propublica.org/article/mumbai-case-offers-rare-picture-of-ties-between-pakistans-intelligence-serv.

68. Rotella, Sebastian, "Four Alleged Masterminds of 2008 Mumbai Attacks Are Indicted in Chicago," *ProPublica*, 25 April 2011, accessed 11 June 2018. https://www.propublica.org/article/four-alleged-masterminds-of-2008-mumbai-attacks-are-indicted-in-chicago.

69. Scott-Clark and Levy, *The Siege*.

70. Ibid.

71. Ibid.

72. Ibid.

73. Riedel, Bruce, "Al Qaeda 3.0: Terrorism's Emergent New Power Bases," *Brookings Institution*, 3 Dec. 2012, accessed 11 June 2018. https://www.brookings.edu/opinions/al-qaeda-3-0-terrorisms-emergent-new-power-bases/.

74. Sharma, Surinder Kumar and Anshuman Behera, *Militant Groups in South Asia*, New Delhi: Institute for Defence Studies and Analyses, 2014.

75. US Department of State, *Country Reports on Terrorism 2013*, April 2014, accessed 11 June 2018. http://www.state.gov/j/ct/rls/crt/2013/.

76. Jamaat-ud-Dawa, accessed 7 Sept. 2016 (link expired). http://www.judofficial.com/en/.

77. US Department of Treasury, "Treasury Designates Lashkar-e-Tayyiba Leadership," 30 Aug. 2012, accessed 11 June 2018. http://www.treasury.gov/press-center/press-releases/Pages/tg1694.aspx.

78. See Tankel, "Lashkar-e-Taiba: Past Operations and Future Prospects;" and Sharma and Behera, *Militant Groups in South Asia*.

79. Khan, "Allah's Army," p. 125.

80. The cable does not explain the empirical underpinning of this estimate. See Subramanian, Nirupama, "No planning' went into action against JuD, says US official," *The Hindu*, 30 March 2011, accessed 11 June 2018. http://www.thehindu.com/news/the-india-cables/lsquoNo-planning-went-into-action-against-JuD-says-US-official/article14966518.ece.

81. Jamaat-ud-Dawa, accessed 7 Sept. 2016 (link expired). http://www.judofficial.com/en/.

82. John, Wilson, "Resurgent Radicalism in Pakistan: A Case Study of Jamaat-ud-Dawa," *CLAWS Journal* (Winter 2008), pp. 60–73.

83. Taqwa Model School, "Taqwa Model School Homepage," accessed 11 June 2018. http://taqwamodelschool.com/.

84. The website provides fees for the Gulshan campus. The monthly fees for beginner to class five run Rs. 18,500 (US$177) in addition to a Rs. 2,000 (US$20) annual fee. Class six through ten is slightly more expensive as are the college fees. It also offers a special Hifz (memorization of the Quran) class which is equivalently expensive. The Taqwa Model School is far more transparent about its fee structures than the top private schools in Pakistan (Beaconhouse, The City School, Lahore Grammar School) which expressly do not publicize their fee structures. However, according to one Beaconhouse fee chart for Bahria Town in Lahore, for beginning through eighth grade, the total monthly fees are around Rs. 13,300 ($127) in addition to a Rs. 800 ($7.65) registration fee and a one-time admission fee of Rs. 20,000 ($191). The monthly fees of class 10 is Rs. 17,885 ($171). Thus the Taqwa schools are price-competitive with this prestigious school system. See Taqwa Model School, "Fee Structure," accessed 11 June 2018. http://taqwamodelschool.com/fee-structure/; and Kaisrani, Hussain, "Beaconhouse School System, Bahria Town Campus (BBTC) Lahore—A successful completion of first year (Admission process, Fee Structure, Suggestions)," blogpost, 21 Aug. 2015, accessed 11 June 2018. http://kaisrani.blogspot.in/2015_08_01_archive.html.

85. Taqwa Model School, "TMS Introduction Video," accessed 11 June 2018. https://vimeo.com/134557405.

86. See Taqwa Model School, "Taqwa Model School Homepage," and "Taqwa Model School Facebook Page," accessed 11 June 2018. https://www.facebook.com/tss.edu.karachi/.

87. See Tankel, "Lashkar-e-Taiba: Past Operations and Future Prospects;" and Fair, C. Christine, *Fighting to the End* and "Leader-Led Jihad in Pakistan: The Case of Lashkar-e-Taiba," in *The Evolution of the Global Terrorist Threat: From 9/11 to Osama bin Laden's Death*, (ed.) Bruce Hoffman and Fernando Reinares, New York: Columbia University Press, 2014, pp. 571–599.

88. See Fair, C. Christine, "Militant Recruitment in Pakistan: Implications for Al-Qa'ida and Other Organizations," *Studies in Conflict and Terrorism*, 27, 6 (Nov./Dec. 2004), pp. 489–504 and "Lashkar-e-Tayiba and the Pakistani State," *Survival*, 53 (Aug. 2011), pp. 1–23.

89. Khan, "Allah's Army," pp. 125.

90. Rana, Muhammad Amir, *The A to Z of Jehadi Organizations in Pakistan*.

91. Yasmeen, *Jihad and Dawah*.

92. It's helpful to provide some sort of benchmark for this figure of 100,000 copies of *al-Dawa*. Pakistan's largest Urdu daily newspaper is the *Daily Jang*, which claims a daily circulation of 850,000. This figure may seem low given that Pakistan's population exceeds 196 million. Newspaper sales will be tempered by relatively low rates of literacy and the ability to purchase them. It turns out that only fifty per cent of adult Pakistanis are literate and about half of the population lives in poverty with one in five persons living on less than $1.25 a day. Even though newspapers such as the *Daily Jang* Pakistan are quite inexpensive (Rs. 12, about 12 cents), illiteracy and poverty constrain the market. Nonetheless about 36 per cent of rural populations and 60 per cent of urban populations report reading newspapers. This tracks with the literacy rates in rural and urban areas generally. And about 30 per cent of the population report reading a periodical at least once a day. See Tankel, "Lashkar-e-Taiba: Past Operations and Future Prospects;" and InfoAsAid, "Pakistan: Media and Telecoms Landscape Guide," *Communicating with Disaster Affect Communities Network*, Jan. 2014, accessed 11 June 2018. http://www.cdacnetwork.org/tools-and-resources/i/20140613150126-rxeiv.

93. Ghazwa refers to the battles in which the prophet Muhammad personally participated. (Ghazwa-e-Hind, a battle to establish Islamic rule declared by the prophet, is a battle-cry of LeT/JuD.)

94. Rana, *The A to Z of Jehadi Organizations;* Tankel, "Lashkar-e-Taiba: Past Operations and Future Prospects."

95. C. Christine, "Not at the Forefront of Flood Relief," *Foreign Policy*, 20 Sept. 2010, accessed 11 June 2018. http://foreignpolicy.com/2010/09/20/not-at-the-forefront-of-flood-relief/.

96. Fair, C. Christine, "Lashkar-e-Taiba: Pakistan's Domesticated Terrorists," *Lawfare*, 29 Dec. 2013, accessed 11 June 2018. https://www.lawfareblog.com/foreign-policy-essay-c-christine-fair-lashkar-e-taiba-pakistans-domesticated-terrorists.

97. Jamaat-ud-Dawa, "FIF is Reality of Jamat-ud-Dawa."

98. Falah e Insaniat Foundation, "Relief Work in Balochistan," *Falah e Insaniat Foundation*, accessed 11 June 2018. http://fifpakistan.blogspot.com/p/services-of-fif-in-baluchistan-falah-e.html.

99. See Falah e Insaniat Foundation, "About Us," accessed 11 June 2018. http://www.devotedtohumanity.org/en/page/about-us.php. Over the course of the summer of 2016 and winter of 2017, I met with representatives from Indian and Bangladeshi intelligence organizations who shared their assessments that FIF was engaging in these activities. American officials also shared with me their belief that FIF was not exaggerating their reach. Thus while I cannot rule out that FIF is engaging in deception, intelligence officials from three countries suspect that these accounts are accurate.

100. As of Dec. 6, 2017, Twitter feed associated with the organization (@FIF_NGO and @SalmanFIF) used display pictures demonstrating their work in Myanmar for the Rohingyas. On 14 Nov. 2017, FIF posted this update to its website along with photos of their efforts and other messages requesting donations for Rohingya relief. "Relief caravan of Falah e Insaniat Foundation has reached in Rakhine State in extremely risky conditions. FIF distributed Millions of cash money and blankets among more than 300 besieged Rohingya Muslims. Head FIF Foreign Affair Shahid Mahmood told that relief activities of FIF for Burmi[sic] refugees are continued. FIF is also distributing dry ration and other items of food and drink. As well as, FIF has started relief activities for besieged Rohingya Muslims in Rakhine State. FIF will soon start its relief activities in whole areas of Burma where Muslims are besieged." See "Rakhine: FIF starts relief activities for besieged Rohingya Muslims," 14 Nov. 2017, accessed 11 June 2018. http://www.devotedtohumanity.org/blog/detail/rakhine-fif-starts-relief-activities-for-besieged-rohingya-muslims.php.

101. See for example, the two-page advertisement in *Invite*, Issue 7 (Oct. 2017), pp. 8–9.

102. One explanation that a Bangladeshi intelligence official offered in Jan. 2018 is that the group is designated rather than specific persons. Countries receiving visa applications from member would not know that they are members unless the individual is designated as well. One Bangladeshi intelligence official explained to me in January 2017, that such persons entered Bangladesh having applied for a visa in which they indicated that they wanted to donate *zakat* to the needy. Once they were in country, they visited Rohingya refugees from Burma, set up their banner and took photos of their activities. Given Bangladesh's history with Pakistani terrorist groups like LeT operating in Bangladesh, it is still surprising that such a person would receive a visa under those grounds. But apparently, this is one way in which individuals associated with LeT are able to enter countries for this kind of work. See United Nations Security Council, "Security Council Al-Qaida Sanctions Committee Adds Four Names to Its Sanctions List, Amends One Entry," 14 March 2012, accessed 11 June 2018. http://www.un.org/press/en/2012/sc10578.doc.htm.

103. Falah e Insaniat Foundation, "Muzaffarabad, Falah-e-Insaniat Foundation Holds Rally," 6 Aug. 2016, accessed 22 Aug. 2016 (link expired). http://www.devotedtohumanity.com/blog/detail/muzaffarabad-falah-e-insaniat-foundation-holds-rally.php.

104. Tankel, "Lashkar-e-Taiba: Past Operations and Future Prospects."

105. Rana, Muhammad *Amir, Gateway to Terrorism*, London: New Millennium Publication, 2003. I try to avoid using Rana as a source. In recent years, I have heard from multiple intelligence sources that Rana is a front organization for the ISI. There are reasons to take this seriously. For one thing, his publication rate is incredible, particularly given his limited English. Moreover, his organization has received extensive funding from China which would not be possible if he were not close to the government.

106. Tankel, *Storming the World Stage*.

107. Nanjappa Vicky, "Terror in the family: Hafiz Saeed's son-in-law Waleed LeT's next chief?" OneIndia.com, 18 Aug. 2016, accessed 11 June 2018. http://www.oneindia.

com/india/terror-in-the-family-hafiz-saeeds-son-in-law-waleed-lets-next-chief-2185 418.html.

108. See Tankel, *Storming the World Stage;* Fair, "Leader-Led Jihad in Pakistan;" and Fair, C. Christine, author fieldwork 2016.

109. Popovic, "The Perils of Weak Organization."

110. Fair and Chalk, *Fortifying Pakistan.*

111. Tankel, "Lashkar-e-Taiba: Past Operations and Future Prospects."

112. According to the UNSC Al-Qaida Sanctions Committee, Haji Muhammad Ashraf was chief of finance for LeT, a position he has held since at least 2003 (UNSC 1267 Committee 2008). Presumably Ashraf has been superseded by Zafar Iqbal in this post.

113. United Nations Security Council, "Zafar Iqbal," 14 March 2012, accessed 11 June 2018. https://www.un.org/sc/suborg/en/sanctions/1267/aq_sanctions_list/summaries/individual/zafar-iqbal.

114. Fair, fieldwork.

115. "Bailed Mumbai suspect Lakhvi's luxury jail time," *BBC*, 10 April 2015, accessed 11 June 2018. http://www.bbc.com/news/world-asia-31606798.

116. "Bailed Mumbai suspect Lakhvi's luxury jail time," *BBC*, 10 April 2015, accessed 11 June 2018. http://www.bbc.com/news/world-asia-31606798.

117. See "Mullah Omar: Taliban leader "died in Pakistan in 2013"," *BBC*, 29 July 2015, accessed 11 June 2018. http://www.bbc.com/news/world-asia-33703097; and "How did jailed Mumbai attacks mastermind become a father?," *The News*, 27 Nov. 2012, accessed 11 June 2018. https://www.thenews.com.pk/archive/print/626776-how-did-jailed-mumbai-attacks-mastermind-become-a-father?

118. United Nations Security Council, "Hafiz Abdul Salam Bhuttavi."

119. I was unable to find this book through various searches on Worldcat. It could be that this volume has not been catalogued by any library.

120. Sharma, Surinder Kumar and Anshuman Behera, *Militant Groups in South Asia,* New Delhi: Institute for Defence Studies and Analyses, 2014.

121. US Department of Treasury, "Treasury Targets Pakistan-Based Terrorist Organizations Lashkar-E Tayyiba and Jaish-E Mohammed," 4 Nov. 2010, accessed 11 June 2018. http://www.treasury.gov/press-center/press-releases/Pages/tg944.aspx.

122. Kahn, Jeremy, "Mumbai Terrorists Relied on New Technology for Attacks," *The New York Times,* 8 Dec. 2008, accessed 11 June 2018. http://www.nytimes.com/2008/12/09/world/asia/09mumbai.html.

123. Glanz, James, Sebastian Rotella, David E. Sanger, "In 2008 Mumbai Attacks, Piles of Spy Data, but an Uncompleted Puzzle," *The New York Times,* 21 Dec. 2014, accessed 11 June 2018. https://www.nytimes.com/2014/12/22/world/asia/in-2008-mumbai-attacks-piles-of-spy-data-but-an-uncompleted-puzzle.html.

124. See Rotella, Sebastian, "Pakistan and the Mumbai attacks: The Untold Story," *ProPublica,* 26 Jan. 2011, accessed 11 June 2018 and "The Man Behind Mumbai," *ProPublica,* 13 Nov. 2010, accessed 11 June 2018. https://www.propublica.org/article/the-man-behind-mumbai.

125. Rotella, "The Man Behind Mumbai."

126. Ibid.

127. US Department of Treasury, "Treasury Designates Lashkar-e-Tayyiba Leadership," 30 Aug. 2012, accessed 11 June 2018. http://www.treasury.gov/press-center/press-releases/Pages/tg1694.aspx.

128. Sharma and Behera, *Militant Groups in South Asia*.

129. United Nations Security Council, "Mohammed Yahya Mujahid," 14 Sept. 2009, accessed 11 June 2018. https://www.un.org/sc/suborg/en/sanctions/1267/aq_sanctions_list/summaries/individual/mohammed-yahya-mujahid.

130. US Department of Treasury, "Treasury Designates Lashkar-e-Tayyiba Leadership," 30 Aug. 2012, accessed 11 June 2018. http://www.treasury.gov/press-center/press-releases/Pages/tg1694.aspx.

131. John, Wilson, "LeT's Social Media Warfare," *Observer Research Foundation*, 3 July 2013. http://www.orfonline.org/research/lets-social-media-warfare/.

132. There are numerous other important personalities, many of whom have been proscribed by the United States and/or the United Nations. I have not been able to ascertain the current status of these persons. See Sharma and Behera, *Militant Groups in South Asia;* and Jamal, Umair, "Analyzing the Role of the Top LeT Ideologue: A Profile of *Amir* Hamza," Militant Leadership Monitor, 3, 6 (2012).

133. South Asia Terrorism Portal, "Lashkar-e-Toiba 'Army of the Pure," accessed 11 June 2018. http://www.satp.org/satporgtp/countries/india/states/jandk/terrorist_outfits/lashkar_e_toiba.htm.

134. "Meet the Lashkar Super Boss," *Rediff*, 15 Nov. 2005, accessed 11 June 2018. http://www.rediff.com/news/2005/nov/15sld2.htm.

135. Tankel, *Storming the World Stage*.

136. Ethnic cleansing in Kashmir usually refers to the exodus of Kashmiri Pandits (Hindus) who left the valley en masse in 1990 as militant violence began ravaging the state. In fact, by 1990 the vast majority (95 per cent) of the 160,000–170,000 Pandits had fled. While much contemporary discussion of Indian-administered Kashmir deliberates upon the fate of Muslims there, there is very little discussion of the Pandits' experiences, much less their ability to return home (Evans 2002).

137. See Popovic, "The Perils of Weak Organization;" Tankel, *Storming the World Stage* and "Lashkar-e-Taiba: Past Operations and Future Prospects."

138. Fair, C. Christine, "Pakistan and the Taliban: Is Past Prologue," *The Diplomat*, 11 (Oct. 2015), accessed 11 June 2018; and Qazi, Shehzad H., "Rebels of the Frontier: Origins, Organisation, and Recruitment of the Pakistani Taliban," *Small Wars and Insurgencies*, 22, 4 (2011), pp. 574–602; and Mir, *Amir, The Fluttering Flag of Jehad*, Lahore: Mashal Books, 2008.

139. Kambere, Geoffrey et al., "The Financing of Lashkar-e-Taiba," *CTX Journal*, 1, 1 (2011), accessed 11 June 2018. https://globalecco.org/ctx-v1n1/lashkar-e-taiba.

140. Sharma, Surinder Kumar and Anshuman Behera, *Militant Groups in South Asia*, New Delhi: Institute for Defence Studies and Analyses, 2014.

141. Sharma, *Militant Groups in South Asia*.

142. See Kambere et al, "The Financing of Lashkar-e-Taiba;" and Rana, *The A to Z of Jehadi Organizations*.

143. Rana, *The A to Z of Jehadi Organizations*.
144. Author fieldwork 2016.
145. Khan, Zaigham, "Interview with Hafiz Mohammed Khan," *The Herald Annual* (Jan. 1998), pp. 131–133.
146. Khan, Zaigham, "From Strength to Strength," *The Herald Annual*, (Jan. 1998), p. 125.
147. Khan, "Allah's Army."
148. Khan, Kamran and John Lancaster, "Extremists Fill Aid Chasm After Quake," *The Washington Post*, 16 Oct. 2005, accessed 11 June 2018. http://www.washingtonpost. com/wp-dyn/content/article/2005/10/15/AR2005101501392.html.
149. Subrahmanian et al, "A Brief History of LeT."
150. Behera provides funding estimates from 2001. She notes that the organization obtained about Rs. 20 crores overall in this year. (One crore equals 10,000,000. Behera does not specify whether these are Pakistani or Indian Rupees and thus I am unable to provide currency conversions for these or the other amounts she presents. This figure includes two crores raised by the department of External Affairs, eighty Lakhs in profit from Dar al Andalus (a Lakh equals 100,000); thirty-five lakhs from the students (education) department; 2.5 crore from animal hide collection; seventy lakhs from the department of women; forty-five lakhs from the Peasant and Labor Wing; and another six crore from other "miscellaneous" enterprises. She also notes that the organization secures contributions from Arab Gulf States among which Saudi Arabia is most prominent. (She does not specify if these bestowals are from the state, non-state organizations or individuals.) In addition, the *tanzeem* has bureaus in European countries which collect contributions for the jihad fund. See Behera, Navnita Chadha. *Demystifying Kashmir*, Washington, D.C.: Brookings Institution Press, 2007; and Jost, Patrick M. and Harjit Singh Sandhu, "The hawala alternative remittance system and its role in money laundering," *Interpol*, Jan. 2000, accessed 11 June 2018. http:// www.peacepalacelibrary.nl/ebooks/files/hawala.pdf.
151. Boone, Jon, "Eid animal slaughter funds Pakistan terror groups," *The Guardian*, 15 Oct. 2013, accessed 11 June 2018. http://www.theguardian.com/world/2013/oct/15/ eid-animal-slaughter-funds-pakistan-terror-groups.
152. Boone, "Eid animal slaughter."
153. "Minimum wage raised to Rs10,000, no additional tax on Rs2.5 million income," 21 June 2013, accessed 11 June 2018. https://tribune.com.pk/story/566389/mini-mum-wage-raised-to-rs10000-no-additional-tax-on-rs2-5-million-income/.
154. "Banned Outfits Raise Cash from Sacrifice Day," *Dawn*, 24 Nov. 2010, accessed 11 June 2018. http://www.dawn.com/news/585173/banned-outfits-raise-cash-from-sacri-fice-day.
155. Bhattacharya, Sanchita. "JuD: The Dependable Terrorist," *South Asia Intelligence Review*, 13, 2 (July 2014), accessed 11 June 2018. http://www.satp.org/satporgtp/ sair/Archives/sair13/13_2.htm.
156. "Pakistan Punjab demands Rs 1 billion from finance ministry to run Hafiz Saeed's JuD, other organisations," *Hindustan Times*, 31 May 2018, accessed 22 June 2018, https://www.hindustantimes.com/world-news/pakistan-punjab-demands-rs-1-bil-

lion-from-finance-ministry-to-run-hafiz-saeed-s-jud-other-organisations/story-3fMC cq7B778y2cmpOUUsKL.html. The federal government had, in February, started confiscating the properties of Saeed's banned outfit Jamaat-ud-Dawa (JuD) and its charity arm Falah-e-Insaniyat Foundation (FIF) across the country during a crackdown on the two organizations, in line with the UN Security Council sanctions list.

157. Khattak, Inamullah, "Why aren't we taking action against Hafiz Saeed, PML-N lawmaker asks," *The Dawn*, 6 Oct. 2016, accessed 11 June 2018, https://www.dawn.com/news/1288400.

158. Abbas, "In God We Trust;" Rana, Muhammad *Amir, The A to Z of Jehadi Organizations in Pakistan*, trans. Saba Ansari, Lahore: Mashal, 2004; Yasmeen, *Jihad and Dawah*.

159. See Abou Zahab, "I Shall be Waiting at the Door of Paradise;" and Adlakha, Joshua, "The Evolution of Lashkar-e-Tayyiba and the Road to Mumbai," Master's thesis, Georgetown University, 2010, accessed 11 June 2018. http://hdl.handle.net/10822/553436.

160. Husnain, Ghulam, "Inside Jihad," *Time*, 5 Feb. 2001, accessed 11 June 2018. http://content.time.com/time/magazine/article/0,9171,97126,00.html.

161. Yasmeen, *Jihad and Dawah*.

162. Tankel, *Storming the World Stage*.

163. See Tankel, "Lashkar-e-Taiba: Past Operations and Future Prospects;" and Fair, "Militant Recruitment in Pakistan."

164. Scott-Clark and Levy, *The Siege*.

165. Rotella, Sebastian, "Mumbai Case Offers Rare Picture of Ties Between Pakistan's Intelligence Service, Militants," ProPublica, 2 May 2011, accessed 11 June 2018. https://www.propublica.org/article/mumbai-case-offers-rare-picture-of-ties-between-pakistans-intelligence-serv.

166. For more information about the structure of the ISI, see Kiessling, Hein, *Faith, Unity, Discipline: The Inter-Service-Intelligence (ISI) of Pakistan*, London: Hurst, 2016; and Sirss, Owen L., *Pakistan's Inter-Services Intelligence Directorate: Covert Action and Internal Operations*, Abingdon: Routledge, 2017.

167. See Fair, C. Christine, "Lashkar-e-Taiba: Pakistan's Domesticated Terrorists," *Lawfare*, 29 Dec. 2013, accessed 11 June 2018. http://www.lawfareblog.com/2013/12/the-foreign-policy-essay-c-christine-fair-on-lashkar-e-taiba-pakistans-domesticated-terrorists/ and "Militant Recruitment in Pakistan."

168. Khan, "Allah's Army."

169. Fair, "Lashkar-e-Taiba: Pakistan's Domesticated Terrorists."

170. Husnain, "Inside Jihad."

171. See Fair, "Lashkar-e-Taiba: Pakistan's Domesticated Terrorists;" Rassler, Don, C. Christine Fair, Anirban Gosh, Nadia Shoeb, "The Fighters of Lashkar-e-Taiba: Recruitment, Training, Deployment and Death," *West Point Combating Terrorism Center*, April 2013, accessed 11 June 2018. https://www.ctc.usma.edu/wp-content/uploads/2013/04/Fighters-of-LeT_Final.pdf; and Tankel, *Storming the World Stage*.

172. Subrahmanian et al, "A Brief History of LeT."

173. Husnain, "Inside Jihad."

174. Tankel, *Storming the World Stage*; Fair, C. Christine, "Lashkar-e-Tayiba and the Pakistani State," *Survival*, 53 (Aug. 2011), pp. 1–23.

175. Husnain, "Inside Jihad."

176. See Rassler et al, "The Fighters of Lashkar-e-Taiba;" Rana, *The A to Z of Jehadi Organizations*; and Tankel, *Storming the World Stage*.

177. Tankel, *Storming the World Stage*.

178. Fair, C. Christine, "Lashkar-e-Tayiba and the Pakistani State," *Survival*, 53 (Aug. 2011), pp. 1–23.

179. See Rassler et al, "The Fighters of Lashkar-e-Taiba;" Tankel, *Storming the World Stage*; and Scott-Clark and Levy, *The Siege*.

180. Khan, "Allah's Army."

181. Ibid.

182. Fair, "Lashkar-e-Tayiba and the Pakistani State."

183. See Asal, Victor, C. Christine Fair, and Stephen Shellman, "Consenting to a Child's Jihad in Pakistan: Insights from Survey Data in Pakistan," *Studies in Conflict and Terrorism*, 31, 11 (2008), pp. 973–994; Abou Zahab, "I Shall be Waiting;" and Khan, "Allah's Army."

184. Abou Zahab, "I Shall be Waiting."

185. See Asal, Victor, C. Christine Fair, and Stephen Shellman, "Consenting to a Child's Jihad in Pakistan: Insights from Survey Data in Pakistan," *Studies in Conflict and Terrorism*, 31, 11 (2008), pp. 973–994; and Abou Zahab, "I Shall be Waiting."

186. "Hafiz Saeed's JuD to contest 2018 Pakistan general elections," *Economic Times*, 3 Dec., accessed 11 June 2018. https://m.economictimes.com/news/international/world-news/hafiz-saeed-to-contest-pakistan-general-elections-next-year/amp_article-show/61897257.cms.

187. Sirohi, Seema, "Pentagon Forces US Congress to Drop Linkage of Pakistan Aid To LeT," *The Wire*, 17 Nov. 2017, accessed 11 June 2018. https://thewire.in/197999/pentagon-forces-us-congress-drop-linkage-pakistan-aid-let/.

188. Constable, Pamela. "Trump's new Afghanistan policy has Pakistan angry and alarmed," *Washington Post*, 29 Aug. 2017, accessed 11 June 2018. https://www.washington-post.com/world/asia_pacific/trumps-new-afghanistan-policy-has-pakistan-angry-and-alarmed/2017/08/29/40e2de88–8cb9–11e7–9c53–6a169beb0953_story.html?utm_term=.7c9cc50f9424.

189. Hussain, Sajjad, "US defence secy meets Pak PM to mend frayed ties," *Outlook*, 4 Dec., accessed 11 June 2018. https://www.outlookindia.com/newsscroll/us-defence-secy-meets-pak-pm-to-mend-frayed-ties/1202293. The odd timing of these events almost prompts the question of whether the Department of Defense cajoled the US Congress to remove the conditionality that Pakistan do more to combat the JuD/LeT with actual knowledge that the JuD was fielding the MML. No doubt Pakistani officials would have justified this move arguing that it was a "deradicalization" plan.

190. John, "LeT's Social Media Warfare."

191. See Qayyum, Tabish. "The ISIS' Footprint in Pakistan: Myth or Reality," accessed 11 June 2018. https://www.academia.edu/31628011/The_ISIS_Footprint_in_Pakistan_Myth_or_Reality.

192. For an alternative view of CPEC and an argument that in fact this project is not going to primarily benefit Pakistan, see Fair, C. Christine, "Pakistan Can't Afford China's "Friendship," *Foreign Policy*, 3 July 2017, accessed 11 June 2018. http://foreignpolicy.com/2017/07/03/pakistan-cant-afford-chinas-friendship/.

193. Hashmi, By Dr. Muzammil Iqbal (Vice President of the MML), "What is Milli Muslim League All About?" *Invite*, Issue No. 7 (Oct. 2017) p. 18.

194. Ghori, Hafeez, "The Rise of MML and the Mainstreaming Debate," *Invite*, Issue No. 7 (Oct. 2017), p. 28.

195. "Aims and Objectives: Milli Muslim League," *Invite*, Issue No. 7 (Oct. 2017) pp. 12–13.

196. *Labbaik* literally means "I am here for you!." Thus a literal translation of this movement's name would be the "'I am here for you O prophet' Movement."

197. Qayyum, Tabish. "The Finality of the Prophethood and the Ideology of Pakistan," *Daily Khabrain*, 4 Oct. 2017, accessed 11 June 2018. http://epaper.dailykhabrain. com.pk/epaper?station_id=13&date=2017-10-05. Trans Moiz Abdul Majid.

198. Qayyum, "The Finality of the Prophethood and the Ideology of Pakistan."

199. Email correspondence with Tabish Qayyum, 26 Nov. 2017.

200. Fair, C. Christine. "The Only Enemy Pakistan's Army Can Beat Is Its Own Democracy," Foreign Policy, 9 Aug. 2017, accessed 11 June 2018. http://foreignpolicy. com/2017/08/09/the-only-enemy-pakistans-army-can-beat-is-its-own-democracy/.

201. "Hafiz Saeed's JuD Launches Political Party in Pakistan."

202. During the month of Nov. 2017, I corresponded with the MML leadership and posed several questions. Despite their initial willingness to engage, they ignored all of my questions.

203. Email correspondence with Tabish Qayyum, 26 Nov. 2017.

204. Shapiro, Jacob N., *The Terrorist's Dilemma: Managing Violent Covert Organizations*, Princeton: Princeton University Press, 2013.

205. Shapiro, *The Terrorist's Dilemma*.

206. The organization also arranges marriages among persons from across the Line of Control. For example, if an LeT cadre is from Pakistan, the organization may arrange his marriage to a girl or young woman from Indian-administered Kashmir and vice-versa. This is a deliberate strategy to strengthen the "Kashmiri" bonds of the organization. LeT comes under perpetual criticism because it is a largely Punjabi organization as I discuss in the next chapter. The organization also encourages cadres to marry the widows of martyrs. See Parashar, Swati, "Gender, Jihad, and Jingoism: Women as Perpetrators, Planners, and Patrons of Militancy in Kashmir," *Studies in Conflict and Terrorism*, 34, 4 (2011), pp. 295–317; Haq, Farhat, "Militarism and Motherhood: The Women of the Lashkar-i-Tayyabia in Pakistan," *Signs*, 32, 4 (Summer 2007), 1023–1046 and "Mothers of Lashkar-e-Taiba," *Economic and Political Weekly*, 44, 18 (May 2009), pp. 17–20; and Abou Zahab, "I Shall be Waiting."

207. Scott-Clark and Levy, *The Siege*.

5. WHO ARE THE SOLDIERS IN THE ARMY OF THE PURE?

1. The author is especially thankful to Nadia Shoib for doing the coding and to Anirban Ghosh for performing the statistical analysis in this section. However, without the support of Don Rassler at West Point's Combatting Terrorism Center this work would not have been possible. This chapter expands upon Fair, C. Christine, "Insights from a Database of Lashkar-e-Taiba and Hizb-ul-Mujahideen Militants," *Journal of Strategic Studies*, 37, 2 (2014), pp. 259–290.

2. Rassler, Don, C. Christine Fair, Anirban Gosh, Nadia Shoeb, "The Fighters of Lashkar-e-Taiba: Recruitment, Training, Deployment and Death," *West Point Combating Terrorism Center*, April 2013, accessed 11 June 2018. https://www.ctc.usma.edu/wp-content/uploads/2013/04/Fighters-of-LeT_Final.pdf.

3. *Mujallah al-Dawah* (renamed *Al-Haramain*) has been Lashkar-e-Tayyaba's and Jamaat ud-Dawa's most important publication. The first issue of the magazine was published in March 1989, and it was edited by Maulana Amir Hamza, the founding ideologue of the JuD. Qazi Kashif Niaz is also believed to have been an editor of *al-Dawa* for a period. The publication is now defunct. Typically, every issue carried articles on what being a Muslim should mean to every believer, drawing especially on the Ahl-e-Hadees school of Islamic jurisprudence. *Al-Dawa* also usually carried reports of jihad (particularly in Indian-administered Kashmir), information about fallen militants, and updates about the workings of all JuD departments. *Al-Dawa* reportedly had a circulation of around 140,000 before it closed. Other LeT linked magazines include: *Ghazwa Times* (renamed *Jarrar*), *Tayyabat* (a bi-monthly magazine for women, which has been renamed *Al-Saffat*), *Voice of Islam* (an English language magazine, which has been discontinued), *Nanhe Mujahid* (a monthly now released under the name *Rozatul Atfal*) and *Al-Ribat* (a monthly magazine in Arabic, which is now titled *Al-Anfal*). Umm-e-Hammad is the compiler of the three-volume series *Ham Ma'en Lashkar-e-Tayyaba Ki*, and is the editor of *Tayyabiat*, LeT's magazine for women, the head of LeT's Women Wing, and a mother of two LeT militants. For background see Naim, C.M., "The Mothers of the Lashkar', *Outlook India*, 15 Dec. 2008, www.outlookindia.com/article.aspx?239238 and Iqtidar, Humeira, *Secularizing Islamists: Jama'at-e-Islami and Jamat'at-ud-Da'wa in Urban Pakistan*, Chicago: University of Chicago Press, 2011, pp. 106–107.

4. Later data may or may not exist. Nonetheless, I am unable to acquire these materials for data extraction, assembly, and analysis.

5. Bueno De Mesquita, Ethan, "The Quality of Terror," *American Journal of Political Science*, 49, 3 (July 2005), pp. 515–530.

6. Author fieldwork in India, Pakistan, and Afghanistan over many years.

7. Khan, Zaigham, "Allah's Army," *The Herald Annual* (Jan. 1998), pp. 123–130.

8. See Tankel, *Storming the World Stage* and "Lashkar-e-Taiba: Past Operations and Future Prospects," *New America Foundation*, National Security Studies Program Policy Paper, April 2011.

9. Fair, Gosh, Rassler, and Shoeb, "The Fighters of Lashkar-e-Taiba."

10. Ibid.
11. Fair, *Fighting to the End.*
12. Fair, *Fighting to the End.*
13. Fair, C. Christine, "The Educated Militants of Pakistan: Implications for Pakistan's Domestic Security," *Contemporary South Asia,* 16 (March 2008), pp. 93–106 and *The Madrassah Challenge: Militancy and Religious Education in Pakistan,* Washington, D.C.: United States Institute of Peace, 2008.
14. Abou Zahab, Mariam, "I Shall be Waiting at the Door of Paradise,", pp. 133–158.
15. Khan, "Allah's Army."
16. See Stern, Jessica, "Pakistan's Jihad Culture," *Foreign Affairs* 79 (2000): pp. 115–126; Winthrop, Rebecca and Corinne Graff, *Beyond Madrasas: Assessing the Links Between Education and Militancy in Pakistan,* working paper 2, Washington, D.C.: Brookings Center for Universal Education, last accessed 11 June 2018. https://www.brookings.edu/research/beyond-madrasas-assessing-the-links-between-education-and-militancy-in-pakistan/; and Mannes, Aaron, John. P. Dickerson, Amy Sliva, Jana Shakarian, and V.S. Subrahmanian, "A Brief History of LeT," in *Computational Analysis of Terrorist Groups: Lashkar-e-Taiba,* New York: Springer, 2013, pp. 23–68; and Haq, Farhat, "Mothers of Lashkar-e-Taiba," *Economic and Political Weekly,* 44, 18 (May 2009), pp. 17–20.
17. Pakistan Bureau of Statistics, "Table 3: percentage Distribution of Population by 10 Years Age and Over by Level Of Education, Sex and Nature Of Activities 2009–2010," in *Labour Force Survey 2009–10*2010, accessed 11 June 2018. http://www.pbs.gov.pk/content/labour-force-survey-2009–10.
18. Fair, *The Madrassah Challenge.*
19. See Abou Zahab, "I Shall be Waiting," pp. 140; and Fair, "The Educated Militants."
20. Khan, "Allah's Army," p. 126.
21. Fair, *The Madrassah Challenge.*
22. Abou Zahab and Roy, *Islamist Networks,* p. 39.
23. Fair, Gosh, Rassler, Shoeb, "The Fighters of Lashkar-e-Taiba."
24. Andrabi, Tahir et al., "Religious School Enrolment in Pakistan: A Look at the Data," *Comparative Education Review,* 50, 3 (2006), pp. 446–77.
25. See Andersson, Neil, Noor Ansari, Ubaid Ullah Chaudhry, Anne Cockcroft, Amir Khan, Deborah Milne, Khalid Omer, "Challenging the myths about madaris in Pakistan: A national household survey of enrolment and reasons for choosing religious schools," *International Journal of Educational Development,* 29, 4 (July 2009), pp. 342–349; and ASER-Pakistan, "Annual Status of Education Report: ASER-Pakistan 2013," Lahore: South Asian Forum for Education Development, 2014, accessed 11 June 2018. http://www.aserpakistan.org/document/aser/2013/reports/national/ASER_National_Report_2013.pdf.
26. Fair, C. Christine, ""Does Pakistan Have a Madrasah Problem? Reconsidering the Securitization of Islamic Education in Pakistan," 19 July 2014, accessed 11 June 2018. http://ssrn.com/abstract=2468620.
27. Abou Zahab, "I Shall be Waiting," pp. 136.

28. Fair, C. Christine, "Who Are Pakistan's Militants and Their Families?", *Terrorism and Political Violence*, 20, 2 (2008), pp. 49–65.

29. Fair, "Who Are Pakistan's Militants."

30. See Haq, "Mothers of Lashkar-e-Taiba;" and Khan, "Allah's Army."

31. Khan, "Allah's Army."

32. Khan, "Allah's Army," p. 127.

33. Ibid.

34. Haq, "Mothers of Lashkar-e-Taiba," p. 19.

35. Ibid.; and Khan, "Allah's Army."

36. Fair, Gosh, Rassler, and Shoeb, "The Fighters of Lashkar-e-Taiba."

37. Ibid.

38. Khan, "Allah's Army."

39. "Australian David Hicks 'relieved "after terror conviction quashed"," *BBC*, 19 Feb. 2015, accessed 11 June 2018. http://www.bbc.com/news/world-australia-31529745.

40. Dertouzos, James N., *The Cost-Effectiveness of Military Advertising: Evidence from 2002–2004*, Santa Monica: RAND Corporation, 2009.

41. Dertouzos, James N. and Steven Garber, *Is Military Advertising Effective? An Estimation Methodology and Applications to Recruiting in the 1980s and 90s*, Santa Monica, CA: RAND Corporation, 2003.

42. Kumar, Anand and Shanker Krishnan, "Memory Interference in Advertising: A Replication and Extension," *Journal of Consumer Research*, 30, 4 (March 2004), pp. 602–611.

43. Hammad, Umm-e, *Hum Ma'en Lashkar-e-Tayyaba Ki* (We, the Mothers of Lashkar-e-Tayyaba), 2, Lahore: Dar-ul-Andalus, 2003, pp. 22.

44. Hammad, *Hum Ma'en Lashkar-e-Tayyaba Ki* (We, the Mothers of Lashkar-e-Tayyaba), pp. 243.

45. To conduct this analysis, we selected a random sample of 120 biographies from among the complete set and translated them in full. Ali Hamza did all of the biography translations unless otherwise noted. I then read them for the thematic content of the motivations. This is the beginning of a much larger project on battlefield motivation that will entail the translation of the full set of biographies.

46. Perhaps one of the most important of such studies is that of Shils and Janowitz (1948), in which they rely upon letters from German soldiers, interrogation reports among others. Such sources are also likely to be biased in various ways. See Shills, Edward A., and Morris Janowitz, "Cohesion and Disintegration in the Wehrmacht in World War II," *The Public Opinion Quarterly* 12, 2 (1948): pp. 280–315. See also Bartov, Omer, "Daily Life and Motivation in War: The Wehrmacht in the Soviet Union," *Journal of Strategic Studies* 12, 2 (1989), pp. 200–214.

47. "Abu Marsad Habeeb ur Rahman," *Mujallah Tayyabaat*, trans Ali Hamza, Dec. 2003, p. 43.

48. Um-e-Abdulrub, "Lanterns of Memory: The Martyrdom of Abu-Zubair rekindled the spirit of Jihad in the family associated with Tehreek-e-Mujahideen," *Mujallah Tayyabaat*, trans Ali Hamza, Jan. 2002, p. 24.

49. Um-e-Musaffra, "The blood struggle of a Martyr is never wasted: Abu Huzaifa Abdul Waheed," *Mujallah Tayyabaat*, trans Ali Hamza, April 2004, pp. 32 and 42; "Abu Quhafa Shaheed Syed Abdul Rasheed bin Tufail ul Rehman Shah," *Mujallah Tayyabaat*, trans Ali Hamza, Jan. 2003, p. 20; Ukht-e-Abdullah Sani, "To realize the status of a martyr, you need to transcend beyond the horizon. To understand the ecstasy of eternal life, you need to sacrifice yourself (Abu Bilal (Umar) & Abu Ququa (Usman))," *Mujallah Tayyabaat*, trans Ali Hamza, Aug. 2004, p. 29.

50. Hafza Hashmi, "Abul Hassan Mohammed Zubair Shaheed," *Mujallah Tayyabaat*, trans Ali Hamza, Aug. 2004, p. 31. Also see Um e Javed, "Memories of Abu Mohammed Askari Mohammed Boota Shaheed," *Mujallah Tayyabaat*, trans Ali Hamza, Feb. 2004, p. 33.

51. "Um-e-Hamaad's Second Son Jawad Ahmad Shaheed: Impressions of Amir Honorable Hafiz Mohammed Saeed Hafza-ullah," *Mujallah Tayyabaat*, trans Ali Hamza, May/July 2000, p. 20.

52. The author of the bio of Abu Abdullah Affan Javed was a fellow fighter with LeT. He says of the martyr that despite myriad physical ailments including asthma, kidney stones and a frail physique, he still entered the battlefield of jihad even though "There were problems as big as mountains in his path but it was the greatest objective of his life and he was determined to achieve it. He body was very weak and thin … Even with so many impediments, he was determined to achieve his objective and he did not take pay much importance to them. His heart was full of his desire for martyrdom. He served the leader for many years by spreading the message of religion and Jihad. But he yearned for martyrdom and he wanted to go to the battlefield. Everyone told him not to do so as how would he cross those mountain passes with such weak physique? But little did they know that when a person dedicates himself whole heartedly to the cause of Allah, then Allah helps such people in secret as well. Allah Almighty also helped this young man and he finished his practical training. After the completion of the training the leader advised him to stay back and spread the message of Jihad. But after his insistence the leader gave him his permission to go for Jihad to follow the example of companions of the holy prophet (PBUH)." Khurrum Shahzad, "Abu Abdullah Affan Javed Shaheed: A Great Honor for Punjab University," *Zarb-e-Tayyaba*, trans Ali Hamza, April 2005, p. 64.

53. Aqsa Dukhter Abdul Rasheed, "Abu Ayub Ansari," *Mujallah Tayyabaat*, trans Ali Hamza, July 2003, p. 23.

54. Inter alia, see Um-e-Shams-ul-Arifeen, "Shams-ul-Arifeen," *Mujallah Tayyabaat*, trans Ali Hamza, Sept. 2004, p. 38; Amir Hamza and Abu Umair Shaheed, "The situation and biographies of martyrs of Battle of Bandipura," *Mujallah ul Dawa*, trans Ali Hamza, Oct. 1994, p. 12; Amir Hamza, "Three Captains and dozens of soldiers of the Army of Nimrod sent to hell by Lashkar-e-Tayyaba in Burgaam," *Mujallah ul Dawa*, trans Ali Hamza, Jan. 1994, p. 4; Qazi Kashif Niaz, "The Whipping of Indian Army by the Wrath of Allah in the form of battle with Lashkar-e-Tayyaba (LeT)," *Mujallah ul Dawa*, trans Ali Hamza, July 1994, p. 5.

55. See, *inter alia*, Sufyan Asghar, "Abu Huzaifa Muhammad Luqman—another honor

for Bahauddin Zakariya University," *Zarb-e-Tayyaba*, trans Ali Hamza, Nov. 2004, p. 28; Salman Nazeer, "Remembering Abu Abdullah Abdul Majeed Tariq the martyr," *Zarb-e-Tayyaba*, trans Ali Hamza, Dec. 2004, p. 35; Mohammad Tayyab, "Abu Muslim Fidai Abdul Waheed Shaheed. A Tale of a Mujahid who battled the infidels for four years," *Zarb-e-Tayyaba*, trans Ali Hamza, Feb. 2005, p. 38; Salman Nazeer, Renala Khurd, "Shaheed Abu Zeeshan. Painful memories and heartwarming tales," *Zarb-e-Tayyaba*, trans Ali Hamza, June 2005, p. 41.

56. See, *inter alia*, Abu Mohsin of Sargodha, "Abu Hanzla Babar Zameer, Bhalwal," *Mujallah ul Dawa*, trans Ali Hamza, Jan. 2001, p. 38; Ukth-e-Abdul Wasaih and Ukht-e-Saad-ul-Rehman, "Another rose blossomed in the Garden of Martyrdom: Abu Ukasha Abdul Rashid Shaheed," *Mujallah Tayyabaat*, trans Ali Hamza, June 2004, p. 42.

57. See, *inter alia*, Ukht-e-Abu Hashim, "Abu Hamza Sayyaf Sani Abdul Rehman," *Mujallah Tayyabaat*, Jan. 2004, trans Ali Hamza, p. 23; Ghazi Faheem Ijaz, "In memory of Shaheed Abu Sufian," *Mujallah ul Dawa*, trans Ali Hamza, Aug. 1994, pp. 31–33; Amir Hamza, "The Invasion of Lashkar-e-Taiba in Occupied Kashmir," *Mujallah ul Dawa*, trans Ali Hamza, Feb. 1994, pp. 4–9.

58. "Abu Hanzul Amjad (martyred)—Those who require truth, do ablution with their blood," *Zarb-e-Tayyaba*, trans Ali Hamza, April 2004, p. 33–35; Abuzar Salafi, "Abu Saraqah Amjad Hussain," *Mujallah ud Dawa*, trans Ali Hamza, Jan. 2001, pp. 34–35; Abu Khalid, "Abu Mursad Zakaullah, Faisalabad," *Mujallah ud Dawa*, trans Ali Hamza, Jan. 2001, pp. 40–4; Um-e-Shams-ul-Arifeen, "Shams-ul-Arifeen," *Mujallah Tayyabaat*, trans Ali Hamza, Sept. 2004, p. 38; Hafza Hashmi, "Abul Hassan Mohammed Zubair Shaheed," *Mujallah Tayyabaat*, trans Ali Hamza, Aug. 2004, p. 31.

59. See *inter alia*, Mohammad Bilal Akram, Abu Bilal Mohammad Ashraf Shaheed: A tale of that Mentor, who left behind an example for his students," *Zarb-e-Tayyaba*, trans Ali Hamza, Sept. 2004, pp. 34–36; "Abu Maooz Mohammad Asghar Shaheed. An excellent student of University of Engineering and Technology Taxila," *Zarb-e-Tayyaba*, trans Ali Hamza, April 2005, pp. 62–64; "Um-e-Hamaad's Second Son Jawad Ahmad Shaheed: Impressions of Amir Honorable Hafiz Mohammed Saeed Hafza-ullah," *Mujallah Tayyabaat*, trans Ali Hamza, May/July 2000, p. 20; Mohammad Akram Zaheer, "Abu Zaraar Qari Mohammad Aslam," *Mujallah ud Dawa*, trans Ali Hamza, Jan. 2004, pp. 28–29.

60. *Inter alia*, Abuzar Salafi, "Abu Saraqah Amjad Hussain," *Mujallah ud Dawa*, trans Ali Hamza, Jan. 2001, pp. 34–35; Master Muhammad Afzal, "Abu Bakr Ammar Anjum Abdul Waris, Sialkot," *Mujallah ud Dawa*, trans Ali Hamza, Jan. 2001, pp. 41–42; Ukth-e-Abdul Wasaih and Ukht-e-Saad-ul-Rehman, "Another rose blossomed in the Garden of Martyrdom: Abu Ukasha Abdul Rashid Shaheed," *Mujallah Tayyabaat*, trans Ali Hamza, June 2004, pp. 42–43, 36.

61. Van Der Veer, Peter, "Ayodhya and Somnath: Eternal Shrines, Contested Histores," *Social Research*, 59, 1 (1992): pp. 85–109; Tilly, Charles, "Contentious Conversation," *Social Research*, 65, 3, *Conversation*(FALL 1998), pp. 491–510; Eaton, Richard M., "Temple desecration and Indo-Muslim states," *Frontline* (Jan. 2001): pp. 70–77; Shah, Ghanshyam, "Contestation and negotiations: Hindutva sentiments and temporal interests in Gujarat Elections," *Economic and Political Weekly* (2002): pp. 4838–4843.

62. Thapar, Romila, *Somanatha: The Many Voices of a History*. London: Verso Books: 2015.

63. See *inter alia, Amir* Hamza and Abu Umair Shaheed, "The situation and biographies of martyrs of Battle of Bandipura," *Mujallah ud Dawa*, trans Ali Hamza, Oct. 1994, pp. 4–9; Ukht-e-Abu Hashi, "Abu Hamza Sayyaf Sani Abdul Rehman," Mujallah Taibaat, trans Ali Hamza, Jan. 2004, p. 23; Muhammad Idrees Shahid, Phalia, "Abu Usman Muhammad Ilyas, Mandi Bahauddin," Mujallah ul Dawa, trans Ali Hamza, Jan. 2001, pp. 31–33.

64. Abou Zahab, "I Shall be Waiting."

65. Saeed, Hafiz Muhammad, *Tafseer Surah at-Taubah*, trans M. Saleem Ahsan, Lahore: Dar-ul-Andulus, 2006.

66. Saeed, *Tafseer Surah at-Taubah*, p. 120.

67. "Lanterns of Memory: The Martyrdom of Abu-Zubair rekindled the spirit of Jihad in the family associated with Tehreek-e-Mujahideen," *Mujallah Tayyabaat*, trans Ali Hamza, May/July 2000, p. 24.

68. "Lanterns of Memory: The Martyrdom of Abu-Zubair rekindled the spirit of Jihad in the family associated with Tehreek-e-Mujahideen," *Mujallah Tayyabaat*, trans Ali Hamza, May/July 2000, p. 24.

69. "Abu Quhafa Shaheed Syed Abdul Rasheed bin Tufail ul Rehman Shah," *Mujallah Tayyabaat*, trans Ali Hamza, Jan. 2003, p. 16.

70. "Abu Quhafa Shaheed Syed Abdul Rasheed bin Tufail ul Rehman Shah," pp. 16–17.

71. Ibid.

72. Ibid., p. 16.

73. Um-e-Musaffra, "Abu Huzaifa Abdul Waheed: The blood struggle of a Martyr is never wasted," *Mujallah Tayyabaat*, April 2004, p. 42. Trans Ali Hamza.

74. Um-e-Musaffra, "Abu Huzaifa Abdul Waheed," p. 32.

75. When al Khansa's brother, Mu'awiyah, was murdered by members of another tribe, she insisted that another brother, Sakhr, avenge his death. Sakhr was wounded while doing so and succumbed to his injuries a year later. She mourned his death by writing poetry for which she became famous. In 629 CE, she met the prophet and converted to Islam. She had four sons, all of whom also converted to Islam as well and subsequently perished in the famed 636 CE Battle of Qadisiyah in which the Muslims conquered Persia. Reportedly, when al Khansa learned the news of her sons' demise, she did not grieve; rather, she exclaimed: "I consider it an honour that they died for the sake of Islam. I ask only that God allow me to meet them in Paradise." She is revered for being the finest poet of classical Arabic and even the prophet Muhammad is known to have requested her to recite her poems frequently, most of which were elegies on her two brothers and slain sons. She is also venerated among *jihadi* circles for her willingness to dispatch her loved ones into battle. For example, Islamic State named a brutal, all-female police squad after her (al-Khansa Brigade) which ensure that female members are fully covered in public, do not wear inappropriate attire (such as high heels), and are accompanied by a male in public. See Eleftheriou-Smith, Loulla-Mae, "Escaped ISIS wives describe life in the all-female al-Khansa Brigade who punish women with 40 lashes for wearing wrong clothes," *Independent*, 20 April 2015, accessed 11 June 2018. http://

www.independent.co.uk/news/world/middle-east/escaped-isis-wives-describe-life-in-the-all-female-al-khansa-brigade-who-punish-women-with-40-lashes-10190317.html. Al Qaeda also produced an internet-based women's magazine under the title of al-Khansa which aims to help them become better fighters. There are numerous accounts of her on the internet and other *jihadi* publications. See Gentry, Caron E. and Laura Sjoberg, *Mothers, Monsters, Whores: Women's Violence in Global Politics*, New York: Zed Books, 2007. See also: Evans, Suzanne, *Mothers of Heroes, Mothers of Martyrs: World War I and the Politics of Grief*, Montreal: McGill-Queen's University Press, 2007, p. 34; and Al-Udhari, Abdullah, *Classical Poems by Arab Women* (Bilingual Edition), London: Saqi Books, 1999.

76. "Abu Ali Ameer Muaviya (martyred)—The rose whose joviality perfumed the paradise of Kashmir," *Zarb-e-Tayyaba*, trans Ali Hamza, Aug. 2004, p. 30.

77. Akram, Mohammad Bilal, "Abu Bilal Mohammad Ashraf Shaheed: A tale of that Mentor, who left behind an example for his students," *Zarb-e-Tayyaba*, trans Ali Hamza, Sept. 2004, p. 34.

78. Rasheed, Aqsa Dukhter Abdul, "Abu Ayub Ansari," *Mujallah Tayyabaat*, trans Ali Hamza, July 2003, p. 23.

79. Abdullah, Hayat, "Abu Abdullah Muhammad Munsha: To pray for Jihad, and to face the opposition of our beloved ones," Mujallah ul *Dawah*, date and year unknown. Trans Ali Hamza.

80. Abdullah, "Abu Abdullah Muhammad Munsha."

81. Haq, "Militarism and Motherhood."

82. It should be noted that Wahhabi and Ahl-e-Hadees followers veil in a similar fashion. See Haq, "Militarism and Motherhood."

83. Haq, "Militarism and Motherhood."

84. Ibid.

85. Hammad, Umm-e, *Hum Ma'en Lashkar-e-Tayyaba Ki* (We, the Mothers of Lashkar-e-Tayyaba) 1, Lahore: Dar-ul-Andalus, 1998, p. 13.

86. Hammad, *Hum Ma'en Lashkar-e-Tayyaba Ki*, p. 15.

87. Ibid.

88. Hammad, *Hum Ma'en Lashkar-e-Tayyaba Ki*, p. 16.

89. Hammad, *Hum Ma'en Lashkar-e-Tayyaba Ki*, p. 17.

90. Ibid.

91. Asghar, Sufyan, "Abu Huzaifa Muhammad Luqman," *Zarb-e-Tayyaba*, trans Ali Hamza, Nov. 2004, p. 28.

92. Um e Abdulrubab, "Abu Saarya Muhammed Tahir," *Mujallah Tayyabaat*, trans Ali Hamza, March 2004, p. 33.

93. Farooq, Amjad. "Abu Ans Shehzad Ghulam Mohammad," *Mujallah ul Dawah*, trans Ali Hamza, Dec. 2003, p. 31.

94. Nazeer, Salman and Renala Khurd. "Abu Zeeshan: Shaheed Abu Zeeshan. Painful memories and heartwarming tales," *Zarb-e-Tayyaba*, June 2005, p. 41. Trans Ali Hamza.

95. Hamza, Amir. "Abu Umair Shaheed," *Mujallah ul Dawah*, trans Ali Hamza, Oct. 1994, p. 7.

96. Um-e-Hamaad's Second Son: Jawad Ahmad Shaheed, "Impressions of Amir Honorable Hafiz Mohammed Saeed Hafza-ullah," *Mujallah Tayyabaat*, trans Ali Hamza, May/July 2000, p. 20.

97. Um-e-Shams-ul-Arifeen, "Shams-ul-Arifeen," *Mujallah Tayyabaat*, Sept. 2004, pp. 38–40. Trans Ali Hamza.

98. Amir Hamza, "Abu Umair Shaheed," *Mujallah ul Dawah*, trans Ali Hamza, Oct. 1994, p. 9.

99. Amir Hamza, "The Invasion of Lashkar-e-Taiba in Occupied Kashmir: Abu Abdul Wahab Sani and Abu Hafz Shaheed," *Mujallah ul Dawah*, trans Ali Hamza, Feb. 1994, p. 9.

100. Ibid.

101. Ibid.

102. Ijaz, Ghazi Faheem, "In memory of Shaheed Abu Sufian," *Mujallah ul Dawah*, trans Ali Hamza, Aug. 1994, p. 31.

103. Um e Abdulrubab, "Abu Saarya Muhammed Tahir," *Mujallah Tayyabaat*, trans Ali Hamza, March 2004, p. 33.

104. Um-e-Shams-ul-Arifeen, "Shams-ul-Arifeen," *Mujallah Tayyabaat*, trans Ali Hamza, Sept. 2004, p. 39.

105. Ukht-e-Shuhdaa, "Abul Qasim Shaheen Shaheed," *Mujallah Tayyabaat*, trans Ali Hamza, May 2004, p. 32.

106. Ibid.

107. Ukth-e-Abdul Wasaih and Ukht-e-Saad-ul-Rehman, "Another rose blossomed in the Garden of Martyrdom: Abu Ukasha Abdul Rashid Shaheed," *Mujallah Tayyabaat*, trans Ali Hamza, June 2004, p. 44.

108. Qazi Kashif Niaz, "The Whipping of Indian Army by the Wrath of Allah in the form of battle with Lashkar-e-Tayyaba (LeT): Abu Abdul Rehman, Dr. Abu Turab, Abu Talha, Abu Baseer and Abu Ali," *Mujallah ul Dawah*, trans Ali Hamza, July 1994, p. 9.

109. Qazi Kashif Niaz, "The Whipping of Indian Army by the Wrath of Allah in the form of battle with Lashkar-e-Tayyaba (LeT): Abu Abdul Rehman, Dr. Abu Turab, Abu Talha, Abu Baseer and Abu Ali," *Mujallah ul Dawah*, trans Ali Hamza, July 1994, p. 9.

110. Ibid., p. 11.

111. See for example "Last will and testament of Abu Ukasha Abdul Rasheed' in which the fighter provides several posthumous instructions "Mother, please have courage when you receive this news and rejoice that Allah has granted you this position of being the mother of a martyr. Offer two prayers as thanks. The brother who is delivering this news, listen to his advice carefully and follow it as well. It is my instructions that sisters should cover themselves as per shariah, and also to offer prayers diligently. *Shariat* should be followed in our household. And the brothers should also accept the path of Jihad. It is my advice to my relatives that they should teach their children Quran. Actually they should make them memorize it and make them an expert in it so that they can have a better life here and in the hereafter." In Ukth-e-Abdul Wasaih

and Ukht-e-Saad-ul-Rehman, "Another rose blossomed in the Garden of Martyrdom: Abu Ukasha Abdul Rashid Shaheed," *Mujallah Tayyabaat*, trans Ali Hamza, June 2004, p. 36.

112. Abou Zahab and Roy, Islamist Networks.

113. "Abu Ali Ameer Muaviya (martyred)—The rose whose joviality perfumed the paradise of Kashmir," *Zarb-e-Tayyaba*, trans Ali Hamza, Aug. 2004, p. 30.

114. Abou Zahab and Roy, *Islamist Networks;* and Khan, "Allah's Army."

115. See inter alia, Um-e-Musaffra, "Abu Huzaifa Abdul Waheed: The blood struggle of a Martyr is never wasted," *Mujallah Tayyabaat*, trans Ali Hamza, April 2004, p. 42; the biography of Abu Turab Dr Mohammad Javed Shaheed in Qazi Kashif Niaz, "The Whipping of Indian Army by the Wrath of Allah in the form of battle with Lashker-e-Taiba (LeT)," p. 7; "Abu Hanzul Amjad Shaheed: Those who require truth, do ablution with their blood," *Zarb-e-Tayyaba*, trans Ali Hamza, April 2004, pp. 33–35; "Abu Zarraar Muhammad Aqeel," *Mujallah al Dawah*, trans Ali Hamza, Jan. 2001, pp. 39–40.

116. Amir Hamza, "Abu Abdullah, Abu Alqama, Abu Jandal and Abu Muawwiyah Shaheed," *Mujallah ul Dawah*, trans Ali Hamza, Jan. 1994, p. 5.

117. See Abou Zahab and Roy, *Islamist Networks*; and Haq, "Militarism and Motherhood."

118. Abou Zahab and Roy, *Islamist Networks*.

119. Ibid.

120. "Biography of Abu Fida'a Masood Salafi," Mujallah Dawa, trans Umber Latafat, Jan. 1995, p. 41.

121. Rana, Muhammad *Amir, The A to Z of Jehadi Organizations in Pakistan*, trans Saba Ansari, Lahore: Mashal, 2004, p. 41.

122. Fair, "Who Are Pakistan's Militants."

123. Um e Abdulrubab, "Abu Saarya Muhammed Tahir," *Mujallah Tayyabaat*, trans Ali Hamza, March 2004, p. 33.

124. Fair, "Who Are Pakistan's Militants."

125. Abou Zahab and Roy, *Islamist Networks*.

126. Levitt, S. D., and Venkatesh, S., "The Financial Activities of an Urban Street Gang," *Quarterly Journal of Economics*, 115, 3 (2000), pp. 755–789.

127. Levitt and Venkatesh, "The Financial Activities."

128. Haq, "Militarism and Motherhood."

129. Quoted in Ibid., p. 1023.

130. Fair, C. Christine and Bryan Shepherd, "Research Note: Who Supports Terrorism? Insights from Fourteen Muslim Countries," *Studies in Conflict and Terrorism*, 29, 2 (Jan./Feb. 2006), pp. 51–74.

131. Fair, C. Christine and Jacob N. Shapiro, "Understanding Support for Islamist Militancy in Pakistan," *International Security*, 34, 3 (2010), pp. 79–118.

132. Fair, C. Christine, Jacob S. Goldstein, Ali Hamza, "Can Knowledge of Islam Explain Lack of Support for Terrorism?," *Studies in Conflict and Terrorism*, 40, 4 (2017), pp. 339–355.

133. Fair, C. Christine, Rebecca Littman, Elizabeth R. Nugent, "Conceptions of Shari'a

and Support for Militancy and Democratic Values: Evidence From Pakistan," *Political Science Research and Methods*, 25 Jan. 2017, accessed 11 June 2018. https://doi.org/10.1017/psrm.2016.55. The following use gender as one of several demographic controls, but do not report the results: Fair, C. Christine, Neil Malhotra, Jacob N. Shapiro, "Faith or Doctrine? Religion and Support for Political Violence in Pakistan," *Public Opinion Quarterly*, 1 Jan. 2012, 76, 4, pp. 688–720 and "Democratic Values and Support for Militant Politics," *Journal of Conflict Resolution*, 58, 5 (2014), pp. 743–770; and Blair, Graeme, C. Christine Fair, Neil Malhotra, Jacob N. Shapiro, "Poverty and Support for Militant Politics: Evidence from Pakistan," *American Journal of Political Science*, 57, 1 (2013), pp. 30–48.

6. THE DOMESTIC POLITICS OF LET

1. See Kapur, Paul S., *Jihad as Grand Strategy: Islamist Militancy, National Security, and the Pakistani State*, New York: Oxford University Press, 2016; and Fair, *Fighting to the End*.

2. See Tankel, *Storming the World Stage* and Fair, C. Christine, "Militant Recruitment in Pakistan: Implications for Al-Qa'ida and Other Organizations," *Studies in Conflict and Terrorism*, 27, 6 (Nov./Dec. 2004), pp. 489–504 and *Fighting to the End*; and Kapur, *Jihad as Grand Strategy*.

3. Fair, C. Christine, "Lashkar-e-Tayiba and the Pakistani State," *Survival*, 53 (Aug. 2011), pp. 1–23.

4. Saifi, Sophia and Juliet Perry, "Pakistan detains alleged Mumbai attack mastermind, Hafiz Saeed," *CNN*, 31 Jan. 2017, accessed 11 June 2018. http://www.cnn.com/2017/01/31/asia/hafiz-saeed-house-arrest-pakistan/.

5. "Hindus protest Hafiz Saeed's house arrest," *Express Tribune*, 2 Feb. 2017, accessed 11 June 2018. https://tribune.com.pk/story/1314323/raising-voice-hindus-protest-hafiz-saeeds-house-arrest/.

6. In 1974 Zulfiqar Ali Bhutto declared the Ahmadis non-Muslim as a sop to Islamist opposition groups.

7. See Metcalf, Barbara, *Islamic Contestations: Essays on Muslims in India and Pakistan*, New Delhi: Oxford University Press, 2004.

8. Waraich, Omar, "Terrorism-Linked Charity Finds New Life Amid Pakistan Refugee Crisis," *Time*, 13 May 2009, accessed 11 June 2018. http://content.time.com/time/world/article/0,8599,1898127,00.html.

9. Khan, Ismail, "The Assertion of Barelvi Extremism," *Current Trends in Islamist Ideology*, 12 (2011), pp. 51–72.

10. Raghavan, TCA, "This political turmoil in Pakistan marks the coming out of the Barelvis," *The Hindustan Times*, 5 Dec. 2017, accessed 11 June 2018. http://www.hindustantimes.com/analysis/this-political-turmoil-in-pakistan-marks-the-coming-out-of-the-barelvis/story-jZJ768gm4YES2TiQf3L7RL.html.

11. Rehman, Zia Ur, "The battle for Kurram." *The Friday Times*, 24, 3 (2012), accessed 11 June 2018. http://www.thefridaytimes.com/beta2/tft/article.php?issue=20120302&page=3.

12. "Hafiz Saeed asks govt to curb foreign bid to bolster IS in Pakistan," *Indian Express*, 17 Oct. 2015, accessed 11 June 2018. http://indianexpress.com/article/world/world-news/hafiz-saeed-asks-govt-to-curb-foreign-bid-to-bolster-is-in-pakistan/.

13. Rabbani, Abul Hassan Mubbashir Ahmed, *Masalah-yi takfir aur is ke usul o zavabit* (The Problem of Takfir and its Principles and Regulations), trans Safina Ustaad, Lahore: Dar-ul-Andulus, 2015.

14. "Hafiz Mohammad Saeed," Pakistan Times, nd, https://www.pakistantimes.com/topics/hafiz-mohammad-saeed/; Fair, C. Christine. "Jamaat-ud-Dawa: Converting Kuffar at Home, Killing Them Abroad," *Current Trends in Islamist Ideology*, vol. 21, forthcoming Oct. 2017.

15. "Jamaat-ud-Dawa will not allow destruction of Hindu temples in Pakistan: Hafiz Saeed," Times of India, May 3, 2016, accessed 11 June 2018. http://timesofindia.indiatimes.com/world/pakistan/Jamaat-ud-Dawa-will-not-allow-destruction-of-Hindu-temples-in-Pakistan-Hafiz-Saeed/articleshow/52089381.cms.

16. Bin Muhammad, Abdussalam, "*Hum Kyon Jihad Kar Rahen Hain?* [Why Are We Waging Jihad?]," trans C. Christine Fair and Safina Ustaad, Lahore: Dar-ul-Andulus, 2004.

17. Takfir is the "Pronouncement that someone is an unbeliever (*kafir*) and no longer Muslim. Takfir is used in the modern era for sanctioning violence against leaders of Islamic states who are deemed insufficiently religious" (Esposito, Joh (ed.), 2017. "Takfir." in Oxford Islamic Studies Online, accessed 11 June 2018. Available at http://www.oxfordislamicstudies.com/article/opr/t125/e2319).

18. "*Wajib ul qatal*" literally means worthy of being killed. However, this translation does not do the phrase justice because it also implies that those who kill persons so deemed will actually receive a boon for doing so.

19. From the earliest years of Pakistan's existence, Islamists lobbied to have Ahmadis declared "non-Muslim" because they do not recognize the ordinal finality of the prophet and recognize a living prophet. Nearly twenty years after these agitations began, Zulfiqar Ali Bhutto—an ostensible liberal—declared them to be non-Muslim in 1974 by constitutionally redefining their status. Prior to this move, Pakistanis considered Ahmadis to be as a sect of Islam. With Bhutto's move, the Ahmadis became a non-Muslim minority overnight despite their prominent role in the movement to secure an independent Pakistan. This constitutional provision also expanded the legal and extra-legal justifications for killing Ahmadis with wanton impunity (Sadia Saeed, 2007, "Pakistani Nationalism and The State Marginalisation of the Ahmadiyya Community In Pakistan," *Studies in Ethnicity and Nationalism*, Vol. 7, No. 3: pp. 132–152).

20. In fact, it has been my experience in dealing with Pakistan various journalist that they are often unable accurately to describe violence perpetrated against Ahmadis because they lack acceptable vocabulary to describe, for example, a massacre at a place of worship without using the word "*masjid*." (The word that is often used by Ahmadis *in lieu* of "*masjid*" is "*ibadat gah*" (literally "place of worship"), although it is not widely known amongst journalists.

21. He explained via email that "There is a consensus on Ahmedis being a Non-Muslim

minority. Constitution of Pakistan is clear on their status. They, like any other minority should have right to practice their faith without posing as Muslims or representatives of Islam, which would stand in violation of Pakistan's constitution." Email correspondence, 26 Nov. 2017.

22. Muhammadi, Ubaidurrahman, *Difa-i-Jihad (Defense of Jihad)*, trans Safina Ustaad, Lahore: Dar-ul-Andulus, 2003.

23. Wagemakers, Joas, "'Seceders" and "Postponers"? An Analysis of the "Khawarij" and "Murji'a" Labels in Polemical Debates between Quietist and Jihadi-Salafis," *Contextualising Jihadi Thought*, Jeevan Deol and Zaheer Kazmi (eds), London: Hurst, 2012, pp-145–164.

24. Wagemakers, "'Seceders" and Posponers"?," p. 152.

25. Wagemakers, "'Seceders" and Posponers"?'

26. Ibid.

27. Rabbani, *Masalah-yi takfir aur is ke usul o zavabit*, pp. 11–12.

28. Ibid., p. 15.

29. Rabbani, *Masalah-yi takfir aur is ke usul o zavabit*, p. 24. Rabbani does not indicate who compiled the volume nor does he offer any information about where one may find it. Unfortunately, there are many similarly named volumes on the internet. My efforts to reach out to the JuD did not bear fruit.

30. It appears that to some degree, Rabani's concerns were misplaced. As evidence that JuD is tied to this volume, he cites a 2013 congressional testimony by Steven Tankel in which he argues that evidence presented by me and a poorly cited, undated essay by Rabbani titled "The Schism of Excommunication" exemplifies the organization's utility to the state. Tankel then claims that "Al-Qaeda refuted points from 'The Schism of Excommunication,' in a book entitled, Knowledgeable Judgment on the Mujrites of the (Present) Age." He does not cite either of these works in full. What does seem clear is that Rabbani appears to misunderstand why Tankel included him in his testimony, which he mistakes for an essay. Rabbani caviled of this: "In an essay by Stephen Tankel titled 'Protecting the Homeland Against Mumbai Style Attacks and the Threat from Lashkar-e-Taiba,' published in the magazine Carnegie, the very first page links our organization to Marja-tul-'Asr." It is impossible to discern if Rabbani is correct because Tankel seems not to possess a copy of Rabbani's Urdu-language essay or the volume in question as evidenced by the lack of a full citation or his inability to provide it when requested. It is most certainly Urdu source material and it is not clear who translated these materials for Tankel or what the Urdu titles are. After extensive discussions with scholars familiar with these publications, I was unable to locate the volume in question, *Knowledgeable Judgment on the Mujrites of the (Present) Age*. I did however find an un-dated Urdu book that takes on Rabbani's speech titled *Murjia Tul Asar ki Talbisat ka ilmi Muhakima*, written by Mohammad Khabeeb Sadeeqi and Hafez Amar Naruqi published by a clearly pro-al Qaeda organization known as the Al Muhadeen Islaami Library (The library of those who embrace the notion of Tawheed).

31. Bin Muhammad, *"Hum Ky'on Jihad Kar Rahen Hain?"*

32. al-Rahman, Rahmat Allah ibn Khalil and Muhammad Ahmad Abdulqadar Malakavi, *Isaiyat? (What is Christianity?)*, Lahore: Dar al Andalus, 2007.

33. Hamza, Maulana Amir, *Shahrah-e-Bahisht* (*Highway to Paradise*), trans Safina Ustaad, Lahore: Dar-ul-Andulus, 2004.

34. Bin Muhammad, "*Hum Kyon Jihad Kar Rahen Hain?*," p. 3.

35. Muhammadi, *Difa-i-Jihad*, pp. 13–14.

36. Ibid., p. 23.

37. Ibid., p. 24.

38. Ibid., p. 26.

39. Dorronsoro, Gilles, *Revolution Unending: Afghanistan, 1979 to the Present*, London: Hurst, 2005.

40. Muhammadi, *Difa-i-Jihad*, p. 41.

41. Ibid.

42. Ibid.

43. Gahlot, Mandakini, "India's Hindu Fundamentalists: People & Power investigates India's Hindu fundamentalists and their influence on the country's government," *Al Jazeera*, 8 Oct. 2015, accessed 11 June 2018. http://www.aljazeera.com/programmes/peopleandpower/2015/10/indias-hindu-fundamentalists-151008073418225.html.

44. This practice continues with alarming frequency in contemporary Pakistan, as detailed by Imtiaz, Saba, "Hindu Today, Muslim Tomorrow," *The Atlantic*, 14 Aug. 2017, accessed 11 June 2018. https://www.theatlantic.com/international/archive/2017/08/hindu-muslim-pakistan/536238/. Forced conversion of Muslims and Christians to Hinduism does happen in India as well. "Indian Agra Muslims fear conversions to Hinduism," *BBC News*, 11 Dec. 2014, accessed 11 June 2018. http://www.bbc.com/news/world-asia-india-30429118.

45. Raghavan, Srinath, "Civil–Military Relations in India: The China Crisis and After," *The Journal of Strategic Studies*, 32 (2009), pp. 149–175.

46. Another plebiscite formula was floated in Nov. 1947 according to which a plebiscite would be held "as soon as possible under the aegis of two persons nominated by the Governments of India and Pakistan, with a person nominated by the Kashmir Government as observer." The plebiscite itself would be conducted by British officers. However, both Indian and Pakistani officials rejected this proposal for various reasons. In addition, both the Maharaja of Kashmir and Sheikh Abdullah opposed the plebiscite for their own personal and political reasons. Nehru remained adamant that a plebiscite would take place once law and order had been restored. While India and Pakistan continued diplomatic discussions about Kashmir, the military battle continued. Nehru resolved that he would follow two parallel courses of action: appealing to the newly-formed United Nations and "complete military preparations to meet any possible contingency." See Whitehead, Andrew, *A Mission in Kashmir*, London: Penguin Global, 2007 and Raghavan, 'Civil-Military Relations in India.'

47. Raghavan, 'Civil-Military Relations in India.'

48. United Nations Security Council, "United Nations Security Council Resolution 47: The India-Pakistan Question," 1964, last accessed 11 June 2018. http://www.un.org/en/ga/search/view_doc.asp?symbol=S/RES/51(1948).

49. India claims that the eponymously named Simla Agreement, which was signed in 1972

by India's Prime Minister Indira Gandhi and Pakistan's President Zulfiqar Ali Bhutto in the northern Indian city of Shimla and formally concluded the 1971 war, obviated this process entirely. In that document, Prime Minister Gandhi and President Bhutto agreed that India and Pakistan would: settle their differences by peaceful means through bilateral negotiations or by any other peaceful means mutually agreed upon between them. Pending the final settlement of any of the problems between the two countries, neither side shall unilaterally alter the situation nor shall both prevent the organization, assistance or encouragement of any acts detrimental to the maintenance of peaceful and harmonious relations (Text of Simla Agreement 1972). India maintains that after Simla the two countries are bound to resolve issues bilaterally, without reference to third parties. Pakistan opposes this interpretation of the Simla Agreement.

50. Per the 1951 census of Pakistan, the total population of the country was seventy-five million, 13 per cent of whom were Hindus, most of whom lived in East Pakistan which numbered forty-two million. See D'Costa, Bina, *Nationbuilding, Gender and War Crimes in South Asia*, New York: Routledge, 2001.

51. As one of the reviewers noted, "Khulna was not 'a village' even in 1949; it was a district capital and more comparable perhaps to an average north Indian mofussil town."

52. Raghavan, 'Civil-Military Relations in India,' p. 185.

53. Sachar, Rajindar, "Sachar Committee Report," Government of India, 2006, accessed 11 June 2018. http://www.minorityaffairs.gov.in/sites/default/files/sachar_comm.pdf.

54. Baloch, Saher, "'Non-Muslims other than Christians have no marriage law of their own'," *Dawn*, 16 Dec. 2015, accessed 11 June 2018. https://www.dawn.com/news/1226582.

55. See US Commission for International Religious Freedom, *Annual Report 2016*, April 2016, accessed 11 June 2018. http://www.uscirf.gov/reports-briefs/annual-report/2016-annual-report; Human Rights Watch, *World Report 2017*, accessed 11 June 2018. https://www.hrw.org/world-report/2017/country-chapters/india; and Amnesty International, *Amnesty International Report 2016/2017*, 2017, accessed 11 June 2018. https://www.amnesty.org/en/latest/research/2017/02/amnesty-international-annual-report-201617/.

56. 'India "to cut Kashmir troops by a quarter,"' BBC, 14 Jan. 2011, accessed 11 June 2018. http://www.bbc.com/news/world-south-asia-12190425

57. Bin Muhammad, "*Hum Kyon Jihad Kar Rahen Hain?*," p. 15.

58. Ibid.

59. Ibid.

60. Muhammadi, *Difa-i-Jihad*, p. 57.

61. This paragraph draws primarily on the author's more than twelve years of fieldwork in Pakistan. Since Dec. 1999, the author has undertaken more than two dozen research trips to Pakistan, Afghanistan, India, and Bangladesh to study Lashkar-e-Taiba and other militant organizations based in and operating out of Pakistan.

62. Fair, C. Christine, "Militant Recruitment in Pakistan: Implications for Al-Qa'ida and Other Organizations," *Studies in Conflict and Terrorism*, 27, 6 (Nov./Dec. 2004), pp. 489–504.

63. It is worth dilating upon the fact that technically speaking neither of these assertions is correct. Pakistan was not founded upon this principle however the Objectives Resolution did declare that Allah is sovereign over the entire university and that Allah has delegated authority to the state of Pakistan, through its people. Bin Muhammad's characterization of the so-called *veer* is also flawed. Prior to 1947, various national flags were proposed with the image of the *charkha* or spinning wheel at the center to signify the means through which Indians could liberate themselves through economic exploitation. After 1947, the Indian parliament took up the issue for the first time in July 1947. The new insignia, the Asoka Chakra, replaced the Gandhian *charkha* because the new symbol reflected an "international period in Indian history." See Bin Muhammad, "Hum Kyon Jihad Kar Rahen Hain?' p. 43; and Roy, Srirupa, "'A symbol of freedom': The Indian flag and the transformations of nationalism, 1906–2002," *The Journal of Asian Studies*, 65, 3 (2006): 495–527.

64. Fair, *Fighting to the End.*

65. Bin Muhammad, *"Hum Kyon Jihad Kar Rahen Hain?,"* pp. 34–35.

66. Ibid., p. 35.

67. Ibid.

68. Fair, *Fighting to the End.*

69. *Kufr* means disbelief in the truth. *Shirk* describes the action of ascribing to humans the attributes of Allah or worshipping them in the way of Allah.

70. Bin Muhammad, *"Hum Kyon Jihad Kar Rahen Hain?,"* p. 42.

71. Rabbani, Abul Hassan Mubbashir Ahmed, *Kalima-go mashrik [The Muslim Polytheist],* trans C. Christine Fair and Abbas Haider, Lahore: Dar-ul-Andulus, 2009.

72. Rabbani, *Kalima-go mashrik,* pp. 15–16.

73. Lashkar-e-Jhangvi, "Shia Wajib Ul Qatal Kiyon (Why Are Shia Deserving of Being Killed)?" Dec. 2008, accessed 11 June 2018. http://www.mediafire.com/download/oiv665tqtvsfve2/Shia+Wajib+Ul+Qatal+Kiyon.pdf.

74. The differences between a *mashrik* and *kafir* are subtle and sometimes the words are used interchangeably. A *mashrik* is one who commits *shirk* by assigning the attributes of Allah to another or by worshiping anything or anyone else but Allah. A *kafir* is one who spreads disbelief in the truth such as one who denies the obligation to pray or pay *zakat*. For this reason, the author uses the expression *"kalima-go"* to distinguish those who claim to be Muslims from those who do not.

75. Muhammadi, *Difa-i-Jihad,* p. 51.

76. Ibid., p. 52.

77. Fair, *Fighting to the End.*

78. Muhammadi, *Difa-i-Jihad,* p. 52.

79. Ibid., p. 53.

80. Ibid.

81. Ibid., p. 54.

82. Ibid., pp. 54–55.

83. Ibid., p. 55.

84. Ibid.

85. Rabbani, *Masalah-yi takfir aur is ke usul o zavabit* (The Problem of Takfir and its Principles and Regulations), trans Safina Ustaad, Lahore: Dar-ul-Andulus, 2015, pp. 24–25.

86. Rabbani, Masalah-yi takfir, pp. 13–14.

87. Ibid., p. 14.

88. Ibid., p. 22.

89. Ibid., p. 14.

90. Ibid., p. 15.

91. Ibid., p. 27.

92. Ibid.

93. Ibid., pp. 27–28.

94. Ibid., p. 36.

95. Ibid., p. 30.

96. Ibid.

97. Ibid.

98. Ibid., p. 30.

99. Ibid., p. 31.

100. Ibid.

101. Ibid., p. 34.

102. Ibid., p. 13.

103. Ibid., p. 18.

104. Ibid., p. 18.

105. See Reeves, Phillip, "In Pakistan, Ultra-Conservative Rivals Attack Moderate Muslims," *NPR Morning Edition*, 28 April 2014, accessed 11 June 2018. http://www.npr.org/2014/04/28/307627337/in-pakistan-ultra-conservative-muslim-movement-grows-stronger; and Khan, Farz, "Failed assassination bid: Key cleric ambushed in Karachi," *The Express Tribune*, 26 Dec. 2012, accessed 11 June 2018. https://tribune.com.pk/story/484521/failed-assassination-bid-key-cleric-ambushed-in-karachi.

106. Bin Muhammad, "*Hum Kyon Jihad Kar Rahen Hain?*," p. 24.

107. Muhammadi, *Difa-i-Jihad*, p. 51.

108. Fair, C. Christine, "Jamaat-ud-Dawa: Converting Kuffar at Home, Killing Them Abroad," *Current Trends in Islamist Ideology*, vol. 22, (November 2017): pp. 58–79.

109. As of July 6 2017 the population of Sindh is estimated to be 50.7 million, according to "Population Clock," Government of Sindh's Bureau of Statistics Planning and Development Department, accessed 11 June 2018. http://sindhbos.gov.pk/development-statistics/.

110. Tahir, Minerwa, "Why is Sindh's Population Data Being Manipulated in the Census?," *The Express Tribune*, 22 March 2017, accessed 11 June 2018. http://blogs.tribune.com.pk/story/47937/why-is-sindhs-population-data-being-manipulated-in-the-census/.

111. "Hindu Population (PK)," The Pakistan Hindu Council, accessed 11 June 2018. http://pakistanhinducouncil.org.pk/?page_id=1592. It is also impossible to verify this estimate because Pakistan has not conducted a census since 1998.

112. Ahmad, Imtiaz, "Child deaths help JuD make inroads into Hindu-majority Pakistan region," *Hindustan Times*, 14 March 2016, accessed 11 June 2018. http://www.hindustantimes.com/world/child-deaths-help-jud-make-inroads-into-hindu-majority-pakistan-region/story-2EIUw2IWWj7EroBKq5HQoJ.html

113. "JuD "teaching" Islam to Hindu flood victims," *Times of India*, 27 Oct. 2011, accessed 11 June 2018. http://timesofindia.indiatimes.com/world/pakistan/JuD-teaching-Islam-to-Hindu-flood-victims/articleshow/10503822.cms.

114. "Charity with a cause from Pakistan," *Asian Tribune*, 20 May 2016, accessed 11 June 2018. http://www.asiantribune.com/node/88981.

115. International Crisis Group, "Pakistan: No End To Humanitarian Crises," Asia Report No. 237, 9 Oct. 2012, accessed 11 June 2018. https://d2071andvip0wj.cloudfront.net/237-pakistan-no-end-to-humanitarian-crisis.pdf.

116. "Bring Back Our Girls: Pakistan's Hindus Struggle Against Forced Conversions," The Wire, 14 Jan. 2017, accessed 11 June 2018. https://thewire.in/rights/pakistan-minorities-girls.

117. Inayat, Naila, "Pakistani Hindus lose daughters to forced Muslim marriages," USA TODAY, 15 Feb. 2017, accessed 11 June 2018. https://www.usatoday.com/story/news/world/2017/02/15/pakistani-hindus-lose-daughters-forced-muslim-marriages/97013614/.

118. Total population is from "Pakistan," Central Intelligence Agency World Fact Book, 15 June 2017, accessed 20 June 2017. https://www.cia.gov/library/publications/the-world-factbook/geos/print_pk.html. Data on Christians is from "Christianity in Pakistan," *Christians in Pakistan*, accessed 11 June 2018. https://www.christiansin-pakistan.com/christianity-in-pakistan/.

119. Abbas, Qaswar, "Hafiz Saeed accuses India of backing twin suicide attacks at Peshawar church," *India Today*, 23 Sept. 2013, accessed 11 June 2018. http://indiatoday.intoday.in/story/hafiz-saeed-india-pakistan-peshawar-church-bombings-terrorist-nation/1/311165.html.

120. Bin Muhammad, Abdussalam, *Hindu Customs Among Muslims*, trans M. Saleem Ahsan, Lahore: Dar-ul-Andulus, 2007, p. 10.

121. Bin Muhammad, *Hindu Customs*, p. 17.

122. This is usually spelled "Sandhya" or "Sandhyavandanam." The author's description is not terribly accurate. These are prayers that are offered in the morning, noon and evening, traditionally offered by Brahmin males. The breathing description likely refers to the practice of *pranayama* (exercises in regulated breathing). For a more accurate description of this, see Narayan, M.K.V., *Exploring the Hindu Mind: Cultural Reflection and Symbolism*, New Delhi: Read Worthy Publications, 2011.

123. Bin Muhammad, *Hindu Customs*, p. 43.

124. Ibid., p. 45.

125. Ibid., p. 48.

126. Ibid., p. 59.

127. Ibid., p. 59.

128. Ibid., p. 59.

129. Ibid., p. 59.
130. Ibid., p. 60.
131. Fair, "Jamaat-ud-Dawa."
132. Hamza, Maulana Amir, *Shahrah-e-Bahisht* (*Highway to Paradise*), trans Safina Ustaad, Lahore: Dar-ul-Andulus, 2004.
133. Hamza, *Shahrah-e-Bahisht*, p. 86.
134. Ibid., p. 121.
135. See Abou Zahab, Mariam, "Salafism in Pakistan: The Ahl-e Hadith Movement," in *Global Salafism: Islam's New Religious Movement*, pp. 126–139; and Fair, C. Christine, "Lashkar-e-Tayiba and the Pakistani State," *Survival*, 53 (Aug. 2011), pp. 1–23.
136. Waraich, Omar, "Terrorism-Linked Charity Finds New Life Amid Pakistan Refugee Crisis," *Time*, 13 May 2009, accessed 11 June 2018. http://content.time.com/time/world/article/0,8599,1898127,00.html.
137. See Khan, Kamran and John Lancaster, "Extremists Fill Aid Chasm After Quake," *The Washington Post*, 16 Oct. 2005, accessed 11 June 2018. http://www.washingtonpost.com/wp-dyn/content/article/2005/10/15/AR2005101501392.html; and Mir, Amir, 'Militant' Philanthropy," *Newsline*, 15 Nov. 2005, accessed 11 June 2018. http://www.newslinemagazine.com/2005/11/militant-philanthropy/.
138. See Andrabi, Tahir and Jishnu Das, "In Aid We Trust: Hearts and Minds and the Pakistan Earthquake of 2005," Policy research working paper no. 5440, *The World Bank*, 2010, accessed 11 June 2018. https://openknowledge.worldbank.org/handle/10986/3922; and Fair, C. Christine, "Not at the Forefront of Flood Relief," *Foreign Policy*, 20 Sept. 2010, accessed 11 June 2018. http://foreignpolicy.com/2010/09/20/not-at-the-forefront-of-flood-relief/.
139. See Ellick, Adam B. and Pur Zubair Shah, "Hard-Line Islam Fills Void in Flooded Pakistan," *The New York Times*, 6 Aug. 2010, accessed 11 June 2018. http://www.nytimes.com/2010/08/07/world/asia/07pstan.html?pagewanted=all&_r=0; and Shah, Saeed, "U.N.-listed 'terror front' group leads flood relief in Pakistan," *McClatchy Newspapers*, 3 Aug. 2010, accessed 11 June 2018. http://www.mcclatchydc.com/news/nation-world/world/article24589408.html.
140. Fair, "Not at the Forefront of Flood Relief."
141. See Sethi, Ali, "Pakistan: Who's Afraid of the ISI?" *The New York Review of Books*, 30 April 2014, accessed 11 June 2018. http://www.nybooks.com/daily/2014/04/30/pakistan-whos-afraid-isi/; Haider, Ejaz, "An Open Letter to General Pasha," *The Express Tribune*, 7 June 2011, accessed 11 June 2018. https://tribune.com.pk/story/184106/an-open-letter-to-general-pasha/; and Yusuf, Huma, "Conspiracy Fever: the US, Pakistan and its Media," *Survival*, 53 (Aug. 2011), pp. 95–118.
142. Siddique, Abubakr, "Pakistani Quake Victims Suffer as Government Denies International Aid," *Radio Free Europe/Radio Liberty*, 16 Oct. 2013, accessed 11 June 2018. http://www.rferl.org/a/pakistan-earthquake-international-aid/25138901.html
143. 'Nov. 2013 Human Rights Report of Balochistan, 2013," Crisis Balochistan, 1 Dec. 2013. http://www.crisisbalochistan.com/secondary_menu/news/november2013humanrightsreportofbalochistan.html.

144. Jafri, Owais, "JuD Plans Development, Welfare Projects in Balochistan," *Express Tribune*, 18 April 2012, accessed 11 June 2018. https://tribune.com.pk/story/366515/jud-plans-development-welfare-projects-in-balochistan/.

145. Jafri, "JuD Plans Development.'

146. Fair, C. Christine and Ali Hamza, "Rethinking Baloch Secularism: What the Data Say," *Peace and Conflict Studies*: Vol. 24, 1 (2017), accessed 11 June 2018. http://nsuworks.nova.edu/pcs/vol24/iss1/1.

147. Blair, Graeme, C. Christine Fair, Neil Malhotra, Jacob N. Shapiro, "Poverty and Support for Militant Politics: Evidence from Pakistan," *American Journal of Political Science*, 57, 1 (2013), pp. 30–48.

148. This section draws upon Fair, C. Christine. "Lashkar-e-Taiba: Pakistan's Domesticated Terrorists," *Lawfare.org*, 29 Dec. 2013. http://www.lawfareblog.com/2013/12/the-foreign-policy-essay-c-christine-fair-on-lashkar-e-taibapakistans-domesticated-terrorists/#.UsGgv7SSkt4.

149. "Bringing back the Dead: Why Pakistan Used the Jaish-e-Mohammad to Attack an Indian Airbase," *The World Post*, 7 Jan. 2015, accessed 11 June 2018. http://www.huffingtonpost.com/c-christine-fair/bringing-back-the-dead-wh_b_8955224.html

150. Mir, Amir, *True Face of the Jehadis*, Lahore: Mashal, 2004.

151. Fair, "'Bringing Back the Dead.'"

152. Krishnan, Ananth, "China defends latest hold on Masood Azhar listing," *India Today*, 8 Feb. 2017, accessed 11 June 2018. http://indiatoday.intoday.in/story/china-masood-azhar-listing-india/1/877671.html.

153. See Roul, Animesh, "Jaish-e-Muhammad's Charity Wing Revitalizes Banned Group in Pakistan," *Terrorism Monitor*, 9, 41 (11 Nov. 2011); Hussain, Zahid, "The return of Masood Azhar," *Dawn*, 8 Oct. 2016, accessed 11 June 2018. http://www.dawn.com/news/1084328; Rodriguez, Alex, "Pakistani militant groups out in the open," *The Los Angeles Times*, 8 May 2010, accessed 11 June 2018. http://articles.latimes.com/2010/may/08/world/la-fg-0508-pakistan-militants-20100508; Roggio, Bill, "Pakistani government refused to move against radical madrassas in Punjab," *Long War Journal*, 22 May 2011, accessed 11 June 2018. http://www.longwarjournal.org/archives/2011/05/pakistani_government_2.php; Kumar, Raksha, "A Pakistani Militant Leader Stirs, Worrying the Indian Government," *India Ink*, 25 Feb. 2014, accessed 11 June 2018. https://india.blogs.nytimes.com/2014/02/25/a-pakistani-militant-leader-stirs-worrying-the-indian-government/?_r=0; Swami, Praveen, "With backing of ISI, Jaish-e-Muhammad rises like a phoenix in Pakistan," *Indian Express*, 11 Jan. 2016, accessed 11 June 2018. http://indianexpress.com/article/india/india-news-india/with-backing-of-isi-jaish-e-muhammad-rises-like-a-phoenix-in-pakistan/; and Mir, Amir, "More power to Pakistan's jihadis," *Asia Times*, 2 Sept. 2011, accessed 11 June 2018 http://www.atimes.com/atimes/South_Asia/MI02Df02.html.

154. See Nicolini, Assunta, "Migration and Militancy Along the Pakistani Border," *Center for Religion and Geopolitics*, 27 April 2015, accessed 11 June 2018. http://www.religionandgeopolitics.org/pakistan/migration-and-militancy-along-pakistani-border; Taqi, Mohammad, "Pakistani Patronage of Haqqani Network Continues Undeterred

as US Turns a Blind Eye," *The Wire*, 18 April 2016, accessed 11 June 2018. https://thewire.in/30099/pakistani-patronage-of-haqqni-network-continues-undeterred-as-us-turns-a-blind-eye/; and Khan, M. Ilyas, "Where have all Pakistan's militants gone?" *BBC.com*, 20 June 2014, accessed 11 June 2018.Nov. 2017. http://www.bbc.com/news/world-asia-28096454.

155. Gall, Carlotta, "Pakistan's Hand in the Rise of International Jihad," *The New York Times*, 7 Feb. 2016, accessed 11 June 2018. https://www.nytimes.com/2016/02/07/opinion/sunday/pakistans-hand-in-the-rise-of-international-jihad.html.

156. See "Banned Jaish-e-Muhammad outfit on recruitment spree in Pakistan," *Business Standard*, 7 Feb. 2017, accessed 11 June 2018. http://www.business-standard.com/video-gallery/world/banned-jaish-e-muhammad-outfit-on-recruitment-spree-in-pakistan-44964.htm; and Swami, Praveen, "Terror targeting India: A lid on Lashkar, Jaish takes jihadi centrestage in Pakistan," *Indian Express*, 7 Feb. 2017, accessed 11 June 2018. http://indianexpress.com/article/india/masood-azhar-terror-targeting-india-a-lid-on-lashkar-jaish-takes-jihadi-centrestage-in-pakistan-4511358/.

7. DEALING WITH LET AND ESCAPING PAKISTAN'S NUCLEAR COERCION

1. Shah, Aqil. "Pakistan's 'Armored Democracy'." *Journal of Democracy* 14.4 (2003), pp. 26–40. International Crisis Group, "Islamic Parties in Pakistan," International Crisis Group Report 216, 12 Dec. 2011, accessed 11 June 2018. https://www.crisisgroup.org/asia/south-asia/pakistan/islamic-parties-pakistan; International Crisis Group, "Elections, Democracy and Stability in Pakistan," International Crisis Group Report 137, 31 July 2007, accessed 11 June 2018. https://www.crisisgroup.org/asia/south-asia/pakistan/elections-democracy-and-stability-pakistan; International Crisis Group, "Pakistan: The Mullahs and the Military," International Crisis Group Report 49, 20 March 2003, accessed 11 June 2018. https://www.crisisgroup.org/asia/south-asia/pakistan/pakistan-mullahs-and-military.

2. Small, Andrew. *The China-Pakistan Axis: Asia's New Geopolitics*. London: Hurst, 2015.

3. Kronstadt, K. Alan. "Direct Overt US Aid Appropriations for and Military Reimbursements to Pakistan, FY2002-FY2018," Congressional Research Service, 28 Nov. 2017. For a scathing exposition of how the Coalition Support Funds are used and abused, see Government Accounting Office, "Combatting Terrorism: Increased Oversight and Accountability Needed over Pakistan Reimbursement Claims for Coalition Support Funds," 24 June 2008, accesed 9 Dec. 2017. http://www.gao.gov/products/GAO-08–806.

4. Fair, C. Christine. "How the US can push Pakistan to abandon its terror proxies," *Live Mint*, 7 Nov. 2016, accessed 11 June 2018. http://www.livemint.com/Opinion/WOhXqDpubUvtmXzdD2iYaP/How-the-US-can-push-Pakistan-to-abandon-its-terror-proxies.html; Perkovich, George and Toby Dalton. *Not War, Not Peace?: Motivating Pakistan to Prevent Cross-Border Terrorism*. New Delhi: Oxford University Press, 2017.

5. US Congress, ""Consolidated Appropriations Act, 2014." 3 July 2014, accessed 11 June 2018. https://www.gpo.gov/fdsys/pkg/BILLS-113hr3547enr/pdf/BILLS-113hr3547enr.pdf.

6. "Pentagon pressures US congress to delink LeT from Haqqani Network," *Pakistan Tribune*, 20 Nov. 2017, accessed 11 June 2018. https://tribune.com.pk/story/1563285/3-pentagon-pressures-us-congress-delink-let-haqqani-network/.

7. For a thorough accounting (through 2013) of the various ways in which the United States used waivers and dubious certifications of compliance to authorize aid to Pakistan that should have been held up had the various conditionalities been honored, see Epstein, Susan B. and K. Alan Kronstadt, "Pakistan: US Foreign Assistance," CRS Report, 1 July 1 2013, accessed 11 June 2018. https://fas.org/sgp/crs/row/R41856.pdf.

8. In late Sept. 2016, the Indian Army publicized that it undertook what it called "surgical strikes" several kilometers into Pakistan-administered Kashmir to punish it for the LeT attack that took place earlier that month at Uri. This was not the first time that the Indian Army undertook such raids, but it was the first time that it publicized doing so. See Swami, Praveen, "India hits Pakistan along LoC, casting spotlight on savage, secret war," *Indian Express*, 29 Sept. 2016, accessed 11 June 2018. http://indianexpress.com/article/india/india-news-india/indian-army-pakistan-surgical-strikes-loc-casting-spotlight-on-savage-secret-war-3055999/; Gupta, Shishir, "LeT, not Jaish-e-Mohammad, involved in Uri terror attack: NIA report." *Hindustan Times*, 22 March 2017, accessed 11 June 2018. http://www.hindustantimes.com/india-news/let-not-jaish-e-mohammad-involved-in-uri-terror-attack-nia-report/story-pcwkG2PSKUy3T-CIQbU5puI.html; Joshi, Shashank. "Everything that we know about India's cross-LoC strikes before Uri," *Scroll India*, 5 Oct. 2016. https://scroll.in/article/818324/everything-that-we-know-about-indias-cross-loc-strikes-before-uri.

9. Singh, Sushant. "PM Modi's 'strategic restraint' choice: A virtue or a necessity?," *Indian Express*, 25 Sept. 2016, accessed 11 June 2018. http://indianexpress.com/article/opinion/web-edits/pm-modis-strategic-restraint-uri-attack-pakistan-a-virtue-or-a-necessity/.

10. "Global Terrorism Database," *National Consortium for the Study of Terrorism and Responses to Terrorism*, accessed 11 June 2018. https://www.start.umd.edu/gtd/.

11. Dashi, Dipak K, "400 road deaths per day in India; up 5% to 1.46 lakh in 2015," *India Times*, 21 April 2016, accessed 11 June 2018. http://timesofindia.indiatimes.com/india/400-road-deaths-per-day-in-India-up-5-to-1-46-lakh-in-2015/articleshow/51919213.cms.

12. "How the 1993 blasts changed Mumbai forever," *BBC.com*, 30 July 2015, accessed 11 June 2018. http://www.bbc.com/news/world-asia-india-33713846.

13. Centers for Disease Control and Prevention, "Motor Vehicle Crash Deaths, 18 July 2016. accessed 11 June 2018. https://www.cdc.gov/vitalsigns/motor-vehicle-safety/index.html.

14. Dashi, Dipak K, "400 road deaths per day in India; up 5% to 1.46 lakh in 2015," *India Times*, 21 April 2016, accessed 11 June 2018. http://timesofindia.indiatimes.com/india/400-road-deaths-per-day-in-India-up-5-to-1-46-lakh-in-2015/articleshow/51919213.cms.

15. Stokes, Bruce, "The Modi Bounce: Indians Give Their Prime Minister and Economy High Marks, Worry about Crime, Jobs, Prices, Corruption," Pew Research Center, 17 Sept. 2015, accessed 11 June 2018. http://www.pewglobal.org/2015/09/17/the-

modi-bounce/; Pew Research Center, "Topline Results: Spring 2015 Survey-Sept. 17, 2015 Release," accessed 11 June 2018. http://www.pewglobal.org/2015/09/17/methodology-14/.

16. Fair, C. Christine, "Prospects for effective internal security reforms in India," *Commonwealth & Comparative Politics*, 2012, 50, 2, pp. 145–170.

17. See Pardesi, Manjeet S., "Is India a great power? Understanding great power status in contemporary international relations," *Asian Security*. 2015. 11, pp. 1–30.

18. World Bank, "Global Economic Prospects," Updated 4 June 2017, accessed 11 June 2018. http://databank.worldbank.org/data/reports.aspx?source=global-economic-prospects&Type=TABLE&preview=on#.

19. SIPRI, "Military expenditure by country as percentage of gross domestic product: 2003–2016," 2017, accessed 11 June 2018. https://sipri.org/sites/default/files/Milex-share-of-GDP.pdf.

20. SIPRI, "Military expenditure by country as percentage of gross domestic product: 2003–2016," 2017, accessed 11 June 2018. https://sipri.org/sites/default/files/Milex-share-of-GDP.pdf.

21. Perkovich and Dalton put forward an extensive suite of investments that India would require to compel Pakistan to cease and desist from using terrorism under its nuclear umbrella. See Perkovich, George and Toby Dalton, *Not War, Not Peace?: Motivating Pakistan to Prevent Cross-Border Terrorism*, New Delhi: Oxford University Press, 2016. Unfortunately, they misdiagnose the policy puzzle as I detail in Fair, C. Christine. "Book Review: Not War, Not Peace? Motivating Pakistan to Prevent Cross-Border Terrorism. By George Perkovich and Toby Dalton," *The Journal of Politics*, 79,2 (2017): pp. e43-e44. However, their assessment of the institutional reforms that India would require are sound despite their various errors of fact and interpretation.

22. Fair, C. Christine, "India and Iran: New Delhi's Balancing Act." *The Washington Quarterly*, Vol. 30. No. 3 (Summer 2007): pp. 145–159; Fair, C. Christine. "When It Comes to Afghanistan, America Should Ditch Pakistan for Iran." *The Nationalist Interest*, 7 Sept. 2015, accessed 11 June 2018. http://nationalinterest.org/feature/when-it-comes-afghanistan-america-should-ditch-pakistan-iran-13788. Rubin, Barnett. "Afghanistan And Considerations Of Supply," *War on the Rocks*, 11 July 2017, accessed 11 June 2018.

23. I explain these issues in Fair, C. Christine. "False Equivalency In The "Indo-Pakistan,"" *War on the Rocks*, 16 June 2015, accessed 11 June 2018. https://warontherocks.com/2015/06/false-equivalency-in-the-indo-pakistan-dispute/; Fair, C. Christine and Sumit Ganguly; "An Unworthy Ally," Foreign Affairs, Vol. 94, No. 5 (Sept./Oct. 2015): 160–170; and Fair, C. Christine and Sumit Ganguly, "Lives on the Line," *The Washington Quarterly*, Vol. 36, No. 3 (Summer 2013):173–184.

24. Shapiro, Jacob N., *The Terrorist's Dilemma: Managing Violent Covert Organizations*, Princeton: Princeton University Press, 2013.

25. Popovic, Miles. "The Perils of Weak Organization: Explaining Loyalty and Defection of Militant Organizations Toward Pakistan," *Studies in Conflict & Terrorism*, Vol. 28, No. 11 (2015): pp. 919–937.

26. Abrahms, Max, and Jochen Mierau. "Leadership matters: The effects of targeted kill-ings on militant group tactics." Terrorism and Political Violence (2015): p. 2, accessed 11 June 2018. http://www.tandfonline.com/doi/abs/10.1080/09546553.2015.1069 671.

27. Johnston, Patrick B. "Does Decapitation Work? Assessing the Effectiveness of Leadership Targeting in Counterinsurgency Campaigns," International Security 36 (2012): pp. 47–79; Price, Bryan C., "Targeting Top Terrorists: How Leadership Decapitation Contributes to Counterterrorism," International Security 36 (2012): pp. 9–46, p. 7.

28. Jaeger, David A. and M. Daniele Paserman, "The Shape of Things to Come? On the Dynamics of Suicide Attacks and Targeted Killings," Quarterly Journal of Political Science 4 (2009), pp. 315–42; Jordan, Jenna, "When Heads Roll: Assessing the Effectiveness of Leadership Decapitation," Security Studies 18 (2009): 719–55; Mannes, Aaron, "Testing the Snake Head Strategy: Does Killing or Capturing Its Leaders Reduce a Terrorist Group's Activity?" The Journal of International Policy Solutions 9 (2008), pp. 40–49; Smith, Megan and James Igoe Walsh, "Do Drone Strikes Degrade Al Qaeda? Evidence from Propaganda Output," Terrorism and Political Violence 25, no. 2 (2013), pp. 311–27.

29. This kind of problem typically arises with quantitative studies in which scholars use extant datasets and, per force, use sub-optimal measures for concepts they wish to test. For exam-ple, if a scholar wants to proxy for group cohesion, they may use a variable on length of time during which the organization did not split. While this measure tells us something about the effects of group cohesion (in that the group did not split), it does not tell us much about the actual factors that produce such cohesion. For a discussion of this, see Long, Austin. "Whack-a-Mole or Coup de Grace? Institutionalization and Leadership Targeting in Iraq and Afghanistan," Security Studies, 23,3 (2014), pp. 471–512.

30. The phrase "large n" refers to studies of many observations which typically employ quantitative analytical means. "Large n" contrast with "small n" studies, which tend to be qualitative analyses of a small number of cases (usually fewer than ten). For more discussion of these issues, see Carvin, Stephanie, "The Trouble with Targeted Killing," Security Studies 21, 3 (July 2012), pp. 529–555; Long, "Whack-a-Mole or Coup de Grace?"; Abrahms and Mierau, "Leadership matters."

31. Byman, Dan, "Do Targeted Killings Work?" Foreign Affairs, 85, 2 (Mar.—Apr., 2006), pp. 95–111.

32. Shapiro, The Terrorist's Dilemma.

33. Austin, "Whack-a-Mole or Coup de Grace?," p. 476.

34. Price, Bryan, "Targeting Top Terrorists."

35. Long, "Whack-a-Mole or Coup de Grace?"

36. Ibid.

37. Fair, C. Christine, Clay Ramsay, Steve Kull, "Pakistani Public Opinion on Democracy, Islamist Militancy, and Relations with the US," Washington D.C.: USIP/PIPA, Jan. 7, 2008, accessed 11 June 2018, https://www.usip.org/publications/2008/02/paki-stani-public-opinion-democracy-islamist-militancy-and-relations-us.

38. Gelpi, Christopher, Peter D. Feaver, and Jason Reifler. *Paying the Human Costs of War: American Public Opinion and Casualties in Military Conflicts*, Princeton: Princeton University Press, 2009.

39. This section draws from and reproduces some materials that have appeared variously in Fair, C. Christine, "Pakistan's Strategic Culture: Implications for how Pakistan Perceives Threats and Counters Them," NBR's Special Report #61 (Seattle: National Bureau of Research, December 2016); Fair, C. Christine, "A New Way of Engaging Pakistan," *Lawfare*, 11 April 2016, accessed 23 June 2018, https://www.lawfareblog.com/new-way-engaging-pakistan; Fair, C. Christine, "Pakistan Will Try to Make Trump Pay," *The Atlantic*, 8 Jan. 2018, accessed 23 June 2018, https://www.theatlantic.com/international/archive/2018/01/trump-pakistan/549887/; Fair, C. Christine, "Pakistani Power Play," 6 November 2012, accessed 23 June 2018, http://foreignpolicy.com/2012/11/06/pakistani-power-play/; Fair, C. Christine, "False Equivalency In The 'Indo-Pakistan' Dispute," *War on the Rocks*, 16 June 2015, accessed 23 June 2018, https://warontherocks.com/2015/06/false-equivalency-in-the-indo-pakistan-dispute/.

40. Ahmed, Mutahir. "IMF and Pakistan." PIDE Lecture Series, 2012, accessed 11 June 2018. http://www.pide.org.pk/pdf/PIDELectureSeries/The%20IMF%20and%20Pakistan%20Seminar%20PIDE%20expansion.pdf; Fair, C. Christine, et al. *Pakistan: can the United States secure an insecure state?* Santa Monica: RAND Corporation, 2010. See Boucher's comments on the US vote at the IMF in 2001 available at "Sept. 11, 2001: Attack on America," State Dept. Daily Press Briefing," 24 Sept. 2001, accessed 11 June 2018. http://avalon.law.yale.edu/sept11/state_dept_brief020.asp. For a countervailing view, see Momani, Bessma, "The IMF, the US War on Terrorism, and Pakistan," *Asian Affairs*, 31, 1 (Spring, 2004): pp. 41–50.

41. Wolfsthal, Jon B. "Keeping a Nuke Peddler in Line," *Los Angeles Times*, 11 Jan. 2004, accessed 11 June 2018. http://articles.latimes.com/2004/jan/11/opinion/op-wolfsthal11.

42. In 2010, I argued that Washington should consider offering a conditions-based civilian nuclear deal centered around ceasing the use of terrorism as a tool of foreign policy, transparency into the A.Q. Khan affairs among other security-related interests. I argued then that if Pakistan were to make incremental progress on any of the conditions, we would all benefit. However, I also argued that Pakistan would be unlikely to ever fulfil these conditions because it is not in Pakistan's interests to do so. Such a rebuff would essentially "call Pakistan's bluff about the rationale for its behavior, motivating the United States to rethink its handling of Pakistan." Fair, C. Christine, "Should Pakistan Get a Nuke Deal? Only if it finally abandons its support for terrorism," *Foreign Policy*, 23 March 2010, accessed 11 June 2018. http://foreignpolicy.com/2010/03/23/should-pakistan-get-a-nuke-deal-2/. In the fall of 2015, the Obama administration floated a plan to bring Pakistan into the "nuclear mainstream." Pakistan flatly rejected it. See Sajjad, Baqir, "PM's US trip to be marked by tense diplomacy," *Dawn*, 16 Oct. 2015, accessed 11 June 2018. https://www.dawn.com/news/1213429; Malik, Mehreen Zahra-Malik and David Brunnstrom, "Pakistan to tell US it won't accept limits on tactical nuclear arms," 21 Oct. 2015, accessed 11 June 2018. http://www.reuters.com/article/us-nuclear-pakistan-idUSKCN0SF2A120151022.

43. Epstein, Susan B., and K. Alan Kronstadt. Pakistan: US foreign assistance." Congressional Research Service, 1 July 2013, accessed 11 June 2018. https://fas.org/sgp/crs/row/R41856.pdf; US Government Accounting Office, "Combating Terrorism: Increased Oversight and Accountability Needed over Pakistan Reimbursement Claims for Coalition Support Funds, July 2008, accessed 11 June 2018. http://www.gao.gov/assets/280/277240.pdf.

44. United Nations Security Council, "Resolution 1373 (2001)," 28 Sept. 2001, accessed 11 June 2018. http://www.un.org/en/sc/ctc/specialmeetings/2012/docs/United%20Nations%20Security%20Council%20Resolution%201373%20(2001).pdf.

45. Haqqani, Hussain, *Magnificent Delusions: Pakistan, the United States, and an Epic History of Misunderstanding*, New York: Public Affairs, 2013.

46. For devastating accounts of Pakistan's apparatus for security governance, see International Crisis Group, "Reforming Pakistan's Prison System," Report 212, 12 Oct. 2011, accessed 11 June 2018. https://www.crisisgroup.org/asia/south-asia/pakistan/reforming-pakistan-s-prison-system; International Crisis Group, "Reforming Pakistan's Criminal Justice System," Report 196, 6 Dec. 2010, accessed 11 June 2018. https://www.crisisgroup.org/asia/south-asia/pakistan/reforming-pakistan-s-criminal-justice-system; International Crisis Group, "Reforming the Judiciary in Pakistan," Report 160, 16 Oct. 2008, accessed 11 June 2018. https://www.crisisgroup.org/asia/south-asia/pakistan/reforming-judiciary-pakistan; International Crisis Group, "Reforming Pakistan's Police," Report 157, 14 July 2008, accessed 11 June 2018. https://www.crisisgroup.org/asia/south-asia/pakistan/reforming-pakistan%E2%80%99s-police.

47. Global Security, "Major Non-NATO Ally (MNNA)," n.d., accessed 11 June 2018. http://www.globalsecurity.org/military/agency/dod/mnna.htm.

48. Tellis, Ashley J. "Are India-Pakistan Peace Talks Worth a Damn?," *Carnegie Endowment for International Peace*, 20 Sept. 2017, accessed 11 June 2018. http://carnegieendowment.org/2017/09/20/are-india-pakistan-peace-talks-worth-damn-pub-73145.

49. Tellis, Ashley J. Tellis, C. Christine Fair, Jamison Jo Medby. *Limited Conflicts Under the Nuclear Umbrella*, Santa Monica: RAND, 2001.

50. United Nations Security Council, "Security Council Committee Pursuant To Resolutions 1267 (1999) 1989 (2011) And 2253 (2015) Concerning Isil (Da'esh) Al-Qaida And Associated Individuals Groups Undertakings and Entities," n.d., accessed 11 June 2018. https://www.un.org/sc/suborg/en/sanctions/1267.

51. Riedel, Bruce, "The China-Pakistan axis and Lashkar-e-Taiba," *Brookings.com*, 26 June 2015, accessed 11 June 2018. https://www.brookings.edu/opinions/the-china-pakistan-axis-and-lashkar-e-taiba/. See also Roggio, Bill. "UN declares Jamaat-ud-Dawa a terrorist front group," *Long War Journal*, 11 Dec. 2008, accessed 11 June 2018. http://www.longwarjournal.org/archives/2008/12/un_declares_jamaatud.php.

APPENDIX 1: NOTES ON TRANSLITERATION AND TRANSLATION

1. Nor do I use the expression "Peace Be Upon Him (PBUH)" after the mention of the prophet Muhammad (or its Arabic variant ṣallā Allāhu ʿalayhi wa-ala ālihi wa-sallam

(abbreviated as SAWS) or its calligraphic equivalent (ﷺ), as is the custom of Muslim writers. This is not intended to offend Muslim readers; rather I find the use of such expressions to be inappropriate in a book authored by a non-believer.

SELECT BIBLIOGRAPHY

Abbas, Azmat, "In God We Trust," *The Herald (Pakistan)* (Jan. 2002), pp. 45–49.

Abbas, Hassan, "Defining the Punjabi Taliban Network," *CTC Sentinel*, 2, 4 (April 2009), pp. 1–4.

Abbas, Qaswar, "Hafiz Saeed accuses India of backing twin suicide attacks at Peshawar church," *India Today*, 23 Sept. 2013, accessed 11 June 2018. http://indiatoday. intoday.in/story/hafiz-saeed-india-pakistan-peshawar-church-bombings-terrorist-nation/1/311165.html.

Abdullah, Hayat, "Abu Abdullah Muhammad Munsha: To pray for Jihad, and to face the opposition of our beloved ones," trans Ali Hamza, *Mujallah ul Dawah*, date and unyear unknown.

Abou Zahab, Mariam, "The Regional Dimension of Sectarian Conflicts in Pakistan," in *Pakistan: Nationalism Without a Nation?* Christophe Jaffrelot (ed.), London: Zed Books, 2002, pp. 115–28.

——, "I Shall be Waiting at the Door of Paradise: The Pakistani Martyrs of the Lashkar-e-Tayyaba (Army of the Pure)," in *The Practice of War: Production, Reproduction and Communication of Armed Violence*, Aparna Rao et al. (eds), New York: Berghahn Books, 2007, pp. 133–158.

——, "Salafism in Pakistan: The Ahl-e Hadith Movement," in *Global Salafism: Islam's New Religious Movement*, Roel Meijer (ed.), London: Hurst, 2009, pp. 126–139.

Abou Zahab, Mariam, and Olivier Roy, *Islamist Networks: The Afghan-Pakistan Connection*, London, Hurst, 2004.

"Abu Ali Ameer Muaviya (martyred)—The rose whose joviality perfumed the paradise of Kashmir," trans Ali Hamza, *Zarb-e-Tayyaba*, Aug. 2004, p. 30.

"Abu Hanzul Amjad (martyred)—Those who require truth, do ablution with their blood,'" trans Ali Hamza, *Zarb-e-Tayyaba*, April 2004, pp. 33–35.

"Abu Maooz Mohammad Asghar Shaheed. An excellent student of University of Engineering and Technology Taxila," trans Ali Hamza, *Zarb-e-Tayyaba*, April 2005, pp. 62–64.

"Abu Marsad Habeeb ur Rahman," trans Ali Hamza, *Mujallah Tayyabaat*, Dec. 2003, p. 43.

Abu Mohsin of Sargodha, "Abu Hanzla Babar Zameer, Bhalwal," trans Ali Hamza, *Mujallah ul Dawa*, Jan. 2001, p. 38.

"Abu Quhafa Shaheed Syed Abdul Rasheed bin Tufail ul Rehman Shah," trans Ali Hamza, *Mujallah Tayyabaat*, Jan. 2003, p. 20.

Afzal, Muhammad, "Abu Bakr Ammar Anjum Abdul Waris, Sialkot," trans Ali Hamza, *Mujallah ud Dawa*, Jan. 2001, pp. 41–42.

Ahmad, Aftab, "At the Time of Independence," *The Express Tribune*, 12 Aug 2014, accessed 11 June 2018. https://tribune.com.pk/story/747233/at-the-time-of-independence/.

Akhtar, Asif Duraiz (Maj. Gen.), "Nation Building," in *Pakistan Army Green Book: Role of Pakistan Army in Nation Building*, Rawalpindi, Pakistan Army Headquarters, 2000, pp. 1–3.

Akram, A. I. (Col), "On Infiltration," *Pakistan Army Journal*, 6, 2 (1964), pp. 1–4.

Akram, Mohammad Bilal, "Abu Bilal Mohammad Ashraf Shaheed: A tale of that Mentor, who left behind an example for his students," trans Ali Hamza, *Zarb-e-Tayyaba*, Sept. 2004, pp. 34–36.

Akram, Muhammad (Lt Col), "Dien Bien Phu," *Pakistan Army Journal*, 13, 2 (1971), pp. 29–37.

Al-Anbari, Khalid bin Ali bin Muhammad, *The Murji'ah of the Era*, trans Abu Hayyaan Salal ibn Ahmad, SalafiManhaj, 2006, accessed 11 June 2018. https://web-beta.archive.org/web/20070927210906/http://www.salafimanhaj.com/pdf/TheMurjiahOfTheEra_ebook.pdf.

Al-Rahman, Rahmat Allah ibn Khalil and Muhammad Ahmad Abdulqadar Malakavi, *Isaiyat? (What is Christianity?)*, Lahore, Dar al Andalus, 2007.

Anbari, Khalid bin Ai bin Muhammad, *The Murji'ah of the Era!*, trans Abu Hayyaan Salal ibn Ahmad, SalafiManhaj.com, 2004, accessed 11 June 2018. https://web-beta.archive.org/web/20070927210906/http://www.salafimanhaj.com/pdf/TheMurjiahOfTheEra_ebook.pdf.

Anwari, Masood Navid (Lt Col), "Deterrence—Hope or Reality," *Pakistan Army Journal*, 29 (March 1988), pp. 45–53.

Arif, Khalid Mahmud (Gen.), *Working with Zia: Pakistan Power Politics, 1977–1988*, New York, Oxford University Press, 1995.

———, *Khaki Shadows: Pakistan 1947–1997*, Karachi, Oxford University Press, 2001.

Asghar, Sufyan, "Abu Huzaifa Muhammad Luqman—another honor for Bahauddin Zakariya University," trans Ali Hamza, *Zarb-e-Tayyaba*, November 2004, p. 28.

Bin Muhammad, Abdussalam, *"Hum Kyon Jihad Kar Rahen Hain? [Why Are We Waging Jihad?]*," trans C. Christine Fair and Safina Ustaad, Lahore, Dar-ul-Andulus, 2004.

——, *Hindu Customs Among Muslims*, trans M. Saleem Ahsan, Lahore, Dar-ul-Andulus, 2007.

East, C.H.A. (Maj.), "Guerrilla Warfare," *Pakistan Army Journal*, 1, 4 (1958), pp. 57–66.

Eaton, Richard M., 'Temple desecration and Indo-Muslim states," Frontline (Jan. 2001), pp. 70–77.

El-Edroos, S.A. (Brig), "Jordan and the Arab-Israeli War, 6–22 October 1973," *Pakistan Army Journal*, 15 (June 1974), pp. 11–35.

El-Edroos, S.A. (Lt. Col.), "General Vo Nguyen Giap and the Viet Nam People's Army," *Pakistan Army Journal*, 6, 1 (1964), pp. 10–17.

——, "Mao Tse-Tung and the Chinese People's Liberation Army (1927–1964)," *Pakistan Army Journal* 6, 2 (1964), pp. 8–28.

El-Edroos, S.A. (Maj.), "Infiltration-A form of attack," *Pakistan Army Journal*, 3, 2 (1961), pp. 3–15.

——, "Afro-Asian Revolutionary Warfare and our Military Thought," *Pakistan Army Journal*, 4, 2 (1962), pp. 26–41.

Fair, C. Christine, "Militant Recruitment in Pakistan: Implications for Al-Qa'ida and Other Organizations," *Studies in Conflict and Terrorism*, 27, 6 (November/Dec. 2004), pp. 489–504.

——, *The Madrassah Challenge: Militancy and Religious Education in Pakistan*, Washington, D.C., United States Institute of Peace, 2008.

——, "Who Are Pakistan's Militants and Their Families?" *Terrorism and Political Violence*, 20, 2 (2008), pp. 49–65.

——, "Lashkar-e-Tayiba and the Pakistani State," *Survival*, 53 (Aug. 2011), pp. 1–23.

——, "The Militant Challenge in Pakistan," *Asia Policy*, 11 (Jan. 2011), pp. 105–137.

——, *Fighting to the End: The Pakistan Army's Way of War*, New York, Oxford University Press, 2014.

——, "Leader-Led Jihad in Pakistan: The Case of Lashkar-e-Tayyaba," in *The Evolution of the Global Terrorist Threat: From 9/11 to Osama bin Laden's Death*, (eds.) Bruce Hoffman and Fernando Reinares, New York: Columbia University Press, 2014, pp. 571–599.

——, "Insights from a Database of Lashkar-e-Tayyaba and Hizb-ul-Mujahideen Militants," *Journal of Strategic Studies*, 37, 2 (2014), pp. 259–290.

——, "Jamaat-ud-Dawa: Converting Kuffar at Home, Killing Them Abroad," *Current Trends in Islamist Ideology*, vol. 22, (November 2017): pp. 58–79.

——, "Pakistan's Nuclear Program: Laying the Groundwork for Impunity," C. Christine Fair in Joseph Liow, Andrew Scobell and Sumit Ganguly Eds. *Routledge Handbook of Asian Security Studies (2nd Edition)*. Abingdon: Routledge, 2017, pp. 126–139.

——, "The Milli Muslim League: The Domestic Politics of Pakistan's Lashkar-e-Taiba," *Current Trends in Islamist Ideology*, 7 May 2018, accessed 11 June 2018. https://www.hudson.org/research/14305-the-milli-muslim-league-the-domestic-politics-of-pakistan-s-lashkar-e-taiba.

Falah e Insaniat Foundation, "Muzaffarabad, Falah-e-Insaniat Foundation Holds Rally," 6 Aug. 2016, accessed 22 Aug. 2016 (link expired). http://www.devotedtohumanity.com/blog/detail/muzaffarabad-falah-e-insaniat-foundation-holds-rally.php.

——, "Relief Work in Balochistan," *Falah e Insaniat Foundation*, accessed 11 June 2018. http://fifpakistan.blogspot.com/p/services-of-fif-in-baluchistan-falah-e.html.

——, "About Us," last accessed 11 June 2018. http://www.devotedtohumanity.org/en/page/about-us.php.

——, "International Services," last accessed 11 June 2018. http://www.devotedtohumanity.org/en/page/international-services.php.

Ganguly, Sumit, *The Crisis in Kashmir: Portents of War, Hopes of Peace*, Cambridge: Cambridge University Press, 1997.

——, *Conflict Unending: India-Pakistan Tensions Since 1947*, New Delhi: Oxford University Press, 2001.

——, "The Crisis of Indian Secularism," *Journal of Democracy*, 14, 4 (2003), pp. 11–25.

——, "Nuclear Stability in South Asia," *International Security*, 33 (Fall 2008), pp. 45–70.

——, editor, *India's Foreign Policy: Retrospect and Prospect*, New York: Oxford University Press, 2012.

Ganguly, Sumit, and S. Paul Kapur, *India, Pakistan, and the Bomb: Debating Nuclear Stability in South Asia*, New York: Columbia University Press, 2010.

Hammad, Umm-e, *Hum Ma'en Lashkar-e-Tayyaba Ki* (We, the Mothers of Lashkar-e-Tayyaba), 1, Lahore: Dar-ul-Andalus, 1998.

——, *Hum Ma'en Lashkar-e-Tayyaba Ki* (We, the Mothers of Lashkar-e-Tayyaba), 2, Lahore: Dar-ul-Andalus, 2003.

——, *Hum Ma'en Lashkar-e-Tayyaba Ki* (We, the Mothers of Lashkar-e-Tayyaba), 3, Lahore: Dar-ul-Andalus, 2003.

Hamza, Amir, "The Invasion of Lashkar-e-Tayyaba in Occupied Kashmir," trans Ali Hamza, *Mujallah ul Dawa*, February 1994, pp. 4–9.

——, "Abu Umair Shaheed," trans Ali Hamza, *Mujallah ul Dawah*, October 1994, p. 9.

Hamza, Maulana Amir, *Shahrah-e-Bahisht* (*Highway to Paradise*), trans Safina Ustaad, Lahore: Dar-ul-Andulus, 2004.

Hashi, Ukht-e-Abu, "Abu Hamza Sayyaf Sani Abdul Rehman," trans Ali Hamza, *Mujallah Tayyabaat*, Jan. 2004, p. 23.

Hashmi, Hafza, "Abul Hassan Mohammed Zubair Shaheed," trans Ali Hamza, *Mujallah Tayyabaat*, Aug. 2004, p. 31.

Hashim, Ukht-e-Abu, "Abu Hamza Sayyaf Sani Abdul Rehman," trans Ali Hamza, *Mujallah Tayyabaat*, Jan. 2004, p. 23.

Haq, Farhat, "Militarism and Motherhood: The Women of the Lashkar-i-Tayyabia in Pakistan," *Signs*, 32, 4 (Summer 2007), 1023–1046.

——, "Mothers of Lashkar-e-Tayyaba," *Economic and Political Weekly*, 44, 18 (May 2009), pp. 17–20.

Haqqani, Husain, *Pakistan: Between Mosque and Military*, Washington, D.C.: Carnegie Endowment for International Peace, 2005.

——, *Magnificent Delusions: Pakistan, the United States, and an Epic History of Misunderstanding*, New York: Public Affairs, 2013.

Hussain, Rizwan, *Pakistan and the Emergence of Islamic Militancy in Afghanistan*, Burlington: Ashgate, 2005.

Ifzal, Muhammad (Brig.), "Concept of Limited War," in *Pakistan Army Green Book 2004: Limited War*, Rawalpindi: Pakistan Army General Headquarters, 2004, pp. 13–21.

Ijaz, Ghazi Faheem, "In memory of Shaheed Abu Sufian," trans Ali Hamza, *Mujallah ul Dawa*, Aug. 1994, pp. 31–33.

Ilahi, Shereen. 2003. "The Radcliffe Boundary Commission and the Fate of Kashmir," *India Review*, vol. 2, no. 1: 77–102.

Iqbal, Shahid (Maj. Gen.), "Doctrinal Aspects of Limited War and Its Applicability in the Region," in *Pakistan Army Green Book 2004: Limited War*, Rawalpindi: Pakistan Army General Head, 2004, pp. 83–89.

Iqbal, Shaukat (Brig.), "Present and Future Conflict Environments in Pakistan: Challenges for Pakistan Army and the Way Forward," in *Pakistan Army Green Book 2008: Future Conflict Environment*, Rawalpindi: Pakistan Army General Headquarters, pp. 43–50.

Iqtidar, Humeira, *Secularizing Islamists: Jama'at-e-Islami and Jamat'at-ud-Da'wa in Urban Pakistan*, Chicago: University of Chicago 2011, pp. 106–107.

Jamaat-ud-Dawa, "FIF is Reality of Jamat-ud-Dawa. Hafiz Saeed," 11 February 2016, accessed 7 Sept. 2016 (link expired). http://www.judofficial.com/en/news/fif-reality-jamat-ud-dawa-hafiz-saeed/.

——, accessed 7 Sept. 2016 (link expired). http://www.judofficial.com/en/.

Jamal, Arif, *Shadow War: The Untold Story of Jihad in Kashmir*, New York: Melville, 2009.

——, *Call For Transnational Jihad: Lashkar-e-Tayyaba 1985–2014*, East Brunswick: AvantGarde Books LLC., 2014.

John, Wilson, "Resurgent Radicalism in Pakistan: A Case Study of Jamaat-ud-Dawa," *CLAWS Journal* (Winter 2008), pp. 60–73.

——, *Caliphate's Soldiers: The Lashkar-e-Tayyeba's Long War*, New Delhi: Amaryllis and the Observer Research Foundation, 2011.

Khalid, Abu, "Abu Mursad Zakaullah, Faisalabad," trans Ali Hamza, *Mujallah ud Dawa*, Jan. 2001, pp. 40–41.

Khan, Zaigham, "Allah's Army," *The Herald Annual* (Jan. 1998a), pp. 123–130.

———, "From Strength to Strength," *The Herald Annual*, (Jan. 1998), pp. 125.

———, "Information Revolution," *The Herald Annual*, (Jan. 1998), pp. 128–129.

———, "Interview with Hafiz Mohammed Khan," *The Herald Annual* (Jan. 1998), pp. 131–133.

Mahmud, Muneer (Brig.), "Low Intensity Conflict-Historical Perspective," in *Pakistan Army Green Book 2002: Low Intensity Conflict*, Rawalpindi: Pakistan Army General Headquarters 2002, pp. 17–23.

Metcalf, Barbara. "Islam and power in colonial India: the making and unmaking of a Muslim princess." The American Historical Review 116.1 (2011): 1–30.

———,*Islamic Contestations: Essays on Muslims in India and Pakistan*, New Delhi: Oxford University Press, 2004

Mir, Amir, *True Face of the Jehadis*, Lahore: Mashal, 2004.

———, 'Militant' Philanthropy," *Newsline*, 15 November 2005, accessed 11 June 2018. http://www.newslinemagazine.com/2005/11/militant-philanthropy/

———, *The Fluttering Flag of Jehad*, Lahore: Mashal Books, 2008.

———, "More power to Pakistan's jihadis," *Asia Times*, 2 Sept. 2011, accessed 11 June 2018 http://www.atimes.com/atimes/South_Asia/MI02Df02.html.

———, "Punjabi Taliban's exit to affect TTP's terror drive," *The News International*, 15 Sept. 2014, accessed 11 June 2018. http://www.thenews.com.pk/Todays-News-2-272864-Punjabi-Talibans-exit-to-affect-TTPs-terror-drive.

Muhammadi, Ubaidurrahman, *Difa-i-Jihad (Defense of Jihad)*, trans Safina Ustaad, Lahore: Dar-ul-Andulus, 2003.

Naim, C.M., "The Mothers of the Lashkar," *Outlook India*, 15 Dec. 2008, www.outlookindia.com/article.aspx?239238.

Nazeer, Salman, 'Remembering Abu Abdullah Abdul Majeed Tariq the martyr," trans Ali Hamza, *Zarb-e-Tayyaba*, Dec. 2004, p. 35.

Niaz, Qazi Kashif, "The Whipping of Indian Army by the Wrath of Allah in the form of battle with Lashkar-e-Tayyaba (LeT): Abu Abdul Rehman, Dr. Abu Turab, Abu Talha, Abu Baseer and Abu Ali," trans Ali Hamza, *Mujallah ul Dawah*, July 1994, p. 9.

Parker, Reuben D. (Lt Col), "Infiltration as a Form of Maneuver," *Pakistan Army Journal*, 6 (June 1964), pp. 1–9.

Paul, T.V., *The Warrior State: Pakistan in the Contemporary World*, New York: Oxford University Press, 2014.

Perkovich, George and Toby Dalton, *Not War, Not Peace? Motivating Pakistan to Prevent Cross-Border Terrorism*, New Delhi: Oxford University Press, 2016.

Philippon, Alix. "The Role of Sufism in the Identity Construction, Mobilization and Political Activism of the Barelwi Movement in Pakistan." *Partecipazione E Conflitto*, Vol. 7. No. 1 (2014): 152–169.

Qazi, Kashif Niaz, "The Whipping of Indian Army by the Wrath of Allah in the form of battle with Lashkar-e-Tayyaba (LeT)," trans Ali Hamza, *Mujallah ul Dawa*, July 1994, p. 5.

Qazi, Shamsul Haq (Lt. Col.), "A Case for Citizen Army," *Pakistan Army Journal* 6 (June 1964): pp. 18–25.

Qazi, Shehzad H., "Rebels of the Frontier: Origins, Organisation, and Recruitment of the Pakistani Taliban," *Small Wars and Insurgencies*, 22, 4 (2011), pp. 574–602.

Rabbani, Abul Hassan Mubbashir Ahmed, *Kalima-go mashrik [The Muslim Polytheist]*, trans C. Christine Fair and Abbas Haider, Lahore: Dar-ul-Andulus, 2009.

———, "Fitna Takfeer [The Civil Strife of Excommunication]," 23 Sept. 2011, accessed 11 June 2018. https://www.youtube.com/watch?v=0Tpc-Hv8NuQ.

———, *Masalah-yi takfir aur is ke usul o zavabit* (The Problem of Takfir and its Principles and Regulations), trans Safina Ustaad, Lahore: Dar-ul-Andulus, 2015.

Rabasa, Angel et al., *The Lessons of Mumbai*, Santa Monica: RAND Corporation, 2009.

Rana, Muhammad Amir, *Gateway to Terrorism*, London: New Millennium Publication, 2003.

———, *The A to Z of Jehadi Organizations in Pakistan*, trans Saba Ansari, Lahore: Mashal, 2004.

Rasheed, Aqsa Dukhter Abdul, "Abu Ayub Ansari," trans Ali Hamza, *Mujallah Tayyabaat*, July 2003, p. 23.

Rashid, Ahmed, *Descent into Chaos*, New York: Viking, 2008.

Rassler, Don, Fair, C. Christine Fair, Anirban Gosh, Don Rassler, and Nadia Shoeb, "The Fighters of Lashkar-e-Tayyaba: Recruitment, Training, Deployment and Death," *West Point Combating Terrorism Center*, April 2013, accessed 11 June 2018. https://www.ctc.usma.edu/wp-content/uploads/2013/04/Fighters-of-LeT_Final.pdf.

Robinson, Cabeiri deBergh, *Body of Victims, Body of Warrior: Refugee Families and the Making of Kashmir Jihadists*, Berkeley: University of California Press, 2013.

Rotella, Sebastian, "Pakistan and the Mumbai attacks: The Untold Story," *ProPublica*, 26 Jan. 2011, accessed 11 June 2018. https://www.propublica.org/article/pakistan-and-the-mumbai-attacks-the-untold-story.

———, "Four Alleged Masterminds of 2008 Mumbai Attacks Are Indicted in Chicago," *ProPublica*, 25 April 2011, accessed 11 June 2018. https://www.propublica.org/article/four-alleged-masterminds-of-2008-mumbai-attacks-are-indicted-in-chicago.

———, "Mumbai Case Offers Rare Picture of Ties Between Pakistan's Intelligence Service, Militants," ProPublica, 2 May 2011, accessed 11 June 2018. https://www.propublica.org/article/mumbai-case-offers-rare-picture-of-ties-between-pakistans-intelligence-serv.

———, "Chicago Terrorism Trial: What we learned, and Didn't, About Pakistan's Terror Connections," *ProPublica*, 9 June 2011, accessed 11 June 2018. http://www.propublica.org/article/chicago-terrorism-trial-what-we-learned-and-didnt.

———, "The Man Behind Mumbai," ProPublica, 13 November 2010, accessed 11 June 2018. https://www.propublica.org/article/the-man-behind-mumbai.

———, "Four Disturbing Questions about the Mumbai Terror Attack," *ProPublica*, 22 February 2013, accessed 11 June 2018. https://www.propublica.org/article/four-disturbing-questions-about-the-mumbai-terror-attack.

Sadeeqi, Mohammad Khabeeb and Hafez Amar Naruqi, "Murjia Tul Asar ki Talbisat ka ilmi Muhakima, Al Muhadeen Islaami Library [The library of those who embrace the notion of Tawheed]," accessed 11 June 2018. http://pdf9.com/download-book-murjia-tul-asar-ki-talbisat-ka-ilmi-muhakima-id-4564.html.

Saeed, Hafiz Muhammad, *Tafseer Surah at-Taubah*, trans M. Saleem Ahsan, Lahore: Dar-ul-Andulus, 2006.

Saeed, Sadia, "Pakistani Nationalism and the State Marginalisation of the Ahmadiyya Community in Pakistan," *Studies in Ethnicity and Nationalism*, 7, 3 (2007), pp. 132–152.

Salafi, Abuzar, "Abu Saraqah Amjad Hussain," trans Ali Hamza, *Mujallah ud Dawa*, Jan. 2001, pp. 34–35.

Salik, Naeem (Brig. Retd), *The Genesis of South Asia Nuclear Deterrence: Pakistan's Perspective*, Karachi: Oxford University Press, 2009.

Salik, Siddiq (Maj. Retd), *Witness To Surrender*, Dhaka: The University Press Limited, 1997.

Scott-Clark, Cathy and Adrian Levy, *The Siege: 68 Hours Inside the Taj Hotel*, New York: Penguin, 2013.

Shafqat, Saeed, "From Official Islam to Islamism: The Rise of Dawat-ul-Irshad and Lashkar-e-Tayyaba," *Pakistan: Nationalism without a Nation*, (ed.) Christophe Jaffrelot, London: Zed Books, 2002, pp. 131–147.

Shahid, Muhammad Idrees, "Abu Usman Muhammad Ilyas, Mandi Bahauddin," trans Ali Hamza, *Mujallah ul Dawa*, Jan. 2001, pp. 31–33.

Shaikh, Farzana, *Making Sense of Pakistan*, New York: Columbia University Press, 2009.

Shapiro, Jacob N., *The Terrorist's Dilemma: Managing Violent Covert Organizations*, Princeton: Princeton University Press, 2013.

Sharma, Surinder Kumar and Anshuman Behera, *Militant Groups in South Asia*, New Delhi: Institute for Defence Studies and Analyses, 2014.

Shahzad, Khurrum, "Abu Abdullah Affan Javed Shaheed: A Great Honor for Punjab University, Zarb-e-Tayyaba," trans Ali Hamza, April 2005, p. 64.

Siddiqa, Ayesha, "Jihadism in Pakistan: The Expanding Frontier," *Journal of International Affairs*, 63, 1 (2009), pp. 57–71.

Sikand, Yoginder, "The Islamist Militancy in Kashmir: The Case of the Lashkar-e-Tayyaba," in *The Practice of War: Production, Reproduction and Communication of Armed Violence*, (ed.) Aparna Rao et al., New York: Berghahn Books, 2007, pp. 215–238.

Swami, Praveen, *India, Pakistan and the Secret Jihad: The Covert War in Kashmir, 1947–2005*, London: Routledge, 2007.

Tankel, Stephen, *Storming the World Stage: The Story of Lashkar-e-Tayyaba*, New York: Oxford University Press, 2011.

——, "Lashkar-e-Tayyaba: Past Operations and Future Prospects," *New America Foundation*, National Security Studies Program Policy Paper, April 2011.

——, "Beyond the Double Game: Lessons from Pakistan's Approach to Islamist Militancy," *Journal of Strategic Studies*, 24 July 2016, accessed 11 June 2018. http://www.tandfonline.com/doi/full/10.1080/01402390.2016.1174114.

Tayyab, Mohammad, "Abu Muslim Fidai Abdul Waheed Shaheed. A Tale of a Mujahid who battled the infidels for four years," trans Ali Hamza, *Zarb-e-Tayyaba*, February 2005, p. 38.

"The situation and biographies of martyrs of Battle of Bandipura," trans Ali Hamza, *Mujallah ud Dawa*, October 1994, pp. 4–9.

Tiwana, Muhammad Nazar (Brig.), "Low Intensity Conflict Genesis of the Concept," in *Pakistan Army Green Book 2002: Low Intensity Conflict*, Rawalpindi: Pakistan Army General Headquarters, 2002, pp. 23–26.

Ukht-e-Abdullah Sani, "To realize the status of a martyr, you need to transcend beyond the horizon. To understand the ecstasy of eternal life, you need to sacrifice yourself (Abu Bilal (Umar) & Abu Ququa (Usman))," trans Ali Hamza, *Mujallah Tayyabaat*, Aug. 2004, p. 29.

Ukht-e-Shuhdaa, "Abul Qasim Shaheen Shaheed," trans Ali Hamza, *Mujallah Tayyabaat*, May 2004, p. 32.

Um-e-Abdulrub, "Lanterns of Memory: The Martyrdom of Abu-Zubair rekindled the spirit of Jihad in the family associated with Tehreek-e-Mujahideen," trans Ali Hamza, *Mujallah Tayyabaat*, Jan. 2002, p. 24.

Um-e-Abdulrubab, "Abu Saarya Muhammed Tahir," trans Ali Hamza, *Mujallah Tayyabaat*, March 2004, p. 33.

"Um-e-Hamaad's Second Son Jawad Ahmad Shaheed: Impressions of Amir Honorable Hafiz Mohammed Saeed Hafza-ullah," trans Ali Hamza, *Mujallah Tayyabaat*, May/July 2000, p. 20.

Um-e-Javed, "Memories of Abu Mohammed Askari Mohammed Boota Shaheed," trans Ali Hamza, *Mujallah Tayyabaat*, February 2004, p. 33.

Um-e-Musaffra, "The blood struggle of a Martyr is never wasted: Abu Huzaifa Abdul Waheed," trans Ali Hamza, *Mujallah Tayyabaat*, April 2004, pp. 32–42.

Um-e-Shams-ul-Arifeen, "Shams-ul-Arifeen," trans Ali Hamza, *Mujallah Tayyabaat*, Sept. 2004, p. 38.

Unnithan, Sandeep, *Black Tornado: The Three Sieges of Mumbai 26/11*, Noida: HarperCollins India, 2015.

Wagemakers, Joas, ""Seceders" and "Postponers"? An Analysis of the "Khawarij" and "Murji'a" Labels in Polemical Debates between Quietist and Jihadi-Salafis," *Contextualising Jihadi Thought*, (eds.) Jeevan Deol and Zaheer Kazmi, New York: Columbia University Press, 2012, pp-145–164.

Wasaih, Ukth-e-Abdul and Ukht-e-Saad-ul-Rehman, "Another rose blossomed in the Garden of Martyrdom: Abu Ukasha Abdul Rashid Shaheed," trans Ali Hamza, *Mujallah Tayyabaat*, June 2004, p. 42.

Waze, Sachin and Shirish Thorat. *The Scout: The Definitive Account of David Headley and the Mumbai Attacks*, New Delhi, Bloomsbury, 2016.

Yasmeen, Samina, *Jihad and Dawah: Evolving Narratives of Lashkar-e-Taiba and Jamat ud Dawah*. London, Hurst, 2017.

Zaheer, Mohammad Akram, "Abu Zaraar Qari Mohammad Aslam," trans Ali Hamza, *Mujallah ud Dawa*, Jan. 2004, pp. 28–29.

INDEX

INDEX